John Louis Rishad Zinkin
Better Governance Across the Board

John Louis Rishad Zinkin

Better Governance Across the Board

Creating Value Through Reputation, People, and Processes

DE G PRESS

ISBN 978-1-5474-1711-7
e-ISBN (PDF) 978-1-5474-0093-5
e-ISBN (EPUB) 978-1-5474-0095-9

Library of Congress Control Number: 2019937878

Bibliographic information published by the Deutsche Nationalbibliothek
The Deutsche Nationalbibliothek lists this publication in the Deutsche
Nationalbibliografie; detailed bibliographic data are available on the Internet at http://dnb.dnb.de.

© 2019 John Louis Rishad Zinkin
Published by Walter de Gruyter Inc., Boston/Berlin
Printing and binding: CPI books GmbH, Leck
Typesetting: MacPS, LLC, Carmel
Cover Image: Gajus/iStock/Getty Images Plus

www.degruyter.com

Praise for *Better Governance Across the Board*

A deeply insightful and comprehensive handbook that provides superb guidance on board responsibilities with persuasive real-life examples. I would thoroughly recommend this book as essential reading for directors who want to know how to effectively raise the level of corporate governance in the boardroom.
— Vincent Loh, Chief Executive, Core Management Consulting; Chairman, Visdynamics Holdings Berhad

A must-read for directors who care about ethical value creation, enhancing corporate reputation and achieving sustainable success. This book provides good experiential learning on corporate ethics and governance through simple, real life examples. It operationalizes values into measurable actions.
— Ewe Hock Ong, Deputy Chairman, Business Ethics Institute of Malaysia

A book which both informs and enlightens directors—providing a clear explanation of their duties, relevant and fascinating case studies, and a wealth of information and checklists which will help them to do a better job. A book which all directors should have at hand as they carry out their work.
— Edward Clayton, SE Asia Lead Partner, PwC Strategy&

John Zinkin's book—*Better Governance Across the Board: Creating Value Through Reputation, People and Processes*—is a must have for any Director, CEO or advisor to boards of directors.

In the seventeen very well-written, inviting, easy-to-read, global, insightful and best in class governance chapters, Mr Zinkin covers all governance topics, including value creation, board and CEO succession, risk governance, pay governance, stakeholders, management accountability, board accountability, and, above all, ethical conduct and the important role of the Board of Directors—all squarely from a highly effective directorial perspective. This governance coverage and depth by a single author is remarkable. John Zinkin's book should be on every Director's and Manager's bookshelf. I highly recommend it!
— Richard Leblanc, Professor of Governance, Law & Ethics York University, Toronto, Canada

This ambitious and comprehensive book is an accessible and valuable contribution to the conversation on corporate governance. For lay readers, it clearly and succinctly lays out the history and importance of governance. For board members, the guide to best practices will substantially improve any board's processes and capabilities. For those who study corporate governance, the solid analysis and advocacy for boards to act more like owners—from succession planning to sustainability—will help them tackle critical issues concerning boards today. In short, it's a work that will be of great use to the vast majority of people who interact with corporations today.

— Dominic Barton, Senior Partner
and former Global Managing Partner, McKinsey & Co

In the 26 years since the Cadbury Report international jurisdictions have revised (and frequently amended) their Corporate Governance codes and even their Companies Acts, the purpose has been to secure better corporate governance, behaviour and performance. John Zinkin has not only written a wonderfully accessible and intellectually rigorous guide to the current state of corporate governance but has created clear guidelines for the six critical areas of director responsibility, among many other board related requirements. He casts his net well beyond the more usual, Anglo-American sphere by drawing on his wide experience of multiple jurisdictions and cultures. A book to be read and kept close.

— Murray Eldridge, Director of Actinium CS and of Perfect People Ltd; Chartered Director and Fellow of the UK Institute of Directors;
Program leader (Strategy, Leadership and Diploma level),
Institute of Directors Chartered Director Program

I find the book an excellent one stop reference. I will certainly get a copy and use it as such a source of reference given its breadth of coverage. My heartiest congratulations.

— Dato Dr. R. Thillainathan, Chairman of the Audit Committee,
Allianz Malaysia Berhad;
Board Member of The Institute for Democracy and Economic Affair;
Member of the Board of Directors of University Malaya

John Zinkin's book aligns very well with our approach at the Thai Institute of Directors: to shift the focus of corporate governance away from shareholder to stakeholder. This will be one of the earliest books to make this point: that the duty of directors is to ensure the company's long-term value creation and that good corporate governance leads to sustainability. It provides practical guidance on what directors should do when fulfilling each of their responsibilities in setting and reviewing strategy, managing risk, planning succession, ensuring internal controls and engaging stakeholders. I enjoyed the book and thoroughly recommend it for any independent director wishing to add value to their board.

— Dr. Bandid Nijathaworn, Immediate Past President
and CEO, Thai Institute of Directors, Bangkok

This is a very well thought out and researched book. It doesn't just deal with the fundamentals (which are good reminders on basic CG tenets) but has many fresh ideas that I would describe as thought leadership material yet can be put into practice. There are many new concepts that I have learnt from reading it and it has practical recommendations. The book is also peppered with great real-life examples of corporate failures and other stories to illustrate points the author wants to emphasise, which make it much more readable than purely intellectual material. I like the way the author starts with the basics of CG concepts and then moves on to how this affects the way a Board operates before discussing the "How" to guide directors in undertaking their responsibilities and finally suggesting what Boards could do differently.

— Sridharan Nair, Managing Partner,
PwC Malaysia

John Zinkin's book highlights some of the many issues in considering corporate governance in an international context. This book is a valuable contribution to issues involved in understanding comparative international corporate governance. It will help those of us who are working actively in this complex, and essentially cross disciplinary field.

— Chris Bennett, Director,
BPA Australasia Pte Ltd

This book looks at governance from an interesting and meaningful perspective. There is something for everyone in the book, both for the experienced and the novice, as the author covers both the fundamental thought processes and the advanced thought processes. The author quotes liberally from several authoritative and persuasive references and these references are listed after each chapter. These references provide an opportunity for readers to "deep-dive" into areas where they seek further information. The author draws on his varied experiences in dealing with boards of directors and I especially found it interesting when he draws on his personal perspectives—often using the first-person perspective. I found the book very readable and informative. It is a good read for those who wish to enhance the value of their nebulous off-balance sheet assets.

— Devanesan J A Evanson, Chief Executive Officer,
Minority Shareholders Watch Group;
formerly Chief Regulatory Officer and Chief Market Operations
of Bursa Malaysia;
President of ACCA Malaysia Advisory Committee

This book adopts a fresh and pragmatic approach to best navigate the demands and challenges of modern CG expectations. It then discusses filters, lenses and analytical models through which this "raw data" should be sifted to reach an informed, effective and comprehensive CG framework and practice. It also addresses a number of enterprises beyond just the for-profit listed companies. And last but not least, in a sign of the turbulent current times and policy issues, the book outlines some potential remedies which would be facilitated by better CG and enhanced cooperation between the private and public sector.

— Youssef Nasr, Chairman of the Board,
Hellenic Bank plc;
Independent Director of Brookfield Asset Management
and Brookfield Property Partners

John Zinkin's latest book brings together all the elements necessary for organizations to be well governed and is a real differentiator beyond the financials. The book highlights what it takes to be ahead; to be an exceptional leader in governance through people, processes and reputation. A must-read for all who want to go beyond traditional corporate governance.

— Tay Kay Luan, Vice Chancellor,
International University Malaya Wales

John Zinkin has approached governance in his latest book from the crucial angle of responsibility. Indeed, responsibility can be deemed the cornerstone of good governance. As John asserts convincingly, good governance is not only about codes and laws, and goes much beyond compliance. Good governance is a key driver of long-term success and for that it needs to rely on the sense of responsibility of the few individuals privileged enough to truly drive that governance. This latest work from John Zinkin combines technical governance with values-based governance to develop an all-encompassing view of what creates great governance and allows board directors to be the impactful stewards of their organization that they want to be.

— Professor Didier Cossin,
President of the Stewardship Institute;
Founder & Director of the IMD Global Board Center;
Professor in Finance and Governance, IMD

The most significant contribution of this book is reflected in the sub-title, the importance of boards recognizing their role in:
- Creating and maintaining corporate reputation; an asset that seldom appears on the balance sheet. In recent years companies have found their market value collapse because of a strategic crisis.
- Valuing members of staff as assets not costs. This can be particularly important in an increasingly high-tech world dependent on skilled and experienced individuals.
- Recognizing the fundamental value of the policies and procedures which get things done in the organization: what the author calls "the glue that holds everything together."

The book is a practical primer for better board performance and long-term strategic success.

— Professor R I (Bob) Tricker D.Litt FCMA CGMA,
author of *Corporate Governance—principles, policies and practices* and
Business Ethics—a stakeholder, governance and risk approach

Acknowledgments

The idea for writing this book came from a short conversation with HRH Sultan Nazrin Muizzuddin Shah of Perak, Malaysia, who suggested it was time for me to write another book on corporate governance.

This book is designed for a global audience. I have been most fortunate to have had the help and advice of my international and local panel of readers without whom this book could not have been written. *Between them, they helped ensure that my thinking was rigorous, that my ideas were relevant both globally and locally; and that my recommendations for directors were practical.* Youssef Nasr helped balance my thinking as the book developed with his international banker's perspective and immense experience of boards. Dominic Barton of McKinsey, Sridharan Nair of PwC, and Edward Clayton of Strategy& provided international professional services firm perspectives based on their unrivalled experience in different jurisdictions. Professors Richard Leblanc, Didier Cossin, and Bob Tricker ensured academic rigor based on their global expertise in corporate governance and their exposure to North American, European, and Asian boards. Vincent Loh helped with the financial discussion and Ewe Hock Ong with ethics. Dr. Bandid Nijathaworn and Devaneson Evanson made sure my thinking reflected their experience of problems faced by boards as former regulators in ASEAN markets, while Chris Bennett, Kay Luan Tay, and Murray Eldridge shared their insights as international trainers of directors and Dr. Thillainathan shared his views as a director of long-standing in leading Malaysian institutions.

I hope I have done justice to their thinking and input and I am immensely grateful for the time and thought they have invested in reading the manuscript, highlighting any flaws in its argument or structure. Any errors are mine alone. If some readers are surprised by the occasional reference to Malaysian best practice, it is the result of my being based in Malaysia, and which I feel may provide a useful and different point of view.

I am very grateful to Tan Sri Zarinah Anwar, former chairman of the Securities Commission Malaysia and current chairman of the Institute of Corporate Directors Malaysia, for investing the time to read my manuscript and trouble to write the foreword to this book.

My thanks also to Jeff Pepper and Jaya Dalal for their invaluable help in developmental editing, Anett Rehner and Angie MacAllister in production, and Denise Pangia for the care taken in doing the thankless task of copy editing. They have been great partners making the book much better as a result.

Finally, I must thank my wonderful wife, Lisa, for her patience and support while I was writing and rewriting chapters of the book in my spare time at her expense!

About the Author

John Zinkin has written three books on CG: *Corporate Governance* (2005), *Challenges in Implementing Corporate Governance: Whose Business is it Anyway?* (2010), and *Rebuilding Trust in Banks: The Role of Leadership and Governance* (2014) published by John Wiley & Sons. He wrote the *FIDE Good Governance Handbook* (2013), designed specifically for Malaysian banks and insurance companies, under the auspices of Bank Negara Malaysia. He is a faculty member of the Institute of Corporate Directors Malaysia (formerly MINDA), Securities Industry Development Corporation, and Pinnacle Perintis. He has contributed a chapter on "Corporate Governance in Asia Pacific" and another chapter on "Corporate Governance in an Age of Populism" for the *Handbook on Corporate Governance, 2nd edition*, edited by Professor Richard Leblanc, due out later in 2019 in the United States, published by John Wiley & Sons.

John was a member of the Malaysian working party in 1999 and was involved in the launch of the Malaysian Code on Corporate Governance in 2000. He was a member of the working party that drew up the Malaysian Corporate Governance Blueprint in 2011 and the revised Malaysian Code on Corporate Governance in 2012.

He speaks regularly on leadership and governance and used to write fortnightly for *The Star* newspaper on governance-related topics (2007–2013). He was voted "Writer of the Year" on CG matters in 2014 by the Minority Shareholders Watchdog Group. His other specialties are "Leading Brand-Based Change," "Reconciling Leadership and Governance," and "Ethics in Business." He has led board effectiveness evaluations in banking, insurance, and government entities and has written codes of conduct and board charters for several development banks. He is a certified training professional who has done extensive training in CG, branding, and leadership. Since 2007 he has trained more than 1,500 directors in CG as well as senior managers of public listed companies. He has trained securities regulators from Cambodia, Hong Kong, Laos, Malaysia, Philippines, Singapore, Thailand, and Vietnam on behalf of the Securities Commission Malaysia and the Australian Government as part of their CG capacity building programs in ASEAN and APEC.

During his career, starting in 1971, John worked in the United Kingdom in fast-moving consumer goods (Unilever), insurance brokering (Hogg Robinson), management consulting (McKinsey), and office products (Rank Xerox) before moving to Hong Kong in 1985 for Inchcape Pacific. There John ran marketing and distribution companies in a variety of industries across the Asia Pacific, before joining Burson-Marsteller in 1997 as the Asia-Pacific Marketing and Change Management Practice Chair where he became interested in CG as a result of client work. John moved to Malaysia in 2001 and from 2001 to 2006, was associate professor of marketing and strategy at Nottingham University Business School, Malaysia Campus, responsible for its MBA program. In 2006 he was asked to set up the Securities Industry Development Corporation, the capital markets training arm of the Securities Commission Malaysia, and in 2011 he was appointed managing director, corporate governance of the Iclif Leadership and Governance Centre under the aegis of Bank Negara Malaysia, responsible for training directors of banks and insurance companies in CG. Since 2013 he works independently as the managing director of Zinkin Ettinger Sendirian Berhad, a boutique consultancy specializing in CG, brand-based change, and ethical leadership.

John is married to a Malaysian. He has Malaysian permanent residency and was awarded a Federal Datukship in 2013 for services to Malaysia. John graduated from Oxford University with a BA in Politics, Philosophy, and Economics (1968) and the London Business School with an MSc in Business Administration (1971).

About the Series Editor

Alexandra Reed Lajoux is Series Editor for De|G PRESS, a division of Walter De Gruyter, Inc. The series has an emphasis on governance, corporate leadership, and sustainability. Dr. Lajoux is chief knowledge officer emeritus (CKO) at the National Association of Corporate Directors (NACD) and founding principal of Capital Expert Services, LLC (CapEx), a global consultancy providing expert witnesses for legal cases. She has served as editor of *Directors & Boards, Mergers & Acquisitions, Export Today,* and *Director's Monthly*, and has coauthored a series of books on M&A for McGraw-Hill, including *The Art of M&A* and eight spin-off titles on strategy, valuation, financing, structuring, due diligence, integration, bank M&A, and distressed M&A. For Bloomberg/Wiley, she coauthored *Corporate Valuation for Portfolio Investment* with Robert A. G. Monks. Dr. Lajoux serves on the advisory board of Campaigns and Elections, and is a Fellow of the Caux Round Table for Moral Capitalism. She holds a BA from Bennington College, a PhD from Princeton University, and an MBA from Loyola University in Maryland. She is an associate member of the American Bar Association and is certified as a Competent Communicator by Toastmasters International.

Foreword

Today's boards are subjected to significantly more public scrutiny. Investors are holding boards accountable for company performance and will not hesitate to take action for governance shortcomings. Increasingly they are measuring the sustainability and impact of their investment along the environmental, social, and governance (ESG) dimensions to help them better determine the future financial performance of companies. They believe that sound corporate governance practices, including how the company manages the environmental and social aspects of its operations, are key to better risk adjusted returns. So, they are scrutinizing the leadership capacity of boards to ensure that boards are capable of overseeing the risks and opportunities that will determine long-term value creation.

Of course, corporate failures will continue to occur; business judgments, no matter how well founded, can still go wrong. A market economy is not infallible; shifting macroeconomic conditions and unknown and unexpected competitive pressures can emerge, but good governance does enable mistakes to be revealed early, facilitates corrections, and generates a process of learning and improvements to discover better solutions to limit the impact of future failures.

Against this background, the role of the board in corporate governance has progressively evolved into one of leadership, taking charge of setting strategies, determining risk appetite of the business, executive compensation and CEO succession, among key responsibilities that traditionally resided with management. Thus, it is increasingly important for the board to work with top management to oversee and deal with the impact of change and respond to ESG risks and opportunities over the long term to ensure sustainable financial performance. Indeed, the responsibility of the board today is to ensure collaborative leadership, working hand in hand with management in deliberating on the most critical company decisions, while avoiding micromanaging. Each party has a responsibility to make the relationship work.

This calls for the directors to be engaged and informed and to educate themselves on the many different facets of the business to enable them to provide value add; thus, the concern of investors on quality and composition of boards, and the importance of alignment of board members' skills with the company's strategy.

Boards therefore need to continually review the standards of their governance practices and their leadership role in ensuring they are the drivers of governance in their businesses. Development of capacity to facilitate professional and ethical management and oversight of companies represents a crucial first line of defense against corporate misbehavior.

This is a book that helps boards to do just this. John Zinkin has dealt comprehensively with the many issues of governance facing boards today and how boards should conduct themselves and respond effectively to the expectations of multiple stakeholders. John highlights the shift in board responsibility from the traditional role of governance to one that increasingly holds boards also accountable for management and the importance of properly documenting the boundaries, if directors are to be protected by the business judgment rule.

With his extensive experience in consulting and training in corporate governance and evaluating board effectiveness, John has developed critical insights into how boards can lead effectively and manage dilemmas that arise. His emphasis on reputation, people, and process as key elements of sustainable long-term value is timely. His guide on how directors can fulfill their responsibilities, and his framework for setting priorities, allocating resources, and reinforcing desired values and behaviors are highly instructive.

John is right in highlighting that boards are only as good as their chairmen, imbued as the chairman is with the responsibility for ensuring that the board works as a cohesive team, ensuring the adoption of all best practices in governance standards, and nurturing a collaborative relationship characterized by honesty, openness, mutual trust, and support. His observations on chairing effective boards are incisive.

This is a book that will benefit directors immensely. Like John's previous book, it is highly readable. John has approached the issues in a very practical manner with ample illustrations that directors will find easy to relate to, while offering suggestions and alternative solutions to problems.

I believe it is a book that directors will return to repeatedly, as it provides valuable reference on a range of issues and challenges they are regularly confronted with in discharging their duties.

—Tan Sri Zarinah Anwar
Chairman, Institute of Corporate Directors Malaysia,
and former chairman of Securities Commission, Malaysia

Contents

Part One: Anatomy of Corporate Governance

Chapter 1: What Is Corporate Governance and Why It Matters — 3
    What Is Corporate Governance? — 3
    Why Corporate Governance Matters — 5
    Two Caveats Regarding Implementation — 11
    Conclusion — 15

Chapter 2: Integrating Ethics and Branding — 19
    The Importance of Culture — 19
    Ensuring an Ethical Basis for the Business — 20
        Ensuring an Ethical Foundation — 21
        Need for an Ethical Framework — 25
        Meeting Client Needs Ethically — 28
        Satisfying Regulations — 31
    Branding — 36
        Company "Brand Promise" Captures Purpose, Values, and Culture — 37
        Company Brands Are Most Valuable — 39
    Conclusion — 39
    Appendix 2.1: The World's Most Valuable Brands — 41

Chapter 3: Redefining the Boundaries of Responsibility — 47
    Boundaries of Board Responsibility: The Traditional View — 47
        Determining the "Purpose" of the Organization — 48
        Defining the Mission, Vision, and Values — 50
    Boundaries of Board Responsibility: Changing Perspectives — 56
    Redefining the Boundaries — 60
    Conclusion — 63

Chapter 4: Chairing an Effective Board — 67
    Getting the Context Right — 67
        Reflecting the Drivers of the Business — 67
        Reflecting the Life-Stage of the Business — 68
        Reflecting the Style of Engagement — 70
    Role of the Board Charter — 71
    Contribution of the Chair to Board Effectiveness — 72
    Role of Board Committees — 76
        Role of the AC — 77
        Role of the RMC — 78

Role of the NC —— 79
Role of the RC —— 80
Conclusion —— 81
Appendix 4.1: Sample Board Charter: Table of Contents —— 82

Chapter 5: Being an Effective Board Member —— 85
Chair and CEO: Two Distinct Roles? —— 85
Role and Responsibilities of the Chair —— 86
Role and Responsibilities of the CEO —— 88
Being an Effective Director —— 91
Being an Effective Board Member —— 98
Reconciling Independence with Deep Understanding of the Business —— 98
Commitment and Passion —— 100
Experience and Appropriate Competence —— 100
EQ —— 101
Conclusion —— 102

Chapter 6: Reconciling Leadership and Governance —— 105
Leadership—An Amoral Force for Change —— 106
Characteristics of Effective Leadership —— 108
Find the Energy to Create a Better Future —— 109
Have a Clear Purpose at All Times —— 109
Lead with Values —— 110
Encourage "Speaking Truth to Power" —— 110
Learn from Failure and Move On —— 110
Develop Co-Leaders and Share Authority and Responsibility —— 111
Move from "I" to "We" Thinking, Creating Conditions for Maximum Collective Success —— 111
Create a Lasting Legacy —— 112
From Success to Failure —— 112
Stan O'Neal and Merrill Lynch —— 113
Dick Fuld and Lehman Brothers —— 115
Fred Goodwin and RBS —— 117
Conclusion —— 119

Part Two: The "Five P" Framework and Good Governance

Chapter 7: Introducing the "Five P" Performance Framework —— 125
Introducing the "Five P" Framework —— 125
The "Five P" Components —— 126
"Purpose" —— 126

"Principles" —— 130
"Power" —— 132
"People" —— 133
"Processes" —— 134
Boundaries of Responsibility for the "Five Ps" —— 135
"Purpose" —— 135
"Principles" —— 136
"Power" —— 136
"People" —— 137
"Processes" —— 137
Conclusion —— 138

Chapter 8: Setting Strategy —— 141
Why Plan? —— 141
Analyzing the External Environment —— 143
Six "Macro Drivers" of Demand —— 143
Analyzing Organizational Capabilities —— 152
SWOT —— 152
Five Forces —— 153
Deciding Where and How to Compete —— 156
Choosing Where and How to Compete —— 156
To Disrupt or Not? —— 158
Low Cost Leadership or Differentiation? —— 160
Conclusion —— 162
Appendix 8.1: Questions Regarding Threats and Opportunities —— 163
Appendix 8.2: Questions Regarding Weaknesses and Strengths —— 164
Appendix 8.3: Questions Regarding Business Model Appropriateness —— 165

Chapter 9: Reviewing Strategy —— 169
Board's Strategy Review Process —— 169
Measures Matter —— 171
Financial Metrics —— 173
Including the "Voice of the Customer" —— 180
Voice of the Customer —— 182
Soft Metrics and KPIs —— 183
Using "Five Ps" to Crosscheck —— 185
Conclusion —— 185
Appendix 9.1: Four Brands' Volume Market Shares Compared —— 186
Calculating Market Share —— 187
Appendix 9.2: Measuring Customer Satisfaction —— 188
Appendix 9.3: Calculating Customer Lifetime Value —— 189

Chapter 10: Managing Risk —— 191
- Role of the Board —— 191
- "Cultural" Risks —— 194
  - Ethics Conflicts —— 195
  - Misaligned Incentives and Strategy —— 197
  - Inappropriate Rewards —— 199
  - Differences of Social Culture —— 200
- Systemic Risks —— 201
  - Herding Behavior —— 201
  - Failure of Systemic Integrity —— 202
  - Moral Hazard —— 203
- "Traditional" Risks —— 203
  - Financial Risk and Credit Risk —— 204
  - Natural Hazards —— 204
  - Physical Security —— 204
  - Legal/Regulatory —— 205
  - Compliance and Fraud —— 205
  - IT and Cybersecurity Risks —— 205
- "Earnings Driver" Risks —— 206
  - Product Innovation —— 206
  - Brand Impairment —— 207
  - Pricing Pressure —— 207
  - Supplier Relationships —— 207
  - Distribution Channels —— 208
  - Alternative Technologies —— 208
  - Customer Churn —— 208
- Using the "Five P" Framework to Cross Check —— 208
  - Purpose —— 209
  - Principles —— 209
  - Power —— 209
  - People —— 209
  - Processes —— 209
- Conclusion —— 210
- Appendix 10.1: Fraud Red Flags —— 211
- Appendix 10.2: "Purpose" Checklist of Questions and Issues —— 213

Chapter 11: Planning Succession; Managing Talent —— 219
- Succession Planning for the Board —— 220
- CEO Succession —— 225
- Remuneration and Performance Measurement —— 229
- Company Succession and Talent Management —— 236
- Using the "Five P" Framework to Cross Check —— 238

Purpose —— 238
Principles —— 238
Processes —— 238
Conclusion —— 239
Appendix 11.1: MCCG 2017 Guidance Regarding INED Tenure —— 240
Appendix 11.2: AICD's 10 Core Director Attributes —— 241
Appendix 11.3: Ten Reasons for CEO Succession Failure —— 244

Chapter 12: Ensuring Internal Controls —— 247
Three Lines of Defense Versus Five Lines of Assurance —— 247
"Minding the Numbers" —— 249
  Unsupported Manual Entry Adjustments —— 249
  Aggressive Revenue Recognition —— 250
  Continuous One-Off, Nonrecurring Charges —— 250
  Regular Changes to Reserve, Depreciation/Amortization or Comprehensive Income Policies —— 250
  Related Party Transactions —— 251
  Complex Structured Products —— 252
  Pension Fund Liabilities —— 253
Compliance —— 256
  Regular Reporting of Key Control Metrics —— 256
  Executives Report Changes to Key Systems, Processes, and People —— 259
  Executives Sign Off on their Financial Statements as Being Accurate —— 260
  Identify and Assess Nonroutine Processes —— 260
  Support Strong Internal Audit Function —— 260
  All Employees Attest their Understanding of the Code of Conduct —— 261
Introducing COSO —— 261
  The Need to Consider Risk When Setting Strategy —— 262
  Risk of Strategic Misalignment —— 262
  Reframing Risk in Terms of Performance —— 262
  Recognizing the Importance of Culture —— 263
  Integrating Internal Control with Risk Management —— 263
Using the "Five P" Framework to Cross Check —— 264
  "Purpose" —— 264
  "Principles" —— 265
Conclusion —— 265
Appendix 12.1: Role of the "Unconscious Mind" in Decision Making —— 266

Chapter 13: Engaging Stakeholders —— 269
Capital Market Discipline —— 269
  Shareholder-Driven Market Discipline —— 269
  Stakeholder-Driven Market Discipline —— 270

Regulatory-Driven Stakeholder Engagement —— 271
Stakeholders Defined —— 272
Engaging with Stakeholders —— 274
    "Purpose" of the Organization —— 276
    Appropriate Time Horizons and Risk Profiles —— 276
Communicating with Stakeholders —— 280
    Communication Chain of Command —— 280
    Taking Responsibility for All Major Announcements —— 282
    Six Principles of Effective Stakeholder Communications —— 282
    Monitoring Stakeholder Relations —— 283
    Using Appropriate Communication Channels —— 284
Using the "Five P" framework to cross check —— 287
    Purpose —— 288
    Principles —— 288
    Power —— 288
    People —— 289
    Processes —— 289
Conclusion —— 289
Appendix 13.1: Questions Regarding Corporate Disclosure —— 291
Appendix 13.2: Questions Regarding Investor Relations —— 293
Appendix 13.3: Questions Regarding Effectiveness of Stakeholder Engagement —— 293

Part Three: Creating Value Through Reputation, People, and Processes

Chapter 14: Focusing on Reputation —— 299
Why Reputation Matters —— 299
    It Increases Growth —— 300
    It Makes it Easier to Recruit and Retain the Best People —— 300
    It Mitigates Risk —— 301
    It Builds Trust Equity —— 301
    It Enhances the Share Price —— 301
Role of Reputation in Determining Strategy —— 302
    Defining a Sustainable Mission —— 302
    Creating a Compelling Vision —— 302
    Reconciling Value Creation, Extraction, and Distribution —— 303
Minimizing Reputation Risk Across the Value Chain —— 305
    Natural Capital/Environment —— 306
    Social Capital/Community —— 308
    Human Capital/Workplace —— 310
Conclusion —— 311

Chapter 15: Investing in People —— 317
    Underlying Assumptions about "People" —— 317
        People as a Cost —— 317
        People Are Disposable —— 319
    How Best to Invest in People? —— 324
        Recognize There Are Several Types of Leadership —— 324
    Conclusion —— 333

Chapter 16: Harnessing Processes to Create Long-Term Value —— 339
    Board Processes to Deliver Long-Term Value —— 339
        Rotating "Devil's Advocacy" —— 340
        Adopting Activity-Based Costing (ABC) —— 341
        "Reframing" Budget and Cost Control Discussions —— 342
        Setting KPIs and Targets Using a Ten-Step Process —— 345
        Adopting an Effective Innovation Process —— 348
        Recruiting More Women Directors —— 353
    "CG Ecosystem" Makes a Difference —— 355
        Effective Regulatory Discipline —— 357
        Professional Boards —— 358
        Professional Intermediaries —— 358
        Educated Investors —— 358
    Conclusion —— 359

Chapter 17: Conclusion: Achieving Better Governance Across the Board —— 363
    CG Matters Regardless of the Type of Ownership —— 363
    Integrating Ethics and Branding —— 363
    Redefining Boundaries of Responsibility —— 364
    Chairing an Effective Board —— 364
    Being an Effective Board Member —— 364
    Reconciling Leadership and Governance —— 365
    "Five P" Framework —— 365
    Setting Strategy —— 365
    Reviewing Strategy Implementation —— 366
    Managing Risk —— 366
    Planning Succession and Managing Talent —— 367
    Ensuring Effective Internal Controls —— 368
    Engaging Stakeholders —— 368
    Focusing on Reputation —— 369
    Investing in People —— 370
    Harnessing Processes to Create Long-Term Value —— 371

Index —— 373

Introduction

Nearly five years have passed since I wrote *Rebuilding Trust in Banks: The Role of Leadership and Governance*, focusing on the problems of governance in banks and what could be done about them. Eight years have passed since I wrote *Challenges in Implementing Corporate Governance: Whose Business is it Anyway?* which dealt with issues faced by publicly listed companies in general. Since 2008 I have led workshops and training programs for more than 1,500 directors, where I have come to appreciate better the dilemmas faced by independent nonexecutive directors as they try to fulfill their fiduciary duty.

These dilemmas have become much more challenging as the context of corporate governance widened from considering how best to deliver shareholder value in a publicly listed enterprise from a legal and accounting perspective in terms of compliance—its primary focus in 1992 when the Cadbury Report was published—to including ethics; reconciling stakeholder expectations and issues of public governance.

Annual reporting requirements have also become more demanding, as listed companies were required to add social and governance reporting sections covering ESG issues in annual reports; and then to adopt integrated reporting to provide greater transparency for investors and analysts. Regulators at first were satisfied with a "comply or explain" approach to adopting best practices outlined in the various codes of corporate governance. When they realized how this was abused by companies adopting third party "cut and paste" generalities in the governance section of the annual report, some regulators, now require listed companies to "apply or explain" instead.

Being an independent director in the twenty-first century has become much more onerous. First, came the changes in legislation and regulation following Enron with the passing of the Sarbanes-Oxley Act in 2002. Second, came the change in the climate of public opinion regarding boards after the Global Financial Crisis in 2008 and extending the fiduciary duty of directors of banks to include depositors and of insurance companies to include policyholders. Third, came Australian rulings in 2011 and 2012 which are regarded by Commonwealth judges as precedents to be considered or as being "persuasive" when passing judgement. These rulings set a much higher standard for the duty of care than existed previously.

As a result of undertaking third party board evaluations with face-to face in-depth interviews of board members and managers reporting to boards, I realized there are significant gaps between the understanding members of the board have of their respective roles and what regulators expect and believe should happen and what happens.

These differences in expectation are made more serious by the fact codes of corporate governance, which are voluntary, are based on a philosophy that "boards govern and direct, management manages"; whereas statute law in many Commonwealth jurisdictions stipulate that "directors manage and direct" the affairs of the businesses for which they are responsible. The higher standard of the duty of care, combined with what some companies acts define as the responsibility of directors, raises the need to redefine the boundaries of responsibility between boards and management.

Given these changes in the corporate governance environment over the past twenty-five years, I felt it would be useful to write a book that:

1. Explains what corporate governance is; why it matters and how its remit has changed in the past twenty-five years; revisiting the role of the board and its component parts, in the much more onerous twenty-first century context.
2. Provides directors with a "how to" guide to help them fulfill their designated six responsibilities: setting strategy, reviewing its implementation, managing risk, planning succession, ensuring internal controls, and engaging stakeholders.
3. Considers three critical areas in value creation that do not feature on company balance sheets as assets—reputation, people, and processes[1] where a change in approach might help avert a "political tragedy of the commons," namely by focusing more on reputation, investing in people as assets rather than treating them as costs, and recognizing the fundamental importance of processes and harnessing them to create long-term value.

Structure of the Book

This book is presented in three parts.

Part One: Anatomy of Corporate Governance

This consists of six chapters. The first two chapters set the "conceptual" framework of corporate governance. The next four chapters explore "operational" considerations affecting boards.

Chapters 1 and 2 broaden the discussion of corporate governance from the traditional, mainly legal, and accounting, compliance-oriented approach for public listed companies, by showing how the definition has changed to cover more areas of responsibility; hence, the double meaning in the title "Better Governance Across the Board." I also highlight the fact standards to which boards and directors are now held have

---

[1] "The two most important things in any company do not appear in its balance sheet: its reputation and its people." Henry Ford, https://www.azquotes.com/quote/1430055. It is ironic that Henry Ford did not mention "processes" when his adaptation of the Swift meat works processes created the revolutionary assembly line, so essential to much of modern manufacturing. So, I would add processes, for it is processes that differentiate "third world mindsets" from "first world mindsets."

been raised dramatically from the 1925 definition of directors' duties to the incredibly challenging standards set by rulings in the twenty-first century, which, from my discussions, many directors have yet to recognize fully.

Chapter 1, "What Is Corporate Governance and Why It Matters" explores the principles of good governance as they apply to all enterprises regardless of whether they are listed, for-profit or not, and regardless of their ownership structure, explaining why in implementation, however, "no one size fits all" jurisdictions or companies. I define what corporate governance (CG) is and why it matters.

Chapter 2, "Integrating Ethics and Branding," introduces the idea of expanding the scope of CG beyond the limited boundaries of board responsibility set by the law and regulations. It discusses the importance of ethics and branding because these two fundamental topics seem so often to be missing from legalistic and accounting-based discussions of corporate governance. I explain why I believe business ethics are essential and go on to explore why ethics are such a difficult area. I provide a five-stage "right-good" decision-making framework, reconciling consequential, duty-based, and personalistic ethics for directors to use when making or reviewing decisions. As far as branding is concerned, I make the case corporate/organization brands are the responsibility of the board as they reflect the mission, vision and values of the enterprise—areas that are for the board to define.

Chapters 3–6 discuss the role and responsibilities of effective boards. I explain the need to define where the boundaries of responsibility lie between boards and management, as a result of differences between what *voluntary* codes of corporate governance recommend and what many *statutory* companies' acts stipulate. I then discuss what it takes to chair an effective board and be an effective board member. I conclude with three case studies where the boards failed to rein in charismatic, domineering CEOs with disastrous results.

Chapter 3, "Redefining the Boundaries of Responsibility" compares the traditional and modern views of the boundaries of responsibility between board and management. This contrasts the traditional view that boards "govern and direct" with the modern view that boards "manage and direct" and makes the case for redefining the boundaries of responsibility clearly, incorporating them into the memorandum and articles of association and board charter, if there is one.

Chapter 4, "Chairing an Effective Board" discusses the context determining different engagement styles of boards with management and explain why different styles are needed at different stages in the enterprise's life stages. This also depends on the constitution of the organization and is covered in what must be in a board charter—the document that determines the roles and responsibilities of the board, its members, and committees. I explore further the role of the chair in ensuring board dynamics and culture are appropriate to demonstrate the immense importance of the chair in ensuring board effectiveness.

Chapter 5, "Being an Effective Board Member" discusses the quite distinct roles of chair and CEO and explains why they should be separated—the norm outside the

United States—an effective chair has a very demanding job when governing the board and is the link between the board and the CEO. An effective chair is a coach and sounding board for the CEO as well as the person who hires and fires the CEO. Conflicts of interest are inevitable if the chair and CEO are one and the same. I also explore what it takes to be an effective director and member of the board.

Chapter 6, "Reconciling Leadership and Governance" explores the role of governance in providing checks and balance to prevent successful, dynamic CEOs from abusing their executive power. Great charismatic leaders who are not subject to checks and balance will fall victim to Lord Acton's saying, "Absolute power tends to corrupt absolutely" and may destroy the businesses they lead. Governance without leadership will result in mundane performance at best. Hence, a key responsibility of boards is to reconcile leadership with governance. The chapter looks at three cases where highly successful CEOs were allowed to destroy the firms they led because of weak boards.

Part Two: The "Five P" Framework and Good Governance

This consists of seven chapters designed to act as a working "how to" guide for directors in fulfilling their six responsibilities outlined in the most up to date codes of corporate governance.

Chapter 7, "Introducing the 'Five P' Performance Framework" introduces a simple framework that directors can use for reviewing any decision brought before the board. The framework consists of five elements that must be aligned if the enterprise is to achieve its designated mission and vision. The five elements are "purpose"; "principles" or values; "power" reflecting the optimum organizational design and associated reporting relationships; "people" in terms of number of employees, competencies and character required to get the job done; and "processes"—the glue that holds everything together. Should any one of the five elements be out of alignment, the organization will fail to achieve its designated mission.

Chapters 8–13 explore how directors can operationalize their six corporate governance responsibilities. They deal in turn with setting strategy, reviewing its implementation, managing risk, planning succession and managing talent, ensuring internal controls, and engaging stakeholders.

Chapter 8, "Setting Strategy" argues it is the responsibility of boards to set strategic direction rather than acting as rubber stamps signing off on what management proposes. Initiating strategy is the primary responsibility of the board, even though in practice most boards are reactive/passive responding to whatever management puts in front of them. It is a fundamental premise of this book that determining and defining strategic direction and priorities is the responsibility of the board and it is the responsibility of the CEO and management to deliver the board-agreed strategic objectives.

Chapter 9, "Reviewing Strategy" explores the five-stage review process for setting strategy, defining the metrics that matter. It examines the financial metrics and categorizes them as metrics for investment and metrics for ongoing operations. It discusses the deficiencies of financial metrics and explores how to include the "voice of the customer" recognizing there are four archetypical customer segments. It discusses the components that make up market share and includes the soft nonfinancial metrics and key performance indicators (KPIs) boards must look at. It shows how the "Five P" framework can be applied to evaluate whether anything has been missed.

Chapter 10, "Managing Risk" discusses the board's role in risk management, dividing risk into three categories: "cultural risks," "traditional risks," and "earnings driver risks."[2] It defines risk and focuses on cultural risks because research suggests these are rarely covered by boards, yet they are often the most material risks. It also explores systemic risks, which are a relatively new area for boards to consider, as a result of the lessons learned in the Global Financial Crisis, where boards also learned to their cost to pay attention to KPI risk and CEO risk. It shows how the "Five P" framework can be applied to evaluate whether anything has been missed.

Chapter 11, "Planning Succession; Managing Talent" discusses succession planning and talent management. It begins by exploring how best to plan succession for the board, discussing criteria for effective directors, using directors' gap analysis in terms of their ability to contribute to board discussions across eleven knowledge and performance parameters. It then deals with CEO succession planning, the problems in recruitment and what to look for in today's CEO. Based on research by INSEAD it argues that effective CEOs today are "chief enabling officers" rather than the traditional "chief executive officers" and explores the seven attributes of such CEOs and how such CEOs behave in times of crisis. It explores the issues surrounding CEO remuneration and discusses the merits of a number of alternative approaches.

It covers four steps in talent management and introduces the concept of feasibility feedback—relating gaps in organizational design and personal development plans to the ability of the organization to achieve the desired business strategy. It shows how the "Five P" framework can be applied to evaluate whether anything has been missed.

Chapter 12, "Ensuring Internal Controls" deals with internal controls. The chapter begins by comparing the three lines of defense and five lines of assurance philosophies. It goes on to look at what matters in the numbers and the seven areas in financial reporting directors must dig into to understand what is really happening if they are to meet the twenty-first century standard for the duty of care. Given the increasing penalties for noncompliance, the chapter explores six practices directors should consider adopting for the audit committee to have effective control. It then briefly

---

[2] Booz Allen & Hamilton (2004), "Too Much SOX Can Kill You: Resolving the Compliance Paradox."

discusses the COSO approach to enterprise risk management. It shows how the "Five P" framework can be applied to evaluate whether anything has been missed.

Chapter 13, "Engaging Stakeholders" discusses stakeholder engagement. This is an area most boards do not spend enough time on. The chapter begins by reminding boards there are other ways stakeholders can penalize bad practices than what investors choose to do, which tends to be the focus of much of the discussions on stakeholder engagement. It then looks at shareholder-driven market discipline, stakeholder-driven market discipline, and regulatory-driven stakeholder engagement. Stakeholders are defined as primary, secondary, and tertiary and their likely impact on the organization is discussed. The three objectives of stakeholder engagement are reviewed: building trust, soliciting support, and creating goodwill. The chapter covers the need to communicate the "ends" of the organization and appropriate time horizons so investors understand what the organization is trying to do. It then deals with the process of effective stakeholder engagement—categorizing stakeholders as advocates, supporters, spectators, saboteurs, and adversaries and discussing how best to deal with each.

Finally, the chapter deals with ways of communicating effectively, discussing the chain of command, the different roles of investor relations and PR, and the need to adhere to the six principles of effective communication.

Part Three: Creating Value Through Reputation, People, and Processes

The three most important contributors to long-term competitive advantage, the three most important assets any enterprise has are its reputation, people, and processes. However, they do not feature on the balance sheet and so are often undervalued or forgotten. Three chapters explore what boards could do differently to create sustainable long-term value provided they give reputation, people, and processes the attention they deserve. They also explore the issue of a "political tragedy of the commons" caused by individual boards focusing on doing what is best for their own organization at the expense of the environment, community, and economy, if all boards were to follow suit.

Chapter 14, "Focusing on Reputation" discusses the need for boards to focus on it when making decisions, particularly now more than 80% of the value of companies is intangible and directors have come to recognize reputation risk is their number one risk. It shows five ways a good reputation improves business and explores its role in setting strategy: defining a sustainable mission, creating a compelling vision, and reconciling value creation and extraction. It discusses how best to minimize reputation risk across the company value chain looking at vulnerabilities in the areas of "natural," "social" and "human" capital; in other words, at the sources of reputation risk in the environmental, social, and workplace practices of the company and how to mitigate them.

Chapter 15, "Investing in People" begins by exploring the paradox that directors regularly say people are assets but treat them as costs. This is because the financials only record people as payroll costs in the income statement and do not show them as assets on the balance sheet. As a result, boards seek to minimize and externalize the costs of people. Employers who offer "psychic" income (vocations and fashion) also underpay, justifying their actions on the grounds of the "psychic income" they offer. As a result of thinking of people as costs, boards tend to treat people as being disposable, especially in Anglosphere economies. This leads to low loyalty and lack of investment in long-term training and long-term relationships, which have been developed successfully by "Rhenish capitalist" economies. This in turn has led to more successful economies and better jobs for the middle- and lower-income groups than has been true of the United States and the United Kingdom. The chapter then goes on to discuss how best to invest in people by recognizing there are four different types of leadership. It argues HR should stop trying to fit "square pegs into round holes," ignoring the importance of default personalities, which make people suited for jobs requiring their default personality. It also makes the case for having two career ladders—a managerial ladder and a technical ladder—in recognition of the fact most people do not want to manage other people.

Chapter 16, "Harnessing Processes to Create Long-Term Value" looks at how boards can use processes differently to create long-term value, recognizing the importance of an external "CG ecosystem" to support their efforts. The chapter begins by recognizing why boards fail and suggests six process changes to help them do better: using "rotating Devil's Advocacy" to create constructive challenge in the boardroom; adopting activity-based costing to understand the true sources of profitability; reframing budget and cost control decisions; setting KPIs and targets using a ten-step process; adopting a systematic and effective innovation process; and last and perhaps most important, recruiting more women to boards.

The chapter then explores what is needed outside companies to reinforce their efforts at good governance. It describes an effective "CG ecosystem" consisting of four factors: effective regulation—IOSCO best practice; professional boards—supported by mandatory training and a qualified roster of directors from whom to choose; professional capital market intermediaries; and educated, financially literate investors. These four factors in turn need to be supported by good public governance; a judiciary that understands commercial law unafraid of enforcing the law, including custodial sentences; and educated investigative business journalists that follow the money wherever it leads, supported by professional external auditors to ensure accurate and timely financial reporting.

Part One: **Anatomy of Corporate Governance**

This part consists of six chapters. The first two chapters set the "conceptual" framework of corporate governance. The next four chapters explore "operational" considerations affecting boards.

Chapter 1
What Is Corporate Governance and Why It Matters

You will find this book to be a global look at governance issues. This chapter is presented in three parts: the first defines corporate governance showing how it has changed over the years to include long-term outcomes and stakeholder considerations, no longer focusing just on satisfying shareholders; the second explores why governance matters; the third discusses two caveats regarding implementation.

What Is Corporate Governance?

Corporate governance (CG) is a relatively recent idea,[i] though the principles on which it is based are as old as humanity's invention of organizations requiring people to come together to achieve a common purpose.

There are too many definitions of CG to do them all justice. The basis for this book is one I like for its completeness:

> Corporate governance is defined as the *process and structure* used to direct and manage the business and affairs of the company towards promoting business prosperity and corporate accountability with the ultimate objective of realising long-term shareholder value while [considering] the interest of other stakeholders.
>
> Corporate governance provides a *framework of control mechanisms* that support the company in achieving its goals, while preventing unwanted conflicts. The pillars of corporate governance such as ethical behaviour, accountability, transparency and sustainability are important to the governance of companies and stewardship of investors' capital. Companies that embrace these principles are more likely to produce long-term value than those that are lacking in one or all.
>
> Proper governance identifies the *distribution of rights and responsibilities* among different participants in the company and outlines among others the rules and procedures for decision-making, internal control and risk management. Corporate governance is not only concerned with shareholder interests but requires balancing the needs of other stakeholders such as employees, customers, suppliers, society and the communities in which the companies conduct their business.[ii] [Emphases mine]

This definition of CG widens the areas of responsibility and accountability of directors to include long-term outcomes and the needs of other stakeholders, going further than just focusing on the needs of shareholders. It reflects the transition from shareholder capitalism of the 1980s and 1990s to stakeholder capitalism in the twenty-first century. This progression can be seen when comparing earlier, narrower definitions of CG, which do not really take stakeholders into account and do not specify the importance of long-term outcomes, for example:

DOI 10.1515/9781547400935-001

> Governance is a system of rules, procedures and processes by which a company is directed and controlled. Specifically, it is framework by which various stakeholder interests are balanced and efficiently and professionally managed.[iii]

> Corporate Governance involves a set of relationships between a company's management, its board, its shareholders and other stakeholders. Corporate Governance also provides the structure through which the objectives of the company are set, and the means of attaining those objectives and monitoring performance are determined.[iv]

These earlier definitions were accepted worldwide and served their purpose well. After all, the Cadbury Committee Report was the foundation document for all CG; the Organization of Economic Cooperation and Development (OECD) Principles of CG were the reference document for regulators in IOSCO.[v] Limited reference was made to stakeholders, reflecting the twentieth century emphasis on shareholders. They also seemed to assume CG frameworks could be applied universally without too much difficulty. As jurisdictions began to take CG seriously, they discovered applying the principles of CG proved to be more challenging than expected. As a result, the OECD redefined CG in 2015, recognizing "one size does not fit all":

> Effective corporate governance requires a sound legal, regulatory and institutional framework that market participants can rely on when they establish their private contractual relations. This corporate governance framework typically comprises elements of legislation, regulation, self-regulatory arrangements, voluntary commitments and business practices that are the result of a country's specific circumstances, history and tradition. The desirable mix between legislation, regulation, self-regulation, voluntary standards, etc., will therefore vary from country to country. The legislative and regulatory elements of the corporate governance framework can usefully be complemented by soft law elements based on the "comply or explain" principle such as corporate governance codes in order to allow for flexibility and address specificities of individual companies. *What works well in one company, for one investor or a particular stakeholder may not necessarily be generally applicable to corporations, investors and stakeholders that operate in another context and under different circumstances.*[vi] [Emphasis mine]

The 2008–2009 Global Financial Crisis highlighted the need to include ethics as an element of good CG and other failures raised questions about should be done about pension funds. I quite like this definition of CG, which recognizes the diversity of jurisdictions, articulates the need to consider ethics, long-term stakeholder expectations, and includes recognizing the rights of workers past, present, and future:

> *Different countries have different ideas as to what constitutes good corporate governance*[1]. ... *In essence we believe that good corporate governance consists of a system of structuring, operating and controlling a company such as to achieve the following:*

---

1 Belinda Gibson formerly of ASIC, the Australian regulator is reported to have said, "the role of a regulator is to match the risk appetite of the society where they regulate," in email correspondence between the author and Chris Bennett on October 6, 2018.

– A culture based on a foundation of sound business ethics fulfilling the long-term strategic goal of the owners while taking into account the expectations of all the key stakeholders, and in particular:
   o Consider and care for the interests of employees, past, present and future
   o Work to maintain excellent relations with both customers and suppliers
   o Take account of the needs of the environment and the local community
   o Maintaining proper compliance with all the applicable legal and regulatory requirements under which the company is carrying out its activities.[vii] [Emphasis mine]

Why Corporate Governance Matters

Too often when discussing the issue of good governance with directors, I have been met with responses that it is a waste of time and effort; it is a regulatory burden[2] which only the largest companies can afford to deal with; that the reporting requirements for public listed companies are increasingly complicated and of relevance only to academics and the odd analyst who has the patience to wade through long documents that are really another form of PR greenwash.

Countering their arguments is made more difficult by the fact that although there is a correlation between good governance and better financial performance over the long term, and there is evidence that good governance leads to better performance, there is also evidence to the contrary. On balance, however, it seems good CG does in fact lead to better results in terms of higher profits and better dividends.[viii]

Aside from the legal requirements of governance, when investors think of the benefits of good CG, they split into three groups:

1. *The first group believes that companies with good CG will perform better over time. In the long run,* it will translate into higher stock prices, with better upside potential. Studies in the United States,[ix] Germany,[x] and India[xi] tended to support this expectation.
2. *The second group sees good CG as being a way of limiting the downside risk* to which companies may be exposed. They believe it will reduce the chances of bad things happening to the company and, if they do happen, the company will recover faster because it has good governance to deal with the problems as they arise.

---

2 Directors should remember when complaining about CG regulatory burdens, regulators respond to political pressure resulting from the public's reaction to scandals. The worse the scandal, the greater the pressure brought to bear on regulators. In a sense, companies have only themselves to blame if the regulatory response is unduly harsh. The scandals that created the demand for CG: Polly Peck and Maxwell in the United Kingdom in the 1990s; Enron in the United States in 2001 and the Global Financial Crisis scandals in the United States and United Kingdom were egregious. I discuss further why we have regulations in Chapter 2.

3. *The third group recognizes the importance of self-fulfilling prophecies.* So, even though they regard CG as a fad, they go along with it because so many investors think it matters, and therefore, they expect share prices to reflect this.[xii]

In the case of public listed companies, there may be another reason why CG can lead to better shareholder value—how accountable boards feel they are to shareholders. Companies where boards felt less accountable performed less well than those where boards took their responsibilities to shareholders more seriously. The American study mentioned earlier[xiii] classified the former group of companies as "dictatorships" (those with the most management power and lowest shareholder rights) and the latter as "democracies" (those with least management power and strongest shareholder rights). The "democracies" appear to have outperformed the "dictatorships" by a "statistically significant 8.5 percent per year" in firm valuations.[xiv] The study also showed that a dollar invested on September 1, 1990 would have grown to US$3.39 in the "dictatorship" portfolio but would have grown to US$7.07 in the "democracy" portfolio by December 31, 1999. The "democracy" portfolio would have outperformed the "dictatorship" portfolio by 9.3 percent per annum.[xv] Two factors may help explain the difference in performance:

1. *Bad investment decisions:* The more firmly entrenched managers are, the more likely they are to invest unwisely from the shareholder's point of view.[xvi]
2. *Agency costs:* Acquisitions create agency costs, particularly when the acquirer has overpaid for the acquired company. Value-destroying capex may thus be one of the reasons for the poorer performance of "dictatorship" companies (as we shall see in Chapter 2). Other agency problems can be caused by low ownership of the projects by managers, high free cash flow being invested in projects of diminishing returns, and unwise diversifications.[xvii] "Dictatorship" companies may not have sufficiently strong checks and balances at the board level to ensure CEOs do not get carried away as a result of past successes. The evidence from the Global Financial Crisis in the cases of Bear Stearns, Merrill Lynch, Lehman Brothers, and Royal Bank of Scotland would suggest shareholders had little say in what happened as their boards were enthralled with CEOs with oversized personalities reinforced by a track record of past success.[xviii]

Even so, it is important to remember good CG does not interest all shareholders equally. Investors with a low portfolio turnover (selling 0–40% of their portfolio within one year) were willing to pay a premium on average of 12% for good CG. On the other hand, investors with a high portfolio turnover rate (41–100% sold within a year) were only willing to pay a 7% premium. High frequency traders, day traders are not interested at all in CG. As long as their profits exceed their commission costs, they are happy.[xix]

The asset management philosophy also affects the attitudes of investors to CG:

> Value investors are interested in the long-term and so are more likely to appreciate good CG than growth investors where the growth in the company can hide failures of CG. Although these errors might cause profits to be lower than they otherwise should be, this does not matter so much when there are high price-earnings multiples justified by prospective earnings growth. In fact, the difference in the two attitudes is best illustrated by the two quotes below, cited in a McKinsey research paper:[xx]
>
> *Value investor*: "A good board may help to lift an underperforming stock and capture hidden value."
>
> *Growth investor*: "One major shareholder...said that he did not want to talk about governance or anything else and had bought our stock only because of the growth trend he foresaw in the industry as a whole."[xxi]

The growth investor's attitude may well explain the willingness of investors to hold Alphabet (Google), Facebook, Alibaba, and other growth stocks where the founders deny the ordinary shareholders a say in the way the business is run through dual class share structures.[xxii] Dual class share structured companies are the ultimate "dictatorship" companies. They include Berkshire Hathaway, Expedia, Fitbit, Ford, Google (Alphabet), GoPro, Hyatt Hotels, Snap, and Under Armour, to name a few.

The defense of such an undemocratic structure is that:

> Recent research[xxiii] suggests that in order to foster innovation, reward for long-term success and job security are important. The way that dictatorship firms are set up facilitates this.
>
> Data suggests[xxiv] that dictatorship firms can increase company value by allowing it to take a long-term view. Hence, shareholders provide capital to dictatorship firms by trusting the skills and vision of the founder and leadership team to identify, invest in, and manage projects that guarantee continual high future growth.[xxv]

Growth "dictatorship" companies can become a problem for shareholders in the following three circumstances:

Growth and innovation slow down
The firm now has fewer investment opportunities—the justification for its undemocratic structure. As a result, cash piles grow and the excess money is invested increasingly ineffectively, instead of being returned to the shareholders who are disenfranchised from pressuring management to do so.

Handling succession
The children of innovator-founders are often not the best people to take over (this is a problem faced by family firms as well). In these circumstances, just as with family

firms, shareholders may be unable to prevent the management being handed on to people who are not best qualified to take over, and there is little they can do about it.

When dramatic change in leadership is needed
This occurs:

> when a dramatic change in the course of action of the company is required—particularly in response to scandals. Since 2010, Facebook has had ten sets of legal issues[xxvi] (excluding the Cambridge Analytica scandal). In a company with strong shareholder rights, it is likely that a change in the executive leadership team would have happened by now. Not all hope for better corporate governance is lost, however. The ride-hailing app company Uber provides an example of how change can still happen,[xxvii] despite having an entrenched leadership team. After several scandals emerged at the end of 2017, its board made former Uber CEO Travis Kalanick step down and revoked his super-voting rights, creating equal voting power among shareholders.[xxviii,xxix]

Increasingly, leading CEOs like Warren Buffett and Jamie Dimon[xxx] argue against companies reporting quarterly earnings on the grounds that such reporting forces CEOs and boards to focus too much on short-term numbers management at the expense of long-term value creation. And yet, regulators introduced quarterly earnings reporting in the name of good governance and transparency to protect investors from managers who were hiding malpractices. The unintended consequence was that:

> Earnings guidance can lead management teams to under-invest in the future and can crimp earnings growth, according to a 2017 FCLT Global report.[xxxi]

Their voices are being heard as fewer and fewer companies in the United States are reporting quarterly earnings according to the 2017 FCLT Global Report cited in the Fortune article:

> The report found fewer than a third of S&P 500 companies still issued quarterly guidance in 2016, down from 36% in 2010. About 31% gave annual earnings-per-share guidance. Companies including Unilever, Facebook, GlaxoSmithKline and BP have scrapped the practice in favor of multiyear outlooks, according to the report.[xxxii]

This is just as well because good CG does matter as is shown in this extract:

> *Corporate governance—the authority structure of a firm—lies at the heart of the most important issues of society* [emphasis mine] ... such as "who has claim to the cash flow of the firm, who has a say in its strategy and its allocation of resources." The corporate governance framework shapes corporate efficiency, employment stability, retirement security, and the endowments of orphanages, hospitals, and universities. "It creates the temptations for cheating and the rewards for honesty, inside the firm and more generally in the body politic." It influences social mobility, stability and fluidity... It is no wonder then, that corporate governance provokes conflict. Anything so important will be fought over... like other decisions about authority, corporate governance structures are fundamentally the result of political decisions.

> Shareholder value is partly about efficiency. But there are serious issues of distribution at stake—job security, income inequality, social welfare. There may be many ways to organize an efficient firm.[xxxiii]

The reader might be forgiven for thinking at this point CG is only relevant to public listed companies. In fact, CG is important to every enterprise that selects and implements strategy, manages risk, plans succession, engages stakeholders, and ensures there are proper controls on how work is done, whether it is listed, incorporated or for-profit.

There are two more reasons why CG matters to any organization:
1. *CG's focus on long-term value creation* reconciles two different perspectives of the "Principal-Agent Conflict"[xxxiv] where the principal, the owner of the business, demands a rate of return the agents, the managers of the business, regard as too ambitious. Managers always ask for more resources with which to do less than the board, under pressure from the owners, will accept. Every year, the budgeting process is one of haggling over what is an acceptable short-term risk-adjusted rate of return. Negotiation in the board forces owners and managers to compromise about where they should be on the risk-adjusted conflict continuum. However, directors, representing the owners, may find it difficult to agree with management for three reasons:
    a. *They may be looking at the problem through "win-lose" lenses*, when a "win-win" solution might be more appropriate.
    b. *Each side may have a different appreciation of the risks involved,* making it difficult for them to decide what is a reasonable rate of return for a given level of risk.
    c. *They may disagree on the appropriate time horizons.*

    Making matters more complicated for directors of listed companies, different classes of owner do not have the same expectations regarding risk and time horizons. There are:
    a. *Shareholders looking for immediate returns* (high frequency traders, day traders).
    b. *Hedge funds and analysts interested in quarterly results.*
    c. *Patient capital:* Buy-to-hold investors, pension funds, insurance companies, and sovereign wealth funds with a long-term view, which may extend beyond the tenure of existing management.

    This leaves directors facing the question: which shareholders should be given priority if they do not all have the same objectives, risk appetites, and time horizons. Perhaps the problem can be resolved if directors reframe the issue as reconciling needs of owners and managers by creating sustainable value. If directors and management can think about how best to create sustainable value rather than arguing about where they stand on the risk-adjusted continuum; if they can focus on moving beyond the boundary set by the risk-adjusted continuum, they may be able to create greater and more sustainable long-term value. This is the prize offered by focusing on CG's long-term focus and its wider remit than just considering maximizing shareholder value.

2. *CG failure can be incredibly expensive.* The failure of Lehman Brothers in 2008 destroyed more value than the five worst natural disasters in human history combined—US$ 691.9 billion versus US$585 billion (Table 1.1). This does not include the social impact around the world caused by the resulting Great Recession: suicides; mental illness; careers destroyed and lower birth rates.

Table 1.1: CG failure can be incredibly expensive[xxxv]

Top Five Natural Disasters	Cost billions	Top Five Failures of CG	Cost $billions
Tohoku earthquake (Japan)	210	Lehman Brothers	691.9
Sichuan earthquake (China)	147	Washington Mutual	328.9
Hurricane Katrina (USA)	144	AIG*	170.0
Northridge earthquake (USA)	43	WorldCom	103.9
Hurricane Andrew	41	Enron	63.4
Total	585	Total	1,357.3

*US$170 billion was injected into AIG to prevent it going bankrupt.[xxxvi]

More worrying than the astonishing cost of the Lehman Brothers debacle is the trend of rising costs of failure. Enron, unprecedented disaster that it was, is only a rounding error when compared with Lehman Brothers seven years later. The reason for the quantum leap in the cost of CG failure is the financialization and globalization of the economy that took place in the intervening years.

When Enron went bankrupt in 2001, it was the most expensive disaster to have occurred in the United States and was only overtaken by Hurricane Katrina (the costs of the 2017 hurricane season have still to be totaled) and 9/11. Yet, 9/11 cost less than Lehman Brothers (Table 1.2), even after all the knock-on costs are taken into account, whereas the loss in value associated with Lehman excludes the knock-on effects of the crisis it precipitated.

Given the potentially expensive downsides posed by failures of CG, perhaps the best way to regard CG, if you are not persuaded by the research that CG does in fact add value in the long-term, is to treat it as an insurance policy to mitigate the downside and to recover faster from a crisis when it strikes.

Table 1.2: Total costs of 9/11

Items	Cost US$ billions
Four aircraft destroyed	0.4
World Trade Center buildings	3.0–4.5
Damage to Pentagon	1.0
Clean-up cost	1.3
Property and infrastructure	10.0–13.0
Federal emergency funds	40
Direct job losses and lost wages	17
Losses to New York City	95
Insurance industry losses	40
Lost air traffic revenue	10
Total	217.7–222.2

Source: Institute for the Analysis of Global Security, "How much did the September 11 attack cost America?"[xxxvii]

Two Caveats Regarding Implementation

Most of the literature on CG and the regulation supporting CG assume it matters because it concerns publicly listed companies with widely dispersed shareholders who need protecting.

This raises two questions.

Does CG matter to 100% owned companies or companies that are not listed (family firms and government statutory bodies that do business)?

From a regulatory, legal and reporting perspective the answer is, as quoted below:

> Obviously, CG is not a problem for the 100 percent owner-manager of a business. Nor is it much of a problem for the majority stockholder (or group) which controls the board of directors and can fire managers at any time [e.g. venture capitalists and family firms] ...So CG is an issue mainly for minority stockholders, in a firm controlled by the managers where there are no significant stockholders that can easily work together[3]. In that situation, the stockholders potentially can

---

[3] During discussions at the OECD Asian Roundtable on Corporate Governance held on November 7, 2018 at the Securities Commission Malaysia, one of the speakers from the OECD argued that the focus on resolving the "principal-agent" conflict resolves a problem that exists, mainly in Anglosphere capital markets because of their widely dispersed shareholder mode. However, this does not exist to the same degree in Asian capital markets where dominant controlling shareholders (either family or government) are the norm who do not face the "principal-agent" conflict to the same extent because their control allows them to behave as owners with "skin in the game."

still exert control to protect their interests but face formidable difficulties (in terms of transaction costs and inadequate incentives) in actually working together.[xxxviii]

From a control and accountability perspective, however, CG would prevent scandals like 1MDB[xxxix] occurring in unlisted government bodies. Whether it would have as significant an impact on family-controlled firms is less clear, given family-controlled companies on average appear to outperform listed companies with widely dispersed shareholders:

> The financial performance of family-owned companies provides support for their strong relative share-price performance. Revenue growth of family-owned companies has been higher than for non- family-owned peers for each of the past ten years, EBITDA margins are higher and cash flow returns are stronger too. In addition, family-owned companies tend to focus more on future growth as below-average pay-out ratios support in-line-to-above capex intensity and above-average R&D spending...
>
> These calculations show a clear "alpha" generated by the family-owned universe. We would specifically highlight the following revenue growth characteristics:
> - For each of the past ten years, family-owned companies have shown stronger revenue growth than their non-family-owned peers.
> - In 2009, when non-family-owned companies experienced a revenue decline of around 7%, family-owned companies still managed to grow their top lines, albeit by just 30 bp.
> - Over the past two years, the family-owned companies have managed to increase their top-line growth differential to 370 bp in 2016 from 320 bp in 2013, and 250 bp in 2014.
> - Family-owned companies generated a high risk-adjusted revenue growth (i.e. annual average revenue growth divided by the standard deviation of this growth), which might indeed be a result of taking more of a longer-term view with regard to investment decisions.
> - We have also analyzed revenue growth differentials between family and non-family owned companies on a regional basis. Generally speaking, we find that the revenue growth "alpha" is apparent across all main regions.[xl]

Is there a need to localize CG to meet emerging market conditions?

Many emerging markets do not just have a preponderance of family firms,[4] but also have entities upon which governments apply pressure in the interests of "national service" at the expense of individual shareholders:

> This is more serious because, in the case of many of these markets, the countries are young, and government believe they have a duty to build their nations through "pillar industries" and other forms of direction of capital to projects whose justification is not only economic.[xli]

---

[4] Family SMEs are the majority in all jurisdictions, not just emerging markets and in the words of the same OECD speaker at the November 7, 2018 conference in Malaysia: "Companies with concentrated ownership are the rule rather than the exception in the 50,000 listed companies worldwide. Companies being owners of other companies is normal in Asia and elsewhere; except in Anglosphere markets."

The scope for bad CG under abusive pressure from the government is a real risk, with the scandal of Malaysia's 1MDB an unfortunate example.[xlii]

As research done by McKinsey in 2001 showed, broadly speaking there are two types of capital markets in the world. Although the study contrasted the "control" model with the "market" model of only the United States and United Kingdom, the *assumptions and structure* of the "market" model are to be found in Canada, Australia, South Africa, New Zealand, and the more developed Commonwealth countries (Singapore and Malaysia), as well as Hong Kong. Their underlying structure and assumptions of how companies operate and how capital markets work differ. The regulatory superstructures built on these foundations also differ between the "black letter law approach" of the United States versus the "principles-based" approach favored by the United Kingdom and the Commonwealth, Japan's combination of both; and the need for each regulatory regime to reflect the levels of maturity of their market and its participants. Undeveloped markets are more likely to focus on "rules-based" approaches, whereas more sophisticated markets are more likely to adopt "principles-based" approaches.

Different market structures lead to different worldviews

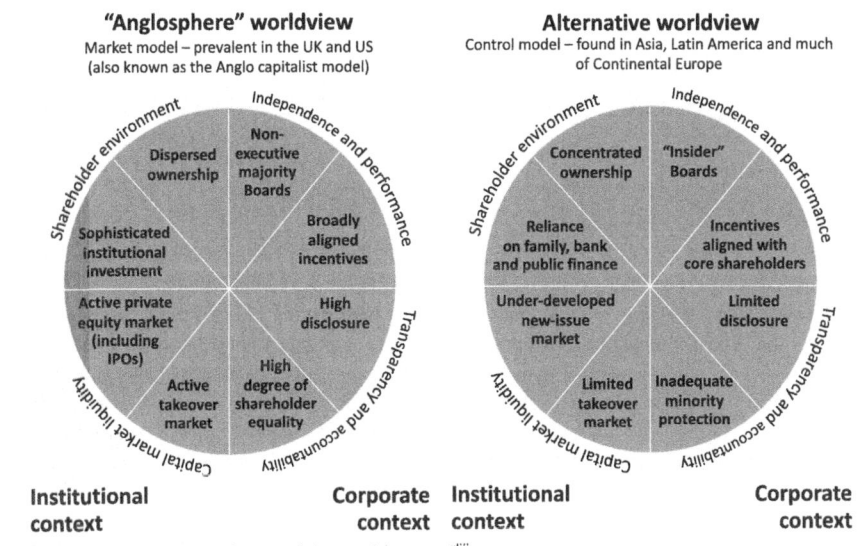

Figure 1.1: Two capital market models: worlds apart[xliii]

As you can see from the institutional contexts (on the left side of both circles) in Figure 1.1, the shareholder environments in the two models are quite different, as are the chances of activist shareholders holding boards to account because of the difference in the liquidity of the two types of market and in the levels of ownership concentration. What about the corporate contexts (on the right side of each circle)? The boards are structured differently, including, in addition, unitary boards in common law jurisdictions, as opposed to two-tier boards in others. This affects their respective levels of independence and the value placed on the importance of shareholder rights and transparency.

Given the disparity in the underlying drivers of board behavior in the two models, CG needs to be localized and can not just be "exported" using the three variants of the "Anglosphere"[5] model: The U.S.'s rules-based "black letter law" or the UK's and the Commonwealth's slightly different "principle-based" approach.

As important, are the differing assumptions owners in Asian markets have regarding INEDs shown in Table 1.3.

There is considerable evidence[6] for the Asian view regarding the ability of family-controlled firms to deliver better long-term value than companies with widely dispersed shareholders.[xliv]

---

5 Although I have chosen to call the "market" model jurisdictions, "Anglosphere," there are three versions: the United States, United Kingdom, and Commonwealth. The United States allows chair-CEOs with boards made up of INEDs with only the CEO as an ED; Delaware's judges interpret the business judgment rule more generously than either the United Kingdom or Commonwealth models because of the emphasis on "black letter law." Like the United Kingdom, the U.S. approach to CG is that "boards govern and direct, management manages." The United Kingdom is the original source of CG codes and recommends separating the chair and CEO, but only expects one third of the board to be INEDs, allowing EDs to be board members. The United Kingdom and Commonwealth approaches to regulation are principles-based unlike the US's rules-based approach. The Commonwealth model shares the same legal system of common law, inherited from the British with judges referring to cases in other Commonwealth jurisdictions. However, leading jurisdictions specify that directors "manage and direct the affairs of the company," putting an extra burden of responsibility on INEDs. They also require the majority of the boards of listed companies to be INEDs.

6 *The CS Family 1000* published in 2017 by Credit Suisse's Research Institute found Asian family-controlled firms outperformed non-family-controlled firms over the period 2006–2017 in terms of returns; 12-month forward P/Es; absolute cash flow return on investment; investment in R&D. They were more long-term focused; with less than 15% using equity funding.

Table 1.3: Different assumptions regarding INEDs[xlv]

"Anglosphere" assumptions	Asian assumptions

1. The model assumes the existence of the "principal-agent conflict" resulting from widely dispersed shareholdings preventing shareholders from behaving like owners. To represent the interests of the owners (especially minorities), the INED must be independent, for without independence the INED can not be effective through the process of fearless, but constructive challenge:
   a. Independence of thought guarantees effectiveness as it allows fresh insights to be brought to the board, allowing proposal to be examined from a perspective that does not reflect vested interests
   b. Constructive challenge leads to better-informed decisions.
	1. In family-founded and led firms, the model assumes limited, if any "principal-agent conflict." Families know better than minority shareholders where the best interests of the firm lie because they have "skin in the game" and lengthy time horizons. Any "principal-agent conflict" is restricted to minority shareholders, represented by INEDs, who do not really understand the business, because they can not give it the time and attention it requires:
	   a. INEDs do not have enough access to key people to overcome asymmetry of information and if they did, it would undermine the chain of command and confuse managers about lines of authority in "high power distance" cultures
	   b. Harmony is crucial and challenge may lead to conflict, which is to be avoided; so, in practice most INEDs will not challenge.

2. The presence of INEDs reminds the board its fiduciary duty is to shareholders as owners and creditors, hence the appointment of INEDs to chair key committees of the board. Independence is essential if there are to be checks and balances on executive power.	2. The best guarantors of the interests of the shareholders are the founding family, whose investment in the firm and commitment to the firm over the long term is greater than that of the minority shareholders who are only interested in short-term performance.

Conclusion

Definitions of CG have evolved over the years to include a wider range of stakeholders and their interests, moving away from just considering shareholders. Increasingly regulators, investors and directors themselves are being forced to recognize the importance of CG, if only because the costs of failure can be so dramatic, not just for the company, but also for the wider economy. These costs are rising because of the increased interconnectedness resulting from the financialization and globalization of business.

Although most of the literature of CG focuses on the problems and issues faced by public listed companies, CG applies to any organization that is trying to achieve an outcome through teams of people who need to be directed effectively to achieve a common objective.

Equally, although most of the literature in English deals with CG in developed markets, with perhaps an excessive focus on "Anglosphere" capital markets, the principles of CG, suitably localized, apply to all markets. From the wider perspective of developing the right strategy, implementing it effectively, managing risk, planning succession and managing talent, ensuring proper internal controls and engaging stakeholders, CG still matters, as we will see in Chapters 8–11, regardless of the ownership structure or the cultural differences between "Anglosphere" capital markets and others. The importance of building a strong ethical foundation to CG should not be forgotten and I deal with this in Chapter 2.

References

i Eells, R.S. (1960), "The Meaning of Modern Business: An Introduction to the Philosophy of Large Corporate Enterprise" (Columbia University Press: New York). This is the first time the concept is mentioned in academic literature. The first time the term is applied to companies is by Sir Adrian Cadbury in the "Report of the Committee on the Financial Aspects of Corporate Governance" in 1992.

ii Securities Commission Malaysia (2017), *Malaysian Code on Corporate Governance*, 1.

iii Cadbury, A. (1992), *The Financial Aspects of Corporate Governance*, December 1, 1992, http://www.ecgi.org/codes/documents/cadbury.pdf, accessed on June 8, 2018.

iv OECD (2015), G20/OECD Principles of Corporate Governance 2015, 9, Columbia University Press:https://www.oecd.org/daf/ca/Corporate-Governance-Principles-ENG.pdf, accessed on August 8, 2018.

v IOSCO stands for the International Organization of Securities Commissions.

vi OECD (2015) op. cit., 13, https://www.oecd.org/daf/ca/Corporate-Governance-Principles-ENG.pdf, accessed on June 8, 2018.

vii https://www.applied-corporate-governance.com/definition-of-corporate-governance/ accessed on June 8, 2018.

viii Hermalin, B. and Weisbach, M. (1991), "The Effects of Board Composition and Direct Incentives on Firm Performance," *Financial Management* 20: 101–12; Shleifer, A. and Vishny, R.W. (1997), "A Survey of Corporate Governance," *Journal of Finance*, LII, No. 2: 737–83; Mitton, T. (2001), "A Cross-Firm Analysis of Corporate Governance on East-Asian Crisis," *Journal of Financial Economics*, May: 5–50; Becht et al. (2003), "Corporate Governance and Control," *Handbook of the Economics of Finance*, Constantinides et al. (eds), Elsevier: North Holland: 3–109; Denis, D. K. and McConnell, J. J. (2003), "International Corporate Governance," European Corporate Governance Institute Working Paper No 05/2003: 1–62; Holderness, C. G. (2003), "A Survey of Block Holders and Corporate Control," *FRBNY Economic Policy Review:* 51–64; Gugler, K. et al. (2004), "Corporate Governance and Globalization," *Oxford Review of Economic Policy* 20, No. 1: 129–56.

ix Gompers, P., Ishii, J., and Metrick, A. (2003), "Corporate Governance and Equity Prices," *The Quarterly Journal of Economics* 118, No. 1: 107–55; Brown, L. D. and Claylor, M. L. (2004), "Corporate Governance and Firm Performance," Working Paper, Georgia State University.

x Drobetz, D., Shillhofer, A., and Zimmermann, H. (2003), "Corporate Governance and Expected Stock Returns: Evidence from Germany," ECGI Working Papers Series in Finance, Number 11/2003, February 2003.

xi Banerjee, A. et al. (2009), "Corporate Governance and Market Value: Preliminary Evidence from Indian Companies," Standard & Poor's, September 2009, at www.standardandpoors.com

xii Zinkin, J. (2010), *Challenges in Implementing Corporate Governance: Whose Business is it Anyway?* (Singapore: John Wiley & Son), 2.

xiii Gompers, Ishii and Metrick, op. cit.

xiv Ibid., 110.
xv Ibid., 120.
xvi Ibid., 131.
xvii Ibid., 132.
xviii Zinkin, J. (2014), *Rebuilding Trust in Banks: The Role of Leadership and Governance* (Singapore: John Wiley & Sons), 25–42.
xix Felton, R., Hudnut, A., and Van Heeckeren, J. (1996), "Putting a Value on Board Governance," *McKinsey Quarterly* 4.
xx Ibid., 171.
xxi Zinkin (2010), op. cit., 4.
xxii The Conversation, "Does Mark Zuckerberg have too much power at the helm of Facebook?" March 28, http://theconversation.com/does-mark-zuckerberg-have-too-much-power-at-the-helm-of-facebook-940032018, accessed on June 9, 2018.
xxiii Baranchuk, N. et al. "Motivating Innovation in Newly Public Firms," SSRN, June 19, 2014, cited in The Conversation, op. cit.
xxiv Martijn Cremers, K. L. et al. (2017), "Staggered Boards and Long-Term Firm Value," *Journal of Financial Economics,* 126, No. 2, November: 422–44, cited in The Conversation, op. cit.
xxv The Conversation, op. cit.
xxvi Blumberg, P. and Bodoni, S., "Facebook Has a Long History of Resolving Privacy Claims on the Cheap," https://www.bloomberg.com/news/articles/2018-03-20/facebook-s-long-history-of-resolving-privacy-claims-on-the-cheap", 21, 2018, https://www.bloomberg.com/news/articles/2018-03-20/facebook-s-long-history-of-resolving-privacy-claims-on-the-cheap, accessed on June 9, 2018, cited in The Conversation, op. cit.
xxvii The Conversation, "Uber gets a backseat driver as Kalanick exits top job," June 21, 2017, https://theconversation.com/uber-gets-a-backseat-driver-as-kalanick-exits-top-job-79854, accessed on June 9, 2018, cited in The Conversation, op. cit.
xxviii Bensinger, G., "Uber Board Approves Series of Corporate Reforms," *The Wall Street Journal,* October 3, 2017, https://www.wsj.com/articles/uber-board-approves-series-of-corporate-reforms-1507073868, accessed on June 9, 2018, cited in The Conversation, op. cit.
xxix The Conversation, op. cit.
xxx "Warren Buffett and Jamie Dimon Really Want Companies to Stop Giving Quarterly Earnings Guidance," *Fortune,* June 7, 2018, http://fortune.com/2018/06/07/buffett-dimon-quarterly-earnings-guidance-short-term-thinking/ accessed on June 8, 2018.
xxxi Ibid.
xxxii Ibid.
xxxiii Gourevitch, Peter A. and Shinn, James (2005), *Political Power and Corporate Control: The New Global Politics of Corporate Governance* (Princeton, NJ: Princeton University Press), quoted in James McRitchie, "Corporate Governance Defined: Not So Easily," https://www.corpgov.net/library/corporate-governance-defined/ accessed on June 8, 2018.
xxxiv Jensen, M. C. and Meckling, W. (1976), "A Theory of the Firm: Governance, Residual Claims and Organizational Forms," *Journal of Financial Economics* 3, No. 4.
xxxv *Source:* BankrutpcyData.com, based on US SEC filings, quoted by PwC in Non-Executive Directors Development Training Program "Is it worth the Risk?" held in Kuala Lumpur over the period 2008–2010, quoted in Zinkin, J. (2014), *Rebuilding Trust in Banks,* 250.
xxxvi Wingfield, B. (2009), "Bankruptcy for AIG", www.forbes.com/2009/03/19/aig-bankruptcy-business-washington-aig.html, accessed on November 24, 2012.
xxxvii Institute for the Analysis of Global Security, "How Much Did the September 11 Attack Cost America?" http://www.iags.org/costof911.html, accessed on June 9, 2018.
xxxviii Scott, K. (2002), "Agency Costs and Corporate Governance," in *The New Palgrave Dictionary of Economics and the Law* (London: Palgrave Macmillan), 26–27, quoted in Wallace, P. and Zinkin, J. (2003), *Corporate Governance* (Singapore: John Wiley & Sons), 2–3.

xxxix "US DoJ charges Jho Low, former Goldman bankers over 1MDB." *The Star*, November 1, 2018, https://www.thestar.com.my/news/nation/2018/11/01/doj-to-move-on-1mdb/, accessed on November 3, 2018.
xl Klerk, E. et al. (2017), "The CS Family 1000," *Credit Suisse Research Institute*, September 2017, 18–19.
xli Zinkin (2010), op. cit., 12.
xlii Shukry, A. and Tan, A. (2018), "Malaysia Premier Says 1MDB Fund Wrongdoing Larger Than Thought," *Bloomberg*, May 16, 2018, https://www.bloomberg.com/news/articles/2018-05-16/declassified-report-on-malaysia-s-1mdb-shows-funding-anomalies, accessed on June 11, 2018.
xliii *Source:* Coombes, P. and Watson. M. (2001), "Corporate Reform in the Developing World," cited in Wallace, P. and Zinkin, J. (2005) *Corporate Governance* (Singapore: John Wiley & Sons), quoted in Zinkin (2010), op. cit.
xliv Klerk, E. et al. (2017), op. cit., 35–37.
xlv Based on "Non-Executive Directors Development" directors training program—run by the author when CEO of Securities Industry Development Corporation with PwC for listed companies on the Malaysian Stock Exchange.

Chapter 2
Integrating Ethics and Branding

This chapter expands the scope of corporate governance (CG) beyond the limited boundaries of board responsibility set by the law and regulations. It is presented in three parts: the first explores the importance of culture; the second, the wider problems of ethics that boards should consider; the shorter third part suggests boards should be more involved in branding their organizations—incorporating ethics into the organizational brand in order to build sustainable value.

The Importance of Culture

Three elements determine the ability of an organization to succeed long-term: first, an ethical foundation; second, satisfying needs of customers; and third, complying with regulations. Figure 2.1 illustrates the interaction between these three elements, its overarching culture, supported by its codes of conduct and compliance, encapsulated in the organization's brand where all three elements converge.

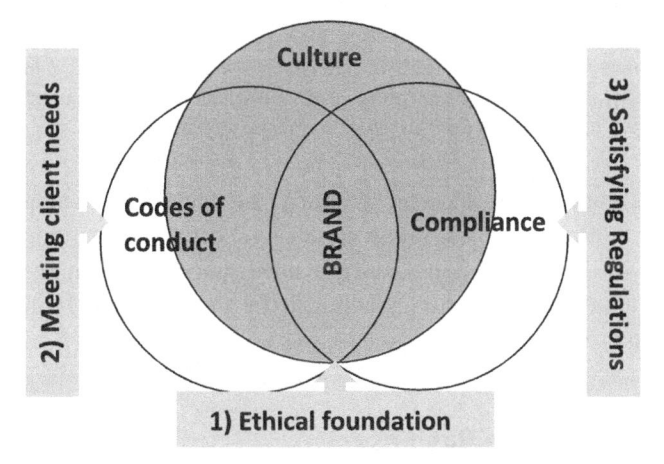

Figure 2.1: Boards must satisfy three operational constraints using culture, codes of conduct, and compliance, captured in the brand

Culture is the responsibility of the board, as are the supporting codes of conduct, defining how customers are treated and the compliance systems to satisfy requirements of regulators. It reflects the priorities of the organization:

> *A company's culture is the environment created by the priorities it sets...in a company's formal mission statement, for example, or in the structure of the organization and the power given to different departments and functions.*[i] [Emphasis mine]

Combined, they reflect and reinforce the culture of the organization and are captured in the company brand (see the section on branding later in this chapter).

The extent to which boards are now held responsible for the culture and codes of conduct of their companies by legislators and regulators is best shown by the following exchange between Marcus Agius, the former independent nonexecutive chair of Barclays during his testimony on July 10, 2012 to the United Kingdom Parliament's Treasury Committee regarding Barclays LIBOR fixing:

> *Michael Fallon:* "If you were concerned... that the bank's funding position should not be misinterpreted, ... why weren't you involved with Mr. Diamond [Barclays CEO] in telling your staff to get involved with the regulatory authorities as a matter of urgency?"
>
> *Marcus Agius:* "...because, for the avoidance of doubt—and maybe I should have made the point earlier—there is of course a distinction between what the board does and what the executive does. The executive is there to run the bank. The board does not run the bank. I stayed unusually connected with the senior management because of my concerns, but I did not make any executive decisions. That was not my job."
>
> *Michael Fallon:* "The question is: what does it say about your senior management team that in the end an instruction to manipulate LIBOR was not questioned? ... *You have overall responsibility for the culture of the bank. That is why you have resigned.*"[ii] [Emphasis mine]

Even though Marcus Agius was the nonexecutive chairman, the line of questioning to which he was subjected indicated an expectation of hands-on behavior regarding Barclay's operations that would be appropriate for an executive director. It also made it crystal clear he was accountable for the resulting failure in the bank's culture. I will discuss this further in Chapter 3.

Ensuring an Ethical Basis for the Business

CG in the past focused on what the law had to say about the responsibilities of boards with the law having little to say about *ethical* business behavior. The law does not claim to be the same as ethics. Behavior can be legal, but not ethical. So, staying within the boundaries of the law provides boards with no guarantee they are behaving ethically. Quite the reverse, many successful corporate lawyers have made their fortunes explaining loopholes in the law allowing businesses to obey the letter of the law, only to violate its spirit.

Ensuring an Ethical Foundation

The following quotation by Edward Freeman explains why directors need to remember there is more to business than just Milton Friedman's profit maximization. It also challenges the cynical view business can not be ethically grounded:

> You may think that business is all about profit, business people are unethical and business in general is a black art of guile and greed. Over the years I have found this to be mostly untrue.
>
> The story that business people are bad and what they do is morally questionable is false. For every Enron, there are 10,000 good companies. *And most companies, like most people, are trying to do the right thing.*
>
> *Business can solve the world's problems.* And more people are coming to believe that. Having observed business for more than three decades, I can tell things are changing. Thousands of new businesses are working to make the world a better place and, most importantly, add real value to our daily lives...
>
> ...The old way of thinking about business presupposes the point of business is to make profits. This is akin to believing that breathing is the purpose of life. *Yes, you have to breathe to live, just as businesses must make profits. But the purpose of business is usually determined by a passionate entrepreneur chasing a dream to change the world...*
>
> ...*Business and ethics go hand in hand.* Sometimes we act for selfish reasons and sometimes for other-regarding interests. Incentives are important, but so are values. Most people tell the truth and keep their promises and act responsibly most of the time. And we need to encourage that behavior. When these expectations are not met, it is not just bad ethics, it is also bad business.[iii] [Emphases mine]

There are many examples of business leaders whose initial drive, when establishing their businesses, was not profit, but to make the world a better place. Akio Morita, the founder of Sony and the father of the Walkman (the first portable audio cassette player and precursor of all MP3 players) wanted his engineers to create a product allowing his daughter to listen to music as she walked to school every day. *He wanted to make a difference in his daughter's day, not make money.* Steve Jobs had a vision of every home having a computer when he founded Apple with Steve Wozniak. He had no idea that Apple would become the most valuable firm in history.[iv] Sergei Brin, co-founder of Google (now Alphabet), likewise had no idea that his company would become the money-making behemoth it now is. *He believed knowledge is a good thing and wanted to help people by making information available to everybody.*[v] Narayana Murthy, CEO of Infosys, when asked what he wanted to achieve when he was founding the company answered:

> We spent a great deal of time thinking about how we would define success. We decided we did not want to become India's biggest company. We did not want to become its most profitable company. *We wanted to become its most respected company.* Everything we would do and every

decision we would make, from the most senior person to the most junior, would be judged on whether it made us more respected or not.[vi] [Emphasis mine]

Perhaps the most famous example of the founder of a great business having objectives that were much more important than making a profit, is General Robert Wood Johnson's *Credo*[1] which has guided Johnson & Johnson since 1935.[vii] It provides, in my opinion, the best justification for making a profit because it allows mistakes to be paid for and enables investment in the future, after which shareholders get a fair return:

We believe our first responsibility is to the doctors, nurses and patients, to mothers and fathers and all others who use our products and services. In meeting their needs everything we do must be of high quality. We must constantly strive to reduce our costs in order to maintain reasonable prices. Customers' orders must be serviced promptly and accurately. *Our suppliers and distributors must have an opportunity to make a fair profit.*

We are responsible to our employees, the men and women who work with us throughout the world. *Everyone must be considered as an individual. We must respect their dignity and recognize their merit.* They must have a sense of security in their jobs. Compensation must be fair and adequate, and working conditions clean, orderly and safe. We must be mindful of ways to help our employees fulfill their family responsibilities. Employees must feel free to make suggestions and complaints. *There must be equal opportunity for employment, development and advancement for those qualified. We must provide competent management, and their actions must be just and ethical.*

We are responsible to the communities in which we live and work and to the world community as well. We must be good citizens—support good works and charities and *bear our fair share of taxes.* We must encourage civic improvements and better health and education. *We must maintain in good order the property we are privileged to use, protecting the environment and natural resources.*

Our final responsibility is to our stockholders. *Business must make a sound profit. We must experiment with new ideas. Research must be carried on, innovative programs developed and mistakes paid for. New equipment must be purchased, new facilities provided and new products launched. Reserves must be created to provide for adverse times. When we operate according to these principles, the stockholders should realize a fair return.* [Emphases mine]

The most surprising paragraph in the *Credo* is the third, explicitly recognizing the obligation to the communities in which Johnson & Johnson operates, including the need to be environmentally responsible—an articulation of the social "license to operate"

---

1 It puts satisfying customers first (like Peter Drucker), respecting employees second, being a good citizen third, and giving shareholders a fair return last (unlike Milton Friedman). For examples of other successful companies that did not put profits first, I suggest reading Jim Collins's book *Good to Great*.

long before the term became popular in 1997.[2] I find it an impressive document; still used as a guiding principle in Johnson & Johnson more than eighty years later.

When I taught strategy at Nottingham University Business School's Malaysia Campus, I was concerned some of what was taught in business schools created a very different mental model from the assumptions of the Johnson & Johnson *Credo*.

Milton Friedman's Profit Maximization

Business schools for years taught maximizing shareholder value was the purpose of business. This assumed, in my view, wrongly, all shareholders have the company's long-term interests at heart. Instead many shareholders want maximum returns in a ninety-day horizon, pressurizing boards to sacrifice long-term considerations for short-term demands: sacrificing employees and harming communities in the interests of shareholder return. When they have no moral compass to remind them how money is made is as important as how much money is made, top managers and boards often succumb to these pressures. The last paragraph of the Johnson & Johnson *Credo* is an effective rebuke to the Friedmanite view that the purpose of business is to maximize shareholder value, arguing in its place they deserve a fair return rather than maximum return. Indeed, when I was doing my MSc in business administration at the London Business School in 1969 that was exactly what we were taught—but that was before Friedman and modern theories of finance.[3]

Coase's Theory of the Firm[viii]

Coase argued that the existence of the firm, what it does, what it chooses to make for itself, and what it contracts out to others to make in its place depends on transaction costs. This argument recognizes correctly externalities must be accounted for, as must

---

[2] The term "license to operate" from a social as opposed to technical perspective was first used by the World Bank in March 1997 at a World Bank conference on "Mining: The Next Twenty-Five Years," cited by Cooney, J. (2016), "Social License to Operate: Revisiting the Concept," Ryerson University, Institute for the Study of Social Responsibility, Ted Rogers School of Management, June 28, 2016.

[3] Interestingly, the current attitude to profit maximization has become much more nuanced: "While it is certainly true that a central objective of for-profit corporations is to make money, modern corporate law does not require for-profit corporations to pursue profit at the expense of everything else, and many do not do so." US Supreme Court (573, US 2014), Burwell v Hobby Lobby quoted by Barker, R. (2016): "The Duties and Liabilities of directors—Getting the Balance Right," in *The Handbook of Corporate Governance*, edited by Leblanc, R. (2016) (Hoboken, NJ: John Wiley & Sons Inc), 254: In the United Kingdom, section 172 of the 2006 Companies Act defines a key duty as being promoting the success of the company for the benefit of the shareholder constituency, although other stakeholders must be considered in decisions (doctrine of enlightened shareholder value). However, it is appropriate for companies to define a different purpose in the articles of association according to Lord Goldsmith, the then UK attorney general when driving the 2006 Companies Act that "for a commercial company, success will usually mean long-term increase in value" DTI, Ministerial Statements 2007.

the increasing burden of managing an ever-larger organization both in terms of the costs of doing so, and the difficulty of managing too large an enterprise. However, at the heart of the analysis is the view that the only thing to hold the different elements of a firm together are cost-related legal contracts, ignoring social relationships based on common interests and trust:

> This thinking underpins the view that a firm is temporary alliance of resources, brought together to get a task done. In other words, the firm is a purely economic instrument. Once the task is completed, the organization is reconfigured to meet the next challenging task. Hence outsourcing, 'offshoring' and down-sizing come easily to Anglo-Saxon managers.
>
> The problem with this idea is that it totally ignores the social aspect of work: that people value and enjoy the relationships they have with each other. That is where this idea goes wrong, at least for most people in most countries outside the English-speaking world...they respect and value the relationships that make work a social activity as well as an economic and legal one.[ix]

Having worked in Asia since 1985, where most people respect and value relationships more than the fine print of contracts, it seems to me this is a serious flaw in Coase's thinking.

Interestingly, the second paragraph of the *Credo* recognizes there is much more to a board's responsibility for its employees than to just see them through the lens of economic and legal contracts for tasks done.

Michael Porter's "Five Forces" Framework
The "Five Forces" framework redefined the nature of competition by recognizing there is a finite amount of market margin in each product market and all players in the supply chain from raw materials to end user or consumer compete for their share of it. If the product market is highly profitable and barriers to entry are low, new players will enter the product market, reducing its profitability. In addition, customers will find substitutes and alternatives to the products they are offered because they are unwilling to pay the prices demanded by their suppliers. It is a powerful insight, forcing directors to recognize their competitors are not just the other firms offering equivalent products in head-to-head competition with them, but also their suppliers and their customers in the fight for their share of market margin. However, this approach is based on a zero-sum, dog-eat-dog mindset, which sees all the participants in the supply chain as rivals rather than collaborators working to create maximum value together. The last sentence of the first paragraph of the *Credo* suggests another way of doing business, one closer to the way the Japanese do business, even though Johnson & Johnson is an American company.

Michael Jensen's and Oliver Williamson's Theories

Jensen argued there is a conflict of interest between managers and owners—the "principal-agent conflict" (discussed in Chapter 1). Managers were expected to look out for their own interests at the expense of shareholders and in the 1970s and 1980s, they did just that, culminating in the infamous leveraged buyout of RJR-Nabisco in 1989.[x]

If directors are to ensure an ethical foundation to their business, they must create their own version of the *Credo*, giving them a framework to resist the pressures to maximize short-term shareholder value at the expense of their customers and partners in the supply chain; of their employees; their communities and the environment; while ensuring a fair return to their shareholders.

Need for an Ethical Framework

Directors need an ethical framework to apply to decision making. When discussing ethics with directors and senior managers, I have found it simplest to explain there are five possible approaches directors could choose.

Machiavellian Ethics

Machiavellian ethics are pragmatic, weighing probable consequences and the likelihood of achieving given outcomes, often regardless of how the ends have been achieved. People practicing this type of ethics argue "the ends justify the means." The merit of this system is that at least any decision being taken can be assessed in terms of whether it will achieve the desired ends; and if it fails this basic test, then it should not be taken. However, in my experience, there are two problems with this approach:
1. It does not recognize organizations need codes of conduct and rules to help people to make predictable and consistent decisions.
2. It can lead to a failure of "Tone at the Top" with people encouraged to "do whatever it takes"—the kind of thinking that contributed to the failures of governance in Wall Street that have hurt us all so badly.

Utilitarian Ethics

These are a more moral extension of Machiavellian ethics, where the outcomes are weighed up by calculating how to "achieve the greatest good for the greatest number" for both the company and its customers. Principles are important only as rules of thumb. The problem with this approach is it encourages the tyranny of the majority and can lead to ignoring the needs of minorities and so be used to justify persecuting minority shareholders, which is poor CG. However, the biggest problem with consequential ethics, when deciding what road to take, is we rarely know what all the longer-term consequences are going to be.[4]

Kantian Rules-Based Ethics
Rules-based ethics (associated with the German philosopher Immanuel Kant) go one step further. They also consider the effect actions have on the rules of the organization and whether they adhere to given principles. This approach tends to be bureaucratic and perhaps overly legalistic, sometimes with a rigid adherence to the rules without due regard for particular circumstances that may justify exceptions. If there are too many exceptions or waivers, the rules themselves and the system they represent are discredited; outcomes become unpredictable; and corruption and free-riding are encouraged.

Rousseau's Social Contract Ethics
Social contract ethics recognize the need for mutuality and reciprocity if companies are to flourish: both within the organization itself, where "Do unto others as you would be done by" is as good a rule as any for behavior; and between the company and the community it serves. They also recognize no company is an island and it must therefore behave responsibly toward the community, minimizing the external costs the company creates, lest it create a "tragedy of the commons" with its associated risk of systemic failure. The problem with this approach is it can lead to tribal thinking within a profession where bad practices are covered up and justified in the name of loyalty to the group—a favorite subject of films with rogue cops protected from Internal Affairs, for example.

Personalistic Ethics
Personalistic ethics reflect what individuals feel about the decisions being taken. As such they often share the following three characteristics:
1. They are driven by the individual's personal sense of virtue and how the decision will reflect on the person's character and sense of self-worth.
2. They may be based on empathy where the decision maker puts himself/herself in the shoes of the other person when deciding what to do.

---

[4] For example, did the United States appreciate that by arming the mujahidin in Afghanistan to defeat the Soviet Union, they were helping create Al Qaeda, leading to 9/11, even though such a decision would have passed any test set by Machiavelli? Equally, when President Obama was persuaded by Vladimir Putin not to bomb Syria after President Assad used chemical weapons on his citizens with the argument that bombing would lead to unpredictable consequences for the entire region, could anybody have foreseen the horrors of the civil war that ensued?

3. They may be based on intuition driven by conscience—asking the question "will I be able to sleep at nights" when deciding.

Board members must be personally comfortable with the decisions they are involved with. The problem is often people who decide on personalistic grounds become impatient with other people calculating what to do, using either a rules-based or utilitarian approach, and may be uncomfortable with Machiavellian thinking.

I found the most helpful way for directors to determine whether a decision is both right and good is a tool to integrate the five approaches to ethics. Think of this as treating each approach as a step in deciding, shown in Table 2.1.

Table 2.1: A five-step approach to making right-good decisions

Type of approach	Questions to test for suitability
Step 1: Effectiveness (Machiavelli):	Will this decision deliver the expected outcome?
	Will the ends at least justify the means?
Step 2: Predictability (Kant):	Does making this decision violate our values, policies and procedures?
	Will it set a precedent we will come to regret?
	Is this the morally right thing to do, regardless of the consequences?
	If it is, will we disregard the consequences?
Step 3: Maximizing utility (Utilitarian):	How will we know if it achieves the greatest good for the greatest number?
	If it does, should we do this, even if it is morally the wrong thing to do?
	Do we really understand all the consequences?
Step 4: Mutuality (Rousseau):	Does society allow it?
	How will our people feel about each other if we do this?
	Will it create friction, if we don't do this?
	What will it do to their feeling of fairness?
Step 5: Self-image (Personalistic):	Will it pass the news headline test?
	Will I be able to sleep at night?
	What do I say to my 8-year old child?

Each step in the five-step process in Table 2.1 provides directors with a go-no-go point of reflection:

First step: The decision must pass the effectiveness test, otherwise why take the action?

Second step: Directors must consider its impact on policies and procedures and if it is morally wrong, does that mean they will not take the action regardless of the consequences—for example, refusing to give a bribe, even if it means losing the contract?

Third step: Directors must appreciate maximizing desirable outcomes based on the consequences of the decision sounds easy in principle, but it faces two problems:

1. The difficulty of appreciating all the longer-term consequences of a decision, consequences not understood properly at the time of the decision.
2. It could justify morally wrong behavior on the grounds of the "greatest good for the greatest number"—for example, agreeing to pay a bribe to keep people in their jobs or the US decision to arm the mujahidin in Afghanistan—that causes unforeseen problems later.

Steps 2 and 3 can often be in conflict with each other and the challenge for directors is how to reconcile the two approaches.

Fourth step: Directors need to consider the impact of the firm on the communities where it operates, lest it puts its social "license to operate" at risk. From an internal perspective, there is a need to consider whether what is being done for one group of employees will cause resentment among other groups.

Fifth step: Directors need to consider how they will feel when the consequences of their decisions become public knowledge. This is sometimes called the "smell test" or the "newspaper headline" test. I think the best test is whether a director will comfortable explaining to a child, maybe his/her own eight-year old son or daughter, what he/she does at the office. If this makes the director feel uncomfortable, it is a strong signal the decision in question fails to meet the personalistic ethics test.

If a decision passes all five go-no-go points, then it will be a right-good decision. Should it fail at any point up the "ladder," it raises a red flag and a probable signal to go no further. In the event this should happen, the director must ensure dissent is recorded in the minutes, even if the majority of the board votes otherwise. If the firm continues on that path and ignores the director's objections, the director may have to resign.

Meeting Client Needs Ethically

Directors are ultimately responsible for ensuring clients' needs are met and satisfied in an ethical manner. Failure to do so can have serious impacts on the degrees of freedom regulators will allow the company.

Goldman Sachs' Abacus deal in 2007 leading up to the Global Financial Crisis was perhaps one of the best examples of this disconnect between legality and ethical behavior.[xi] Goldman was accused of deliberately mis-selling collateralized debt obligations (Abacus) to an Australian hedge fund as a great deal, knowing full well they would lose money, because they (Goldman) had created the product to benefit the counter-party (Paulson's hedge fund).

> The U.S. Securities and Exchange Commission claims Goldman misled institutional investors in the Abacus deal by failing to disclose that hedge fund manager John Paulson was shorting the synthetic collateralized debt obligation and also had help [from Goldman] to pick the underlying portfolio of 90 mortgage-backed securities...
>
> ...The SEC said institutional investors lost $1 billion on the deal, while Paulson's hedge fund, Paulson & Co, made $1 billion from shorting the transaction.[xii]

Perhaps the most extraordinary feature of the way Goldman behaved in this and the Timberwolf case was the extent to which it was in absolute violation of its own professed business principles shown in Table 2.2.

Given this kind of behavior, where practice was so different from the published code of conduct and where UBS, Lloyds-TSB, Citi, and Deutsche,[xiii] also violated their professed business principles, I am not surprised many people believe business and business ethics are a contradiction in terms; that people will do whatever it takes to meet their targets and make the profits demanded of them by shareholders who do not care how the money is made.

In their defense of Goldman to Congress, the lawyers were able to make the case although what they had done was unethical, it was not illegal. Senator Carl Levin's outraged reaction was in that case the law needed to be changed. Goldman's lawyers won the battle and lost the war, as this finding was one of the reasons in 2010 for Congress passing the Dodd-Frank Act—the law restricting the freedom of banks to trade derivatives through the so-called Volcker Rule.[5]

---

5 "The Dodd-Frank Act...is a United States federal law that places regulation of the financial industry in the hands of the government. The legislation, which was enacted in July 2010, created financial regulatory processes to limit risk by enforcing transparency and accountability. Other provisions of Dodd-Frank include the creation of the Financial Stability Oversight Council (FSOC), which is tasked with monitoring the financial stability of large companies whose failure would negatively impact the United States economy and the Volcker Rule which requires financial institutions to separate their investment and commercial functions."

Table 2.2: Goldman's professed business principles versus their practices

Goldman's professed business principles[xiv]	Goldman's practices exposed by Carl Levin[xv]
What Goldman's Code of Conduct said: "It has often been said that one person can cause more harm to Goldman Sachs from a single bad decision than good to the firm over the course of a career. As stewards of the firm's success, our actions each day have a profound impact. No financial incentive or opportunity—regardless of the bottom line—justifies a departure from our values. *In fact, loosening our ethical standards in pursuit of business is a betrayal of our duty to clients, shareholders and colleagues and compromises everything we aspire to as a firm.*"[xvi] [Emphasis mine] "The scope of our business means that delivering outstanding client service may at times generate real or perceived conflicts for the firm. We are committed to addressing such conflicts with all appropriate disclosure and transparency. *If a transaction generates a conflict that can not be addressed, we would prefer to lose the business than to abandon our principles.*"[xvii] [Emphasis mine] "Our clients' interests always come first Our experience shows that if we serve our clients well our own success will follow."[xviii]	Below is an extract of Senator Carl Levin's questioning of Lloyd Blankfein, CEO of Goldman's, when Blankfein was testifying to Congress on April 27, 2010: "We've heard in earlier panels today example after example where Goldman was selling securities to people, and then not telling them that they were taking and intended to maintain a short position against those same securities... I'm deeply troubled by that. And it's made worse when your own employees believe that those securities are junk, or a piece of crap, or a shitty deal—words that those e-mails show your employees believed about a number of those deals... Billion-dollar Timberwolf...a senior executive called it a shitty transaction, but the Goldman sales force was told that it was a priority item for two straight months. Goldman sold $600 million in Timberwolf securities to clients, while at the same time holding a short position... And I'd like to ask you whether or not you believe that Goldman, in fact, treated those clients properly... *How—given that kind of a history here, going heavily short in the market... on these specific examples, to be betting against the very securities which you're selling to your clients, and internally your own people believe that these are crappy securities—how do you expect to deserve the trust of your clients*? And is there not an inherent conflict here? And I'd like to ask you whether or not you believe that Goldman, in fact, treated those clients properly. And, as you say, if clients believe we don't deserve their trust, you're not going to survive... ... Do you see a problem? You don't tell them that this is a security which incorporates or which in some way references a whole lot of bad stuff in your own inventory—bad lemons, I think the word was called. You don't—you don't—you're out there looking around. Over and over again—we have e-mails—you're out there looking around for buyers of stuff, whether it's junk or not junk, where you are betting against what you're selling. You are intending to keep the opposite side. *This isn't where you're* just selling something from your inventory. This is where you are betting against the very product you are selling. And you're just not troubled by it. That's the bottom line. There's no trouble in your mind or heart." [Emphases mine]

Perhaps the board's problem results from the difference between Peter Drucker's view of what the business of business is and Milton Friedman's. Peter Drucker believed the purpose of business was to create satisfied customers,[xix] whereas Milton Friedman argued the purpose of business was to maximize shareholder value by maximizing profits.[xx] Peter Drucker based his thinking on the importance of the customer as the primary stakeholder:

> *It is the customer who determines what a business is. It is the customer alone whose willingness to pay for a good or service converts economic resources into wealth, things into goods.* What the business thinks it produces is not of first importance—especially not to the future of the business and to its success... *What the customer thinks he/she is buying, what he/she considers value, is decisive—it determines what a business is, what it produces and whether it will prosper.*
>
> The customer is the foundation of the business and keeps it in existence. He alone gives employment. *And it is to supply the customer that society entrusts wealth-producing resources to the business enterprise.* [Emphases mine][xxi]

Goldman's behavior ignored Peter Drucker's thinking, instead reflecting Milton Friedman's view that profit maximization was the purpose of business. Lloyd Blankfein, Goldman's CEO, hid behind *caveat emptor*, which requires the buyer to take all the risks of acquiring a *not* "fit for purpose" product.[xxii]

When it is a) obvious how a product or service is supposed to perform, and b) its ability to do so can be measured almost immediately, *caveat emptor* is not too one-sided an approach to satisfying a customer. However, if the product or service is extremely complex and there is asymmetry of understanding between the buyer and seller; or if it takes a long time to know whether the product performs as promised by the seller, then *caveat emptor* is an unfair one-way bet in favor of the seller.

One of the consequences of the financial services industry creating complex, opaque products that were difficult to understand and evaluate, is directors of financial institutions now have a dual fiduciary duty: the traditional duty to shareholders and a new one to depositors in banks and policy holders in insurers. They are also expected to explain the benefits and drawbacks of their products in simple language laymen can understand, in an attempt to minimize the previous legal practice of "hiding in plain sight" warnings of what could go wrong in the fine print of long and difficult to understand legalese.

Satisfying Regulations

In my training sessions with directors, the standard complaints about regulations are they impose unnecessary costs on doing business; they are wrongly conceived; or lead to a box-ticking mentality destroying thoughtful applications of principled behavior.

It is worth restating why we need regulations, given the prevailing view in some parts of the world that a bonfire should be made of regulations.[xxiii] At its simplest, we need laws to feel safe from arbitrary action by the state, as the French philosopher Montesquieu put it:

> In every government there are three sorts of power: the legislative; the executive in respect to things dependent on the law of nations; and the executive in regard to matters that depend on the civil law...
>
> ...The political liberty of the subject is a tranquility of mind arising from the opinion each person has of his safety. In order to have this liberty, it is requisite the government be so constituted as one man need not be afraid of another.[xxiv]

In many emerging markets, regulations are, however, sometimes viewed as an opportunity for patronage, bribery and corruption. In the case of patronage, regulations may be used to channel business opportunities to cronies by giving them unfair advantages.[6] In the case of bribery and corruption, every rule provides an opportunity for a negotiated workaround and payoff to the officials responsible for enforcing the rules. Anyone who has tried to get an import license for many emerging markets will know exactly what I mean.

So why do we need regulations? Perhaps the best answer I can provide is by looking more carefully at what Adam Smith, the so-called father of unfettered competition, actually thought:

> According to Adam Smith, markets and trade are, in principle, good things—provided there is competition and a regulatory framework that prevents ruthless selfishness, greed and rapacity from leading to socially harmful outcomes. But competition and market regulations are always in danger of being undermined and circumnavigated, giving way to *monopolies that are very comfortable and highly profitable to monopolists and may spell great trouble for many people*. In Smith's view, political economy—as an important, and perhaps even the most important, part of a kind of master political science, encompassing the *science of the legislator*—has the task to fight superstition and false beliefs in matters of economic policy, to *debunk opinions that present individual interests as promoting the general good and to propose changing regulatory frameworks*

---

6 "The dynamics of corruption in the public sector can be depicted in a simple model. The *opportunity* for corruption is a function of the size of the rents under a public official's control, the *discretion* that official has in allocating those rents, and the *accountability* that official faces for his or her decisions. Monopoly rents can be large in highly regulated economies and, as noted above, corruption breeds demand for more regulation. In transition economies economic rents can be enormous because of the amount of formerly state-owned property essentially 'up for grabs.' The discretion of many public officials may also be large in developing and transition economies, exacerbated by poorly defined, ever-changing, and inadequately disseminated rules and regulations." World Bank, *Helping Countries Combat Corruption: The Role of the World Bank*, http://www1.worldbank.org/publicsector/anticorrupt/corruptn/cor02.htm, accessed on June 15, 2018.

for markets and institutions that help to ward off threats to the security of society as a whole and provide incentives such that self-seeking behavior has also socially beneficial effects[xxv] [Emphases mine]

We need government regulation for the following reasons:

Market Failure
To protect society from the effects of market failure caused by:
- Firms ignoring the social costs of their actions because there are no pricing mechanisms to reflect the harmful externalities they create through pollution, congestion and the "Tragedy of the Commons."
- The tendency of markets to overshoot in the good times, leading to wasted resources and undershoot in bad times, leading to excessive economic losses.
- The difference in time horizons and required rates of return for providing "social goods" such as infrastructure, education and health investments, where private firms can not participate without government intervention and support. For example, the ubiquitous Internet and GPS would never have been created if it had not been for the U.S. government's investment in them through DARPA.[xxvi]

Social Harm
To protect society as a whole from the harmful effects of unscrupulous, selfish and rapacious individuals and organizations; the more harmful the effect, the greater the need for regulation.

Rent-Seeking
To protect consumers and clients from the consequences of monopolistic or oligopolistic behavior, seeking to increase their economic rents by:
1. Raising prices to unjustified levels
2. Restricting access to goods and services through artificial barriers to entry (particularly true of professional services)
3. Limiting innovation by delaying or eliminating newly competitive ways of doing things
4. Mis-selling products and services

Vested Interests
To distinguish between the interests of vested interests and those of society.

To define the "rules of the game" and create level playing fields.

Given regulations are needed, the question arises "how best to regulate?" Essentially there are two approaches to regulation: rules-based and principles-based. Table 2.3 compares and contrasts the two.

Table 2.3: Rules-based and principles-based regulations compared[xxvii]

Rules-based regulations	Principles-based regulations
1. Address the "what" and "how" question	1. Addresses the "why" question
2. Clear what is permitted and what is not	2. Sometimes unclear what is permitted
3. Risk of form over substance	3. Substance above form
4. Box-ticking rather than exercising judgment by directors	4. Requires exercise of judgment above all
Risk of "breaking the law legally" to get around the spirit of the law by focusing on the wording.	*Risk of poor execution because of insufficient detailed direction on "how to implement."*

Rules-based regulations may lead to all the defects attributed to regulations by libertarians: burdensome, over-complicated to implement; easy for clever lawyers to get around by finding loopholes in the wording;[7] and, more seriously, focusing on the legalistic aspects of rules-based regulation allows directors to find ways of gaming the system rather than preventing the problems from arising in the first place:

> The greater the number of laws, rules and regulations, the more people ignore the ethical consequences and focus on compliance only...The legalistic culture of the US gives people a strong motive to shuffle off responsibility to others and cover their back.[xxviii]

Sheila Bair, a former FDIC chairman, supported this view and argued as follows against rules-based regulations:

> Other types of regulation—those that seek to define the kinds of activity that are allowed and not allowed among market participants—are also important but less effective in my view...The more regulators try to answer these questions, the more prescriptive the rules become, adding complexity, new opportunities for gaming, and unnecessary constraints on beneficial product innovation. *But tell a mortgage lender that whatever lending standard it uses, it will be on the hook for 5 to 10 percent of the losses if the borrower can't afford his adjusted payments, the lender will have economic incentives to resolve these issues on his own in a way that reduces the likelihood that the borrower will default.*[xxix](Emphasis mine)

---

7 This is the drawback of "black letter" law.

The problem posed by principles-based regulations, however, is they do not help compliance officers draw up effective codes of conduct and other compliance mechanisms.[8]

More seriously, this is not just a problem for Internal Audit and compliance officers, it is also a problem for judges when they review cases of failed CG. In determining the level of liability of directors for failing to manage and direct[9] the business of the company properly, they need to know, step by step, how decisions were taken; what information was asked for; how it was reviewed; what advice was sought; and whether directors exercised due diligence in coming to their conclusions. It is only by so doing, they can decide directors are protected by the "business judgment" rule[xxx] when considering whether they have fulfilled their fiduciary duties. Principles are important as an ethical frame of reference, but in coming to a judicial determination, what matters is a rules-based approach.

There is an added complication in recommending the best way to use regulations to control behavior, namely not all cultures regard regulation and its enforcement in the same way. By and large, the world can be divided into two groups—universalists and particularists—and they each have quite different approaches to regulation, shown in Table 2.4.

Table 2.4: Impact of different approaches to regulations[xxxi]

Universalists (Rule of Law)	Particularists (Rule of Man)
1. Nobody is above the law	1. The law is what those in power say it is
2. What is good and right can be defined and always applies regardless	2. Attention to obligations of relationships and special circumstances
3. No exceptions to the rules. Similar treatment for all in the same category	3. Waivers to rules because exceptional circumstances always exist
4. Level playing field	4. Handicaps
5. Use legal proceedings to ensure promises are kept	5. Personal relationship is the basis for keeping promises
6. Rules only apply *within* categories; exceptions apply *outside* categories	6. *Must sustain or protect this personal relationship no matter what the rules say*

This difference in approaches explains in part why some countries have a more "elastic" approach to regulations than others; always ready to find reasons "why

---

8 When discussing the role of compliance in achieving good CG, the chief compliance officers from three leading banks in Malaysia were unanimous people in the middle and lower levels of their companies need to know exactly what they can and can not do in quite specific ways, if Internal Audit is to do its job properly reporting to the board. They do not find a principles-based approach helpful in doing their job of enforcing desired behavior.
9 Several leading Commonwealth jurisdictions stipulate in their companies acts that directors "manage and direct the affairs of the business."

the rules do not apply in these particular circumstances." Directors who grew up in and operate in such countries have no difficulty accommodating the demands of particularists, just as directors who only operate in universalist cultures understand how to behave.

Ethics in principle are relatively easy, but in practice are complicated. They are even more difficult when the cultural differences in assumptions about ethical behavior are considered, as the "Moral Machine" research by MIT[xxxii] demonstrates, using AI for the programming choices on who to kill and who to save self-driving cars should make, because of cultural differences across the world.[10] Directors of multinational firms who operate in different cultures and employ people from different cultures, sometimes operating outside their cultural frame of reference need to recognize the real difficulties of reconciling different approaches if they are to operate both ethically and successfully in locations where a particularist culture prevails.

Branding

You may be surprised to see branding as part of CG. Perhaps you will argue branding is the responsibility of the Marketing department and not of the board. You might support this assertion by pointing out marketing directors do not sit on boards. This is perhaps surprising given Peter Drucker's assertion about marketing:

> Because the purpose of business is to create a customer, the business enterprise has two—and only two—basic functions: marketing and innovation. Marketing and innovation produce results; all the rest are costs. *Marketing is the distinguishing, unique function of the business.*[xxxiii] [Emphasis mine]

There are two additional reasons why I believe branding should be regarded as part of CG and a responsibility of the board:
1. The company "brand promise" captures the company's purpose—who the company is, who the company serves, what the company does—and its values; reflecting its unique culture, codes of conduct and compliance.
2. The most valuable brands are company brands and not product brands.

---

[10] "The Moral Machine took ...nine different comparisons shown to polarize people: should a self-driving car prioritize humans over pets, passengers over pedestrians, more lives over fewer, women over men, young over old, fit over sickly, higher social status over lower, law-abiders over law-benders? And finally, should the car swerve (take action) or stay on course (inaction)?" The research found individualistic cultures were more likely to save the young over the old and choose to save more lives; communitarian cultures the reverse. Cultures with weaker institutions and respect for the law were more tolerant of jaywalkers; there was even a difference between countries in choosing to save passengers rather than pedestrians.

Perhaps it helps to explain why a brand is much more than just a logo or tagline:

> A brand is a set of differentiating promises that link a product to its customers. The brand assures the customer of consistent quality plus "superior" value—for which the customer is willing to give loyalty and pay a price that results in a reasonable return to the brand *Young & Rubicam*.

Table 2.5 compares the difference between great, long-lived brands and products.

Table 2.5: Brands and products compared

Characteristics of great long-lived brands	Characteristics of products
A brand is the *relationship* between the user and the product/service: 1. Exists in customers' minds 2. Provides emotional and functional value 3. Timeless; evergreen; not subject to product life cycle	A product provides the user with functional, tangible benefits: 1. Made in a factory 2. Has functional value 3. Transient; perishable; subject to product life cycle

Company "Brand Promise" Captures Purpose, Values, and Culture

The "brand promise" should be simple, distinctive, relevant, and motivating and combines:

- *Function:* what the organization/product has to offer to its customers and how it delivers that promise and its impact on the employees through the demands made of them to deliver that promise.
- *Differentiation:* the offer compared to the competitive set demonstrating its superiority and relevance to its customers and to its employees by answering two questions better than its rivals:
    1. "What's in it for me as a customer?"
    2. "What's in it for me as an employee?"
- *Personality:* the traits of the brand and what it is like to do business with it as a customer and what it is like to work for as an employee.
- *Source of Authority:* the reason why people should believe the claims being made in terms of:
    1. The consistency of performance of the products/services offered to its customers both functionally and emotionally.
    2. The quality of customer experiences at all the 'touch points' where customers are in contact with the company, its policies and procedures, reflected in its code of conduct.

3. The consistent experiences employees have working for the company and their ability to deliver the "on brand" behavior promised by the company.
4. The experience stakeholders and the communities where the company operates have of the impact of the company on their interests.[xxxiv]

Developing "function," "'differentiation," "personality" and "source of authority" properly requires considering the company's purpose, mission and values, how it does business and with whom it does business—its ethical foundation. It also requires defining what the company has to offer its employees and how it will engage with its stakeholders, maintaining its social "license to operate." Answering these questions requires the board to consider the impact of its chosen strategy and risk appetite, its succession planning, its internal controls to reinforce the company culture and how it will satisfy regulators (illustrated earlier in Figure 2.1).

There is another reason why I believe the company brand is too important for the board to ignore. It is intimately linked to the reputation of the organization as a whole and any "off brand" behavior can have serious consequences for the company's market capitalization. For example, on the day the CEO of Audi was arrested for his alleged involvement in the Volkswagen "dieselgate" scandal,[11] the market value of Volkswagen, the parent of Audi, dropped by three percent on the news.[xxxv] This explains why company branding is too important to leave to the marketing director. Boards must ensure alignment between the branding they desire and the reputation they have—otherwise paradoxes like Samsung will occur where the brand is strong with customers, and yet the company gets mired in controversies over corruption and governance.[xxxvi] Chapter 14 looks at how boards should focus on reputation, given it is the most important asset of the enterprise.

Figure 2.2[xxxvii] shows how these four elements combine to yield the "Brand Promise" at the center, by integrating all four elements into one memorable "evergreen" proposition, such as Disney's "family fun and magic" or BMW's "ultimate driving machine":

---

[11] On October 16, 2018, Audi was fined US$926 million over the dieselgate scandal by the EU regulators. Reints, R. (2018), "Audi Fined US$926 Million Over Volkswagen Diesel Emissions Scandal," *Fortune,* October 16, 2018, http://fortune.com/2018/10/16/audi-volkswagen-emissions-scandal/, accessed on October 17, 2018.

Function	Differentiation
• What do the organisation's products/services have to offer? • How does it deliver these offerings?	• The organisational product Unique Selling Proposition (USP) • USP's customer relevance and competitive superiority • USP's relevance for employees
Personality	**Source of authority**
• The perceived traits and characteristics of the brand • What is it like to do business with? • What is it like to work for?	• Track record and legacy • Consistency in "living the brand values" reflected in company Culture, Codes of Conduct and Compliance

(Center: Company Brand Promise)

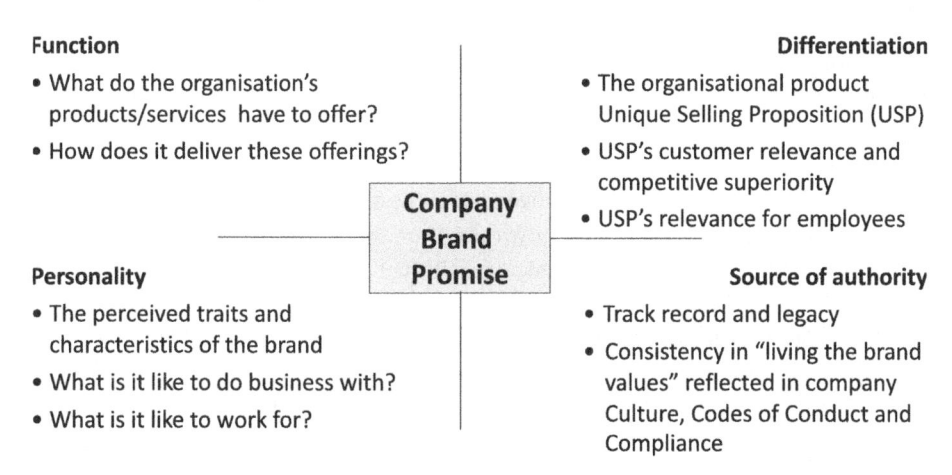

Figure 2.2: Creating the company brand promise

Company Brands Are Most Valuable

When we think of brands, typically most of us will think of purely product brands like Marlboro for cigarettes, Tide and Persil for washing powder, Dove for beauty products, KitKat or Mars for confectionery, or Camry and Lexus for cars. Yet, the surprising fact is that such brands are rare in the 100 most valuable brands in the world. There is one in the top twenty; only thirteen in the top 100. This may explain why there are so few marketing directors on boards. Instead, as Appendix 2.1 shows, corporate brands dominate the 100 most valuable brands globally: eight of the top ten; fourteen of the top twenty; and forty-eight of the top 100. "Corporate/Product" brands, where it is difficult to distinguish between the company brand and the product brand, have one in the top ten, five in the top twenty and forty in the top 100.

Conclusion

Ensuring their company satisfies the needs of customers in ethical ways is the responsibility of the board, as are its culture and its codes of conduct, defining how customers are treated. Directors must pay attention to their compliance systems to satisfy requirements of regulators. Combined, they reflect and reinforce the culture of the organization and are captured in the company brand promise. In today's more demanding environment, directors are held accountable for the behavior of operations to ensure they reflect an ethical foundation to their business.

This, in turn, requires directors to recognize there is more to doing business than just maximizing shareholder value. Perhaps the best example of how a business can reconcile the different stakeholder interests successfully to create long-term value is

Johnson & Johnson's *Credo*, written in 1935. Its continued success requires directors to at least question whether there is not more to running a company successfully than the theories of Friedman, Coase, Jensen, Williamson, and Porter.

There is a need for an ethical framework to help directors make right-good decisions. It can be achieved by using a five-step process that works its way up from considering effectiveness to predictability, then from to maximizing utility to ensuring mutuality, ending with how the directors will feel about their self-image once the decision has been taken.

It is essential clients' needs are satisfied ethically and the role of regulations is to help companies do this. There are two approaches to regulations (principles vs. rules-based), each with its own issues; directors need to find the best way to reconcile them. This is made more difficult by the fact the world divides into universalists and particularists who view the role and relevance of regulations differently and directors need to reconcile these different worldviews as well, if they employ people from the two different backgrounds.

Finally, directors are the custodians of their corporate brand. This is because the corporate brand promise captures what makes the organization unique in terms of what it does, whom it does business with and how it does that business. It is also about how the company interacts with its stakeholders. It ensures its employees understand what is in it for them to work for the company and provides the reasons why its stakeholders should believe the claims it makes. Failure to deliver the brand promise affects the market value of the company and can destroy its social "license to operate."

Appendix 2.1: The World's Most Valuable Brands[xxxviii]

Rank	Name	Type of brand	Industry	$bn
1	Apple	Corporate	Technology	182.8
2	Google	Corporate	Technology	132.1
3	Microsoft	Corporate	Technology	104.9
4	Facebook	Corporate	Technology	94.8
5	Amazon	Corporate	Technology	70.9
6	Coca-Cola	Corporate/Product	FMCG	57.3
7	Samsung	Corporate	Technology	47.6
8	Disney	Corporate	Leisure	47.5
9	Toyota	Corporate	Automotive	44.7
10	AT&T	Corporate/Product	Telecom	41.9
11	McDonalds	Corporate	Restaurant	41.4
12	GE	Corporate	Conglomerate	37.2
13	Mercedes-Benz	Product	Automotive	34.4
14	Intel	Corporate	Technology	34.1
15	Louis Vuitton	Corporate/Product	Luxury	33.6
16	Cisco	Corporate	Technology	32.4
17	IBM	Corporate	Technology	32.1
18	Nike	Corporate/Product	Apparel	32.0
19	Verizon	Corporate	Telecom	31.4
20	BMW	Corporate/Product	Automotive	31.4
21	Oracle	Corporate	Technology	30.8
22	Marlboro	Product	Tobacco	26.6
23	SAP	Corporate	Technology	26.2
24	Honda	Corporate/Product	Automotive	24.3
25	Budweiser	Product	Beer	25.5
26	Walmart	Corporate	Retail	24.9
27	Visa	Corporate/Product	Financial services	24.5
28	Amex	Corporate/Product	Financial services	23.1
29	Pepsi	Corporate/Product	Beverages	18.4
30	L'Oréal	Corporate/Product	FMCG	17.2
31	Nescafe	Product	Beverages	17.1
32	Gillette	Product	FMCG	17.1
33	Home Depot	Corporate	Retail	16.4
34	Starbucks	Corporate	Restaurants	16.2
35	Hermes	Corporate	Luxury	15.3
36	Gucci	Corporate/Product	Luxury	14.9
37	Audi	Corporate/Product	Automotive	14.8
38	Accenture	Corporate	Business services	14.8
39	ESPN	Corporate	Media	14.6
40	IKEA	Corporate	Retail	14.5
41	Frito-Lay	Product	FMCG	14.4
42	Ford	Corporate	Automotive	14.1
43	Wells Fargo	Corporate	Financial Services	13.5

Rank	Name	Type of brand	Industry	$bn
44	UPS	Corporate	Transportation	13.3
45	CVS	Corporate	Retail	13.2
46	Zara	Corporate/Product	Retail	13.0
47	H&M	Corporate/Product	Retail	13.0
48	Siemens	Corporate	Conglomerate	12.8
49	Mastercard	Corporate/Product	Financial services	12.4
50	HP	Corporate	Technology	12.4
51	JP Morgan	Corporate	Financial services	11.9
52	HSBC	Corporate	Financial services	11.9
53	Nestle	Corporate/Product	FMCG	11.7
54	Fox	Corporate/Product	Media	11.7
55	Netflix	Corporate	Media	11.5
56	Chevrolet	Product	Automotive	11.5
57	Pampers	Product	FMCG	11.4
58	Porsche	Corporate/Product	Automotive	11.0
59	Cartier	Corporate/Product	Luxury	10.6
60	BOA	Corporate	Financial services	10.4
61	Red Bull	Product	Beverages	10.4
62	eBay	Corporate	Technology	10.3
63	Sony	Corporate	Technology	10.2
64	Chase	Product	Financial services	10.2
65	Citi	Corporate/Product	Financial services	10.1
66	Colgate	Corporate/Product	FMCG	10.0
67	Danone	Corporate/Product	FMCG	10.0
68	Adidas	Corporate/Product	Apparel	9.5
69	Lexus	Product	Automotive	9.5
70	Nissan	Corporate/Product	Automotive	9.4
71	Rolex	Corporate/Product	Luxury	9.3
72	T-Mobile	Corporate	Telecom	9.0
73	Kraft	Corporate	FMCG	8.8
74	Corona	Corporate/Product	Beer	8.8
75	Hyundai	Corporate	Automotive	8.7
76	Santander	Corporate	Financial services	8.7
77	BASF	Corporate	Conglomerate	8.6
78	Lowe's	Corporate/Product	Retail	8.5
79	Huawei	Corporate	Technology	8.4
80	Adobe	Corporate/Product	Technology	8.3
81	FedEx	Corporate	Transportation	8.3
82	Heineken	Corporate/Product	Beer	8.2
83	Goldman Sachs	Corporate	Financial services	8.2
84	Kellogg's	Corporate/Product	FMCG	8.2
85	Boeing	Corporate/ Product	Aerospace	8.1
86	Costco	Corporate	Retail	8.0
87	Chanel	Corporate/Product	Luxury	8.0
88	Lancôme	Product	FMCG	8.0

Rank	Name	Type of brand	Industry	$bn
89	Nivea	Corporate/Product	FMCG	7.9
90	Volkswagen	Corporate	Automotive	7.9
91	Lego	Corporate/Product	Leisure	7.8
92	Panasonic	Corporate/Product	Technology	7.8
93	Philips	Corporate/Product	Conglomerate	7.7
94	RBC	Corporate	Financial services	7.7
95	Allianz	Corporate	Financial services	7.6
96	Uniqlo	Corporate/Product	Apparel	7.5
97	Walgreens	Corporate/Product	Retail	7.5
98	PayPal	Corporate	Financial services	7.5
99	Dell	Corporate/Product	Technology	7.5
100	KFC	Product	Restaurants	7.4

References

i Hindle, T. (2008) *The Economist Guide to Management Ideas and Gurus*, (London: Profile Books Ltd.), https://books.google.com.my/books?id=Bk2KAgAAQBAJ&pg=PT62&lpg=PT62&d-q=hindle+tim+An+organisation+creates+its+culture+by+the+priorities+it+sets&source=bl&ots=p-JgwRPytg3&sig=YYAcVuSKXzROE, accessed on October 6, 2018.

ii "Fixing LIBOR," Treasury Committee Evidence, July 10, 2012, quoted in Zinkin. J. (2014), *Rebuilding Trust in Banks: The Role of Leadership and Governance* (Singapore: John Wiley & Sons), 100.

iii Freeman, R. E. (2014), "Is Profit the Purpose of Business?" *Darden Ideas to Action,* University of Virginia, Darden School of Business, August 8, 2014, https://ideas.darden.virginia.edu/2014/08/is-profit-the-purpose-of-business/, accessed on June 14, 2018.

iv Somer, J. and Russell, K., "Apple Is the Most Valuable Public Company Ever. But How Much of a Record Is That?" *New York Times,* December 21, 2017, https://www.nytimes.com/interactive/2017/12/05/your-money/apple-market-share.html, accessed on September 30, 2018.

v "Enlightenment Man," *The Economist Technology Quarterly,* December 6, 2008, 27, cited in Zinkin, J. (2010), *Challenges in Implementing Corporate Governance: Whose Business is it Anyway?* (Singapore: John Wiley & Sons), 23.

vi Narayana Murthy answering a question from the floor at the World Capital Market Symposium, Kuala Lumpur, September 3, 2015.

vii "Our Credo," https://www.google.com/search?q=jnj+credo+pdf&oq=J%26Credo&aqs=chrome.2.69i57j0l5.16516j0j7&sourceid=chrome&ie=UTF-8, accessed on June 14, 2018, quoted in Zinkin (2010), op. cit., 22.

viii Coase, R. (1937), "The Nature of the Firm," *Economica* 4 (November), 386–405, cited in Zinkin (2010), op. cit., 34.

ix Zinkin, (2010), op. cit., 34–35.

x Burroughs, B. and Helyar, J. (1990), *Barbarians at the Gate* (New York: Harper Collins).

xi MacDonald, E. (2011), "Goldman Sachs Accused of Misleading Congress, Client," *Fox Business,* April 14, 2011. Accessed January 7, 2013, www.foxbusiness.com/markets/2011/04/14/old-man-sachs-accused-lying-congress, cited in Zinkin, J. (2014), *Rebuilding Trust in Banks: The Role of Leadership and Governance* (Singapore: John Wiley & Sons), 138.

xii Goldstein, M. (2014), "Abacus might have had other benefits for Goldman," *Reuters,* April 24, 2010, https://www.reuters.com/article/us-goldman-circular-exclusive/abacus-might-have-had-other-benefits-for-goldman-idUSTRE63M4U820100424, accessed on June 11, 2018.

xiii Zinkin (2014), op. cit., 53–55.

xiv Goldman's Business Principles.

xv https://www.c-span.org/video/?293196-3/goldman-sachs-ceo-testifies-financial-crisis, accessed April 27.

xvi Lloyd Blankfein, Introduction to the *Goldman Sachs Code of Business Conduct and Ethics*, (2012), 2, accessed on December 17, 2012, http://www.goldmansachs.com/investor-relations/corporate-governance/corporate-governance-documents/revise-code-of-conduct.pdf

xvii Introduction to the *Goldman Sachs Code of Business Conduct and Ethics*, 3, accessed on December 17, 2012, http://www.goldmansachs.com/investor-relations/corporate-governance/corporate-governance-documents/revise-code-of-conduct.pdf

xviii *The Goldman Sachs Business Principles*, accessed on December 20, 2012, http://www.goldmansachs.com/investor-relations/financials/current/annual-reports/2011-annual-report-files/GS_AR11_Business_Principles.pdf.

xix Kotler, P. (2010), "Peter Drucker, The Grandfather of Modern Marketing," Presentation by Philip Kotler, Drucker Celebration, Vienna, November 20, 2009.

xx Friedman, M. (1970), "The Social Responsibility of Business is to Increase its Profits," *New York Times*, September 13, 1970, 12.

xxi Drucker, P. (1955), *The Practice of Management* (Oxford: Butterworth Heinemann), 35, quoted in Zinkin, op. cit., 24.

xxii Lloyd Blankfein's testimony to Congress, https://www.c-span.org/video/?293196-3/goldman-sachs-ceo-testifies-financial-crisis, accessed on April 27.

xxiii For an excellent discussion of the case for and against government regulations, read the *New York Times*, https://www.nytimes.com/2013/06/02/opinion/sunday/sunday-dialogue-more-regulation-or-less.htmlLetters to the Editor, Sunday Dialogue, "More Regulation or Less?" *New York Times*, June 1, 2013, accessed on June 15, 2018.

xxiv Baron de Montesquieu (1748), translated by Nugent. T. (1899), *The Spirit of the Laws*, Volume 1 (New York: The Colonial Press), 151.

xxv Kurz, H. D. (2015), Abstract of "Adam Smith on markets, competition and violations of natural liberty," *Cambridge Journal of Economics*, 40, No. 2, March 1, 2016, 615–638, https://academic.oup.com/cje/article-abstract/40/2/615/2605099, accessed on June 15, 2018.

xxvi "15 Astounding Technologies DARPA is Creating Right Now," *Business Insider*, http://www.businessinsider.com/15-current-darpa-innovations-2014-7/?IR=T, accessed on June 15, 2018.

xxvii Zinkin, J. (2014), "Ethics in Business", Corporate Directors Advanced Programme. August 12, 2014, Kuala Lumpur, Malaysia.

xxviii Persaud, A. and Plender, J. (2007), *Ethics and Finance: Finding a Moral Compass in Business Today* (London: Longtail Publishing, 2007), 5–8.

xxix Bair, Sheila, "Bull By The Horns: Fighting to Save Main Street from Wall Street and Wall Street from Itself," (New York: Free Press, 2012), 324.

xxx "The *business judgment rule* is a presumption that in making a *business* decision, the directors of a corporation acted on an informed basis, in good faith and in the honest belief that the action taken was in the best interests of the company." https://www.google.com/search?q=business+judgement+rule&oq=business+judgement&aqs=chrome.0.0j69i57j0l4.10186j0j7&sourceid=chrome&ie=UTF-8, accessed on June 16, 2018.

xxxi Based on Trompenaars, F. and Hampden-Turner, C. (2006), *Riding the Waves of Culture: Understanding Cultural Diversity in Business*, Second Edition (London: Nicholas Brealey Publishing), 29–48.

xxxii Hao, K. (2018), "Should a Self-Driving Car Kill the Baby or the Grandma? Depends on Where You Are from," October 24, 2018, *MIT Technology Review*, October https://www.technologyreview.com/s/612341/a-global-ethics-study-aims-to-help-ai-solve-the-self-driving-trolley-problem/, accessed on October 28, 2018.

xxxiii Trout, J. (2006), "Peter Drucker on Marketing, *Forbes*, July 3, 2006, https://www.forbes.com/2006/06/30/jack-trout-on-marketing-cx_jt_0703drucker.html#10a8a625555c, accessed on October 6, 2018.

xxxiv Zinkin, J. (2018), "Marketing for SMEs," Department of Trade and Industry, Philippines workshop, Peninsula Hotel, Manila, May 30, 2018.

xxxv Petroff, A. (2018), "Audi CEO Rupert Stadler arrested in Germany," *money.cnn.com*, June 18, 2018, http://money.cnn.com/2018/06/18/investing/audi-ceo-arrested-volkswagen-rupert-stadler/index.html, accessed on June 19, 2018.

xxxvi Boxall, A. (2018), "Samsung's Jailed Chairman Freed after Sentence Reduced and Suspended," *Digital Trends,* February 5, 2018, https://www.digitaltrends.com/mobile/samsung-group-offices-raided-korea-political-scandal-news/, accessed on November 19, 2018.

xxxvii Petroff (2018), op. cit.

xxxviii "The World's Most Valuable Brands: 2018 Ranking," *Forbes* https://www.forbes.com/powerful-brands/list/#tab:rank, accessed on June 17, 2018.

Chapter 3
Redefining the Boundaries of Responsibility

This chapter is presented in three parts: the first explores the traditional view of the boundaries of the board's responsibility; the second explains the somewhat different twenty-first century perspective and the challenges it presents directors; and the third suggests a way of redefining those boundaries, resolving the dilemma faced by directors, caused by the change in expectations.

Boundaries of Board Responsibility: The Traditional View

Boards exist because companies are legal entities distinct from the people who own and the people who operate them. This is to protect owners from unlimited liability while giving management the freedom to act. Boards exist when ownership is too dispersed for owners to direct and manage companies on their own. Boards also exist because family firms go to the market for extra funding or because they welcome the additional challenge they receive from their boards when they are listed; allowing them to move to the next level of professionalism as a result of having to answer to the market.

Collectively, boards have the authority needed to direct and govern the organization and with that authority comes board accountability to the members of that organization (shareholders of a company or members in a cooperative, commune or club).

The board sits at the top of the chain of command and, as a result, the board:[i]
1. *Can not abdicate its prerogatives and "hand them over" to the chair or CEO*, since they are either employed by the board or one of its component parts (contradicting Michael Jensen's assertion American CEOs do not have a boss;[ii] they do—the board—but in the cases he referred to, the boards were not competent).
2. *Must be able to control what it does before it can control anybody else*, hence the immense importance of the chair in governing the board, discussed in Chapter 4.
3. *Has authority; it does not merely advise or supervise*. It has six specific core responsibilities: setting strategy, reviewing its implementation, managing risk, planning succession, and ensuring effective internal controls and engaging stakeholders (these are covered in more detail in Chapters 8–13).
4. *Is the sole source of authority in the company*; no group or persons other than the owners, has any authority, unless the board has specifically granted it to them, officially in the board charter (or memorandum and articles of association).
5. *The board must be more than just a reactive final authority, waiting for management to propose and for the board to decide*, if it is to prevent catastrophic failures of corporate governance (CG) on its watch. The board must be able to initiate

as well as respond to the demands and agenda of the CEO and line management (this is one of the reasons why the chair must be responsible for the board meeting agenda).

As a result, the board can not blame the chair or the CEO or any committee for a breach of CG:

> It alone is accountable and so a failure to perform by the Chair, by the CEO, by any committee, or by the company itself, is a failure of the board. The board cannot escape from this responsibility, though whenever there have been major failures of CG, the boards have initially tried to blame the CEO or the CFO rather than admitting that they have failed. Equally it is crucial to remember that boards only have authority as a group; nobody on the board has any authority unless the board has specifically granted it.[iii]

Before I explore where boundaries should be drawn between the board and management in fulfilling its six responsibilities, there are two underpinnings of strategy that are, in my view, the exclusive prerogatives of the owners of the organization, whether the owners are founders, family, government, dispersed shareholders, or members. These are: determining the "purpose" of the organization; and defining its mission, vision, and values as a result.

Determining the "Purpose" of the Organization

The "purpose" statement must define what will make the organization unique: the beneficiaries it chooses to serve, the difference in their lives it aspires to create, and the resulting satisfaction they will experience. It must also define precisely who will benefit from the activities, how that will be achieved and at what cost. When boards develop their "purpose" statements, they must bear the following in mind:[iv]

1. *"Purpose" objectives are long-term* and should consider the potentially changing needs and profiles of the organization's beneficiaries over time. They also should not be limited by the constraints of the organization's current design and staffing—organizations must be able to adapt[v] if they are to survive and create long-term value.
2. *"Purpose" is not the same as strategic plans*—the plans are the means to achieve the "purpose." The temptation to confuse activities and intentions with the prescribed results is to be resisted.
3. *"Purpose" demands a great deal of time understanding what is being asked of the organization*: what is doable, who are the prospective beneficiaries, how should priorities be set between competing groups of beneficiaries, what do the owners really want and how does the board reconcile their different priorities, what are the costs involved and over what timescale, and how does the organization respond to these issues without losing its sense of purpose.

4. *"Purpose" must recognize it will legitimately differ depending on the ownership structure of the organization.* Illustrative long-term "purposes" for public listed firms, family firms and government invested firms are compared in Table 3.1.

Table 3.1: Differences in organizational "purpose"[vi]

Public-traded firm	Family firm	State-owned firm
Level 1 "The ultimate aim of the company is return on shareholder equity better than the return for firms of similar risk characteristics."	*Level 1* "The overall aim of our company is shared family wealth and work."	*Level 1* "The ultimate purpose of state ownership of enterprises should be to maximise value for society, through an efficient allocation of resources."[vii]
Level 2 "Risk characteristics for comparison will include similar size, industry, and maturity of market. Better return will mean above the median for such firms, rather than above the average."	*Level 2* "Our first priority is the family stays together, with appropriate, satisfying and rewarding work for every adult member who chooses to work in the company. Our second priority is that the worth of the company, and the worth of each family member's shares grows at a rate comparable to indexed funds."	*Level 2* "Our first priority is to promote and create business and job opportunities in our industry and provide quality products and services at a fair price. Our second priority is to enlarge the country's industrial base and ensure a clean and safe environment."

Given the differences in "purpose" between these three "pure" ownership structures, you can imagine the stresses placed on the board when a family firm goes public and the board has to reconcile the differences between the interests of dispersed shareholders who have little or no emotional "skin in the game" and the interests of the family, especially if the founder is still active in the company. Equally, there are tensions between the desired "purposes" that must be reconciled by the board between either a listed or family firm and a government investment in the company. The government has different objectives and timescales, as illustrated by Petronas's[1] mission statement:

> Our objective is to contribute to the well-being of the people and the nation...PETRONAS' contributions—designed to assist in enhancing the quality of life of the people and help in the develop-

---

[1] Petronas is Malaysia's national oil and gas company, which has an excellent independent-minded board and senior management who have successfully ensured it was not abused as a platform for patronage, unlike some other national oil and gas companies.

ment of the nation—include the provision of quality petroleum and related products and services at a fair price; promoting and creating business and job opportunities in the petroleum industry; enlarging the country's industrial base; and ensuring a safe and clean environment.[viii]

Given this was still Petronas's mission statement in 2007, it is not surprising Petronas was involved in the construction of Malaysia's new capital in Putrajaya; in the building of the iconic Kuala Lumpur Twin Towers and in the bailout of MISC, the national shipping line. Malaysians, as a nation, benefitted from Petronas's largesse. Had Petronas been a listed company, Malaysian shareholders might well have been willing to trade-off the benefits to them as citizens against higher dividends or capital gains as investors. However, that consolation would not apply to foreign investors and this is one of the problems faced by state-owned enterprises (SOEs) when listing on international exchanges.

The reason why it is the board's responsibility to agree "purpose" and reconcile any conflicts between them is that the CEO can only be instructed what he or she is expected to deliver, once the board, as the representative of the owners, achieves agreement.

Defining the Mission, Vision, and Values

Given it is the role of management to deliver the mission, vision and values and the time horizons involved are greater than the normal CEO's contract, it is hardly surprising I regard it as the prerogative of the board to define them. The additional reason for arguing this is an area for the board to decide is succession planning and talent management must reflect what the chosen mission and vision are. Key people must be recruited, retained, promoted, and even terminated in accordance with where the company is going (mission and vision) and how they are expected to behave (values). While the mission and vision may change over time, the values are evergreen and must be a key element in the screening criteria by which the NC decides who to hire, promote and terminate, if the board is serious about ensuring the right "tone at the top." Getting this right needs the board to:

1. *Define a sustainable mission and vision* protecting both the company's financial viability and its long-term social "license to operate." The board must answer the following four questions to do this:
    a. Choose what the senior people in the organization must do, ensuring their personal purpose and values align with those of the organization.
    b. Make sure the society within which the organization operates will accept its activities and allow them to continue long-term.
    c. Evaluate whether the identified opportunities have the scale to make good business sense.

d. Assess whether the organization has the necessary competencies to make a success of the opportunities.

Two examples of founders who answered all these questions, are Henry Ford and Michael Marks and Thomas Spencer, the founders of Marks and Spencer (M&S), one of the most successful department stores of the twentieth century, though in serious difficulties since 2000:

Henry Ford:

> I will build a motor car for the great multitude... it will be so low in price that no man making a good salary will be unable to own one—and enjoy with his family the blessing of hours of pleasure in God's great open spaces. When I'm through everybody will be able to afford one, and everyone will have one. The horse will have disappeared from our highways, the automobile will be taken for granted and we will give a large number of men employment at good wages.

Henry Ford was quite explicit about his mission and vision: he defined the beneficiaries of his endeavors: "the great multitude"; he defined the difference in their lives he would make: "enjoying God's great open spaces with their families"; he even defined his measures of success: everyone would own a car and the horse would have disappeared from the highways, solving an apparently insoluble environmental problem[2] and a "large number of men would be employed at good wages." He succeeded beyond his wildest dreams, as a result, replacing one environmental problem with another. He invented a new way of assembling cars, thereby answering the fourth question about the necessary competencies without which he would not have been able to mass produce cars.

M&S:

> The business of Marks and Spencer, they decided, was not retailing. It was social revolution... to subvert the class structure of nineteenth-century England by making available to working

---

[2] "In 1898, the first international urban-planning conference convened in New York. It was abandoned after three days, instead of the scheduled 10, because none of the delegates could see any solution to the growing crisis posed by urban horses and their output. The problem did indeed seem intractable. The larger and richer that cities became, the more horses they needed to function. The more horses, the more manure. Writing in the Times of London in 1894, one writer estimated that in 50 years every street in London would be buried under nine feet of manure. Moreover, all these horses had to be stabled, which used up ever-larger areas of increasingly valuable land. As the number of horses grew, ever-more land had to be devoted to producing hay to feed them (rather than producing food for people), and this had to be brought into cities and distributed—by horse-drawn vehicles. It seemed that urban civilization was doomed." http://www.thefreemanonline.org/columns/our-economic-past-the-great-horse-manure-crisis-of-1894/#

class and lower middle-class customers upper-class goods in superior quality but at a price the customers could afford... This then yielded specific marketing and innovation objectives, and also objectives in respect to productivity, to people and social responsibilities.[ix]

M&S was incredibly successful in the twentieth century: customers loved its value for money; people loved working for M&S; and it was innovative, particularly with its introduction of ready-to-eat quality meals, copied by all its rivals. It answered all four questions. However, it was too successful. It achieved its mission of breaking down the visible class barriers in England; people were no longer immediately identifiable by the clothes they wore or the food they ate. Like NASA, after putting a man on the moon, M&S has been struggling to redefine its purpose and find a new long-term mission. I believe it can only regain its previous iconic status when its board redefines its mission and vision, with a new compelling moral purpose. It is no longer enough to aim to be the best or most profitable department store in the world.

2. *Define values that translate into measurable and observable behavior:* I am always surprised by the number of times directors can not tell me what the values of their organization are, let alone explain to me what they mean in terms of expected behavior. If values are to mean more than motherhood statements on mugs, mouse pads and wall posters in reception, they must be translated into measurable and observable behavior, discussed in employee appraisals and personal development plans. This requires the values to be:

   a. Translated from the normally used abstract nouns into action statements describing desired behavior and performance expectations.

   Take for example "innovation" as a declared value: the subordinate is entitled to ask, "what does that mean exactly; how will I know if am being innovative; by what standard am I being judged; and what target do I need to meet this year, as I progress toward meeting the standard?"

   Equally, the supervisor must be able to explain what the standard for innovation is—the objective level of performance every employee is ultimately expected to meet; what the target for the individual, who is being reviewed, is currently; and where that individual stands in terms of achieving the standard which applies to all employees. As a result, the supervisor can agree an action plan with the subordinate to help him or her attain the required standard by an agreed time.

   So, continuing with the example of "innovation," the translation of the abstract noun into an action statement could be defining innovation as coming up with an idea to improve the product offered, or the process used or improving the place of work. Defining the standard requires setting a time frame and a quantity/number of events that are measured/observed. Thus, the board could define their expectations of "innovation" as follows:

> We expect every employee to suggest at least three new ways each year of improving either our products, our processes or our workplace. Employees who suggest ideas will be rewarded $X for every idea that is implemented.

Now imagine you are about to have an informal mid-year progress review with two of your subordinates: one has already come up with two new ideas that have been accepted; the other has yet to suggest even one.

You can have an easy discussion with the first because she is well on the way to meeting, maybe exceeding, her target—the expected standard of three new implemented ideas. You can either encourage her to overachieve or else suggest she can now focus her energies elsewhere.

In the case of the other subordinate, you review her performance, reminding her that her target is to achieve two new ideas this year on her way to reaching three by next year. You can point out time is running short for her to meet her target of two new implemented ideas this year. As a result of this discussion, you can agree an action plan to help her meet her target, while there is still enough time.

In both cases, you have had a valuable review of performance helping each subordinate in their own way. More important, the reviews are not subjective. Both subordinates will understand why you have evaluated them differently; removing any suspicion of favoritism.

b. *Embedded into the code of conduct:* For employees to internalize values, they must inform everything they do. The best way for the board to achieve this, once they have translated abstract values into observable, measurable behavior, is to incorporate them explicitly into the company's code of conduct, applying to everyone in the organization, including the board members themselves. As a result, employees know exactly what they are expected to do and how to behave, as well as what will lead to sanctions and even dismissal.

In his pathbreaking analysis, Professor Bob Tricker, the so-called grandfather of CG, described the board as having four responsibilities: formulating strategy, making policy and plans, monitoring and supervising, and providing accountability. This is shown in Figure 3.1.

54 — Chapter 3: Redefining the Boundaries of Responsibility

	Outward looking	Inward looking
Forward looking	1. Formulates strategy	2. Makes policy and plans
Backward looking	3. Monitors and supervises	4. Provides accountability

Based on: Tricker, R.I. (1994), *International Corporate Governance: Text, Readings and Cases*, Prentice Hall, Singapore, p. 149
Figure 3.1: The four roles of the board[x]

Boxes 1 and 2 and are forward and outward looking, reflecting the assumption boards "govern and direct." Boxes 3 and 4 are backward and inward looking, reflecting the role that boards oversee management and are held accountable for whatever happens on their watch.

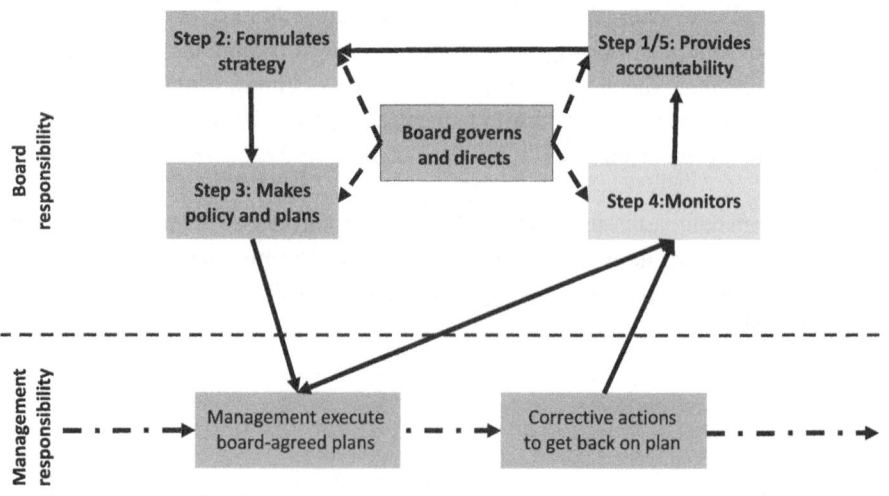

Based on: Tricker, R.I. (1994), *International Corporate Governance: Text, Readings and Cases*, Prentice Hall, Singapore, p. 150
Figure 3.2: Demarcation between board and management responsibilities

However, as Figure 3.2 shows, Professor Tricker belonged to the school of thought that believed "boards govern and direct, management manages" and it was the responsibility of the CEO to operationalize the four quadrants, a view shared by John Carver as well:[3]

> The nature of board work, then, is not management one step up but ownership one step down.[xi]

> The board of directors has the important role of overseeing management performance on behalf of shareholders…[but] corporate directors are diligent monitors, but not managers, of business operations.[xii]

The board governs and directs in five steps: It provides accountability from the beginning (step 1), based on which the directors formulate the strategy (step 2) and its supporting policy and plans (step 3). These are then implemented by the CEO and the management team, and the board monitors performance (step 4), providing feedback to management who then take corrective action to get back on plan. The board continues to monitor (still step 4) and take accountability for any material variance from plan when answering to shareholders (step 5). Based on the outcome, they will then restart the cycle, with the reformulation of strategy based on what was or was not achieved. Indeed, nearly every code of CG assumed boards govern and direct in this manner, managers manage, and boards should not second-guess line management. Although the explanation below regarding the boundaries of responsibility was for nongovernmental organizations (NGOs), it applies equally well to for-profit organizations:

> Governance and management are not the same things. Governance is about vision and organizational direction as opposed to day-to-day management and implementation of policy and programs… In most civil society organizations, governance is provided by a board of directors, which may also be called the management committee, executive committee, board of governors, board of trustees, etc. This group oversees the organization, making sure it fulfills its mission, lives up to its values and remains viable for the future…Although by no means an exhaustive list, essentially, the board has the responsibility to:

---

3 "Policy Governance calls for the board to delegate authority for all management performance to the chief executive officer function…The CEO is the link in the chain of command that connects the board to the rest of management. Therefore, in giving instructions and judging performance, the board speaks with one group voice only to this one person." Carver, J. and Oliver, C. (2002), Boards That Create Value: Governing Company Performance from the Boardroom (San Francisco: Jossey-Bass), 46. "The board should elect members who understand and respect the difference between governance and management. Choose wisely, seeking as directors individuals who bring no personal agendas, understand the role of management in large, complex organizations, and have a desire to work as part of the board-management team. Then conflicts between the board and management will be rare." Bader, B. S. (2008), "Distinguishing Governance from Management," http://trustees.aha.org/boardculture/archive/Great-Boards-fall-2008-reprint-distinguishing-governance-and-management.pdf, accessed on July 3, 2018.

- Define expectations for the organization:
  - Set and maintain vision, mission, and values
  - Develop strategy (e.g., long-term strategic plan)
  - Create and/or approve the organization's policies
- Grant power:
  - Select, manage and support the organization's chief executive
- Verify performance:
  - Ensure compliance with the governing document (e.g., charter)
  - Ensure accountability and compliance with laws and regulations
  - Maintain proper fiscal oversight

Management takes direction from the board and implements on a day-to-day basis. Management has the responsibility to:

- Communicate expectations—mission, strategy, policies—to the entire staff;
- Manage day-to-day operations and program implementation to fulfill the expectations
- Report results to the board.

When the balance between the responsibilities of the board and management is established and functioning well, the organization is better able to:

- Meet the expectations of clients, beneficiaries and other stakeholders;
- Deliver quality programs that are effective and efficient; and
- Comply with laws, regulations and other requirements.[xiii]

Boundaries of Board Responsibility: Changing Perspectives

Most companies did not have properly audited accounts before the collapse of Swedish Match in March 1932 when its founder Ivar Kreuger was found shot dead in a hotel bedroom in Paris. It took its collapse[xiv] for the U.S. Congress to pass securities laws in 1933,[xv] which required disclosure of all material information to prospective buyers of securities and in 1934,[xvi] creating the Securities and Exchange Commission (SEC), designed to ensure greater transparency and less manipulation of securities in the secondary market. This was successful in getting U.S. companies to use the generally accepted accounting principles (GAAP).

American auditors were only required to accept responsibility for the veracity of audited accounts in the 1970s and 1980s.[xvii] The next step in raising the responsibility bar for boards came in the United Kingdom with the publication of the Cadbury Report in 1992, where Sir Adrian Cadbury quoted U.S. experience with audit committees and recommended all listed companies should have one:

Since 1978, the New York Stock Exchange has required all listed companies to have audit committees composed solely of independent directors and the 1987 report of the American Treadway Commission concluded that audit committees had a critical role to play in ensuring the integrity of US company financial reports. While experience of audit committees in this country is shorter, it is encouraging, and around two-thirds of the top 250 UK listed companies now have them in place.

Experience in the United States has shown that, even where audit committees might have been set up mainly to meet listing requirements, they have proved their worth and developed into essential committees of the board. Similarly, recently published research in the United Kingdom concludes that the majority of companies with audit committees are enthusiastic about their value to their businesses. They offer added assurance to the shareholders that the auditors, who act on their behalf, are in a position to safeguard their interests.

The Committee therefore recommends that all listed companies should establish an audit committee.[xviii] [Emphasis mine]

The failures of Enron in 2001 and WorldCom, Global Crossing, Tyco and Adelphia in 2002 in the United States were the drivers of the next round of increasingly intense scrutiny of the board and its internal audit processes, as well as the role of external auditors, leading to the passage of the Sarbanes-Oxley Act in 2002.[xix]

After the collapse of Enron, the U.S. Business Roundtable in 2002 defined the responsibilities of the board as having the following primary oversight functions:[xx]
1. Select, evaluate, and if needed, replace the CEO. It should also plan succession and determine management compensation.
2. Review, approve, and monitor operating plans, budgets, major strategies, and plans, including assessing risk and continuity planning.
3. Ensure the integrity and clarity of financial statements and the independence of the appointed external auditors.
4. Provide advice and counsel to senior management.
5. Review and approve company actions.
6. Nominate a recommended slate of directors for shareholder approval.
7. Review the adequacy of systems to comply with all applicable laws and regulations.

No mention here of managing the business. In fact, it is still possible as late as 2005 for a director to conclude that boards "govern and direct, management manages":

In short, *it is not the responsibility of the board to run the company. That is the job of management*. Instead, directors have the difficult job of ensuring that those running the company run it as effectively as possible. Even before the passage of the Sarbanes-Oxley Act, there have been important discussions from many different quarters regarding how to build the most effective board of directors. The question is how best to structure a board to effectively exercise their responsibilities. *The truth of the matter is that while a well-structured board will better enable more efficient oversight, it does not guarantee quality performance.*[xxi] [Emphases mine]

While the UK Companies Act 2006 does not state the board is responsible for running the company, it does encourage directors to adopt a proactive approach to CG, requiring INEDs to enquire into and gain an informed understanding of the conduct of the company. The standard to which they are now held is best illustrated by the words of Lord Goldsmith, the UK Attorney General, during the debate on the 2006 Companies Act:

> The duty does not prevent a director from relying on the advice of work of others, but the final judgment must be his responsibility... As with all advice, slavish reliance is not acceptable, and obtaining of outside advice does not absolve directors from exercising their judgment on the basis of such advice.

In the Commonwealth (countries of the former British Empire), however, leading jurisdictions have taken a much more demanding view, stating categorically, in statute law, directors are responsible for the management of the affairs of their companies, shown in Table 3.2.

Table 3.2: Directors are responsible for managing the company

Jurisdiction	What the law says	Relevant Act
Australia	The business of a company is to be managed by or under the direction of the directors.[xxii]	Corporations Act 2001, section 198a (1)
Canada	Duty to manage or supervise management 102 (1) Subject to any unanimous shareholder agreement, the directors shall manage, or supervise the management of, the business and affairs of a corporation.[xxiii]	Canadian Business Corporations Act 1985, amended 2018, section 102 (1)
Hong Kong	Powers and duties of directors 82. Subject to the provisions of the Ordinance, the memorandum and articles and to any directions given by special resolution, the business and affairs of the company shall be managed by the directors, who may exercise all the powers of the company.[xxiv]	Companies Ordinance, Cap 32, Schedule 1, Section 82, updated in 2010
Malaysia	(1) The business and affairs of a company shall be managed by, or under the direction of, the board of directors (§211.1)) (2) The board of directors has all the powers necessary for managing and for directing and supervising the management of the business and affairs of the company subject to any modification, exception or limitation contained in this Act or in the constitution of the company (§211.2))	Companies Act 2016, section 211

Table 3.2 (continued)

Jurisdiction	What the law says	Relevant Act
New Zealand	128 Management of company (1) The business and affairs of a company must be managed by, or under the direction or supervision of, the board of the company. (2) The board of a company has all the powers necessary for managing and directing and supervising the management of, the business and affairs of the company.[xxv]	Companies Act 1993, section 128
Singapore	157A Powers of directors (1) The business and affairs of a company shall be managed by, or under the supervision of, the directors.[xxvi]	Companies Act, section 157 A 1) current version as at October 18, 2018
South Africa	66. (1) The business and affairs of a company must be managed by or under the direction of its board, which has the authority to exercise all of the powers and perform any of the functions of the company, except to the extent that this Act or the Memorandum of Incorporation provides otherwise. [xxvii]	Companies Act 2009, section 66 (1)

The standard to which they are held in Australia and other Commonwealth countries where Australian rulings are regarded as either precedent or "persuasive" is best illustrated by the words of Justice Middleton in the Centro case:

> Nothing that I decide in this case should indicate that directors are required to have infinite knowledge or ability. Directors are entitled to delegate to others the preparation of books and accounts and the carrying on of the day-to-day affairs of the company. *What each director is expected to do is to take a diligent and intelligent interest in the information available to him or her, to understand that information, and apply an enquiring mind to the responsibilities placed upon him or her.* [Emphasis mine]

The James Hardie case in 2012 is another Australian ruling that raised the bar dramatically for directors' duty of care. The James Hardie board were found negligent and severely sanctioned because they had signed off on the minutes of the previous board meeting, and as a result, were deemed to have *agreed retrospectively* to a misleading press release to the Australian Stock Exchange.[4] Boards would therefore be well advised to read the minutes of the previous meeting carefully, before approving them, instead of nodding them through with a show of hands.

Redefining the Boundaries

The real question then, is what does the law regard as "managing"? Whenever I have explained to directors the Malaysian Companies Act 2016 holds them responsible for managing the business, and that the words "managed by" precede "or under the direction," which means that a judge will look into their management practices as a priority, their reaction is one of shock. The majority signed up to become directors on the assumption that "boards govern and direct, management manages." The issue becomes one of redefining where the boundaries of responsibility between board and management lie. Table 3.3 suggests how the six core responsibilities of the board divide into actions of the board and those of line management.

---

4 In 2011, ASIC sued James Hardie Industries Ltd. (JHIL) in a civil case against its directors regarding a stock exchange press release concerning the funding of asbestos liabilities incurred by the company, which stated the provisions made were "fully funded" to cover the liabilities. In fact, this proved to be wrong, but not through malpractice. However, the court found the ASX release misleading by conveying that material available to JHIL provided basis for certainty that the funds made available were "sufficient" to meet all legitimate present and future asbestos claims. This even though both CEO and all the directors or the majority believed with certainty amount was "sufficient" and JHIL had received expert advice from PwC and Access Economics that supported their statement with certainty that the amount was "sufficient." The board appealed to the High Court, arguing they could not possibly have approved the announcement and the change of wording from "sufficient" to "fully funded," as it had been modified by management subsequent to the meeting and before release. To prove their case, they pointed out there were other inaccuracies in the minutes and errors in the approval process that cast doubts on reliability of the minutes. The High Court, however, upheld the original ruling in May 2012. It viewed the Board's approval of the minutes at the subsequent meeting as acceptance of the recorded events.

Table 3.3: Redefining the boundaries of responsibility

Six core responsibilities	Board's role	Management's role
1. *Sets strategy*	Board as a whole: 1. Formulates strategy, policies, and plans 2. Challenges management's plan assumptions, priorities, and options 3. Reviews the business plan and budget and sets targets for management (Discussed further in Chapter 8)	CEO and senior management: 1. Coordinate the development of business plan and budget across all BUs 2. Execute strategy and plans for company based on board-agreed direction and executive limitations 3. Report to the board on progress
2. *Reviews strategy implementation*	Board as a whole: 1. Reviews, approves and provides feedback on corporate KPIs and targets 2. Reviews results quarterly, discusses material variances, and ensures corrective actions are taken if required 3. Follows up (Discussed further in Chapter 9)	CEO and senior management: 1. Establish corporate KPIs 2. Cascade KPIs throughout organization 3. Monitor KPIs monthly with BUs, investigate variances and develop corrective actions if required 4. Report to the board on progress
3. *Manages risk*	Board working through the AC or RMC: 1. Sets the company's risk parameters; 2. Understands major risk exposures and ensures appropriate risk mitigation approach is in place; 3. Considers the risk factors in all major decisions. (Discussed further in chapter 10)	CEO and senior management: 1. Analyze and quantify the company's risks 2. Manage all risks within the boundaries set by the board; 3. Instill risk management culture throughout organization 4. Implement ERM and COSO frameworks

Table 3.3 (continued)

Six core responsibilities	Board's role	Management's role
4. *Plans succession*	Board working through the NRC: 1. Selects and proactively plans CEO succession 2. Reviews the performance management philosophy 3. Evaluates CEO 4. Endorses the development plan of people in pivotal positions 5. Understands the pool of future leaders 6. Sets remuneration policies (Discussed further in Chapter 11)	CEO, HR, and senior management: 1. Develop and implement the company's performance management system 2. Evaluate leadership performance and potential of all executives 3. Identify top talent pool and closely manage their performance and development plans 4. Recommend remuneration to the board for key executives.
5. *Ensures internal controls*	Board working through the AC: 1. Ensures through the appointment of an independent, experienced external auditor that the financial statements represent a "fair view" of the business 2. Ensures IA have the resources and credibility to carry out appropriately scoped internal audit plan 3. Approves code of conduct and compliance processes applying to all employees and the board 4. Establishes an effective whistle-blower policy and confidential reporting channels to the AC 5. Ensures adoption of and adherence to COSO framework. (Discussed further in Chapter 12)	CEO, CFO, CIO and Head of IA: 1. Ensure written SOPs, SLAs, policies, and procedures are in place and reviewed regularly 2. Ensure IT systems support reporting and information needs correctly 3. Establish written code of conduct 4. Train employees regularly in code of conduct 5. Ensure code of conduct and compliance are being followed 6. Identify weaknesses and take corrective action 7. Enforce code of conduct and compliance 8. Report through IA to the AC on progress and any issues

Table 3.3 (continued)

Six core responsibilities	Board's role	Management's role
6. *Engages shareholders and stakeholders*	Chair working with company secretary, corporate affairs, PR, and investor relations: 1. Chairs general meetings (AGM and EGM) 2. Ensures all shareholder views are represented and shareholders are treated equally 3. Balances and manages economic impact of stakeholder interests on shareholder value 4. Ensure all laws and regulations are followed correctly 5. Engage with the community to maximize social "licence to operate" 6. Supports management in handling key stakeholders (Discussed further in Chapter 13)	CEO and CFO: 1. Understand needs of shareholders and communicate key decisions in transparent manner to all employees 2. Ensure all disclosures or any other regulatory or statutory requirements are fulfilled 3. Manage all stakeholder interests within boundaries agreed with the board 4. Ensure company obeys environment, safety, and health laws and regulations

The crucial point is not whether the demarcation above is absolutely correct, but that it should be documented in the board charter and or memorandum and articles of association. If this is done, should directors ever have the misfortune to be hauled up in front of a judge, they can show they fulfilled their responsibilities, as laid down by their company's constitution. If they can demonstrate that, they will likely be covered by the "business judgment rule" and prove they have not been negligent or of acting in bad faith.

Conclusion

The board sits at the top of the organization and is accountable for everything that happens on its watch. The board does not just advise or supervise; it has six core responsibilities: setting strategy, reviewing its implementation, managing risk, planning succession, ensuring sound internal controls, and engaging stakeholders. Collectively, it is the sole source of authority and can not blame the chair, CEO or its committees for failures of CG. *The buck stops with the board.*

The board has two prerogatives. The first is determining the "purpose" of the organization. This takes a great deal of thought, effort and time and is affected by the ownership structure of the organization. "Purpose" differs greatly if the company is owned by dispersed shareholders from those that suit a family firm or a government-owned entity. If the company has a mixed ownership (public listed family firm or government listed company), the board alone can reconcile the inherent conflicts and then instruct line management on what is expected. In deciding on "purpose," the board must take a long-term view and not be constrained by the existing configuration of resources and competencies. The second prerogative is defining the company's mission, vision and values, which are essential if the board is to preserve and strengthen its social "license to operate." This determines whether the company can create long-term value. It defines with whom the company chooses to do business, how it will do that business and whom it employs and rewards. Key to this, is the board translating its agreed values into measurable, observable behaviors embedded in its code of conduct and these form the basis of appraisals and personal development plans.

Traditional thinking describes the board as having four roles: formulating strategy, making policy and plans, monitoring and supervising performance, and providing accountability. This view clearly separated governance from managing. Yet over the past thirty years or so, there has been a shift away, at least in leading Commonwealth jurisdictions, toward a view that holds boards responsible for the management of the business.

This shift requires boards to redefine the boundaries of responsibility between directors and management and for these redefined boundaries to be clearly documented in the company's constitution, if directors are to be protected by the business judgment rule, when in front of a judge.

References

[i] Carver, J. and Oliver, C. (2002), Corporate Boards That Create Value (San Francisco: Jossey-Bass), 6, cited in Wallace, P. and Zinkin, J. (2005), Corporate Governance, Singapore: John Wiley & Sons), 43–44.
[ii] Jensen, M., quoted in Gillespie, J., and Zweig, D., (2010), Money for Nothing: How the Failure of Corporate Boards is Ruining American Business and Costing Us Trillions (New York: Free Press), 19.
[iii] Carver and Oliver (2002), op. cit., 44.
[iv] Based on Carver, J. and Carver, M. M. (1997), Reinventing Your Board (San Francisco: Jossey-Bass), 139–141, cited in Wallace and Zinkin (2005), op. cit., 48–49.
[v] Harford, T. (2011), Adapt: Why Success Always Starts with Failure (London: Little Brown).
[vi] Based on Wallace and Zinkin (2005), op. cit., 57.
[vii] OECD (2015), OECD Guidelines on Corporate Governance of State owned Enterprises, 2015 Edition (Paris: OECD Publishing), 17, https://www.oecd-ilibrary.org/docserver/9789264244160-en.pdf?expires=1542261379&id=id&accname=guest&checksum=29D7D3455C42A7989C3D141939B2AAC9, accessed on November 15, 2018.
[viii] Petronas Mission Statement, quoted by Zinkin. J. (2007), "Getting from Good Governance to Good Results," Securities Commission, Emerging Market Programme, Kuala Lumpur, November 23, 2007 .

ix Drucker, P. F., Management Challenges for the 21st Century (Oxford: Butterworth Heinemann), 86, 93–94.

x Based on R. I., Tricker (1993). International Corporate Governance: Text, Readings and Cases (Singapore: Prentice Hall), 149.

xi Carver, J. and Oliver, C. (2002), Boards That Create Value: Governing Company Performance from the Boardroom (San Francisco: Jossey-Bass), xxii.

xii Business Roundtable (2012), quoted by Useem, M., Carey, D., Charan, R. (2016), "Boards that lead," in The Handbook of Corporate Governance, edited by Leblanc, R. (Hoboken, NJ: John Wiley & Sons), 42.

xiii FHI 360, USAID, Capable Partners Development Program (CAP) (2009), "Governance, Management and the Role of a Board of Directors," NGOConnect eNews Issue number 12, May 2009, 1–2. http://www.ngoconnect.net/documents/592341/749044/Governance+-+Governance,+Management+and+the+Role+of+a+Board+of+Directors, accessed on July 3, 2018.

xiv Partnoy, F. (2009), The Match King (London: Profile Books), 203–225.

xv 1933 Truth in Securities Act, Title I of Pub. L. 73–22, 48 Stat. 74, codified at 15 U.S.C.§77a et seq.,

xvi Securities Exchange Act of 1934, Pub. L. 73–291, 48 Stat. 881, enacted June 6, 1934, codified at 15 U.S.C.§78a et seq.

xvii Clikeman, P. M. (2008), Called to Account: Fourteen Financial Frauds that Shaped the American Accounting Profession (Routledge), 3, 9, 13, 17, 20, 46.

xviii Cadbury, A. (1992), Report of the Committee on the Financial Aspects of Corporate Governance (London: The Committee on the Financial Aspects of Corporate Governance and Gee and Co. Ltd), 26–27; http://www.ecgi.org/codes/documents/cadbury.pdf, accessed on July 4, 2018.

xix Moeller, R. R. (2004), Sarbanes-Oxley and the New Internal Auditing Rules (Hoboken, NJ: John Wiley & Sons), 2.

xx The Business Roundtable (2002), Principles of Corporate Governance, May 2002, 4–8, cited in Green, S. (2005), Sarbanes-Oxley and the Board of Directors: Techniques and Best Practices for Corporate Governance (Hoboken, NJ: John Wiley & Sons), 27.

xxi Green (2005), op. cit., 28.

xxii Australian Government, Federal Register of Legislation, Corporations Act 2001, https://www.legislation.gov.au/Details/C2018C00031, accessed on July 4, 2018.

xxiii Canada Business Corporations Act (R.S.C., 1985, c. C-44), last amended on May 1, 2018. http://laws.justice.gc.ca/eng/acts/C-44/page-15.html#h-18, accessed on July 4, 2018.

xxiv Companies Ordinance, Cap 32, Schedule 1, December 10, 2010, https://www.cr.gov.hk/docs/Cap32_Sch1_10Dec2010_e.pdf, accessed on October 18, 2018.

xxv Companies Act 1993, http://legislation.govt.nz/act/public/1993/0105/188.0/DLM320642.html, accessed on July 4, 2018.

xxvi Companies Act 1967, https://sso.agc.gov.sg/Act/CoA1967, accessed on October 18, 2018.

xxvii Companies Act 2009, Government Gazette, Cape Town, volume 526, No32121 April 9, 2009. http://www.cipc.co.za/files/2413/9452/7679/CompaniesAct71_2008.pdf, accessed on July 4, 2018.

Chapter 4
Chairing an Effective Board

This chapter is presented in four parts: the first sets the context against which board effectiveness is measured, the second explores the role of the board charter in setting the framework for the board's operations, the third explores further the immense contribution of the chair, and the fourth discusses the roles of committees in making boards effective.

Just as there is "no one size fits all" solution for good corporate governance (CG), there is no one way a board should engage with management.

Getting the Context Right

The most effective engagement style depends on the unique circumstances faced by the company and its management—the context which drives the way the company operates and the resulting board dynamics, where the company stands in its life-stage, and on the quality and experience of the management. The first responsibility of the chair is to ensure that the appropriate model applies. In making this choice, the chair can use three approaches.

Reflecting the Drivers of the Business[i]

Is it market driven, shareholder driven, organization driven or socially driven? Figure 4.1 provides a framework for choosing the most appropriate board focus—internal versus external, and the level of involvement necessary to create good board dynamics.[1]

---

[1] In Malaysia GLCs are government-linked companies; GLICS are government-linked investment companies; GLCs are like state-owned enterprises (SOEs) in China; GLICs are more like sovereign wealth funds.

DOI 10.1515/9781547400935-004

```
                Market driven              Less involved           Shareholder driven
                Small firms                     ▲                  Large firms
                Fast-moving industries          │                  Capital intensive

                        CEO dominant:           │    Checks and balance:
                        Dependent directors     │    Independent directors
        Internal focus ◄───────────────────────┼────────────────────────► External focus
                        Consensus oriented:     │    Owner dominant:
                        Stakeholder buy-in      │    Dependent directors

                Organization driven             │                  Socially driven
                Protected bureaucracy           ▼                  Family firms
                Knowledge intensive       More involved            GLCs/GLICs
```

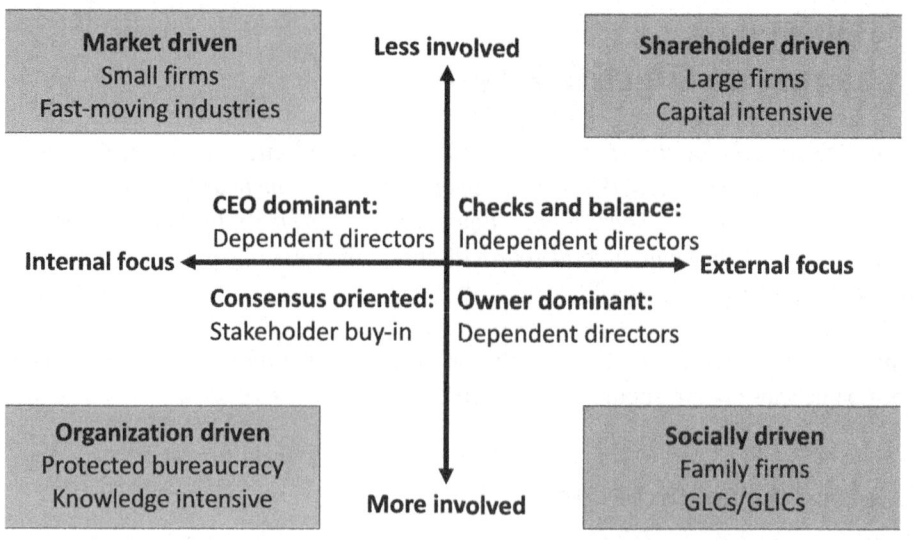

Figure 4.1: Choosing the best approach based on the drivers of the organization

The research undertaken by IMD[ii] identified two levels of board involvement where the chair and the board need to focus on the CEO as the center of decision making, with dependent directors, but requiring different levels of board involvement:

1. *Socially driven firms* requiring more input from the chair and the board and an external focus.
2. *Market driven firms* requiring less input from the chair and board and an internal focus.
3. *Shareholder driven firms* obviously demand checks and balance provided by independent directors and an engaged board, led by an involved chair with an external focus.
4. *Organization driven firms* tend to be introspective and political, hence the need for an internal focus and a higher level of involvement by the board and chair. The chair must appreciate the context she or he faces in order to recruit appropriate directors to ensure good board dynamics.

Reflecting the Life-Stage of the Business

Is the company a start-up, in its growth phase, mature or in decline? This model provides four styles of engagement and board dynamics: scout, challenger, watchdog, or VIP board.[iii]

1. *Scout boards* are high on providing advice, mentoring, and coaching and relatively low on monitoring and control and are appropriate for start-ups where the founders

are young and the chair is the so-called adult supervisor in the room, for example, Eric Schmidt's appointment when Sergei Brin and Larry Page founded Google:[iv]

> Halfway into the interview, [Charlie] Rose brought up Schmidt's appointment, asking, "What's the idea behind that—I mean, you guys couldn't run it yourself?" To which Brin responded, "Parental supervision, to be honest." Rose laughs hard, and asks Page, "Do you agree with that—you guys need adult supervision?" Page: "I don't know if I'd say *need*, but it's really nice to have." Rose: "It's beneficial." Page: "Yeah."

It is important for the chair and directors to recognize when they need to move to becoming a "challenger" board. Scout boards are excellent at giving visionary founder entrepreneurs the support an encouragement they need to get the enterprise off the ground. However, once the enterprise is listed, different rules apply and if the scout style continues for too long, the company can be put at risk by the eccentric behavior of an undisciplined founder, illustrated by what happened to Uber with Travis Kalanick[v] and Tesla with Elon Musk,[vi] where both had to step down from being chairs of the companies they founded.

2. *Challenger boards* are "engaged" boards. They partner with the CEO to provide insights and support on key decisions and their implementation. They recognize a dual responsibility to guide and support the CEO, and to evaluate him or her. Board meetings reflect two-way discussions in an atmosphere of mutual respect. Typically, successful "challenger" boards oversee the growth and maturity stages of the company's development.

3. *Watchdog boards* are "intervening" boards. They are intensely involved in discussions with both the CEO and senior management with frequent meetings. The atmosphere of such meetings is often adversarial, low on trust and respect for the management, as a result of previous crises where the board has felt let down by management—typically such boards are the result of the consistent failure of management to meet their financial targets, falling share prices or else a PR disaster. "Watchdog" boards usually operate in mature companies beginning to show signs of decline.

4. *VIP boards,* so-called trophy boards, are populated by the "great and good of the land" who do not have the time or the interest to get properly involved. Such boards often preside over state-owned enterprises (SOEs) where the directors feel their positions are a reward for past service, often not realizing being a director is a burdensome responsibility; requiring hard work to ensure the future success of the company. Such boards operate in mature companies whose stability makes the directors think they are safe bets. Yet the very fact the board is a disengaged

trophy board that "stays out of the way"[2] may precipitate the demise of the company, as happened with Enron.

Reflecting the Style of Engagement

Board dynamics can be classified according to where the board sits on a spectrum of five styles of engagement; ranging from the "passive" board (similar to the VIP trophy board) to the "operating" board (like the scout board) as follows:[vii]

1. *"Passive" boards:* Such boards function at the discretion of the CEO. They are characterized by limited participation in decision making and limited activity and accountability. They serve to ratify whatever the management proposes; and are similar to VIP boards:

    > If directors lack independence, they work for management, rather than the other way around.[viii]

2. *"Certifying" boards:* Such boards certify the CEO is doing what the board expects to the shareholders. They can attest to the fact the CEO and management are capable of taking necessary corrective action when it is needed. They rely on INEDs who also meet independently without the CEO in attendance. They are willing and able to replace management to be credible to shareholders. Their relationship with management is conditional and at arm's length.

3. *"Engaged" boards:* Such boards partner with the CEO to provide insight, advice, and support to the CEO and management on key decisions and implementation. They recognize they have a responsibility to oversee the CEO and company and must reconcile this dual role of guiding/supporting as well as overseeing and

---

[2] Michael Useem, Dennis Carey, and Ram Charan argue boards have a choice in how they wish to operate. They classify boards into four similar types as Steger and Amann, based on their choices. Boards can choose to:
1. *Take charge:* Such boards are responsible for: the central business idea; selecting the CEO; ensuring board competence, structure and modus operandi; ethics and integrity; remuneration; and crisis management.
2. *Partner:* Such boards are responsible for strategy, associated capex and execution; financials and shareholder value; stakeholder engagement; risk management; resource allocation; M&A; talent management and succession planning.
3. *Monitor:* Such boards are responsible for shareholder value, execution, and operations.
4. *Stay out of the way:* Such boards are responsible for execution, operations, delegating executive authority, taking no strategic decisions—all excluded by board charter.

"Boards that lead" in *The Handbook of Corporate Governance*, edited by Leblanc, R. (Hoboken, NJ: John Wiley & Sons), 32.

judging the CEO. Board meetings are characterized by useful, two-way discussions of key issues/decisions facing the company; and are similar to "challenger" boards.
4. *"Intervening" boards:* Such boards operate in crisis mode: the board becomes intensely involved in discussions of key decisions facing the organization and in decision making, with frequent and intense board meetings called on short notice; and are similar to "watchdog" boards.
5. *"Operating" boards:* Such boards make key decisions; management implements. They are fairly common in early "start-ups" where board members are selected to "fill gaps" in management experience; and are similar to "scout" boards.

Although there are these three ways for the chair to think about the best way of getting the board to interface with management, in the end what really drives the most effective way to chair a board is agreement on the strategy of the company and having the right board composition. It is the chair's responsibility, with the help of the Nomination Committee, if there is one, to ensure the board is of the right size with the right balance of skills, personalities and experience (covered in more detail in Chapter 11).

Role of the Board Charter

During my discussions with directors, I have been surprised by how few directors know what the constitution of their company is, when asked. Perhaps it is because they do not think of the memorandum and articles of association or the board charter, if there is one, as being the company constitution, or perhaps it is because they have not read it carefully. In any case, it is essential directors familiarize themselves with the company constitution. Some regulatory regimes now favor board charters over the traditional memorandum and articles of association.[ix]

Developing the board charter is the responsibility of the chair, working with the company secretary and general counsel in the initial phase; and then "socializing" the proposed draft with the CEO and the other members of the board. Once their feedback has been incorporated, the final version should be formally tabled for approval by the board, and when that is granted, the board charter should go on the company website.

Table 4.1 shows what the board charter must cover.

Table 4.1: Board charter contents

1) Roles	2) Functions
a. Board composition	a. Good governance and culture
b. Role of the board	b. Reputation, ethics and compliance
c. Role of the chair	c. Policy and strategy
d. Role of the CEO	d. Risk management
e. Role of directors	e. Regulatory compliance
f. Role of committees	f. Stakeholder engagement
3) Processes	4) Ensuring efficiency
a. Board meetings	a. Succession planning
b. Committee meetings	b. Directors' selection
c. Decision making	c. Directors' remuneration
d. Monitoring	d. Board evaluation
e. Financial reporting	e. Directors' assessment
f. Nonfinancial reporting	f. Directors' training and development

Source: *Malaysian Corporate Governance Blueprint 2011*, 26.

As you can see, the board charter is designed to deal with four themes from a regulatory perspective, defining: the roles of the different components of the board, the functions of the board, the processes of the board, and what is needed to ensure the board operates efficiently. (Appendix 4.1 features a sample board charter table of contents for reference.)

Contribution of the Chair to Board Effectiveness

From discussions with directors and doing board evaluations, I find boards are only as good as their chairs. This is because effective chairs:

1. *Define the overarching purpose and values for the board:* It is the job of chairs to reconcile the need to satisfy the shareholders' demand for maximum value creation with the constraints presented by taking a stakeholder-friendly approach. At the same time, chairs must promote the highest standards of CG, demanding at a minimum compliance with the requirements of relevant regulations/legislation and the provisions of the relevant CG code, insisting on the highest standards of integrity and honesty.
    Effective chairs create a climate of trust between EDs and INEDs; minimize the information asymmetry between EDs and INEDs, allowing INEDs to contribute in a professional atmosphere of constructive challenge.
2. *Understand the drivers of the business:* Effective chairs learn about the industry and the business, applying the same level of due diligence in achieving a detailed understanding of what makes the company successful, as if the company was

a target for acquisition. Chairs need the right due-diligence mindset,[x] ensuring appropriate conversations with management and outside experts to appreciate the business drivers, its strengths, weaknesses, opportunities and threats.[xi] Then chairs should ensure the directors are able to take a "deep dive" into the drivers and levers of the business, its risks and opportunities, by creating off-site opportunities for detailed discussions with management and outside experts.

3. *See the "big picture":* It is the job of chairs to pull together what the specialists in management and on the board say and then connect the dots:

> A second chairmanly attribute is the ability to integrate, to pull together the different threads of a complex issue, so that it acquires coherence. The skills of management are becoming increasingly specialized and so the fields of experience of directors are tending to become narrower. As a result, their approach to issues is likely to be determined in fair measure by their particular expertise. Chairmen, however, have to see the business as a whole, in the context of its environment, and need to integrate the skills and perceptions of all those seated at the board table.[xii]

4. *Are open to new ideas and able to explain the company's actions and intentions,* where the consequences of decisions on the people they affect has been carefully assessed.

5. *Engage regularly with the CEO and management:* Effective chairs meet regularly with the CEO and management, having made it crystal clear they have no desire to become the CEO, recognizing the roles of chair and CEO are separate and complementary so that the CEO does not feel threatened by the Chair engaging with senior management. Such interactions should cover:
   a. High level discussion of the primary role of the board and performance expectation expectations and evaluation criteria
   b. Asking questions and above all listening
   c. Acting as sounding board for the CEO
   d. Coaching the CEO

6. *Define standards for creating value:* Effective chairs set standards for the performance of the board and perhaps the best approach is to adopt that used by private equity and by focusing on the drivers of value and risk:

> Overall it seems that PE governance overcomes the principal-agent problems with management through an "encourage and challenge" approach.[xiii]

> Similarly, most companies manage value and performance via their financial systems and budgeting processes. Most have succeeded with this basic management task, yet few have specifically targeted the value drivers and leverage points for value creation and growth. In contrast, *top performers [emphasis added] simultaneously target value creation drivers and focus on "risks that matter" to achieve superior financial performance, organizational effectiveness, and value growth.*[xiv]

Effective chairs do this by:
a. *Monitoring the value creation process robustly:*[xv]
   i. Insisting the board must regularly review a value maximizing plan with clearly stated milestones, timelines, and individual accountabilities.
   ii. Working with the CEO to ensure frequent, timely, and accurate information.
   iii. Placing the review of progress against plan as the primary topic on the agenda, giving it the right amount of time for review and inviting people below the CEO who can "move the needle" to present.
   iv. Leading directors to get more involved and engaged in their questioning and challenge processes on the basis that "trust, but verify" is the best way to oversee management.
   v. Always seeking continuous improvement in performance and processes.[xvi]
b. *Ensuring strict management accountability:* Effective chairs expect to see achievement of key milestones with corrective action to be taken when problems arise; they follow up, tracking progress in the minutes, closing the file when the action has been successful.
c. *Influencing director succession and remuneration plans*[xvii] (covered in detail in Chapter 11).
7. *Set the board agenda:* Effective chairs take the time to think through what should be on the agenda, after consultation with the CEO and company secretary. In so doing, chairs must consider the concerns of all board members and reconcile the need to take enough time to discuss future strategic direction with the need to review current and past performance.[3] At the same time, chairs must set the correct boundary for discussion and review between what is the responsibility of the board and what is the responsibility of management to avoid second-guessing the CEO (I covered this earlier in Chapter 3).
8. *Manage the business of the board:* Effective chairs allow enough time for discussion of difficult and sensitive topics; knowing when to allow overruns and where to recover the extra time elsewhere in the agenda. Chairs are responsible for the proper structuring of the agenda: the difficult, contentious topics coming immediately after "matters arising" for discussion and decision making (while directors are still fresh), with topics clearly designated as either for decision or for

---

[3] From my discussions with directors, I believe boards spend too much time reviewing past performance, focusing on internal matters and not enough time on looking at the external forces that affect the business and at the future, which after all is what the word "direction" requires. An analogy might be driving a car, looking in the rearview mirror rather than watching the road ahead and then wondering why there was an accident.

information. When necessary, chairs can arrange informal pre-briefings to ensure INEDs have a thorough understanding of the issues without being pressured into making poor decisions by unrealistic deadlines.

9. *Ensure accurate, timely and clear information:* Effective chairs recognize directors need time to absorb the information contained in board papers. Typically, papers are received five working days before board meetings. Ten days is leading practice. Another leading practice is the calendarization of major topics.[4] In this way, chairs and company secretaries ensure management have the maximum time to prepare and have no excuse for late submission of papers.

10. *Create positive board dynamics:* Effective chairs recognize the critical importance of achieving the right interpersonal dynamics for the board to operate both effectively and in the best interests of the shareholders. Even Warren Buffett admits to the pressures collegiality brought to bear on him when decisions were made that were not in the best interests of the shareholders:

> Too often I was silent when management made proposals that I judged to be counter to the interest of shareholders. In those cases, collegiality trumped independence [and a] certain social atmosphere presides in the boardroom where it becomes impolitic to challenge the chief executive.[xviii]

Chairs must know when and how to rein in directors who are grandstanding, going over old ground or going off at a tangent. It is a delicate, but essential task given the limited amount of time devoted to typical board meetings. At the same time, it is the chair's job to make sure every director contributes to the discussion—even the ones who are disruptive—and then to be able to synthesize the various points that have been made into an effective summary the company secretary can minute accurately. Doing this well, may require the chair to speak last, so directors feel free to express their opinions. It is so much harder to do this if the Chair has begun the discussion, indicating a strong preference for a particular point of view.

Finally, chairs must decide which engagement style is appropriate to get the best board-management dynamics; and once that choice has been made, to ensure

---

4 For example, HR matters are discussed in the second board meeting of the year, while IT topics are discussed in the third board meeting of the year, and so on.

all directors adhere to it. Few things are more confusing and demotivating to management than to find themselves being treated differently by different directors.[5]

Role of Board Committees

I discuss briefly the role of four committees: Audit (AC), Risk management (RMC), Nomination (NC), and Remuneration (RC) committees; briefly, because their roles and responsibilities are discussed in greater detail in chapters 10–12. In many companies, the AC and RMC are combined, as are the NC and RC to form the NRC. In most jurisdictions, only the AC is mandated; there are still some countries that do not require an AC and very few countries mandate the existence of the NRC.[xix]

The decision to have a separate RMC depends on the size of the company and the cost of reporting relative to the revenues of the business.[xx] If the cost of having a separate RMC can be justified, then it makes good sense because the mindset of the AC is focused on the past and on looking inside the company: to establish what happened and what went wrong in the processes and policies of the business. The mindset of the RMC is quite different; it is future-oriented and needs to consider what is happening outside the company, as well as inside it. It needs to ask the question "what could happen?" rather than "what happened?"' and "what impact will it have and how can we mitigate that impact?" rather than "what can we learn from what happened?" This not to say it is bad practice to combine the AC with the RMC, but merely to highlight it requires the same people to wear different hats when thinking about audit and risk.

As a general observation, committees aid and extend the capacity of the board but do not substitute for it. This means their recommendations must be referred back to the full board for approval. From a control point of view the committees must provide the board with both verbal and written reports after each committee meeting. This is to ensure all directors on the board have a good understanding of the deliberations of their colleagues so that they are not relying on them blindly. Committees must follow agreed, written terms of reference (TOR) which are to be found in either memorandum and articles of association (the constitution of the company) or in the board charter,

---

5 For example, one board I assessed had one third of its directors behaving as "watchdogs," while the rest of the board were acting as "challengers." The "watchdog" directors went into too much detail and were regarded by their "challenger" colleagues as disruptive, as well as abusive; while the "challengers" were regarded as being too soft on management by their "watchdog" peers, allowing them to get away with poor performance when compared with their peer companies. Management were confused and demoralized and tried to play the two factions off each other. That such a situation could persist was the result of the chair finding calling to order the "watchdog" minority too difficult because he believed in harmony and saving face. This was a clear example of the difficulty chairs often face when trying to separate cognitive conflict (disagreement about ideas) from affective conflict (dislike of people).

if there is one, which nowadays replaces the memorandum and articles of association as the source of all authority for the company. Committees should consist of a majority of INEDs with access to executives and professional advisers when needed, with agreed budgets to pay for such access. Committee meetings are formal, with agendas, minutes and records of attendance and voting. Committee performance and the suitability of their TOR should be evaluated annually by the board and the results reported in the annual report for public listed companies.

So, what are the specific responsibilities of the AC, RMC, NC, and RC?

Role of the AC

The work of the AC splits into two: working with the external auditors and working with the internal auditors. To do his effectively, the AC must have members who are financially literate, and in some jurisdictions, one must be a qualified accountant:

1. *Working with external auditors:* the AC has five responsibilities when working with the external auditors:
    a. Appoint the external auditors and agree their remuneration: this requires the AC to review the previous year's audit, discuss the coming year's audit proposal, and assess the independence of the external audit team and its experience and competence.
    b. Agree the scope of the audit: this requires the AC to review and understand the proposed audit plan, understand the expectations of the work done by the auditors, and evaluate how the key risk areas will be covered by the plan.
    c. Ensure the independence of the external auditors, checking all matters that affect auditor independence, including other work done and the rotation of the audit lead partner to prevent management capture through too long a relationship with management.
    d. Review the audit findings and recommendations: this requires the AC to review the audited financial statements, discuss the audit findings and any disagreements with management, meeting the auditors without management being present to discuss any difficulties experienced by the external auditors during the audit and any other concerns they might have.
    e. Discuss internal control issues, fraud or illegal acts; follow up with management any recommendations made in the management letter from the external auditors.
2. *Working with internal auditors (IA):* The AC has three responsibilities when working with IA:
    a. Oversee the control structure to ensure operational effectiveness to protect company assets from misappropriation: This requires the AC to determine the adequacy of the scope of work; functions and resources for the IA

team. The AC must ensure IA has the authority and necessary resources and access to management to carry out the audit. The AC then reviews the IA programme of work and results of the audit where needed; and ensures corrective actions are taken as recommended by IA by following up as appropriate.
b. Ensure IA is adequately resourced and able to undertake its activities independently and objectively: This requires the AC to review the performance appraisals of the IA team and to approve the appointment, promotion or termination of senior IA team members, conducting exit interviews with departing members of IA to establish potential areas of weakness and improvement.
c. Review and follow up on any issues raised by internal/external auditors or whistle-blowers, reporting to regulatory authorities if necessary.

These are the responsibilities of a standalone AC that does not include risk management in its TOR. If the AC has to cover risk management as well, then the eight responsibilities of the standalone RMC (in the next section) would be added to those of the AC.

Role of the RMC

The RMC has eight responsibilities to complement the activities of the AC, covered in more detail in Chapter 10:
1. *Ensure the organization has a comprehensive risk management policy.*
2. *Appreciate risk management is a dynamic process reflecting changes in markets and external and internal forces.* This requires members of the RMC to keep up to date with latest developments and get independent expert advice rather than relying only on what management provides.
3. *Consider the effectiveness of the policy, including IT and cybersecurity risks.*
4. *Consider risks posed by relationships with significant vendors, consultants, and changes in customers.*
5. *Review management reports on their assessment of risks.*
6. *Appreciate the difference between macroprudential and microprudential risks* and their different impacts on the company.
7. *Understand the scope of external audit and IA reviews* associated with financial reporting and all other processes covered by the enterprise risk management framework.
8. *Review reports on the findings and recommendations,* together with management's response and follow up to ensure corrective actions are taken in a timely manner.
9. *Hire outside experts and consultants when needed.*

If the board decides that having a separate RMC is not warranted, then these responsibilities would be added back to those of the AC.

Role of the NC

The NC has four responsibilities, covered in more detail in Chapter 11. They are:
1. *Ensure appropriate board composition and skills:* This requires the NC to determine the right size of the board[6] and the most appropriate combination of skills and balance to maximize board effectiveness, taking into account the need for suitable staffing of the board committees. The NC is also required to recommend suitable training and development for directors.
2. *Recommend candidates for key posts after considering the views of shareholders, regulators and the CEO.* It helps if the NC has targets to meet for diversity and inclusion, often the case in leading companies.
3. *Conduct annual board evaluation:* The NC should evaluate the performance of individual directors and the board annually in association with the chair to assess the effectiveness and independence of INEDs. The NC must then report the results in the annual report, if the company is listed.

---

[6] Research suggests boards are less effective if there are fewer than seven members because there are not enough directors to staff the relevant committees and more than eleven directors because they become unwieldy. It has been suggested that the optimum size is ten (Korn Ferry, "29th Annual Board of Directors Study," 2002). Subsidiary boards can be smaller because they have access to advice and expertise of main board directors, though this can create conflicts of interest. The following is a good explanation why there are upper and lower limits to the size of an effective board:
"Up to a certain point, large boards can have a number of benefits. Larger size may facilitate the board's resource-gathering function, since a larger number of directors will usually translate into more interlocking relationships with other organizations that may be useful in providing resources such as customers, clients, credit, and supplies. Larger boards with diverse interlocks are also likely to include a greater number of specialists—such as investment bankers or attorneys—who bring special expertise to the table.
On the other hand, a number of considerations suggest that small boards may be preferable. Large boards tend to be contentious and fragmented, which would reduce their ability collectively to monitor and discipline senior management. In such cases, the senior managers can affirmatively take advantage of the board through coalition building, selective channelling of information, and 'dividing and conquering.'" http://www.professorbainbridge.com/professorbainbridgecom/2009/05/Board-size-is-there-an-optimum.html, accessed on April 20, 2016.

4. *Develop and review succession plan and talent management:* This requires the NC to approve senior management positions as part of the succession plan; the succession plan must also cover the appointment and replacement of directors considering regulatory term limits. In terms of managing the talent pipeline, the NC is required to identify the talent pool and ensure appropriate personal development plans, taking into account the current and future needs of the company, assessing progress on the replacement chart for key individuals. The NC is also responsible for reviewing the company personnel policies, including recruitment, promotion, rotation, and termination. It helps if the NC has diversity and inclusion targets management must meet.

Role of the RC

The RC has four responsibilities. They are:
1. *Recommend a suitable remuneration policy for the board:* This comes in two parts—developing packages for executive directors and for INEDs and nonexecutive directors who are no longer independent:
    a. Packages for EDs: This requires the RC to link reward to individual and company performance to reinforce "pay for performance," based on salary scales which are appropriate for the size of the company and the lines of business it has. The RC must ensure packages do not reward excessive short-term risk taking that could harm the company long term.
    b. Packages for INEDs, including attendance allowances for attending both board meetings and committee meetings on which they sit.[7] The vexed question RCs face is whether to pay each INED differently, based on their unique contribution or whether to pay all board members the same fee on the grounds of equity, with any differences reflecting the result of different attendance and allowances, as well as the premium paid to chairs of committees.
2. *Evaluate the performance of the CEO:* The RC must evaluate the CEO's performance against agreed KPIs and achieve the right balance between long and short-term objectives.
3. *Establish and review incentive plans and stock options to achieve shareholder alignment:* The RC must ensure the packages do not reward unduly risky behav-

---

[7] The difficulty in settling on packages for INEDs is they need to consider the *complexity* of the role; the *opportunity cost* of the INED's time; the burden of *responsibility*; the *time needed* to be spent to do the job; the *experience/expertise* that each INED brings to the board and finally the chemistry and fit (*X factor*) of each INED with the rest of the board. This can be summarized in the mnemonic CORTEX. Personally, I favor paying INEDs differentially based on their unique contribution to creating value. I recognize this is not normal practice.

ior and the packages are seen to be equitable across different grades and lines of business. As part of ensuring the packages are fair to shareholders, the RC must assess the impact of pay-plans under different scenarios to avoid abusive "golden parachute" pay-outs to undeserving departing CEOs.
4. *Ensure plans are appropriate to recruit and retain necessary talent:* The RC must regularly review market conditions with consultants, using appropriate peer comparators and setting sensible pay reference points. Above all, the RC must develop transparent "pay for performance" programs for senior executives, taking into account the increasing unhappiness of shareholders at the excessive levels of CEO pay,[8] reflected in the growth of "say on pay" revolts by shareholders against the packages of top executives.[xxi] The enormous increase in CEO pay in the US does not make sense when compared with the past.[9] The failure of the RCs and their advisers to rein in CEO pay matters because it puts capitalism at risk and may explain some of the discontent in the United States and United Kingdom with the current economic system.

Conclusion

The chair must decide on the best way for the board to work with management. In making this choice, the chair can use one of three approaches reflecting: the drivers of the business; life-stage of the business or most suitable engagement style. The chair is also responsible, with the help of the company secretary and general counsel, for developing the board charter as the constitution of the company. This must cover the board's roles, functions, and processes, with a focus on ensuring efficiency of operations.

The chair's personal contribution to the effectiveness of the board is immense: defining the board's purpose and values; applying his or her understanding of the drivers of the business; seeing the "big picture"; being open to ideas whatever their source; engaging regularly with senior management; defining the standards for creat-

---

[8] "In 1992...CEOs held 2 percent of the equity of US corporations, today [2003], they own 12 percent, which is one of the most spectacular acts of appropriation in the history of capitalism," Brenner, R. (2003), "Towards the Precipice," *London Review of Books* 25, No. 3, quoted in Doogan, K. (2009), *New Capitalism? The Transformation of Work*, Polity Press.

[9] "While the 2016 CEO-to-worker compensation ratio of 271-to-1 is down from 299-to-1 in 2014 and 286-to-1 in 2015, it is still light years beyond the 20-to-1 ratio in 1965 and the 59-to-1 ratio in 1989. The average CEO in a large firm now earns 5.33 times the annual earnings of the average very-high-wage earner (earner in the top 0.1 percent) ... CEO pay continues to be dramatically higher now than it was in the decades before the turn of the millennium: in 1995, the CEO-to-worker pay ratio was 123-to-1; in 1989, it was 59-to-1; in 1978, it was 30-to-1; and in 1965, it was 20-to-1." Mishel, L. and Scheider, J. (2017), "CEO Pay Remains High Relative to the Pay of Typical Workers and High-Wage Earners," *Economic Policy Institute, July 20, 2017,* https://www.epi.org/publication/ceo-pay-remains-high-relative-to-the-pay-of-typical-workers-and-high-wage-earners/, accessed on June 27, 2018.

ing value; setting the board agenda, managing the business of the board and ensuring accurate and timely information; and last and most important, creating positive board dynamics within the board and between the board and management *maximizing constructive cognitive disagreement over ideas and minimizing disruptive affective disagreement about personalities.* In so doing, the chair is aided by the AC, RMC, NC, and RC.

Appendix 4.1: Sample Board Charter: Table of Contents

1. **Introduction**
    1.1. Complementarity to existing laws and Articles of Association
    1.2. Statement of commitment to good corporate governance
2. **Composition of board, positions and committees**
    2.1. Board profile, size, skills and independence
    2.2. Appointment, term of office and resignation of directors
    2.3. Chair
    2.4. CEO
    2.5. Company Secretary
    2.6. Committees
3. **Board general duties and powers**
    3.1. General duties and powers
    3.2. Supervision of management
    3.3. Duties regarding the members and performance of the board
    3.4. Other duties
    3.5. Supervision of financial reporting
    3.6. Duties regarding nomination and assessment of the external auditor
    3.7. Compensation of board members
4. **Board meetings and decision making**
    4.1. Meeting frequency, notice, agenda, and venue
    4.2. Board attendance and admission
    4.3. Chairing the meeting and reporting
    4.4. Decision making in the board
5. **Other provisions**
    5.1. Conflicts of interest of board members
    5.2. Remuneration of board members
    5.3. Directors' induction, ongoing training, and education
    5.4. Other positions
    5.5. Holding and trading securities
    5.6. Confidentiality
    5.7. Miscellaneous

Appendices:
Appendix 1: Policies regarding board governance processes
Appendix 2: Policies regarding board-CEO linkage
Appendix 3: Policies regarding CEO limitations
Appendix 4: Audit committee TOR
Appendix 5: Nomination & remuneration committee TOR
Appendix 6: Board risk management committee TOR
Appendix 7: List of approvals required by the board
Appendix 8: Policies regarding independent external auditor
Appendix 9: Ten core values of directors

References

[i] Steger, U. and Amann, W. (2008), *Corporate Governance: How to Add Value* (Chichester: John Wiley & Sons), 19, cited in Zinkin, J. (2010). *Challenges in Implementing Corporate Governance: Whose Business is it Anyway?* (Singapore: John Wiley & Sons), 55.
[ii] Ibid.
[iii] Ibid., 22.
[iv] Austin, S. (2011), "About Eric Schmidt's Adult Supervision Comment," *The Wall Street Journal*, January 20, 2011, https://blogs.wsj.com/venturecapital/2011/01/20/about-eric-schmidts-adult-supervision-comment/, accessed on June 23, 2018.
[v] Newcomer, E. and Stone, B. (2018), "The Fall of Travis Kalanick Was a Lot Darker and Weirder Than You Thought," *Bloomberg*, January 18, 2018, https://www.bloomberg.com/news/features/2018-01-18/the-fall-of-travis-kalanick-was-a-lot-weirder-and-darker-than-you-thought, accessed on October 6, 2018.
[vi] "Elon Musk: Tesla Boss Mocks US Regulator Days after Settlement," *BBC News*, October 5, 2018, https://www.bbc.com/news/business-45754299, accessed on October 6, 2018.
[vii] Lorsch, J., Nadler, D. A., and Behan, B. (2005), *Building Better Boards: A Blueprint for Effective Governance* (San Francisco: Jossey-Bass).
[viii] Leblanc, R. (2016), "Director Independence, Competency and Behavior," quoted in *The Handbook of Corporate Governance*, edited by Richard Leblanc (Hoboken, NJ: John Wiley & Sons), 164.
[ix] For example, the Malaysian Companies Act 2016 does away with the need for memorandum and articles of association, replacing them with the board charter.
[x] Wolfe, H. D. (2016), "The Non-Executive Chairman," quoted in *The Handbook of Corporate Governance*, edited by Richard Leblanc (Hoboken, NJ: John Wiley & Sons), 89.
[xi] Ibid., 90.
[xii] Cadbury, A. (2002), *Corporate Governance and Chairmanship: A Personal View* (London: Oxford University Press), 104–105.
[xiii] Acharya et al., "Corporate Governance and Value Creation" quoted by Wolfe, H. D. (2016), quoted in *The Handbook of Corporate Governance*, op. cit., 89.
[xiv] Abstract of a *Directors & Boards Magazine* webinar, "Board Risk Management: How Boards Rate Themselves," March 22, 2012, quoted by Wolfe, H. D. (2016), op. cit., 91.
[xv] Wolfe (2016), op. cit., 94.
[xvi] Ibid., 98.
[xvii] Ibid., 94–97.
[xviii] Buffett, W. (2002), Letter to Berkshire Hathaway Shareholders, quoted by Useem, M., Carey, D., Charan, R., (2016), "Boards that Lead" quoted in *The Handbook of Corporate Governance*, op. cit., 27.

xix The Growth and Emerging Markets Committee of the International Organization of Securities Commissions (2016), *Report on Corporate Governance: Final Report*, (OICU-IOSCO), 28, file:///D:/IOSCO%20GEM%20CGTF%20REport.pdf, accessed on June 27, 2018.

xx Ibid., 65.

xxi For example, Bradshaw, B. et al. (2018), "AstraZeneca Suffers Pay Revolt as Sales Suffer," *The Telegraph*, May 18, 2018, https://www.telegraph.co.uk/business/2018/05/18/astrazeneca-may-face-pay-revolt-sales-disappoint/, accessed on June 26, 2018; "Persimmon Hit by Investor Revolt over Executive Pay," *BBC News*, April 25, 2018, https://www.bbc.com/news/business-43891134, accessed on June 26, 2018; Gray, A. and Foley, S. (2016), "Citigroup Shareholders in Rebellion over Executive Pay," *Financial Times*, April 27, 2016, https://www.ft.com/content/b28d4f34-0bcb-11e6-9456-444ab5211a2, accessed on June 26, 2018; Stothard, M. (2015), "Activist Shareholders Lead New French Revolution of Pay Excess," *Financial Times*, May 10, 2015, https://www.ft.com/content/f58f103e-f569-11e4-8c83-00144feab7de, accessed on June 26, 2018.

Chapter 5
Being an Effective Board Member

This chapter is presented in three parts: the first explores the roles of the chair and CEO and why they should be kept separate, the second looks at the roles of directors—independent and nonindependent—and the third concludes with the qualities/attributes that make a board member effective.

Being an effective board member has never been harder. Legislative, regulatory, and political expectations of directors keep getting more demanding as a result of scandals in the twenty-first century and their rising costs, paid for by taxpayers or employees who lose their jobs and pensions as a result. The spotlight has fallen on the effectiveness of chairmen, on CEOs whose performance does not reflect the increases in their remuneration and on the role of directors, the independent nonexecutives (INEDs). The pain and costs of failures of corporate governance (CG) seem to fall on people who are not board members, whereas board members have seemed to be able to walk away scot-free from the disasters for which they were responsible.[1] Hence the increased focus on the effectiveness of board members.

Chair and CEO: Two Distinct Roles?

There is a difference of opinion and practice regarding the need to separate the chairmanship from the CEO between the United States and other jurisdictions.

In 2014 in the United States, only 26% of companies in the SP 500 had split the two roles.[i] By comparison, 79% of the largest British businesses named an outside chairman in their annual reports, according to the Millstein Center.[ii] In Canada, 84% were split in 2013.[iii] The Australian,[iv] Hong Kong,[v] Indian,[vi] Malaysian,[vii] New Zealand,[viii] Singaporean,[ix] and South African[x] Securities Commissions expect/encourage the roles to be split. One of the key reasons for this is the inherent conflict of interest in one person fulfilling both roles:

> If the CEO is also setting the agenda for the board, there is an inherent conflict because the board is supposed to supervise the CEO.[xi]

However, there are a number of additional reasons why the roles should be split. The chair and the CEO have two quite distinct responsibilities: The chair is responsible for ensuring the board is governed properly and acts as the link between the board and the CEO; while the CEO is responsible for satisfying board-agreed organizational

---

[1] This was particularly resented in the United Kingdom when Carillion went bankrupt in 2018.

objectives and delivering key performance indicators (KPIs) within board-defined constraints. From my experience, for these responsibilities to be undertaken properly, there is not enough time for one person to do them both.

Role and Responsibilities of the Chair

The chair's responsibilities relate to governing the board and to engaging with internal and external stakeholders.

Ensuring the Board Is Properly Governed
1. Leading the board so it can fulfill its responsibilities
2. Setting the board agenda and ensuring directors receive complete and accurate information on time
3. Leading board meetings and discussions
    a. Encouraging active participation and constructive challenge and the expression of diverse views[2]
    b. Managing the board-management interface
    c. Engaging stakeholders and communicating their views to the board
    d. Leading the board in establishing and monitoring good CG in the company[xii]

Another way of looking at the chair's board governance responsibilities is as follows. The chair:
1. Chairs the meetings
2. Keeps in touch with directors between meetings
3. Presides over board evaluations
4. Takes resulting actions to enhance director effectiveness
5. Presides over new director recruitment
6. Oversees corporate governance
7. Oversees stakeholder engagement[xiii]

---

[2] This is a much more complex task than many people realize because the chair must do two distinct things to ensure constructive debate and challenge do not become dysfunctional or formal lip service to the idea.
The first is to ensure disagreements do not reflect personal antipathy or past baggage. They must not be allowed to become emotional and affective reflections of how the protagonists feel about each other as individuals. That is often challenging when there are real issues people feel strongly about, especially if they have different interests in mind.
The second is to uncover deep-seated disagreements about ideas to ensure the process of challenge is thorough, but without allowing the disagreements to move from issues of fact and interpretation. This is particularly difficult to do, if one of the protagonists has come to his/her point of view, as a result of personal experience and who therefore finds it difficult to disentangle disagreement about the idea being discussed from an attack on their personal life experience.

Fulfilling the Company's Ten Fiduciary Duties[xiv]
The chair is responsible for ensuring the board proactively:
1. Promotes a good CG culture to reinforce ethical, prudent, and professional behavior with the help of the CEO
2. Ensures the agreed strategy supports long-term value creation considering economic, environmental, and social considerations with the help of the CEO
3. Reviews, challenges management proposals, and monitors implementation with the help of the relevant board committees
4. Supervises and evaluates management performance with the help of the nomination and remuneration committees (or the combined nomination and remuneration committee)
5. Ensures a sound framework of internal controls and risk management with the help of the audit committee
6. Establishes an appropriate risk appetite given the nature of the business with the help of the risk management committee
7. Ensures there is an appropriate risk management framework to assess and manage financial and nonfinancial risk with the help of the risk management committee
8. Ensures orderly succession plans so that senior management has necessary skills and experience with the help of the nomination committee
9. Ensures effective stakeholder engagement with the help of investor relations
10. Ensures the integrity of the company's financial reporting with the help of the audit committee

The Link Between the Board and the CEO
When it comes to dealing with the CEO on behalf of the board, the chair is responsible for the board-CEO linkage. This requires the chair to create a close relationship of trust with the CEO, providing guidance, support, and advice when needed, but without encroaching on the CEO's areas of executive responsibility. The chair is also responsible on a continuing basis for making sure the board is monitoring the performance of the CEO and for advising and coaching the CEO regarding any identified shortfalls. If they are serious and insoluble, the chair must find a replacement, either getting the CEO to leave voluntarily or by termination. The chair works with the Nomination Committee, if there is one, to do this.

The chair must work with the CEO to ensure there is an effective succession plan to ensure a deep enough bench of talent and experience to replace the CEO in the event of an emergency, as well as having a long-term succession plan for senior management and pivotal positions in the company. If the CEO's post becomes vacant, it is the responsibility of the chair, working with the Nomination Committee, to find an appropriate replacement as quickly as possible.

Energizing Internal Stakeholders with the Help of the CEO[xv]

The effective chair achieves this, working closely with the CEO, by:
1. Setting the long-term vision with milestones, targets, and agreed action plans
2. Inspiring and energizing groups
3. Setting and achieving new higher performance standards
4. Ensuring key players understand their roles and what is in it for them
5. Holding individuals accountable for results
6. Respecting and being respected by those who are led

Engaging External Stakeholders

The effective chair has the relevant experience and maturity to be able to:
1. Accept personal responsibility when challenged by activist shareholders[xvi]
2. Communicate and meet regularly with shareholders[xvii] and not just at the annual general meeting (AGM)
3. Ensure shareholder communications do not break the law regarding "fair disclosure"[xviii]

Role and Responsibilities of the CEO

The CEO is the servant of the board. It is the job of the CEO to satisfy board-agreed organizational objectives and deliver KPIs within board-defined constraints. Yet there is a widely held view, at least in the United States, that, in practice, the CEO of a public listed company has no boss.[3] If this is correct, imagine how much worse the CG is likely to be if the CEO is also the chair, responsible for choosing the board—Lord Acton's prophecy that "absolute power tends to corrupt absolutely" is so much more likely to materialize.

In well-governed companies, the board is answerable to the owners of the company; the CEO is answerable to the board; and the board respects the chain of command, delegating its authority to the CEO who leads the organization below him or her. CEOs do have a boss (the board) and their role can be divided into three: what

---

[3] "In the publicly held corporate model, the CEO has no boss. We pretend that the CEO has a boss. We pretend that it is the board of directors. But it almost never is. Basically, the board of directors of most organizations, even the so-called independent directors, see themselves as employees of the CEO. Mostly, the only times CEOs of publicly held organizations have a boss is when a sufficiently large crisis occurs. At that point boards often wake up, but by then it is often too late—much of the damage has already been done." Jensen, M., quoted by Gillespie, J. and Zweig, D. (2010), *Money for Nothing: How the Failure of Corporate Boards is Ruining American Business and Costing Us Trillions* (New York: Free Press), 97.

they must do when answering to the board, what they do when working with the board, and what they do working without the board:

Answering to the Board

The board's authority granted to executive management is delegated through the CEO, who alone has the authority to implement agreed policies and is solely answerable to the board for achieving the organization's board-agreed "purpose," while staying within the executive limitations placed on him or her. *This means the CEO is not allowed by the board to do anything:*

1. *Without considering the effect on long-term shareholder value* of the consequences of health, safety, and environmental regulations and any other laws, political actions, and financing strategies
2. *That is likely to cause the company to become financially distressed* as a result of the chosen financing strategy (e.g., being excessively leveraged)
3. *Where the CEO's personal risk preferences are misaligned* with those of the shareholders when managing the company risks
4. *That damages the company's assets* (people, reputation, and other intangible and tangible assets) by being inadequately maintained, unnecessarily put at risk or left unprotected
5. *That puts employees or subcontracted third parties at risk* through undignified, inequitable, unfair, unsafe treatment, or conditions
6. *That is illegal, unfair, unjust, dishonest,* or involves coercion and physical violence
7. *That permits payments or considerations that are disproportionate* to the contribution made toward achieving agreed board goals

These executive limitations on the CEO are essential, if the board is to be held accountable for the corporate culture, codes of conduct, compliance, and brand (discussed in Chapter 2).

In addition, the CEO must report to, and advise the board at each board meeting on issues affecting the organization's board-agreed "purpose," covering:

1. *Anything with a material impact on company performance*—any potential strategic or political development that could affect the company's social "licence to operate"
2. *Recommending appropriate corrective actions* to deal with underperformance
3. *Any material issues affecting shareholders* and the capital markets where shareholders have a traded interest
4. *Succession planning and talent management programmes,* reflecting any changes in organization design for the future, ensuring continued value creation
5. *The effectiveness of the company and management* in implementing agreed strategy and tactics against board-agreed KPIs and milestones

Working with the Board
The CEO has three responsibilities when working with the board:

Setting direction: The CEO must articulate the company mission and vision in a compelling and distinctive way, making it clear what constitutes both success and failure. This call to action must engage both minds and, more important, hearts. It must provide a clear "line of sight" between the grander design and objectives of the company to divisions, departments, and the individuals who will make it happen (covered more detail in Chapter 7).

Articulating the organization's values: The CEO is responsible for articulating the values of the organization—the moral compass by which employees determine how to behave, to each other, to their customers, suppliers and other external stakeholders. Articulated properly, values must be translated into KPIs and observable measurable behavior and performance that are essential for effective appraisals and personal development plans. In addition to articulating the values of the organization, the CEO must be seen to be living them—that is what is meant by the "tone at the top." An effective CEO must "walk the walk and talk the talk." Nothing is more corrosive for sustainable ethical behavior than the hypocrisy of "don't do as I do, do as I say":

> Where there are no proper values, people will focus on the ends and ignore the means by which they are achieved. They will cut corners and put the safety of both employees and customers at risk. They will justify unacceptable working conditions on grounds that the bottom line demands them.[xix]

Allocating the organization's resources: This means deploying people, cash and technology as required. Perhaps the most critical is ensuring there is a proper talent pipeline and systematic succession planning process. These are essential to prevent discontinuities in strategic direction, lapses in adherence to values and failures in implementing strategy in an increasingly competitive and rapidly changing world (covered in more detail in Chapter 11).

Working Without the Board
Working alone with the authority delegated by the board, the CEO must set performance expectations; protect the company reputation; represent the organizational brand values to all employees; and create an integrated communication architecture for all stakeholders:

Setting performance standards: It is the CEO's job to agree the KPIs with management. Many of these will be financial (margins, returns on assets, levels of working capital, debt-to-equity ratios, etc.). These are lagging indicators, measuring past performance, but leading indicators are also needed because they can provide important early warnings of potential trouble to come. That is the idea behind balanced scorecards. Moreover, CEOs now must worry about environmental, social, and governance (ESG) reporting and the "triple bottom line."

Protecting the company reputation: As a leader, the CEO must be able to communicate to employees what makes their organization special; where they fit in delivering its mission and vision; and how the values of the organizational brand align with their own personal values. This is essential for reinforcing coherence and internal consistency in objectives and strategies to prevent employees becoming confused and embittered as a result.

Representing the brand to employees: The CEO needs to give employees reasons to believe in the company: what it stands for, who it does business with, and how it does that business. They also need an answer to the question "what is in it for me to work for this company?" and "does what I am doing comply with the code of conduct" (covered in Chapter 1).

Creating an integrated communication architecture: Companies have multiple audiences: employees, customers, investors, analysts, media, suppliers, unions, regulators, legislators, civil society (principally NGOs), and the community at large. Each of these groups has its own agenda and interests. Yet, the CEO must ensure there is no dissonance, no confusion about what the company is doing and what it stands for. This requires the CEO to ensure there is an integrated communication architecture to reinforce the integrity and coherence of the messages to different audiences. This is critical if the company is intending to have an initial public offering (IPO), change its strategy or if its social "licence to operate" is under threat as a result of social, legislative or regulatory changes.

Being an Effective Director

In law there is no distinction between executive director (ED) and independent non-executive director (INED). Both are held to the same standards, even though INEDs have less access and detailed understanding of what is happening in the business than EDs. The fact twenty-first century CG expectations of directors are much more demanding than those of the twentieth century is a serious matter for INEDs because they are now being treated as if they had equal access and a granular understanding of the company's business model, drivers of profitability and industry issues as EDs, when they do not. These standards to which they are now held are quite different from those applied in the 1925 landmark case defining what directors were supposed to do, compared in Table 5.1.

Table 5.1: Twentieth century and twenty-first century standards of performance compared

Twenty-first century standard of performance	Twentieth century standard of performance
UK Companies Act 2006[xx] "The duty does not prevent a director from relying on the advice of work of others, but the final judgment must be his responsibility… *As with all advice, slavish reliance is not acceptable, and obtaining of outside advice does not absolve directors from exercising their judgment on the basis of such advice.*" [Emphasis mine] **Centro Property [ASIC v Healey] (2011)**[xxi] "Nothing that I decide in this case should indicate that directors are required to have infinite knowledge or ability. 　　Directors are entitled to delegate to others the preparation of books and accounts and the carrying on of the day-to-day affairs of the company. 　　What each director is expected to do is *to take a diligent and intelligent interest in the information available to him or her, to understand that information, and apply an enquiring mind to the responsibilities placed upon him or her.*" [Emphasis mine]	**Equitable Fire Insurance (1925)**[xxii] "In discharging the duties of his position thus ascertained must, of course, act honestly; but he must also exercise some degree of both skill and diligence." However, there were three provisos: 1. A director need not exhibit in performing his duties a greater degree of skill than may reasonably be expected from a person of his knowledge and experience. 2. A director is not bound to give continuous attention to the affairs of his company. 3. In respect of all duties that, having regard to the exigencies of business, and the articles of association, may properly be left to some other official, a director is, in the absence of grounds for suspicion, justified in trusting that official to perform such duties honestly.

The responsibilities of directors have not just become more onerous because of the higher standards to which they are now held, but also because the scope and remit of CG is much wider than before.

Directors are now expected to consider stakeholders as well as shareholders in order to create and maintain sustainable value. They are required to ensure there is an ethical basis for their business and the way in which business is done, achieved by creating and satisfying the needs of customers and by working within the constraints set by the law and regulations. Directors are also expected to be accountable for reconciling leadership and governance, as well as the branding of their organization and its impact on market capitalization.

Being an effective director requires the director to:
Understand the role and responsibilities of a director:
I think it helps to define who directors are when discussing their roles and responsibilities. By law, a director is:

> Any person occupying the position of director of a corporation by whatever name called and includes a person in accordance with whose directions or instructions the directors of a corporation are accustomed to act and an alternate or substitute director.[xxiii]

The surprising point is that to be deemed a director, you do not actually have to sit on the board of the company you advise. As long as the company is accustomed to acting according to your instructions, you are a director of that company. So, advisers and so-called shadow directors are accountable for the actions of that company.

Directors can of course delegate authority for the performance of some of their duties, but they can not delegate the responsibility for ensuring those duties are carried out properly. The buck stops with the board and the directors, regardless of whether they are EDs, INEDs, alternates, acting directors, "shadow directors," or advisers whose advice is normally followed.

The difference between EDs and INEDs is EDs are on contracts with responsibilities for the operations of part of the company and answer to the CEO, with the CEO in turn answering to the board; whereas INEDs answer to the board and shareholders for ensuring the EDs and management adhere to the board-agreed direction and policies of the company.

INEDs are expected to undertake two distinct roles:
To act as business advisers and coaches to the CEO: This involves providing fresh perspectives and inputs based on their experience and expertise by challenging management's strategy and proposals constructively to help it make better decisions. To do this well, INEDs must thoroughly understand developments and trends in the industry of the company; stay current and well informed on how these will affect the company; and how management intends to respond so it can continue to create value. This requires a thorough appreciation of the motivation, capacity and capabilities of the CEO and senior management, as well as of the organization's ability to deal with the threats and opportunities provided by its environment from political, economic, social, technological, legal, and environmental perspectives.

To act as overseer/watchdog: This relates to strategy, performance and risk management, succession and talent management, internal controls, cybersecurity, and compliance. INEDs must fully understand where management stands on delivering agreed strategies and plans, ensure the company has the skills and competences needed to deliver its business strategy now and in the future, and appreciate how the company's systems of internal control and compliance affect the ability of the company to create sustainable value without endangering its social "licence to operate."

In exceptional circumstances, the board, including the INEDs, may be required to take a "hands-on" approach and manage the company. For example, when General Motors applied for Chapter 11 in 2010, the board had to step in after the departure of Rick Wagoner, the CEO. After the resignation of Bob Diamond, the CEO, and Jerry Del Missier, the COO of Barclays in 2012, the board had to step in and take control.

Understanding the duties of a director: Directors have fifteen primary duties:[xxiv]
Looking after the company's best interests:
1. *Fiduciary duty:* Looking after the company's best interests. This requires directors to "exercise their powers at all times for a proper purpose and in good faith in the best interests of the company." Directors must exercise bona fide discretion in what they consider—not what a court may consider—is in the best interests of the company.[xxv] This is the so-called business judgment rule sometimes allowing directors to often get off scot-free when they clearly failed to fulfill their fiduciary duty, as was the case with the boards of Citigroup, Bear Stearns, and Lehman Brothers in 2008.[4] The business judgment rule also explains why the board of Disney in 2005 were not held liable for paying Michael Ovitz US$ 150 million for only fourteen months of service as CEO![5]

---

4 Minow, N. (2016), "The business judgment rule provides that if directors follow the usual procedures, the courts will not second-guess their decisions, even when they turn out to be wrong. In theory, this makes sense but in practice it has resulted in an orientation toward the three C's: checklists, consultants, and compliance. It has been a bonanza for investment bankers, lawyers and auditors." Because of this rule as interpreted by the Delaware Chancery Court, Citigroup, Bear Sterns, and Lehman Brothers boards have got away scot-free. "The Rise and (Precipitous, Vertiginous, Disastrous) Fall of the Fiduciary Standard," quoted in *The Handbook of Corporate Governance*, edited by Richard Leblanc (Hoboken, NJ: John Wiley & Sons), 244.
5 The business judgment rule can sometimes be a "get-out of jail card" for directors, especially for U.S. companies based in Delaware. In 2005 Disney decided to offer Michael Ovitz a $150 million termination package after only fourteen months service as CEO. The directors were not held to be liable, despite mistakes because "Delaware law does not—indeed, the common law can not—hold fiduciaries liable for a failure to comply with the aspirational ideal of best practices." In re The Walt Disney Company Derivative Litigation, 907 A.2d 693,760 (Del. Ch., 2005), cited by Coffee, J. C. (2016), "Litigation Governance: Taking Accountability Seriously" (Columbia Law and Economics Working Paper No 359. European Corporate Governance Institute Law Working Paper No 145/2010), 5, quoted in *The Handbook of Corporate Governance*, op. cit., 256.

2. *Acting in good faith but without collateral purpose* where best interest lies but motivated by some improper purpose.[xxvi] Clearly, acting in accordance with their fiduciary duty requires some further explaining. So, what exactly does being a fiduciary mean? I think the following definition is helpful:

> A similar fiduciary duty can be held by corporate directors, seeing as they can be considered trustees for stockholders if on the board of a corporation, or trustees of depositors if [serving] as director of a bank. Specific duties include:
> - The duty of care, which applies to the way the board makes decisions that affect the future of the business. The board has the duty to fully investigate all possible decisions and how they may impact the business; If the board is voting to elect a new CEO, for example, the decision should not be made based solely on the board's knowledge or opinion of one possible candidate; *it is the board's responsibility to investigate all viable applicants to ensure the best person for the job is chosen.*
> - The duty to act in good faith. Even after it reasonably investigates all the options before it, the board has the responsibility to choose the option it believes best serves the interests of the business and its shareholders.
> - The duty of loyalty. *This means the board is required to put no other causes, interests, or affiliations above its allegiance to the company and the company's investors.* Board members must refrain from personal or professional dealings that might put their own self-interest or that of another person or business above the interest of the company.
> - *If a member of a board of directors is found to be in breach of his fiduciary duty, he can be held liable in a court of law by the company itself or its shareholders."* [xxvii] [Emphases mine]

I tend to agree with the argument the business judgment rule seriously undermines the concept of fiduciary as originally defined:

> Economic terms like agency costs and moral hazard make the betrayal of beneficiaries' interests into an inescapable cost of doing business, even suggesting it is their own fault. It is time to reject compliance-oriented, lowest common denominator approach and return to the strong, unequivocal words of Cardozo, to speak again of being above the morals of the marketplace, and of the "punctilio of honor the most sensitive."[xxviii]

So, what exactly did Supreme Court Justice Cardozo say in the ground-breaking 1928 U.S. Supreme Court decision in the case of Meinhard v Salmon?[xxix]

> Not honesty alone, but the punctilio of an honor the most sensitive, is then the standard of behaviour. As to this there has developed a tradition that is unbending and inveterate. Uncompromising rigidity has been the attitude of courts of equity when petitioned to undermine the rule of undivided loyalty by the "disintegrating erosion" of particular exceptions. Only thus has the level of conduct for fiduciaries been kept at a level higher than that trodden by the crowd. It will not consciously be lowered by any judgment of this court. Salmon had put himself in a position in which thought of self was to be renounced, however

hard the abnegation. A loyalty that is undivided and unselfish. The rule of undivided loyalty is relentless and supreme.

3. *Duty of care, skill, and diligence:* This requires EDs and INEDs to be diligent, take the time needed, and know the laws that affect the company.[6] What does this mean exactly? Being diligent requires a director to take an "intelligent interest in the information available to him or her, to understand that information, and apply an enquiring mind to the responsibilities placed upon him or her";[7] attend the requisite number of board meetings;[8] devote enough time to remain familiar with nature of the company's business, its business model, and the drivers of profitability, including appreciating the impact of the political, legal, and social environment in which it operates.[9] Directors are also expected to be up to date on the statutory and regulatory requirements affecting the company.[10] Directors' level of care, skill, and diligence is determined:
   – Objectively where a director has additional knowledge, skill and experience, that director will be assessed against a reasonable person who has that additional knowledge, skill and experience (the minimum standard);
   – Subjectively, the actual knowledge and experience of a director is to be considered (the additional standard)
4. *Avoiding conflicts of interest:* Directors must refrain from or prevent acts that adversely affect decision-making and avoid all conflicts of interest. Should conflicts arise, directors must declare them to the board and if they are deemed to be material, recuse themselves from the discussion, leaving the boardroom and

---

[6] The laws include environmental regulations, occupational health and safety laws, contract law, third party liability, anticorruption and bribery laws, AMLA and FATCA, and religious laws wherever they apply.

[7] At least in Commonwealth jurisdictions, this means meeting the much more demanding twenty-first century standard, as opposed to the twentieth century standard, as set out in the UK Companies Act debate, section 173 in 2006, and in Justice Middleton's Centro judgment in Australia [ASIC v Healey] in 2011. In that decision, Justice Middleton held the directors to be negligent because although they had sought advice on a material matter from the CFO and their auditors, Deloitte, that the accounting treatment used was correct, they had not personally looked at every page of the financial statements in the report relating to that matter and were thus negligent when the treatment proved to be wrong.

[8] The memorandum and articles of association and board charters of companies usually stipulate the number of board meetings directors must attend, failing which, they automatically vacate their positions.

[9] The standard of familiarity expected of directors has also risen dramatically in the twenty-first century and the time devoted to the company is now expected to be around forty days per directorship (stipulated in the UK's 2009 *Walker Report—Review of corporate governance in UK banks and other financial industry entities: Final recommendations*, and implied in Bursa Malaysia's Listing Requirements which forbid an INED of a public listed company to sit on more than five boards).

[10] It is the responsibility of the company secretary to update the board and other officers of the company regarding statutory and regulatory changes.

abstaining from voting. However, their recusal does not affect the quorum. If there is a continuing or systemic conflict of interest, directors should resign, after considering the impact of resignation on the board members and shareholders.

5. *Requiring consent of a general meeting:* Directors and officers of the company shall not, without the consent or ratification of a general meeting, use company property; use any information acquired by virtue of their positions as directors or officers of the company; use an opportunity of the company which they became aware of in the performance of their functions as directors or officers of the company; engage in business which is in competition to gain a benefit for themselves or any other person or cause harm to the company.
6. *Declarations:* Directors must declare fully to the board all dealings in company shares.
7. *Material transactions:* Directors must record material transactions in the interests register.
8. *Improper use of position:* Directors must avoid improper use of their positions or information for personal use.[xxx]

    Remuneration: Ensure remuneration is fair to the company (the directors clearly failed to do this in the Home Depot-Nardelli or Disney-Ovitz cases[11]).
9. *Keeping records:* This is one of the most onerous duties of a director; and the penalties for getting it wrong have risen dramatically, as a result of the collapse of Enron in 2001 and the subsequent passage of the Sarbanes-Oxley Act in 2004. Directors have a duty to:
    − Ensure proper accounting records are kept
    − Ensure adequate measures are in place to detect/prevent false accounting
    − Prepare and issue the annual report and audited financial statements to be presented at the AGM within six months of the company year-end
    − Ensure financial reports comply with approved accounting standards
10. *Dealing with shareholders:* The board is required to determine and certify reasonable consideration for the issue of shares or the repurchase of shares on issue. It must also, through the Company Secretary, respond appropriately to written

---

11 "Boards are prone to give away the shareholders' store. A 2004 study of CEO employment agreements [in the US] in large companies showed that 96 percent of the CEOs with such contracts could not be fired 'for cause' for incompetence, and 49 percent even after they breached their fiduciary duties. Michael Jensen, a former Harvard Business School professor and corporate governance expert says, 'Understand that if I fire you for something other than "for cause" as specified in your contract, I have to pay you the total compensation associated with your contract for its entire life, including bonuses, etc. CEO Bob Nardelli received more than $200 million in severance pay when he was dismissed from Home Depot "without cause," and Michael Ovitz received $130 million after being fired in 1996 for incompetence but "without cause" after 14 months on the job as president of the Walt Disney company. He received more pay for being fired than he would have received had he remained employed for his entire contract,'" Gillespie, J., and Zweig, D. (2010), *Money for Nothing: How the Failure of Corporate Boards is Ruining American Business and Costing Us Trillions* (New York: Free Press), 19.

requests for information by shareholders. Directors must ensure the company actions do not harm shareholders and creditors; maintain the company's solvency and reputation by making sure the company does not incur an obligation, unless there are reasonable grounds for believing the company can meet that obligation

11. *Fulfill specific duties in the event of a takeover*
12. *Observe confidentiality*
13. *Disclosing information only with the authority of the board.* Directors may only disclose confidential information to a shareholder or group of shareholders with whom the director has a special relationship with the express authority of the board. *This includes nominee directors who must remember their duty is to act in the best interests of the company on whose board they sit and not in the interests of their nominator.* Failure by the nominee director to do so is to commit an offence.[12]
14. *Avoiding insider trading:* Directors must ensure listed companies have an approved procedure for buying and selling shares in the company by directors, their relatives, and associates. Directors should notify the board of any intended transaction by them, their relatives, and associates. Failure to get prior board approval would be constituted as "insider trading" and would be to commit an offence.
15. *Ensuring all classes of shareholders are treated fairly in accordance with their respective rights.*

Being an Effective Board Member

Being an effective board member depends on the following.

Reconciling Independence with Deep Understanding of the Business

It is one of the ironies of CG, INEDs are expected to combine a deep understanding of the business with an independence of mind. In theory, there is no contradiction; people who know the business really well are able to ask the penetrating and challenging questions regulators assume come with independence and independent thought.

---

12 For example, Section 217 of the Malaysian Companies Act 2016 states, "1) A director who was appointed by virtue of his position as an employee of a company, or who was appointed by or as a representative of a member, employer or debenture holder, *shall act in the best interest of the company and in the event of any conflict between his duty to act in the best interest of the company and his duty to his nominator, he shall not subordinate his duty to act in the best interest of the company to his nominator.*" (§217. 1) [Emphasis mine] "2) A director who contravenes this section commits an offence and shall, on conviction, be liable to imprisonment for a term not exceeding five years or a fine not exceeding three million ringgit [ca. US$750,000 at the June 25, 2018 exchange rate] or both." (§217. 2)

In fact, the theory presupposes they can only ask such questions and provide effective guidance to management if they have that deep understanding of the business. Yet, it ignores the issue of how do INEDs get this deep understanding that allows them to ask such questions.

The only ways INEDs can get this level of required deep understanding are to have worked with the company before, to be either a supplier or a client of the company or to be on its board for a considerable time. The first three ways, by definition, rule out the prospective director as an INED. The fourth is time-limited; in many jurisdictions, INEDs are deemed to no longer be INEDs after they have been on the board for nine years[13] on the grounds they are too familiar and cosy with management. Whilst understandable, this is a fallacious argument. I know INEDs who were not truly independent thinkers, never challenging the CEO constructively from day one—they were chosen deliberately by the CEO to be supporters. I also know some excellent INEDs who had been on their boards for more than nine years (i.e., before the tenure limit was introduced) and who had not lost their capacity of independent thought.

Given the new twenty-first century standards to which INEDs are now held, they must spend much more time on the company's business. They also face much more severe sanctions than before. The combination of more time needed and greater risks faced, means INEDs now expect to be well paid. Gone are the days of the English country gentleman acting as director for a pittance, and yet the ability of a director to get up and leave the board without worrying about the financial implications of resigning were at the heart of the concept of an INED. Given how much more they are paid (rightly so), this raises the question of the adverse financial consequences of resigning or getting a bad reputation for being a maverick director.

Reconciling these contradictory trends is not easy, and INEDs will remain in a difficult position for some time:

> While it is unrealistic (and probably understandable) to think that society will choose to relieve many legal burdens from directors any time soon, it should also be recognized that *a combination of limited liability for shareholders and maximum liability for directors is unlikely to be a sustainable model of successful business organization over the longer term.*[xxxi] [Emphasis mine]

What makes matters worse for INEDs is there are so many ways independence of spirit can be undermined:[xxxii]
1. Gifts, benefits, entertainment and company resources provided for the INED (tickets, jobs for friends, and holidays with the CEO)
2. A corner office provided for the INED chair, with a secretary and research staff
3. Company benefits and resources provided for the INED's friends

---

13 In some it is after six years.

4. INED paid above-market rate fees
5. INED serves on another board with fellow director
6. INED is beholden to a shareholder for position on board without being a nominee director officially
7. Consulting fees awarded in addition to director fees
8. INED has a shared school, university, military, or social background
9. INED is being assessed by colleagues for quality of work
10. Management capturing the INED (e.g., CFO privately lobbying AC chair over the treatment of the accounts)

Commitment and Passion

I have met some INEDs who feel their presence on the board is a reward for past service to the government of the day: they may be ex-civil servants, army or police generals, diplomats, and politicians. Such INEDs often do not realize being an INED is hard work and an onerous responsibility, requiring both commitment to the company and passion and belief in what the company is trying to do. For management to respect the contribution of INEDs, these are essential.

Experience and Appropriate Competence

This is a complex topic (covered further in Chapter 11). However, the experience and competences the mix of directors must bring to the board as a collective can be split into core and desired competences:[xxxiii]

1. *Core competences:* These include enterprise leadership, board governance, understanding of the industry and the company, setting and reviewing strategy, financial literacy, and creating value.
2. *Desired competences:* In their discussions at the board, directors need to have access to the following competences, which may be provided by the directors themselves or by advisers to the board (it is important to remember boards must have access to expert skills and the CEO must provide for such access in the budget):
   a. The directors, between them, should be able to provide the desired competences in: accounting via the AC; capital allocation and markets for strategy; HR, performance management and remuneration via the NRC; marketing and sales; organizational and operational skills for strategy and budget reviews; risk management via the AC or RMC; controls and compliance via the AC.
   b. Using advisers, the board must have access to advice on tax and audit; advocacy, government and regulatory lobbying advice; PR, communication

and reputation management via corporate communications; IR and stakeholder engagement via investor relations and the chair's office; legal and regulatory via the general counsel; sustainability, climate change and CSR via the chair's office, though in some leading companies the board has an ESG committee to deal specifically with these topics; IT, cybersecurity and data protection via the chief technology officer, though there is a growing recognition boards should have a member responsible for this area.

EQ

INEDs may be able to challenge management because they bring a different, independent perspective to the discussion; they may be committed and passionate about the business; they may have relevant experience and be competent, but *if they do not have good EQ, they will fail*. They must appreciate what is effective constructive behavior and understand how to "disagree without being disagreeable":

> The objective of board debates is to maximise cognitive conflict (debates about ideas), and minimise affective conflict (agreement/disagreement based on personal liking/disliking). Finding this sweet spot is the challenge for the Chair, and all directors.[xxxiv]

Effective constructive behavior: there are ten manifestations of EQ valued by boards:[xxxv]
1. Understanding and respecting the distinct roles of the board and management (covered earlier in Chapter 3)
2. Understanding and committing to fiduciary duties and corporate policies, once appointed to the board
3. Respecting management's and fellow directors' expertise and viewpoints, deferring to and relying on expertise as appropriate, though this should not become uncritical over-reliance on the advice of others; directors are expected to "trust but verify"
4. Constructive skepticism to challenge management's assumptions
5. Promoting open discussion and debate, making sure discussion does not become personal
6. Listening to all points of view, controlling oneself to avoid grandstanding and taking too much of the board's limited time
7. Committing to work toward consensus after informed deliberation
8. Developing and maintaining trust between peers and management
9. Preserving board confidentiality
10. Preparing for meetings and sticking to the agenda

Dissenting effectively:[xxxvi] When directors find they disagree with their colleagues, they have three choices:

1. Abstaining or voting against the proposal, if there is genuine disagreement
2. Requesting their abstention or voting against the proposal be recorded in the minutes to express disapproval and to protect themselves against future liability
3. Resigning when they believe management is not dealing with directors, shareholders or public in good faith; information is inadequate, incomplete or incorrect; their point of view is being disregarded entirely (it is usually sensible to seek legal advice before resigning)

Conclusion

The twenty-first century standards to which boards are being held are much more demanding. This means there is greater focus than ever on directors being effective board members. It also means the spotlight is firmly on the two key members of the board: The chair and the CEO.

The chair is responsible for ensuring the board is properly governed (covered earlier in Chapter 4), fulfilling ten fiduciary duties, acting as the link between the board and the CEO, energizing internal stakeholders with the help of the CEO, and engaging external stakeholders.

The CEO, on the other hand, *is answerable to the board* for achieving the organization's agreed "purpose," while working within executive limitations set by the board, reporting to the board on issues affecting the organization's board-agreed "purpose." The CEO *works with the board* in setting the company direction; articulating its values; and allocating resources to create long-term value. In addition, the CEO *has board-delegated authority to work alone* on setting performance standards; protecting the company's reputation; representing the organizational brand to employees, leading by example and setting the appropriate "tone at the top"; and creating an integrated communication architecture, guaranteeing the company speaks with one voice to its many audiences.

There are three important reasons for keeping these two roles separate:
1. Both are very demanding jobs and the role of the chair is underrated. It is my contention that one person can not do both roles justice—hence the need for separation.
2. Combining the two roles into one, puts too much power and control into the hands of a single individual and is an invitation to become an "imperial CEO."
3. Even if the temptation to abuse such power were resisted, there remains the conflict of interest in having the same person reviewing the performance of the person being reviewed.

Having a lead independent director to evaluate the chair-CEO goes some way to resolving this but does not provide an effective answer to the first two reasons for keeping the two roles apart.

Being an effective director requires directors to understand their two roles: to act as business advisers and coaches to the CEO, while at the same time also being overseers and watchdogs. These roles can sometimes be in conflict, discussed earlier in Chapter 3. In addition, directors must fulfill their duties as fiduciaries, most important of which, are the duties of care, loyalty, skill, and diligence.

To be an effective INED means being an effective member of the board, characterized by four attributes: the ability to reconcile independence of mind with a deep understanding of the business; commitment to and passion about what the company does; experience and appropriate competence; and above all, good EQ.

References

[i] Mercer Newsroom (2016), "Prevalence of Combined Chairman/CEO and Non-Executive Chairman Roles Holds Steady in 2015. Mercer Analysis Finds," https://www.mercer.com/newsroom/prevalence-of-combined-chairman-ceo-and-non-executive-chairman-roles-holds-steady-in-2015-mercer-analysis-finds.htm, accessed on June 22, 2018.

[ii] Schwartz, S. K. (2012), "Tipping Point for Combined Chairman and CEO?" *CNBC*, November 15, 2012, https://www.cnbc.com/id/49829626, accessed on June 22, 2018.

[iii] Spizzirri, A. (2014), "CEO/Chair Structure in Canada compared to US in 2013," Rotman School of Management, Clarkson Centre for Board Effectiveness, January 2014, 1.

[iv] Australian Institute of Corporate Directors (2106), ASX Corporate Governance Council's Corporate Governance Principles and Recommendations 3e (2014), Recommendation 2.5., cited in *Role of the Chair: Governance Relations*, March 13, 2016, 2, https://aicd.companydirectors.com.au/-/media/cd2/resources/director-resources/director-tools/pdf/05446-3-13-mem-director-gr-role-of-the-chair_a4-web.ashx, accessed on October 18, 2018.

[v] Hong Kong Clearing and Exchanges Limited (2017), *Listing Rules, Interpretations and Guidance*, Principle A-2-1, *Thompson Reuters Governance*, http://en-rules.hkex.com.hk/en/display/display_viewall.html?rbid=4476&element_id=4661, accessed on October 18, 2018.

[vi] Thakur, J. (2018), "SEBI Moves to Separate Chairman-CEO Post in Companies; Not Everything from the West Is Best," *FIRSTPOST*, September 6, 2018, https://www.firstpost.com/business/sebi-moves-to-separate-chairman-ceo-post-in-companies-not-everything-from-the-west-is-the-best-5124461.html, accessed on October 18, 2018.

[vii] Securities Commission Malaysia (2012), Corporate Governance Blueprint, 2011, 32.

[viii] Eliot H. (2015), "Chairman vs CEO: Who's Right and Who's Responsible?," *Idealog*, June 16, 2015, accessed on October 18, 2018, https://idealog.co.nz/workplace/2015/06/chairman-vs-ceo-whos-right-and-whos-responsible, accessed on October 18, 2018.

[ix] SGX, *Rulebook, Board Composition and Guidance*, Guidelines 3.1, http://rulebook.sgx.com/en/display/display_plain.html?rbid=3271&element_id=5886&record_id=7641&print=1, accessed on October 18, 2018.

[x] Stockhan, M. (2013), "Split Decisions: The Pros and Cons of Separating CEO and Chairman Roles," *Corporate Compliance Insights*, July 9, 2013, https://www.corporatecomplianceinsights.com/split-decisions-the-pros-and-cons-of-separating-ceo-and-chairman-roles/, accessed on October 18, 2018.

[xi] Schwartz, S. K. (2012), "Tipping Point for Combined Chairman and CEO?" *CNBC*, November 15, 2012, https://www.cnbc.com/id/49829626, accessed on June 22, 2018.

xii Securities Commission Malaysia (2017), *Malaysian Code of Corporate Governance*, 15.
xiii Zinkin, J. (2014), "Corporate Directors Onboarding Programme," Kuala Lumpur, April 16, 2014.
xiv Based on Securities Commission Malaysia (2017), *Malaysian Code of Corporate Governance*, 14.
xv Wolfe, H. D. (2016) "The Non-Executive Chairman," quoted in *The Handbook of Corporate Governance*, edited by Richard Leblanc (Hoboken, NJ: John Wiley & Sons), 102.
xvi Wolfe (2016), op. cit., 105.
xvii Ibid., 106, 110.
xviii Ibid., 110.
xix Zinkin, J. (2010), *Challenges in Implementing Corporate Governance: Whose Business is it Anyway?* (Singapore: John Wiley & Sons), 64.
xx Lord Goldsmith, UK Attorney General during debate on UK Companies Act 2006, section 173.
xxi Justice Middleton, Centro judgment in Australia [ASIC v Healey] in 2011.
xxii Lord Justice Romer, Re Equitable Fire Insurance, 1925.
xxiii Malaysian Companies Act 2016, section 1.
xxiv Based on Financial Institutions Director's Education Programme (2012), *FIDE Good Governance Handbook, Part 1: Being an Effective Director* (Kuala Lumpur, Malaysia: Iclif Leadership and Governance Centre), 16, 9–10.
xxv Re Smith and Fawcett Ltd [1942] Ch 304.
xxvi Howard Smith v Ampol Petroleum Ltd [1974] AC 821.
xxvii http://www.investopedia.com/terms/f/fiduciary.asp
xxviii Minow (2016), op. cit., 247.
xxix US Supreme Court Justice Cardozo, B. (1928), Meinhard v Salmon, 164 N.E. 545 (N.Y.1928), quoted by Minow, N. (2016), op. cit., 239.
xxx Regal (Hastings) Ltd v Gulliver [1942] 1 ALL ER 37B.
xxxi Barker, R. (2016), "The Duties and Liabilities of Directors—Getting the Balance Right," quoted in *The Handbook of Corporate Governance*, op. cit., 64.
xxxii Leblanc, R. (2016), "Director Independence, Competency and Behavior," quoted in *The Handbook of Corporate Governance*, op. cit., 164.
xxxiii Ibid., 172–173.
xxxiv Bennett, C. (2018), in email correspondence with the author on October 5, 2018.
xxxv Gregory, H. J. (2016), "The Challenge of Director Misconduct," quoted in *The Handbook of Corporate Governance*, op. cit., 226–229.
xxxvi Ibid., 229–230.

Chapter 6
Reconciling Leadership and Governance

This chapter is presented in three parts: the first deals with the nature of leadership and why it is morally neutral, the second defines the characteristics of effective leaders and why checks and balances are needed to save them from themselves, and the last explores how the lack of effective corporate governance (CG) allowed three highly successful CEOs to destroy the companies they led. It concludes with the need to reconcile leadership and governance for sustainable value to be created.

In this chapter, I argue the recent failures of corporate governance in banking were mainly failures of leadership caused by "great bad" or "dissonant" leaders who were successful leaders originally, but who went astray, leading their organizations into disaster because they were not subjected to the checks and balances of good CG.

They passed Jack Welch's five tests of powerful leadership.[i] They had great ideas and passion, which they were able to impart to the rest of the organization; they had energy, they were able to energize their subordinates, they were able to execute, and they had edge. Yet these attributes by themselves did not protect them from ultimate failure.

This is the result of Lord Acton's famous adage: "absolute power tends to corrupt absolutely."[ii] Without a system of governance to control the actions of CEOs, they can end up believing their own propaganda. The more successful they are initially, the greater risks they run and get away with, the greater the temptation to believe they are right and others are wrong, the greater the temptation to continue with a strategy past its sell-by date. There is no countervailing power, no effective system of checks and balances, to suggest the time may have come for them to reconsider their assumptions or to hold them back from continuing to gamble recklessly with the future of their organizations or taking actions promoting their own interests ahead of those of the organization.

In business, if we focus only on CG, without recognizing the leadership needed to align and energize employees, we may get mediocre performance at best. Quick and decisive action in business has been the justification in the past for combining the roles of chairman and CEO in U.S. companies.[1] When it works well, it produces great results, as do all benevolent dictatorships.

---

[1] In 2017, Facebook defended this practice as follows: "We do not believe that requiring the Chairman to be independent will provide appreciably better direction and performance, and instead could cause uncertainty, confusion, and inefficiency in board and management function and relations." Niu, E. (2018), "Activist Investors Are Pushing for a New Facebook Chairman," The Motley Fool, October 18, 2018, https://finance.yahoo.com/news/activist-investors-pushing-facebook-chairman-182300127.html, accessed on October 18, 2018.

It is the role of the board to help the company's management decide on the business the company is in, its beneficiaries and the difference the company will make to their lives with the return it can expect to earn as a result. It is also the role of the board to decide the company's values its risk appetite and risk management; and its succession planning, including appointing and sacking the CEO. In doing this, boards must challenge the CEOs' mental models constructively, because it is the mental model the CEO brings to the company that determines success or failure.[2] Yet, as will become clear, when companies have failed, boards have not done this for a variety of reasons, among which, the most important was the dominance of the CEO—in effect, powerful leadership without adequate CG.

Leadership—An Amoral Force for Change

Modern writers on leadership often define it as being an exercise where followers have a choice to be led or not; so-called transformational leadership introduced in 1987 by James McGregor Burns.[iii] Warren Bennis reinforced this approach when he proposed so-called authentic leadership in 1989.[iv] Both defined leadership as an exercise of power over others based on mutual advantage:

> Leaders engage others by creating shared meaning, speaking in a distinctive voice, demonstrating the capacity to adapt and having integrity.[v]

Leaders who coerced their followers, or worse still obliterated them, were not leaders; they were defined as "power wielders" by Burns.

> Power wielders may treat people as things; leaders may not.[vi]

Yet we all know and have experienced the dark side of leadership. Historians and political scientists have long studied it extensively and neutrally:

> Historically, political theorists have been far more interested in the question of how to control the proclivities of bad leaders than in the question of how to promote the virtues of good ones. Influenced by religious traditions that focused on good and evil, and often personally scarred by war and disorder, the best political thinkers have had a rather jaundiced view of human nature.[vii]

---

[2] "The CEO's personality determines the mental framework he brings to the situation. This framework shapes his problem-solving approach and influences his discernment. If competitive intelligence is defined as the sum of executive and corporate intelligence then selecting and applying contextual mental models, making these visible, and creating an emotionally intelligent organisational environment are expressed in strategic decision-making." Wallace, E. and Rijamampianina, R. (2005), "Strategic Decision Making with Corporate Emotional Intelligence," Problems and Perspectives in Management, 3/2005, 83.

Machiavelli was quite clear that effective leadership was an amoral activity in his advice to the rulers of Florence when he wrote:

> Cruelties can be called well used (if it is permissible to speak well of evil) that are done at a stroke, out of the necessity to secure oneself and then are not persisted in but are turned to as much utility for the subjects as one can. Those cruelties are badly used which, though few in the beginning, rather grow with time.[viii]

You might well ask: why do leaders lead and followers follow? The answer is self-interest. Leaders and followers engage in a compact designed to protect all against the anxieties caused by disorder and death. It is this that unites the thinking of Hobbes,[ix] Locke,[x] and Rousseau.[xi] Their positions, however, differ greatly on the emphasis placed on the obligations they believe leaders must fulfill; and levels of coercion leaders must use, if they are to maintain legitimacy in the eyes of their followers.

Most modern writers tend to ignore the fact history is full of effective leaders who led their followers, not by example, but through fear and coercion—so-called dissonant leadership. They focus instead on "resonant leadership."[3]

At the individual level, "dissonant" or "great bad" leaders may still satisfy a need for certainty, simplicity, and security. People follow them because the cost of not following is often too high. Resistance can create confusion and uncertainty, the very states of mind most people want to avoid—so resistance is doubly hard.

We need leaders to make sense of the world; because they do not accept that the world is random;[xii] we need plausible causal explanations; however improbable they might be. It is the way our brains are hardwired.[xiii] In an increasingly uncertain world, leaders are assumed to know what they are doing.[xiv] The angst we experience when we do not understand what is happening makes us all the more likely to turn to a person with the appearance of being strong and certain.[xv] This helps explain the continued strength of the totalitarian Chinese leadership; the return of authoritarian leadership in Russia, Turkey, and the Philippines; and the rise of right-wing populist leaders across Europe, the unexpected outcome of Brexit in the United Kingdom, and the election of Donald Trump in the United States in 2016.

---

3 "A recent study done at Case Western Reserve University found a relationship between resonance and effective leadership:
"Being resonant means that a leader is empathetic and has a high emotional intelligence level. A dissonant style, on the other hand, is more authoritarian and objective...
What this means is that resonant leaders activate attention, social awareness, and positive relationships in their employees, while dissonant leaders trigger negative emotions, disregard, limited attention, and decreased social awareness.
Resonant leadership styles also help build trust through the release of oxytocin in their brains and the brains of others." The HR and Employee Engagement Community, The Basis of Leadership is Born in the Brain: Why Leaders Should Care about Neuroscience, https://gethppy.com/leadership/basis-of-leadership-neuroscience, accessed on June 20, 2018.

Leaders have to do demanding work: engaging stakeholders; understanding different perspectives and time horizons.[xvi] The results may be highly uncertain and the data needed to make decisions may be ambiguous. This explains the "Iron Law of Oligarchy," which postulates that people divide naturally into leaders and led.[xvii] Most people do not want to have to deal with ambiguity or with the anxiety caused by the fear of failure. So, they delegate decision making to people who are not too worried about getting the answers right, if they are right more often than half the time. This division of labor or specialization means leaders get better at tolerating ambiguity and followers get worse, demanding ever greater certainty; certainty only leaders can provide. Whether such leaders turn out to be good or bad people depends on other factors. They will, however, become better decision makers and may be tempted to become more autocratic, as predicted by Lord Acton.

Bad leaders make a compact with their followers, who, in return, allow them to behave in increasingly arbitrary and autocratic ways over time. To understand this dynamic better, we must divide followers into three groups.[xviii] Each group is quite rational in its accommodation of evil leadership:

Acolytes: These are true believers, "advocates," who get behind the leadership—either because they genuinely believe it is the right thing to do, or because they get so much personal benefit from being seen to be enthusiastically aligned.

Evil-doers: These "supporters" follow orders because that is what they are supposed to do. They take part as efficiently and effectively as they can, because they are measured and rewarded accordingly.

The silent majority: These "spectators" go along with what is being done because it is too much effort or too risky personally to stand up and be counted, but they do not believe in what is being proposed. They neither take part in, nor stop what is being done.

Characteristics of Effective Leadership

Effective leadership can be divided into two approaches: "resonant" leaders or "great good" leaders and "dissonant" or "great bad" leaders. I agree with Barbara Kellerman that the tendency to only consider "resonant" leadership is a mistake because both styles of leadership need to be compared so we can learn from the mistakes of "dissonant" leaders.[4]

So, what are the characteristics of "resonant" leadership and how do they compare with "dissonant" leadership? And how do we prevent "great good" leaders from becoming "great bad" leaders over time?

Resonant, "great good" leaders exhibit the following characteristics."[xix]

Find the Energy to Create a Better Future

Effective leadership is almost always based on the fundamental values of the person who becomes a leader—either because their personal values have been grossly violated (e.g., Mahatma Gandhi, Nelson Mandela, and Martin Luther King); or because their values are endorsed to the point where they believe they can make the world a better place by "going the extra mile" (e.g., Steve Jobs or Jack Ma). This energy then translates into a purpose, which gives meaning to their existence, focusing their energy on what matters.

Have a Clear Purpose at All Times

Such leaders articulate the business purpose by explaining the vision and defining the mission. In so doing, they must provide a clear "line of sight" linking the business purpose to all individuals working for the organization, so employees understand the consequences of success, and, equally important, of failure. Finally, everybody in the organization must know "what is in it for them personally"; appreciate their responsibility for making the vision happen; and understand the milestones and timetable for action for which they will be held accountable.

---

4 Redefining leadership as being good leadership creates three major problems:
   1. It is confusing because for most people the word "leader" refers to "any individual who uses power, authority, and influence to get others to go along." When we talk of evil political leaders like Hitler, Stalin, and Mao, we still call them "leaders" and not "power wielders."
   2. It is misleading since "leadership can be considered the exercise of influence, or a power relation, or an instrument of goal achievement, or a differentiated role. The point is that each of these definitions is value-free. It makes no sense therefore to distinguish between leaders and power-wielders. In fact, to compare them is not to compare apples and oranges, but apples and apples."
   3. It does a disservice since we need to learn about good leadership by studying both *what makes good leaders and what makes bad leaders so that we can avoid their mistakes.*

Kellerman, B. (2004), *Bad Leadership: What It Is, How It Happens, Why It Matters* (Boston: Harvard Business School Press), 13.

Lead with Values

Such leaders are positive role models, personally living the values of the business and applying its code of conduct to all without exceptions. They treat everyone with respect, regardless of where they are in the organizational hierarchy or whether they agree. When assessing people, they look at the drivers of performance rather than results; they focus on "how" results are achieved, as well as "what" has been achieved. Finally, they make explicit what behavior is expected, by recognizing publicly examples of desired behavior; and as important, by spelling out what will lead to termination through the effective application of the code of conduct.

Encourage "Speaking Truth to Power"

Such leaders do not confuse loyalty with stifling disagreement. Instead they welcome divergent perspectives and encourage subordinates to speak up early enough for them to be able to take corrective action as a result. They do not "shoot the messenger," to do so would only cut off all early warnings of impending trouble. They appreciate the perils of groupthink, recognize the constraints imposed on thinking "out of the box" by the "legacy effect," and value scenario thinking and the use of premortems to minimize risk. Above all, they value constructive "devil's advocacy" to help validate their thinking. Alfred Sloan, the founder of General Motors, said after his first board meeting when all the directors had agreed with his proposal:

> If we are all in agreement on the decision—then I propose we postpone further discussion of this matter until our next meeting *to give ourselves time to develop disagreement and perhaps gain some understanding of what the decision is all about.*[xx] [Emphasis mine]

Learn from Failure and Move On

Such leaders understand past success can be the cause of future failure. They recognize all good strategies have a "sell-by" date and appreciate the difficulties created by groupthink and the "legacy effect" in handling issues in innovative ways. Most important, they know the best way to learn is from our mistakes and recognize the importance of encouraging people to move out of their comfort zones, by focusing on what was learned when things go wrong rather than pointing fingers in "blame frame" mode. When giving feedback, they give "feed forward"—helping people learn from both the good and bad things that have happened.[5]

Develop Co-Leaders and Share Authority and Responsibility

Such leaders delegate but do not abdicate responsibility. They develop their subordinates by rotating them through different jobs: staff and line, function and geography, getting them to report to different types of superior, testing both their technical and people skills, and their ability to reconcile short and long-term objectives. They recruit people who are smarter than they are. They share credit and take the blame when things go wrong.

Move from "I" to "We" Thinking, Creating Conditions for Maximum Collective Success

Such leaders empower colleagues and subordinates; they recognize the importance of teams and the contribution of others. Above all, they appreciate the importance of the "ecosystem" within which they work and harness the value it creates through the systems and processes it brings to bear on decisions they take. They can make good use of the "legacy effect," its ability to create a common set of values and purpose, while minimizing its stranglehold on "out of the box" and original thinking.

---

[5] Perhaps the best examples of this approach are the stories about Tom Watson Jr., CEO of IBM (1956–1971) and Thomas Edison:
"A young executive had made some bad decisions that cost the company several million dollars. He was summoned to Watson's office, fully expecting to be dismissed. As he entered the office, the young executive said, 'I suppose after that set of mistakes you will want to fire me.' Watson was said to have replied, 'Not at all, young man, we have just spent a couple of million dollars educating you.'"

The other classic example of being willing to move on and learn from mistakes is Thomas Edison, when he was still trying to invent the electric lightbulb: "I have not failed. I've just found 10,000 ways that won't work." Thomas Edison also demonstrated a great response to adversity, which complements Watson Jr.'s actions.

When his factory was burned down, with much of his life's work inside, Edison said: "There is great value in disaster. All our mistakes are burned up. Thank God we can start anew."

Schein, E. H. (1985), Organizational Culture and Leadership (San Francisco: Jossey-Bass) quoted in "Characteristics of Leadership: Seeing Things Differently," The Happy Manager, https://the-happy-manager.com/articles/characteristic-of-leadership/, accessed on June 21, 2018.

Create a Lasting Legacy

Such leaders understand their own mortality, recognizing the need for institutions and processes that provide independent checks and balances on their ability to act. They welcome executive limitations, realizing their successors maybe less competent or more corrupt than they are:

> I am here to reinforce a culture. I have to make sure we are a company that will last after me. I don't want to be here another 20 years. Forget about another 200 years. It's really about trying to build a culture that will last longer than the business. That will make it very hard for the next guy to screw up.[xxi]

Table 6.1 compares the two styles of leadership.

Table 6.1: "Great good" and "great bad" leadership compared

"Great good" (resonant) leaders	"Great bad" (dissonant) leaders
1. Find the energy to create a better future	1. Find the energy to create change, though often not for the better
2. Have a clear purpose at all times	2. Have a clear purpose at all times
3. Lead with values and by example	3. Lead through fear and force
4. Welcome the "courage to speak truth to power"	4. Discourage dissent and shoot the messenger
5. Learn from failure	5. Punish failure
6. Recruit coleaders and share authority and responsibility	6. Centralize control and authority; are bottlenecks in decision making
7. Move from "I" to "We" thinking and create collective success	7. Manipulate their followers for self-serving agendas
8. Create a lasting legacy	8. Fail to create a legacy

Independent checks and balances are essential, if "great good" leaders are to resist the temptation of becoming "great bad" leaders. Medieval monarchs understood this temptation and used court jesters to act as a mirror in which to look to stop them from abusing their powers.

I strongly believe *good CG provides essential checks and balance to prevent CEO abuse of power*. All "great good" leaders need a system of checks and balance to prevent them from becoming "great bad" leaders who lead their organizations to failure.

From Success to Failure

For me, one of the most important lessons of the Global Financial Crisis was that charismatic, domineering CEOs could lead their organizations to collapse because of weak CG. The more successful they had been, the greater their downfall. There was no effective CG to protect them from themselves, as I hope to illustrate with the cases of Stan O'Neal of Merrill Lynch and Dick Fuld of Lehman Brothers in the United States; and Fred Goodwin of Royal Bank of Scotland (RBS) in the UK.

If you have read *The Big Short*,[xxii] *The Age of Greed*,[xxiii] *Bull by the Horns*,[xxiv] or *Too Big to Fail*[xxv] or watched CNBC's program *House of Cards*[xxvi] you will know, the collapse of the subprime mortgage market was foreseen by those who understood what was really happening in the U.S. property market. The signs had been in the wind since as early as 2004. So, it is somewhat surprising these three CEOs appear to have taken no notice of the omens. Or perhaps rather than ignoring them, maybe they felt, as Dick Fuld of Lehman Brothers felt, their firms would survive any downturn.[6]

The case of Fred Goodwin in the United Kingdom is different; it was only partly related to problems in the United States, but mainly due to following a growth strategy that turned out to be wrong-headed. The final straw was the disastrous acquisition of ABN-Amro, which brought RBS to its knees. However, Goodwin's *behavior* was similar to that of O'Neal and Fuld, as I hope will become clear.

Stan O'Neal and Merrill Lynch[xxvii]

Stan O'Neal was the first African-American CEO of a Wall Street institution. Clearly talented, he did not welcome divergent points of view, was secretive, chose the wrong strategy, and reacted inappropriately when the crisis hit Merrill Lynch.

As chairman, CEO, and president of Merrill Lynch for six years, he held more power in his hands than normal. He demanded such a high level of loyalty from his key management team they were called "The Taliban" and he was nicknamed "Mullah Omar."[xxviii] As chair, he personally handpicked eight of the ten independent directors on Merrill Lynch's board,[xxix] perhaps to minimize the amount of challenge he would face regarding his decisions. If he distrusted people, he would force them out of the company, saying, "Ruthless isn't always that bad."[xxx]

He overhauled the company, aiming to catch up with Goldman Sachs, by redirecting the firm into ever riskier but more profitable lines of business. He introduced proprietary trading so that Merrill Lynch made US$7.5 billion from trading its own and "its clients" money in 2006, up from US2.6 billion in 2002. He made the business riskier by ramping up its use of leverage and entered the mortgage backed securities

---

[6] "The previous summer, when housing prices started to plummet and overextended banks cut back sharply on new lending, Fuld had proudly announced: 'Do we have some stuff on the books that would be tough to get rid of? Yes. Is it going to kill us? Of course not.' The firm seemed impregnable then. For three years Lehman had made so much money that it was being mentioned in the same breath as Goldman Sachs, Wall Street's great profit machine." Andrew Ross Sorkin, *Too Big to Fail* (New York: Viking, 2009), 11.

(MBS) market. In 2003, the company was insignificant in the collateralized debt obligations (CDO) market; by 2005 it was number one.

He continued this drive away from Merrill Lynch's traditional lines of expertise, buying up mortgage servicers and real estate firms; finally buying First Franklin, a leading subprime mortgage lender, for US$1.3 billion.[xxxi]

When the market started to deteriorate in 2006, O'Neal replaced his most able risk manager, Jeffrey Kronthal, with a young derivatives trader from London who had no experience of the CDO market. Kronthal's mistake was to try to constrain O'Neal's ambition to become the leading mortgage lender, regardless of the riskiness of the business.

To make matters worse, Merrill Lynch then created US$44 billion in CDOs—three times as much as in 2005. Doubters were silenced by O'Neal's intolerance of dissent and by the huge bonuses triggered by the US$700 million in fees arising from CDOs, *even if they had yet to be sold*. In 2006 O'Neal got US$46 million in bonus and the inexperienced derivatives trader got more than US$20 million. In 2007 Merrill Lynch underwrote more than US$30 billion of CDOs, ignoring their greater risk because risk management no longer had an independent voice.

As trouble began, the head of the mortgage division left to set up his own hedge fund. The two managers left behind in charge of the business wrongly advised the board on July 21, 2007 that the resulting exposure was US$77 million saying it was well hedged.

During August and September the position got worse and by the beginning of October the projected loss was US$5 billion; not US$77 million. By the end of October the expected loss was US$7.9 billion. The final write-down on failed investments was US$8.4 billion—the largest loss in Merrill Lynch's ninety-three years of existence.

O'Neal's reaction was to withdraw, brooding while he played golf, often by himself during the working week:

> During August and September 2007, as Merrill was losing more than $100 million a day, O'Neal managed to play at least twenty rounds of golf and lowered his handicap from 10.2 to 9.1.[xxxii]

The final straw was O'Neal's unauthorized overture to Wachovia about a merger without the board's approval. Had it been agreed, he would have received a pay-out of US$274 million if he left when the deal was completed. When they found out, the board allowed O'Neal to "retire" with an exit package of US$161.5 million, on top of the US$ 70 million he had already received during his tenure as chair and CEO.[xxxiii]

It is truly sad a man who had started so well, setting Merrill Lynch on an apparently stellar path of success should end up with a former coworker saying to the *New Yorker*:

> I wouldn't hire Stan to wash windows. What he did to Merrill Lynch was absolutely criminal.[xxxiv]

It could have been avoided, had he welcomed dissent from subordinates and chosen a competent and engaged Board. They could have prevented him from rushing into disaster, following a strategy past its sell-by date, *with no proper assessment of its attendant risks.*[xxxv]

Dick Fuld and Lehman Brothers[xxxvi]

Dick Fuld had good grounds for believing in his judgment.[xxxvii] He revived a capital-starved Lehman Brothers when it was spun off by American Express. He cut headcount dramatically to make it profitable and became the public face of the new bank. He took a contrarian position, when the collapse of Long Term Capital Management nearly took down the market in 1998 and Lehman prospered. He led the company through the tragedy of 9/11 and the ensuing difficulties when they had to abandon their offices. He bought the new headquarters of Lehman Brothers, which proved to be a good investment. He understood the dangers of leverage, but believed he had enough capital to withstand a run and continued to take leveraged bets. As he put it, leverage was like:

> Paving roads with cheap tar. When the weather changes the potholes will be there deeper and uglier.[xxxviii]

As the CEO of Lehman, Fuld followed the same strategy as O'Neal, investing aggressively in mortgage underwriting to catch up with Goldman Sachs and Morgan Stanley, without paying attention to the risks of this strategy. Mike Gelband, his head of risk, warned him to reverse his exposure to MBS in 2005. He was soon gone. So was Madelyn Antonic, Lehman's risk manager after she criticized the aggressive risks taken in MBS:

> Those who disagreed were thought disloyal and dissent was stifled. In the face of growing risk, Fuld raised the stakes further and earned a $35 million bonus that year. In 2007, he went on a real estate buying spree, buying buildings in the United States and overseas, even as markets were weakening. He kept issuing CDOs as well. As the markets became nervous, he chose to double down.[xxxix]

Fuld was the "outside face" of Lehman, relying on his COO, to be its "inside face." However, the COO's style seems to have been rather brutal and eccentric as far as hiring and promoting people went, so when the property bubble burst and hit Lehman, very few people in the crucial commercial real estate business actually had any experience of property. The appointment of Erin Callan as the CFO made matters worse as she had no experience of treasury or accounting—key areas if Lehman was to survive the crisis. Her appointment proved to be the red flag David Einhorn, an influential hedge fund manager controlling over US$6 billion of assets, was looking for.[xl]

Fuld's intemperate reaction to an article in the *Wall Street Journal* (WSJ) revealing his plans to link up with Korean sources of capital[xli] further undermined Lehman's credibility. As a result of this leak, Fuld decreed nobody was to speak to the WSJ again;

perhaps not the wisest move at a time when being on good terms with the WSJ could help improve the climate of opinion in financial circles.[xlii]

Fuld was by now caught in the trap of many successful, hard-charging and charismatic leaders. He appears to have been poorly served by key lieutenants on whom he relied and who were out of their depth, making the wrong calls and appointing unsuitable people, as is shown by this excerpt of a conversation between him and Skip McGee, quoted in *Too Big to Fail*:

> 'You've not been served well by your COO. He's in over his head. He's not minding the store. He's made some horrible personnel decisions, and he's not watching your back on risk.'
>
> Reminding McGee that, as a member of the executive committee, he was responsible for making key decisions along with everyone else, Fuld said, "The entire executive committee is the risk committee."
>
> McGee, realizing that he was not getting his point across, stated carefully, "You are a wonderful leader, but when the books are written, your Achilles' heel will be that you have a blind spot for weak people who are your sycophants."[xliii]

The board is supposed to protect the CEO from the forcefulness of his or her personality in such circumstances. Although the CEO is supposed to be the servant of the board, this is extremely difficult in practice; especially when the CEO is also the Chair who appointed the directors. Unfortunately, the Lehman board was one of the weakest boards in Wall Street and Fuld had intended it to be that way.

With the exception of Jerry Grundhofer, who had only been on the board for 6 months, none of the directors had any experience of structured products. The ineffectiveness of the Lehman board is highlighted in a lawsuit filed by the New Jersey Department of Investment, claiming board and management misrepresentation lost the state pension fund US$118 million:

> The supine Board that defendant Fuld handpicked provided no backstop to Lehman's executives' zealous approach to the Company's risk profile, real estate portfolio, and their own compensation. The Director Defendants were considered inattentive, elderly, and woefully short on relevant structured finance background. The composition of the Board according to a recent filing in the Lehman bankruptcy allowed 'Fuld to marginalize the Directors, who tolerated an absence of checks and balances at Lehman.' Due to his long tenure and ubiquity at Lehman, defendant Fuld has been able to consolidate his power to a remarkable degree. Defendant Fuld was both the Chairman of the Board and the CEO... The Director Defendants acted as a rubber stamp for the actions of Lehman's senior management. There was little turnover on the Board. By the date of Lehman's collapse, more than half of the Director Defendants had served for twelve or more years.[xliv]

Once again, the question we should ask is would Fuld have behaved differently if his board were competent enough and independent enough to challenge him constructively? Would Lehman Brothers still exist? Might the GFC have been avoided?

Fred Goodwin and RBS[xlv]

Goodwin was not a banker, but a chartered accountant and had no banking qualification. He was named "Businessman of the Year" by Forbes' global edition in 2002,[xlvi] "European Banker of the Year" in 2003, knighted for his services to banking in 2004, awarded an honorary doctorate by St Andrews University and an honorary fellowship by London Business School in 2008. His success up to 2007 is shown in Figure 6.1 of RBS's EPS growth.

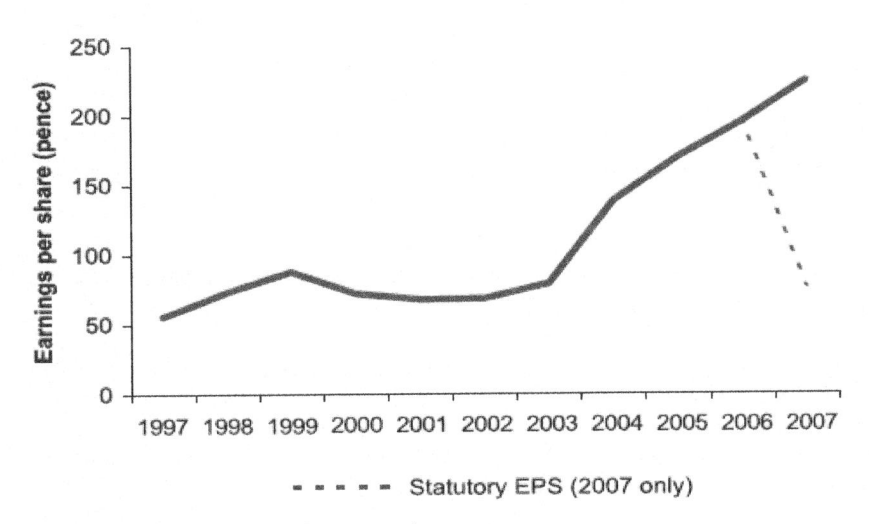

Source: 1997–2007 RBS annual reports and accounts.

Figure 6.1: RBS EPS Growth 1997–2007

Goodwin was labelled "the world's worst banker" by the end of 2008. What changed? Daniel Gross makes a compelling case[xlvii] for this on four counts:

Mergers and acquisitions were used to fuel growth. These became more problematic after the initial success of the hostile NatWest takeover for £26.4billion in 2000. In 2004, Cleveland-based Charter One Financial was bought with US$10.3 billion to expand RBS's footprint in the U.S. rustbelt. In November 2007 came the biggest banking merger in history, with disastrous results. In the words of the new RBS chairman at the 2009 AGM:

> I don't think there can be any doubt that the key decision that led RBS to its difficulties was the acquisition of ABN AMRO. That is the painful reality that we can now do nothing to change. *With the benefit of hindsight, it can now be seen as the wrong price, the wrong way to pay, at the wrong time and the wrong deal.* [Emphasis mine].

He overcommitted to investment banking, trading in structured products with poor credit controls. The extent to which this was a problem is shown by the following comment:

> Under Goodwin, the bank expanded trading and investment in derivatives, boosting derivatives assets 44 percent to 483 billion pounds in the first half of 2008. That was more than the bank's 443 billion pounds of net deposits.
>
> Meanwhile, its reserves of Tier 1 capital, a measure of financial strength and the vital reserve set aside to cover losses, was the lowest among its U.K. rivals at the start of 2008.[xlviii]

He built expensive headquarters in Stamford, Connecticut costing US$ 500 million just in time for the collapse, which would prove too large to use.

In June 2008 he raised £12.3 billion at 200p a share, having told shareholders in February 2008 that no additional capital was needed. The rights issue was designed to shore up the balance sheet suffering from £6bn-worth of write downs, a third of which were from ABN AMRO. However, between June and October RBS lost more than 80% of its market capitalization.[xlix]

Why did Goodwin persist in acquiring banks and in expanding infrastructure at the wrong time? Partly it was a case of:

> vaulting ambition which overleaps itself, of hubris brought low by the very qualities which led to such stellar success,[l] but it was also because Goodwin and his predecessor George Mathewson were in a hurry to take a boring local bank and turn it quickly into a regional and then global bank. Goodwin was executing his predecessor's vision according to Simon Maughan at MF Global Securities, who is quoted as saying:
>
> He [Goodwin] was exactly the right person because he would not suffer fools or listen to detractors, but just pursue the grand aim to take RBS to the top table.[li]

Why did nobody challenge him? Where was the board? The Financial Services Authority (FSA) in its investigation into why RBS failed suggested challenging Goodwin constructively might have been quite difficult:

> The risks that can emerge when there is a dominant CEO are not merely ones of difficult relationships between the CEO and the Board, staff, shareholders and regulators. More seriously they can also result in a lack of effective challenge by the board and senior managers to the CEO's proposals, resulting in risks being overlooked and strategic mistakes being made.[lii]

Goodwin's personal bias toward optimism was reinforced by information being provided to the board, emphasizing good news and perhaps de-emphasizing the bad.

The RBS Group Internal Audit Report of July 2008 to the Chairman pointed out they felt executive management had too much control over the information presented to the Board, "too often with 'good news' reporting and decisions presented as a fait accompli."[liii] A case in point cited by the internal auditors was a report to the Board regarding the performance of the Citizens business in October 2007, which stated that overall it would meet its budget for that year. Apparently, a number of directors had taken this as a positive report, whereas the reality was so different that the internal auditors concluded that "making any reassuring statements, at the September Board and in October to the Group CEO, would be incautious at best."

The FSA cites three reasons for the poor quality of the board's decision making:
1. *Excessive confidence in their ability to acquire another bank in a hostile takeover* because of "the firm's track record of successful acquisition and integration, particularly of NatWest, and the CEO's personal contribution to it."
2. *An extraordinary level of groupthink and lack of rigorous analysis.* The FSA report noted it is difficult to reconcile the lack of rigorous testing, questioning, and challenge with what they would expect of a board involved in deal of such strategic importance—reflecting an extraordinary level of groupthink.
3. *Insufficient discussion of the risks involved to identify "show-stoppers,"* given its complexity, scale, and how it was financed. Instead the focus was on identifying scope for synergies and cost cutting. The board appears to have taken too much comfort from the fact that ABN AMRO was regulated by the DNB (the Dutch banking regulator) and the FSA; that it filed its records with the U.S. SEC; that it conformed with Sarbanes-Oxley requirements; from rating agency reports and from the fact that their great rival Barclays was persisting in their bid. This even though the minutes of the March 28, 2007 Board record that the CEO:

> provided background to the project...*A bid for [ABN AMRO] was not seen as a "must do" deal.* The CEO advised the Board that "execution risk would be high" and that "any bid for [ABN AMRO] and subsequent integration would be more difficult than previous transactions."

> However, the *Review Team has not found evidence that the Board undertook any penetrating analysis of the risks on an enterprise-wide basis in respect of capital and liquidity.*[liv] [Emphases mine]

Conclusion

Quick and decisive action in business has been the justification in the past for combining the roles of chair and CEO in U.S. companies. When it works well, it produces great results. However, if the incumbent is corrupt, incompetent, or takes excessive risks, it is disastrous. Companies need good CG to protect them from the follies of the corrupt, incompetent, or excessively risky but powerful CEOs. Leadership and CG must be reconciled, if companies are to avoid bad leadership and failures of CG on the one hand; and good CG with mediocre performance on the other.

When trying to understand why Stan O'Neal, Dick Fuld, and Fred Goodwin failed, three things stand out:
1. None of them followed Alfred Sloan's policy of ensuring they had strong boards;
2. They demonstrated the characteristics of "great bad" leaders;
3. There were no effective checks and balances to protect them from themselves.

Their dominant personalities and past track records of success, combined with weakness of their boards, denied them the chance to pause and reflect carefully whether what they wanted to do still made sense.

References

i Becker, S. (2016), "Jack Welch: These Five Traits Define a Powerful Leader," *Money and Career Cheat Sheet,* June 17, 2016, https://www.cheatsheet.com/money-career/jack-welch-traits-powerful-leader.html/?a=viewall, accessed on June 19, 2018.
ii https://acton.org/research/lord-acton-quote-archive
iii McGregor Burns, J. (1978), *Leadership* (New York: Harper Collins, 1978).
iv Bennis, W. (1989), *On Becoming a Leader* (New York: Basic Books, 1989).
v Kellerman, B. (2004), *Bad Leadership: What It Is, How It Happens, Why It Matters* (Boston: Harvard Business School Press, 2004), 9.
vi Ibid., 8.
vii Ibid., 5.
viii Machiavelli, N. (1998), *The Prince* (Chicago: University of Chicago Press, 1998), 37–38.
ix Hobbes, T. (1651), *Leviathan* (1651).
x Locke, J. (1690) *Second Treatise on Civil Government* (1690).
xi Rousseau, J-J. (1762), *The Social Contract or Principles of Political Right.*
xii Taleb, N. N. (2001) *Fooled by Randomness: The Hidden Role of Chance in the Markets and Life* (New York: W.W. Norton, 2001); Taleb, N. N. (2010), *The Black Swan: The Impact of the Highly Improbable* (New York: Random House, 2010).
xiii Kahneman, D. (2011), *Thinking, Fast and Slow* (London: Allen Lane, 2011).
xiv Milgram, S. (1974), *Obedience to Authority: An Experimental View* (New York: Harper & Row, 1974).
xv Lipman-Blumen, J. (2001), "Why Do We Tolerate Bad Leaders—Magnificent Uncertitude, Anxiety and Meaning," in *The Future of Leadership,* eds. Warren Bennis et al. (San Francisco: Jossey-Bass, 2001).
xvi Jacques, E. (1990), "In Praise of Hierarchy," *Harvard Business Review,* January 1990.
xvii Michels, R. (1962), *Political Parties* (New York; Free Press, 1962), 66.
xviii Kellerman, B. (2004), *Bad Leadership: What It Is, How It Happens, Why It Matters* (Boston: Harvard Business School Press, 2004), 25–27.
xix The first seven characteristics are based on Peshawaria, R. (2011) "Too Many Bosses, Too Few Leaders" (New York: Free Press, 2011). They were summarized in an article on August 22, 2011 by Jason Moser in "Motley Fool" entitled "Lessons for Leaders."
xx www.brainyquote.com/quotes/quotes/a/alfredpsl194029.html#fzMXMKty3pvGPiRW.99
xxi Claud del Vecchio, CEO of Brooks Brothers, quoted in *Button-Downs and Tweeds, Reclaimed,* by Teri Agins, *New York Times International Edition,* April 23, 2018, 8.
xxii Lewis, M. (2010), *The Big Short: Inside the Doomsday Machine* (New York: W.W. Norton, 2010).
xxiii Madrick, J. (2011), *The Age of Greed* (New York: Alfred Knopf, 2011).

xxiv Bair, S. (2012), *Bull by the Horns: Fighting to Save Main Street from Wall Street and Wall Street from Itself* (New York: Free Press, 2012).
xxv Ross Sorkin, A. (2009), *Too Big To Fail* (New York: Viking, 2009).
xxvi David Faber, D. (2009), *The House of Cards*, http://www.cnbc.com/id/28892719/House_of_Cards
xxvii For a fuller discussion of the events leading up to the collapse of Merrill Lynch, please refer to Zinkin, J. (2014), *Rebuilding Trust in Banks: The Role of Leadership and Governance* (Singapore: John Wiley & Sons), 28–30.
xxviii Ross Sorkin, A. (2009), *Too Big to Fail* (New York: Viking, 2009), 144.
xxix Gillespie, J. and Zweig, D. (2010), *Money for Nothing: How the Failure of Corporate Boards Is Ruining American Business and Costing Us Trillions* (New York: Free Press, 2010), 6.
xxx Ross Sorkin, A. (2009), 144.
xxxi I am indebted to Andrew Ross Sorkin for his analysis of what went wrong at Merrill Lynch in *Too Big to Fail* (New York: Viking, 2009), 142–147.
xxxii Gillespie and Zweig (2010), op. cit., 7.
xxxiii Ibid., 7.
xxxiv Ross Sorkin (2009), op. cit., 147.
xxxv Zinkin (2014), op. cit., 30.
xxxvi For a fuller discussion of the events leading up to the collapse of Lehman Brothers, please refer to ibid., 33–37.
xxxvii Ross Sorkin (2009), op. cit., 11–28.
xxxviii Ibid., 14.
xxxix Madrick (2011), op. cit., 386.
xl Ross Sorkin (2009), op. cit., 107.
xli Craig, S., "Lehman Is Seeking Overseas Capital: As its Stock Declines, Wall Street Firm Expands Search for Cash, May Tap Korea," *Wall Street Journal*, June 4, 2008, accessed on January 3, 2013, http://online.wsj.com/article/SB121253687372943195.html
xlii Ross Sorkin (2009), op. cit., 111.
xliii Ibid., 118.
xliv Wayne, L. (2009), "New Jersey Sues Over its Lehman Losses," *New York Times*, March 17, 2009, and *The Supine Board*, New Jersey complaint (2009), 111 cited in Gillespie and Zweig (2010), op. cit., 16.
xlv For a fuller discussion of the events leading up to the takeover of RBS by the UK government, please refer to Zinkin (2014), op. cit., 37–42.
xlvi "Fred Goodwin, Chief Executive of Royal Bank of Scotland, Has Been Selected as Forbes Global's Businessman of the Year in Recognition of the 'Brilliantly Strategised Hostile Takeover' of NatWest Three Years Ago." Helen Dunne, "Royal Bank's Fred 'the Shred' Wins Forbes Accolade," *The Telegraph*, December 28, 2002, accessed on January 5, 2013, http://www.telegraph.co.uk/finance/2837654/Royal-Banks-Fred-the-Shred-wins-Forbes-accolade.html
xlvii Daniel Gross, "Who's the World's Worst Banker?" *Slate*, December 1, 2008, accessed on January 17, 2013, http://www.slate.com/articles/business/moneybox/2008/12/whos_the_worlds_worst_banker.html
xlviii Simon Clark, "Goodwin's $140 billion Binge May Doom RBS to Nationalization," *Bloomberg*, November 24, 2008, accessed on January 4, 2013, http://www.bloomberg.com/apps/news?pid=newsarchive&sid=a_6BKzvwAYCY&refer=uk
xlix Arnott, S. (2008), "The Rise and Fall of 'Fred The Shred,'" *Bloomberg Business Week*, October 14, 2008, accessed on January 4, 2013, http://www.businessweek.com/stories/2008-10-14/the-rise-and-fall-of-fred-the-shredbusinessweek-business-news-stock-market-and-financial-advice
l Ibid.
li Ibid.

lii FSA Board Report, *"The Failure of the Royal Bank of Scotland,"* www.fsa.gov.uk/rbs, December 2011, 233.
liii RBS Group Internal Audit Report cited in FSA Board Report (2011), "The Failure of the Royal Bank of Scotland," www.fsa.gov.uk/rbs, December 2011, 237.
liv Ibid., 228–229.

Part Two: The "Five P" Framework and Good Governance

The following seven chapters are designed to act as a working "how to" guide for directors in fulfilling their six responsibilities outlined in the most up to date codes of corporate governance.

Chapter 7
Introducing the "Five P" Performance Framework

This chapter is presented in three parts: the first introduces the "Five P" performance framework; the second discusses the "Five Ps": "purpose," "principles," "power," "people," and "processes"; and the third concludes with a discussion of where the boundaries of responsibility lie between the board and management for each of the "Five Ps."

Introducing the "Five P" Framework

Once the board has decided on the enterprise's mission and vision, it must ensure the organization's "purpose" reflects that agreed mission and vision—in other words, decide with whom it will do business and with whom it will not. Next, it must articulate its values or "principles," defining how it will do business and what it stands for.

Once these two steps have been taken, the board must decide on the organizational design or structure needed to allocate resources effectively and to determine appropriate reporting relationships and job descriptions—that is, the "power" structure of the organization. The "power" structure then needs to be staffed with suitable "people" and the whole entity needs "processes" to hold it together. The "Five P" performance framework captures the board's need to define "purpose," "principles," "power," "people," and "processes"; providing five lenses through which the board can review the company's performance, establishing where things are going according to plan or where more investment and corrective actions are needed.

Figure 7.1 shows how the board-defined mission and vision can only be achieved if the organization's "Five Ps" are aligned properly. If any one of the "Five Ps" is misaligned and does not point toward the mission and vision, they will not be achieved. This is because the "Five Ps" interact with each other, either reinforcing or weakening the organization's ability to set priorities appropriately and allocate resources accordingly. Working together, however, they determine and reinforce acceptable behavior and values. Working separately, they will create inconsistent behavior and undermine the values of the organization.

Aligning the organization to achieve the mission and vision

Source: Zinkin, J. (2014), *Corporate Directors Onboarding Program*, Kuala Lumpur, April 16, 2104
Figure 7.1: The "Five P" framework: Five lenses to track performance

The "Five P" Components

What each of the "Five Ps" covers:

"Purpose"

The best way for directors to ensure the enterprise's purpose will be aligned with their mission and vision when starting on its journey is to ask a series of questions of management. It is also important each time directors review proposals brought to them by management, they ask these questions again to reassure themselves the organization is not straying from its originally intended destination, even if the justification is that such a diversion will be very profitable. If these six questions sound like "Blue Ocean" strategy questions, it is because the thought process is similar. The questions are as follows:

Who Are the Intended Beneficiaries of Our Organization?
You may be asking yourself why "beneficiaries" rather than "customers"? There are two reasons for my choosing "beneficiaries":
1. *Corporate governance (CG) applies to more than just companies with customers in the traditional sense of the word;* it also applies to membership organizations, charities, collectives, nongovernmental organizations (NGOs), and religious organizations.

2. *Modern stakeholder capitalism requires directors to consider the interests of all stakeholders.* Consequently, the board must include customers, employees, suppliers, and the communities where they operate in deciding who are the intended beneficiaries and how to reconcile their different considerations. Environmentalists would argue they must also regard Nature as a potential beneficiary. Economists would suggest the externalities created by proposed activities must also be considered even though they have yet to find a satisfactory way of accounting for their costs.

What Difference in their Lives Are We Hoping to Make?

This question requires the board to think carefully about the impact and change they want to make on their stakeholders and to think about how to reconcile the different needs of each. It also forces directors to consider how sustainable such differences will be; to consider issues like congestion, pollution, and public health consequences of the products and services they offer and the effect on people of the way they make and sell such products.

What Value Will they Place on that Difference?

This question forces boards to consider once more Peter Drucker's quote in Chapter 2:

> *It is the customer who determines what a business is. It is the customer alone whose willingness to pay for a good or service converts economic resources into wealth, things into goods.* What the business thinks it produces is not of first importance—especially not to the future of the business and to its success… *What the customer thinks he/she is buying, what he/she considers value, is decisive*—it determines what a business is, what it produces and whether it will prosper.[i] [Emphases mine]

It is essential boards understand what stakeholders value; it is even more important they understand this can change dramatically over time. I cover this in more detail in Chapter 8.

How Will We Make that Difference?

Companies have choices. Directors need to decide on the following options before considering the issues covered under "power" later in this section:

1. *How to avoid being "stuck in the middle":* This is one of the most difficult decisions boards face. Ever since Michael Porter argued firms either can achieve competitive advantage by being low cost leaders or by differentiating their offer,[ii] management has been concerned with the problem of being "stuck in the middle." Although there is merit in his argument, it is not the whole story, as the following quote makes clear:

Being stuck in an unattractive business without a viable exit is one of the worst situations for a firm. Think of nuclear power and petrochemical plants, and many manufacturing operations whose owners face exit costs that can ruin the economics of a business as it approaches its end. Another example is the minority investor who is stuck in an underperforming private firm—even if a minority investor wanted to exit, his or her investment could be stranded if the securities are illiquid...A technology company can become stuck because of a commitment to obsolete technology. Many of these examples of "stuckness" arise because managers made an inflexible commitment to what they thought would always be an attractive business.

Irreversible market positions entail commitments that expose the firm to risks. In contrast, flexible positions can be altered as conditions change. You can think of flexibility as a call option on an alternative strategy—it is enabled, for instance, by holding excess manufacturing capacity, excess inventory, or excess cash.

The challenge for business leadership is not to avoid the middle, but rather, to develop flexibility—such as a sensible "Plan B"—if the dice turn against you. The middle is bad if you are *stuck* in some important way. The inability to respond flexibly and appropriately to new competitive conditions is the grave threat.[iii]

So, when boards consider how they will make the difference that will create happy stakeholders, they do not just need to decide what the basis of their offer is: low cost leadership; differentiation or focus. They need also to remember the need for flexibility in case the assumptions they make about the attractiveness of the industry they enter or are in deteriorates; and they have no easy way out because they are held hostage by their earlier decisions.

2. *To be first to market or follower:* Many believe that it is important to have first mover advantage. Historically, some companies have demonstrated they were good at being first movers: Sony in its heyday and Apple. Others chose to be rapid followers, learning from the mistakes of first movers, notably Exxon and Matsushita. This was understandable as there have been many times when being first creates unexpected headaches: there may be unexpected technological glitches that need fixing, allowing the company that is second into the market to benefit from the mistakes of the first. For example, Boeing's 707 benefitted greatly from the metal fatigue problems of de Havilland's Comet, the first passenger jet plane. Even though the Comet's problems were fixed, its reputation was tarnished and the 707 went on to dominate market.[iv] Sometimes it is just that the market is not yet ready, and it needs the competitive noise and investment when the second player overwhelms the first. Who remembers that P&G's *Pampers* was in fact late into the disposable diaper market (the first successful disposable diaper was *Paddi* launched in the UK in 1950 and in the United States in 1951[v]) or that Lever Brothers' *Comfort* was second into the UK fabric conditioner market (Boots, the chemist, being the first with their own label product)? MS-DOS was not the first PC operating system, nor was it the best, but by making it available to all IBM compatible PCs, Bill Gates was able to capture undreamed of network effects defeating Xerox and IBM's alternative offers, leading to the Wintel near-monopoly of combined chip (from Intel) and operating system (Windows). I will cover this in more detail in Chapter 8.

3. *To brand or not to brand:* Table 7.1 shows the arguments for and against branding, which directors must consider when they are deciding how they wish to make the difference in the lives of beneficiaries.

Table 7.1: To brand or not to brand[vi]

Benefits of branding	Drawbacks of branding
1. Potential to escape the product life cycle 2. Creation of barriers to switching 3. Potential for economies of scale and scope 4. Control of the brand's destiny 5. Leverage over distributors and retailers via demand pull	1. Need to invest heavily in R&D, market development and A&P 2. Need to recover high fixed costs 3. Country of origin may be a problem 4. May be difficult to recover from any problems associated with the brand, especially if the product brand and the organization brand are the same

The second consideration when thinking about branding is which type of brand sponsorship should the company opt for. Table 7.2 shows the benefits and drawbacks of the three types of sponsorship the board can choose.

Table 7.2: Three types of brand sponsorship[vii]

Benefits	Drawbacks

1. *Manufacturer's brand*
  a. Control
  b. Demand pull power
  c. Ability to extend the brand
2. *Own Label (distributor's brand)*
  a. No need to invest in brand
  b. Demand created by distributor
  c. Ability to extend the brand as distributor grows
  d. Limited reputation risk
3. *Licensed brand (franchise)*
  a. Control of format
  b. Rapid growth
  c. Limited capex
	1. *Manufacturer's brand*
	  a. Cost of control
	  b. Need for marketing skills
	  c. Reputation risk if brand has problems
	2. *Own Label (distributor's brand)*
	  a. No control over own destiny
	  b. Competition on cost and reliability only
	  c. Focus on functionality only, no emotional value created
	3. *Licensed brand (franchise)*
	  a. Dependent on franchisees delivering uniform experience
	  b. Potential for problems where franchisee is well connected politically and vice versa

How Much Will it Cost to Achieve that Difference?

The answer to this question depends on the choices of the board regarding how it will make the difference in the lives of its chosen beneficiaries: its organizational design;

its staffing levels; its remuneration and pensions policies; where it chooses to locate its production; its cost of capital; and whether and when it is able to capture economies of scale, scope, and learning, taking into account the lifetime of its investments and their rate of obsolescence. It also depends on how it finances its investments, itself a reflection of the riskiness of the projects and the choices it makes between debt and equity; how much of the debt is long term and how much short term; the credit terms it gets from its suppliers and the credit terms it offers its customers.

What Return Can We Expect as a Result?
Directors need to think not just about the operational ratios involved (breakeven, contribution to fixed costs, gross margin, net margin, EBITDA, ROS, ROA, ROI, ROCE, and ROE), but also about matching the risk appetite of the investors/shareholders they answer to. This means thinking carefully about whether the shareholders have realistic expectations of the business risk-reward ratio and what level of leverage makes sense. It also means thinking about transfer pricing policies and where to pay taxes to optimize shareholder returns.

Getting the operational ratios wrong will lead to losses and eventual bankruptcy. Getting ROE wrong will lead to shareholders selling down their holdings if too low; and a crash if the company is over-leveraged in the event of a liquidity crunch. Being too clever over tax and transfer pricing will alienate governments and their taxmen. All these considerations are too important to be left to management and are the responsibility of the board, advised by the CEO, CFO, accountants, lawyers, and bankers.

Johnson and Johnson's *Credo*, discussed in Chapter 2, is as good an example as any of the founders answering these questions.

"Principles"

These are the values at the heart of the way the organization functions. They determine what kind of business the board chooses to do and with whom it will do business. In the Muslim world, the board needs to consider whether what the company does and the products it offers and where it chooses to invest are Shariah compliant. In the non-Muslim world, the tests are more likely to come under the label of "socially responsible investing." The "principles" determine:

What the Company Stands for and its Culture
Some companies have good reputations for honest dealing, creating quality products, treating their employees well, and being good corporate citizens. Others do not. The difference comes from their "principles"—the values they profess and live by. The late Professor Sumantra Ghoshal was of the view business schools were teaching the wrong values and since the 1980s companies have been behaving less well than

before,[viii] hence the need for more intrusive regulation; this was particularly true of financial services.

> Firms whose managers act on the principle that employees are self-interested opportunists who must be forced to do their job will tend to create just that. Conversely a company that functions on the basis of trust and co-operation creates a system in which honest, co-operative people flourish. Self-fulfilling prophecy makes every company a force for either good or ill.
>
> Since the 1980s, the assumptions baked into the management model are the pessimistic ones. In the crash of 2008 we can see where the template based on them (incentives, compliance with letter rather than spirit, rejection of ethical considerations) leads. If the 21st century that management makes possible is to end happily, managers will have to absorb its most important lesson from the 20th: *what matters most in management is not what you make but what you believe.*[ix] [Emphases mine]

The key point is companies get what they expect: if they do not believe employees will work based on trust, collaboration and values, but only based on greed and self-seeking, they will develop reward and recognition systems that reinforce such behavior; they will promote the selfish and greedy who believe the way to the top is the way shown in *The Apprentice*. The reverse is also true:

> How we do business—and what business does to us—has everything to do with how we think about business, talk about business, conceive of business, practice business. If we think, talk, conceive, and practice business as a ruthless, cutthroat, dog-eat-dog activity, then that, of course, is what it will become. And so, too, it is what we will become, no matter how often (in our off hours and personal lives) we insist otherwise. If, on the other hand, business is conceived—as it often has been conceived—as an enterprise based on trust and mutual benefits, an enterprise for civilized, virtuous people, then that in turn, will be equally self-fulfilling. It will also be much more amiable, secure, enjoyable, and last, but not least, profitable.[x]

The "Tone at the Top" and the "Tone in the Middle"
It is not enough for the board to exhort employees to behave with integrity. The board, the chair, the CEO, and all directors must abide by the values they declare they believe in. Directors need to be covered by the code of conduct in exactly the same way as the rest of the organization. They must think hard about what should be in the code of conduct; review it on a regular basis; and give the compliance function and internal audit the authority, resources, and tools to do their job properly, lest the "tone in the middle" becomes a source of malfeasance.

Careers of Employees and How they Are Treated
Talent management must reflect the needs of the business strategy (defined by the board-agreed "purpose"). However, the board must also ensure the people who are recruited and promoted share the same values as those of the company. This is essen-

tial if the "tone at the top" is to be preserved. For example, Barclays in the UK was a Quaker-founded bank, which for 300 years had great "principles." By promoting Bob Diamond to CEO, Barclays traditional values were destroyed:

> To the extent that the enlarged group had common values, they were built around the pursuit of bonuses. In the years after the financial crisis Barclays was to be plagued by revelations about traders manipulating the Libor interest rate—the reference point for everything from credit-card rates to student loans and mortgages—along with many other forms of market malpractice. At the same time the retail bank gulled hapless customers into buying toxic derivatives.[xi] [Emphasis mine]

Being a Responsible Citizen
This recognizes if the company is to maintain its social "licence to operate," the board must consider the needs of the community in which it operates and of the impact the company has on the environment in terms of degradation, pollution, and congestion. This also requires the board to think carefully about the conditions prevailing in its supply chain, including the working conditions at its suppliers and the ways its suppliers do business. I discuss this in more detail in Chapters 14, 15, and 16.

"Power"

This deals with questions regarding organizational design, job descriptions, roles and responsibilities, and reporting relationships, as well as how people are treated by their superiors, hence the term "power."

When it comes to the most appropriate organizational design, this will first of all be determined by the business strategy agreed by the board. As a result, boards must ensure whatever organizational design they approve, it will be sufficiently flexible to avoid the problem of so-called stuckness, if the business strategy requires a change of direction. Perhaps the most obvious questions in this regard for directors to answer are the following.

To Make or Buy?
If Ronald Coase is to be believed this is merely a matter of cost (already discussed in Chapter 2). However, there is much more to this decision; directors must consider whether by choosing to outsource they are losing control of key intellectual property or losing a core competence leaving them exposed later when the unexpected happens, because although the competence was not core, it was mission-critical. They must also consider what such a decision does to the company's breakeven point and how that affects its profitability, depending on the cyclicality of the business.

To Do R&D or License?

The considerations here are similar to those in the decision to brand or not, except the answer involves investing in jobs and physical infrastructure. Companies doing their own R&D have to invest a great deal of time, effort, and money (all scarce resources) with no certainty the investment will bear fruit. If they have deep pockets and can survive the likelihood that for every success, they will have to finance ten failed projects, then choosing to do their own R&D makes sense. This is true if the resulting patent protection creates a fifteen (United States) or twenty-year (United Kingdom) monopoly for them[xii] before copycats flood the market with cheaper versions of their product. However, if time is of the essence, or if the company does not have the financial or human resources to do the R&D, then licensing is a sensible solution.

To Own Fixed Assets or Rent/Lease Them?

The choice will determine the breakeven point and profitability of the P&L and it will also affect the asset intensity of the business, maybe yielding a ROA that is higher than if the assets were fully owned, depending on tax treatment of leases. It might also affect the "stuckness" of the business, by removing a barrier to exit, depending on the length of the rental or lease agreement. In any event, the board needs to answer this question, particularly if it is in the retail or airline business where sale and leaseback are popular. The decision will make a difference to the organization design as well. Owned assets need employees to look after them differently from leased or rented ones.

To Go Direct, Through Distributors, Franchisees, or Via the Internet?

The answer to this question has a huge impact on the size of the sales force and on the physical assets (bricks and mortar) the board needs to worry about.

"People"

There are three questions directors must answer, with the help of the NRC and HR:

Do We Have the Right Number of People?

In answering this question directors must consider the current business strategy and how they expect it to evolve over time and how that will affect the "power" structure—the organizational design of the company. This will determine the number of jobs/roles needed to fulfill the agreed mission and vision, and if not, what can be done about it.

Do Our People Have the Right Skills and Competencies to Do the Job Properly?

Too often when people are recruited or promoted, the most important criterion is their ability to perform the job based on their past performance,[1] without paying enough attention to whether the nature of the job is changing. This means the board must insist there is an up-to-date competency dictionary used in assessing the current skills base of its key employees. Even if such a dictionary exists, directors must recognize in some industries change is so rapid, some of yesterday's competencies may no longer be suited for today's responsibilities and certainly will not be suited for tomorrow's. However, there will always be a set of core competencies that remain relevant regardless of the changing environment, in particular the leadership competencies.

Do Our People Have the Right Character to Work in Line with Our "Principles"?

It is my belief we often hire and promote people based on their ability to meet targets they are set; their past track record; or their apparent list of competencies, without considering enough whether they have the right character to fit with the "principles" espoused by the organization. Too often, we excuse people whose behavior does not fit with our values either on the grounds of their seniority or on their ability to make a positive impact on the short-term bottom line. Yet what every board must emphasize is how results are achieved is as, or more, important than what results are achieved. If this is not done, directors run the risk of being guilty of "the folly of rewarding A while hoping for B,"[xiii] dealt with in the next section.

"Processes"

These are the glue that binds the organization together. They are also one of the differentiators between advanced and emerging economies and between universalist and particularistic approaches to how things should be done. Universalist organizations believe the rules and procedures apply regardless of who is involved, whereas particularists will always find reasons why *in these particular circumstances* waivers can apply. Universalists depend on explicit shared knowledge of how things are done in the form of manuals, regulations, and laws, whereas particularists rely on relationships and the tacit knowledge of how things are done. Universalists depend more on *technical knowhow*, whereas particularists depend more on *technical know who*.

To be effective as the glue that binds, processes must include strategic planning, budgeting, and financial reporting; board-approved policies and procedures, regularly inspected by internal audit who report to the audit committee on lapses and

---

[1] This explains the famous "Peter Principle," which states people are promoted to their level of incompetence.

loopholes and the corrective action being taken. They also include all forms of internal formal and informal feedback mechanisms, covering reward, remuneration, and appraisal systems; the setting and review of KPIs and scorecards; as well training and personal development schemes; career development and talent management; and appropriate documentation of SOPs and SLAs.

It is essential the measurement and remuneration processes align with the mission and vision, if the board is to avoid falling into the trap of "rewarding A while hoping for B," shown in Table 7.3.

Table 7.3: "Rewarding A while hoping for B"[xiv]

What we hope for	What we often reward
1. Sustainable growth	1. Quarterly earnings
2. Teamwork	2. Individual effort; bell curve
3. Meeting challenging "stretch" objectives	3. Achieving goals; "making the numbers"
4. Maximizing productivity	4. Maximizing Hay points
5. Achieving total quality	5. Shipping on time
6. Candor; welcoming the messenger of bad news	6. Agreeing with the boss; "shooting the messenger"

Boundaries of Responsibility for the "Five Ps"

In Chapter 6, I discussed the need for redefining the boundaries of responsibility between the board and management. The same issues apply when using the "Five P" framework. I am therefore drawing the boundaries between the board and management for each of the "Five Ps" as follows:

"Purpose"

Table 7.4 shows the split between the board's strategic responsibility and management's operational responsibility.

Table 7.4: "Purpose" defines the businesses the company is in

Board's strategic responsibility:
1. Define and quantify who are designated beneficiaries and what difference in their lives they make
2. Establish the value beneficiaries will place on the difference provided by the product/service offered—how much is it worth to them?
3. Determine the cost of delivering the product/service offered
4. Define the resulting rate of return
5. Evaluate whether the company succeeded in meeting these criteria and take appropriate corrective action

Management's operational responsibility:
1. Adhere to board-determined "purpose" parameters
2. Execute accordingly

"Principles"

Table 7.5 shows the split between the board's strategic responsibility and management's operational responsibility.

Table 7.5: "Principles" deliver the mission and vision ethically

Board's strategic responsibility:
1. Define values in terms of desired, observable, measurable behavior
2. Establish standards for each category of behavior applicable to all, including clear definitions of unacceptable behavior

Management's operational responsibility:
1. Set targets for individuals and review performance regularly as part of the appraisal process
2. Agree personal development plans with targets for improvement and agreed action plans as a result of appraisals
3. Follow up and take corrective action if needed. Explain sanctions, when setting KPIs and targets; enforce when they are not met

"Power"

Table 7.6 shows the split between the board's strategic responsibility and management's operational responsibility.

Table 7.6: "Power" supports the mission and vision structurally

Board's strategic responsibility:
1. Specify organization design and structure to meet agreed strategic objectives including resources needed and the timeline for completion
2. Establish and protect an ethical culture in which constructive challenge from subordinates is welcome
3. Lay down standards for "speaking truth to power"

Management's operational responsibility:
1. Establish formal criteria and reward mechanisms to encourage bringing up bad news early rather than "shooting the messenger"
2. Apply the same transparent standards regardless of position and seniority

"People"

Table 7.7 shows the split between the board's strategic responsibility and management's operational responsibility.

Table 7.7: "People" to get the jobs done ethically

Board's strategic responsibility:
1. Based on job evaluation studies, decide on the number and type of positions needed to fulfill current and future mission and vision
2. Define the desired character of individuals joining the organization
3. Review and update desired competencies
4. Develop succession plan and talent management strategy

Management's operational responsibility:
1. Use succession planning and personal development plans to ensure positions are filled in a timely manner with people who have:
   a. Defined competencies to do the job
   b. Appropriate prior experience to step up
   c. Right character with integrity and courage to speak truth to power
2. Ensure the talent pipeline satisfies the changing needs of the organization

"Processes"

Table 7.8 shows the split between the board's strategic responsibility and management's operational responsibility.

Table 7.8: "Processes": The glue that binds

Board's strategic responsibility:
1. Ensure "processes" (policies, procedures, and feedback mechanisms) support and enhance "purpose" (mission, vision) and "principles" (values)
2. Agree "processes" recognizing they affect the other four "Ps" and are the glue that ensures organizational alignment to its mission and vision
3. Approve a written, trained, and attested code of conduct
4. Ensure compliance mechanism is in place with confidential whistle-blowing procedures

---

Management's operational responsibility:
1. Develop SOPs and SLAs in line with board-approved policies
2. Check for any misalignment with the mission and vision and amend accordingly
3. Check for noncompliance and take corrective action including enforcement.

Conclusion

The "Five P" performance framework captures the need for the board to define "purpose," "principles," "power," "people," and "processes." It provides five lenses through which the board can review performance; establishing whether things are going according to plan; and where more investment and corrective actions are needed, if they are not. It also helps directors assess new proposals brought to the board by management, allowing directors to check whether all aspects of the organization are aligned with the board-agreed mission and vision. If any of the five elements are not aligned, directors have an early warning system of potential failure.

As far as the boundaries of responsibility between the board and management are concerned, the board has the strategic responsibility for defining and overseeing critical elements in each of the five Ps, while management is responsible operationally for making sure they are implemented.

References

[i] Drucker, P. (1955), *The Practice of Management* (Oxford: Butterworth Heinemann), 35, quoted in Zinkin, J., op. cit., 24.
[ii] Porter, M. (1985), *Competitive Advantage: Creating and Sustaining Superior Performance* (New York: The Free Press), 41–42.
[iii] Bruner, B. (2012), "Stuck in the Middle? Take the Flexible Approach," January 16, 2012, https://blogs.darden.virginia.edu/brunerblog/2012/01/stuck-in-the-middle/,a guest post quoted by Symonds, M., *Forbes*, February 24, 2012, https://www.forbes.com/sites/mattsymonds/2012/02/24/stuck-in-the-middle-take-the-flexible-approach/#4d1184142ebd, accessed on July 5, 2018.
[iv] Lienhard, J. "No 112: The Comet Failures," *Engines of our Ingenuity*, University of Houston, https://www.uh.edu/engines/epi112.htm, accessed on July 6, 2018.

v "Valerie Hunter Gordon, Inventor of the Disposable Nappy—Obituary," *The Telegraph*, October 20, 2016, https://www.telegraph.co.uk/obituaries/2016/10/20/valerie-hunter-gordon-inventor-of-the-disposable-nappy—obituary/, accessed on July 7, 2018.

vi Zinkin, J. (2018), "Marketing for SMEs," Department of Trade and Industry Philippines Workshop, Peninsula Hotel, Manila, May 30, 2018.

vii Ibid.

viii Ghoshal, S. (2005), "Bad Management Theories Are Destroying Good Management Practices," *Academy of Management Learning & Education* 4, No. 1: 75–91.

ix Caulkin, S. (2012), "The Wrong Direction: Management Has Lost its Way—And its Power Has Sent Business Down a Dangerous Road, *FT Business Education*, December 3, 2012, 12.

x Solomon, R. C. (1999), *A Better Way to Think About Business: How Personal Integrity Leads to Corporate Success* (New York: Oxford University Press, 1999), xxii.

xi Plender, J. (2018), "Barclays, the bank that overreached," *Financial Times*, July 4, 2018, https://www.ft.com/content/0bc94580-7466-11e8-b6ad-3823e4384287, accessed on July 5, 2018.

xii Evans B. (2011), "Duration of a UK Patent," Lawdit Solicitors, February 25, 2011, https://www.lawdit.co.uk/reading-room/duration-of-a-uk-patent, USPTO, "Patent Term, Calculator," https://www.uspto.gov/patent/laws-and-regulations/patent-term-calculator accessed on July 6, 2018.

xiii Kerr, S. (1995), "On the Folly of Rewarding A While Hoping for B," *Academy of Management Executive*, February 1995, 9, 1.

xiv Ibid.

Chapter 8
Setting Strategy

This chapter is presented in four parts: the first makes the case for planning strategy, the second deals with the external environmental analysis directors need to consider when setting strategy, the third covers the internal organizational analysis, and the fourth explores where and how best to compete.

Why Plan?

At its simplest level, when setting strategy, the board must answer four questions: What do we want to achieve? How are we going to do it? Who is going to do it? By when does it need to be done?

When the planning process is done well, it creates enormous value because it provides a common set of goals and objectives around which the diverse parts of the organization can coalesce. It becomes a common "language" to be used across all divisions and departments whose day-to-day activities may be very different, where the thread of continuity between them may not be immediately obvious. This common "language" translates into comparable metrics, usually financial, which are, by definition, neutral and intentionally lacking emotions coloring the picture to the detriment of the whole. It forces everybody involved to articulate their basic assumptions in answering the questions:

1. How did we get here: what are the legacy effects (good and bad)?
2. Where are we trying to go?
3. What needs to change and how much resistance to change will there be?
4. What should we focus on?
5. What resources are needed?
6. What are our priorities?
7. What are the associated risks with each of the assumed scenarios?
8. What is the time frame for action?
9. Who is accountable and for what?
10. What happens if we fail?

It forces the enterprise to think about the future in a structured way, based on analysis, and to prepare for possible changes ahead of time. It helps the process of allocating resources, recognizing future demands on resources might not be the same as current demands, enabling the orderly transition of resources rather than a panic-stricken reaction to changed circumstances. Perhaps most important of all, the discussion of the assumptions and the possible scenarios and outcomes allows different constituencies within the company to listen to each other and agree a common posi-

tion, allowing everybody to get behind the agreed direction, once all have had their say. Such an approach recognizes explicitly the numbers are less important than the assumptions and chosen scenarios underlying them. This allows the board to:
1. Challenge management assumptions in the formulation of their plans
2. Review performance intelligently, distinguishing between deviation from plan caused by wrong assumptions from deviation caused by poor execution

Finally, this entire process must lead to effective implementation: to action, review, applying lessons learned, and more effective future implementation.

Good strategic planning is essential for directors to have the relevant assumptions and facts to hand when deciding what they want to achieve and how best to go about it. This requires four steps: analyzing the organization's external environment, analyzing the organization's internal capabilities, and working out where and how to compete. *The board must never be fooled by advisers and management into thinking there was nothing wrong with the strategy; the problem was implementation. A strategy is only ever as good as its implementation.*

Before starting to analyze the external environment, directors need a stakeholder analysis to ensure what they choose fits with the needs of their stakeholders. These differ depending on the type of organization on whose board they sit. Table 8.1 shows some of the different considerations that will affect how their organizations can compete.

Although these different stakeholder contexts affect directors' deliberations when setting strategy, the need to reconcile efficiency and effectiveness remains the same across the board. So, it is not a choice between "either or" but a case of "both and."

Table 8.1: Different stakeholder contexts compared

Multinational and multilocal firms	Public sector firms	Family firms and SMEs	Professional service firms
The importance of the *corporate structure*: 1. Centralized or decentralized 2. Divisionalized by product group or geography 3. Portfolio decisions with different costs of capital, risk profiles, and cash generation 4. Impact of cross-border issues of culture and law	The importance within a *political context* of: 1. Government changes in priority 2. External constraints or guidelines on decision making set by government 3. Competition for scarce government resources 4. Captive "citizen market" as opposed to customers with choice	The importance of *individual expectations* of: 1. Founders 2. Owners 3. Family members	The importance within a *partnership context* of: 1. Externally set expectations and standards of professional associations 2. Need to reconcile interests of client leaders, practice chairs, and office managers

Analyzing the External Environment

It is logical to start with the external environment in the board's strategy deliberations if, like me, you agree with Peter Drucker's view, quoted in Chapter 2:

> *It is the customer who determines what a business is. It is the customer alone whose willingness to pay for a good or service converts economic resources into wealth, things into goods. What the business thinks it produces is not of first importance—especially not to the future of the business and to its success... What the customer thinks he/she is buying, what he/she considers value, is decisive—it determines what a business is, what it produces and whether it will prosper.* [Emphases mine]

For a start, it reminds directors and management forcefully it is customers who pay for everything in the P&L, including their salaries and pensions. Without customers, there is no revenue; without revenue there is no business. More important, it forces the board to think about external forces driving demand.

To this end, the board should first consider the six "macro drivers" of demand; second, understand the competitive environment for satisfying that demand; and third, appreciate the threats and opportunities created by the external environment and the weaknesses and strengths[1] within the organization affecting its ability to satisfy the identified demand profitably and sustainably.

Six "Macro Drivers" of Demand

Boards must consider the impact on their organization of the political, economic, social, technological, legal, and environmental (PESTLE) trends and developments, affecting demand for their products and services, when setting strategy.

Political Developments

Boards must stay up-to-date regarding the political climate and its impact on economic policy globally as well as nationally and locally. This means understanding not just the attitude of the national and regional/state governments of the day to the industry in which the company operates, as well as to the company itself, but also the

---

[1] This is normally termed SWOT analysis, putting strengths and weaknesses first; followed by opportunities and threats. I have always preferred to view this the other way around because the SWOT approach allows the company to believe all is well for too long, given natural inertia and the constraints posed by the legacy effect on changing how business is done.

In my experience of managing change, starting with the external threats and then considering the opportunities and looking at the weaknesses before looking at the strengths reduces the chances of organizational complacency and creates a greater sense of urgency in the board and with management. Instead of SWOT analysis, I call it TOWS analysis.

attitude of the opposition and regulators to the drivers of economic performance. This covers industrial policy, competition policy, trade policy covering balance of payments, tariffs, and currency as well as nontariff barriers; interest rates and employment rates.

Boards must keep abreast of the governmental developmental agenda and priorities to see how they can fit in with them or else lobby against them. This means having up-to-date connections with key civil servants and ministers, while not jeopardizing relations with the opposition in case the government changes. This requires a good understanding of who key decision makers and influencers are and what matters to them and is best done by corporate affairs, reporting to the chair. How to do this, is covered in more detail in Chapter 13.

Good examples of the importance of understanding what is happening in the political sphere are the UK's vote for Brexit and the election of Donald Trump in the United States in 2016. Regardless of your political beliefs and affiliation, it is obvious these unexpected results have an enormous, as yet unquantifiable, impact on business assumptions about the global and domestic economy and trade; support for certain industries; the approach to regulations; and taxes. Equally, the unexpected change of government in Malaysia in 2018 raised question marks over projects backed by the Chinese government, leading to cancellation or rescheduling of work contractors were expecting to have on their books. It also led to major changes in the appointments of directors in government linked entities. *Directors ignore the importance of political developments at their peril.*

Economic Trends

The board must appreciate what is happening globally, nationally and locally to affect the economic well-being of the company's clients and their demand for its products and services. This means thinking about the impact of changes in growth rates on inflation, interest rates and costs:

1. *In a rapidly growing economy:* This is likely to lead to higher inflation, higher interest rates, shortages of skills, and key inputs both for the company's customers and for the company itself. Inflation may offer opportunities to take on more debt, as it erodes the cost of borrowing. Rapid growth may also require changes in product mix and lines of business as different parts of the economy grow faster than others.
2. *In a stagnant economy:* The emphasis will likely switch to cost cutting to improve earnings and to prepare for signs of a downturn, caused by other companies in the value chain following the same policies. This, reduces their demand upstream as they cut costs, putting further pressure on other members of the value chain downstream to cut costs as well.
3. *In a recession or depression:* Will declining GDP lead to deflation, near zero interests and liquidity problems? Will this force price cuts because of weaker purchas-

ing power, leading to poorer profits and weakened balance sheets? The board needs to consider whether it should deleverage as the company's interest cover shrinks and deflation makes debt more expensive. If the balance sheet is strong, does this provide an opportunity for the board to buy up weaker competitors to increase market share or take out excess capacity? On the other hand, if the balance sheet is weak, should the board seek a buyer with a stronger balance sheet to take over the company? What should the board do about long-term investments, such as R&D or advertising and marketing, when profitability is under pressure? Finally, should the company change its product mix in anticipation of clients trading down because they too are feeling the pain?

Social Trends
In setting and reviewing strategy, the board needs to be very clear about its assumptions regarding the effects of changing demographics in terms of population, life expectancy, life-stage, and lifestyle. It also must consider the effects of changes in education and levels of disposable income on market sizes and relative attractiveness; demand for the company's products and services; the ability to recruit and retain skilled staff; and to employ the right people at the right cost in the right jobs.

Most of the major changes in demand for products and services in the last 100 years have been caused by key sociocultural megatrends. It is the responsibility of directors to follow what is happening around them to be able to "connect the dots," regarding the threats and opportunities such megatrends offer:
1. *Rapid urbanization:* This has not just created cities and all the obvious products and services they rely on and the business opportunities that go with that; it has also changed how we eat and buy our food.
2. *Greying populations and rising health consciousness:* These are increasingly a crucial issue for governments worried about looking after the sick, aged, and infirm.
    Politicians struggle with the taxation and resource implications of us living longer, demanding access to better and more expensive treatments. The obvious beneficiaries of this megatrend are Health Maintenance Organizations (HMOs) and insurance companies that have created new ways of looking after the chronically ill.
    Increased life expectancy in all developed countries, however, has created several other business opportunities that did not exist seventy years ago, for example, cruises; education for the elderly; gyms, spas, and "functional" or nutraceutical foods.
3. *Emancipation of women and the breakdown of the extended family:* Taking the United Kingdom as an example, in 2012 only 65,000 people were employed in domestic service. In 1901, 1.5 million were employed in domestic service, the

majority living in with their employers, attending to their every whim—the subjects of the globally popular TV programme *Downton Abbey*.[i] This megatrend created markets for household appliances; microwavable meals (predicted by Peter Drucker in the 1950s), "snacking and grazing"; and crèches.[ii]

4. *Changing nature of work:* Since World War II there have been major changes in the nature of work and they have in turn created new business opportunities; including new business models; and different expectations of what it means to be employed. We now have a mass leisured class with paid holidays. Travel and tourism have become the biggest employer worldwide, representing 10.2% of global GDP and 296 million jobs in 2016.[iii]

We also have the end of life-time employment, the advent of the gig economy and the threat of robotization and artificial intelligence eliminating a large number of repetitive jobs in the not-too-distant future. Given that many of these jobs will be the so-called bullshit jobs,[2] their disappearance may not be a great loss to the economy. However, boards will have to think about how best to redeploy the displaced workers, if political social contracts are to be preserved and a "political tragedy of the commons" is to be averted.

5. *The growth of "civil society" and "stakeholder capitalism"*: Boards must review regularly the effect "civil society" has on the company's social long-term "licence to operate" with respect to changes in regulations regarding occupational health and safety regulations, as well as product liability and environmental issues. However, they also need to consider carefully whether they believe they should operate according to the principles driving Kraft Heinz or those adopted by Unilever, illustrated by the failed attempt by Kraft Heinz to take over Unilever in 2017:

> There seems to be little doubt that corporate raiders are no longer seen as swashbuckling heroes admired for liberating unrealised shareholder value. Rather they are starting to be seen as contributors to a growing anti-business sentiment and resentment of a "corporate elite" whose only interest is to enrich the already wealthy at the expense of everyone else. Or, as the Financial Times suggests in the article *"Kraft Heinz/Unilever: nowhere men,"* investors with a short-term profit maximisation focus have come to epitomise the "citizens of nowhere" style of capitalism that has helped trigger populist revolts across the globe. Reflecting the public mood, governments may no longer be willing to tolerate the loss of jobs and expertise to enrich shareholders in the short-term. The United Kingdom's government has responded to the Kraft Heinz bid by pledging to draft proposals on how to manage controversial takeover bids.
>
> But this bid was but one skirmish in a long battle. It is far from clear whether it is the Unilever or the Kraft Heinz business model that will be successful in the long-term.

---

2 "The answer, claimed Graeber, is that a great many jobs in the managerial, clerical, sales and service sectors are not real jobs with genuine utility, but, rather, ones whose purpose is unclear to almost everyone, including those doing them. These jobs Graeber termed "bullshit jobs." Anthony, A. (2018), *The Guardian*, May 27, 2018.

The takeover bid has focused attention on the fact that Unilever's margins are lower than those of its peers. Pressure has started to mount on the company to improve its capital efficiency and increase value for existing shareholders. For Unilever, this raises uncomfortable questions. To what extent can it improve short-term performance without compromising its view of long-term value creation? Since the creation of sustainable social and environmental value is a much vaguer and less easily quantifiable (though arguably more important) benefit than the delivery of short-term financial value, can Unilever, and must it, do better at making the non-financial value it is delivering more visible, more understandable and more appealing to shareholders? And even if it manages to do that, is there a bid price at which Unilever's shareholders will yield to a raider irrespective of the social consequences?[iv]

This is perhaps the most important socially determined question facing today's boards, as they ponder strategy: can they reconcile the Kraft Heinz view of their role or the Unilever view?

Technological Developments
As directors, when we think of technology, typically we think of innovative products; it less usual for us to think of innovative processes, which can be just as important. In addition, we are now accustomed to think of innovation as being "disruptive" because so much is written about disruption in the press and in IPO documentation of prospective unicorns. However, we must never forget incremental innovation created by technological advances.

Technology developments affect incumbents in three ways: creating better ways of doing the same thing, putting pressure on margins of incumbents; creating new ways of serving existing needs, threatening incumbents with obsolescence; or providing a new solution to a latent need, creating a new business opportunity for incumbents, if they are agile enough to change their business model to capture it:

1. *Better ways of doing the same thing*—two examples make the point: global supply chains and Dell's business model.

    The invention of global supply chains is an example of doing the same thing in better ways; moving goods from one place to another. It depended on a number of improvements in its component elements: faster and ever larger ships; faster turnaround times in ports as a result of containerization, which in turn allowed multimodal freight methods to be developed; reinforced by the computerization and telecommunication technologies to allow RFID track and trace systems, letting suppliers and clients know exactly where their goods are. This meant less money tied up in goods in transit. It also meant companies could locate their manufacturing in distant clusters where labor was not just cheaper, but also supported by a concentration of skilled suppliers, most notably in the Pearl River Delta of China.

    This set of improvements in moving goods rapidly from one place to another created the global supply chains, allowing multinationals to relocate factories to places where the efficiencies of scale and scope are such it makes sense to ship products half way round the world. The impact on players within the global supply chains was to erode margins unless they adapted and adopted the new ways of doing things. Ports like London that refused to allow containerization, because of union pressure, were replaced by new ones, like Felixstowe, that welcomed it.

One of the most interesting examples of a new way of satisfying existing needs is the process innovation used by Michael Dell to turn the supposed strength of incumbents in the PC market into a critical weakness.

When Dell entered the PC market, buyers of PCs were experienced enough to know what they wanted. They could specify what they needed, rather than relying on the value-added resellers of IBM, HP, and Compaq to tell them what they needed. These resellers were regarded as a source of competitive strength. This was true in the earlier period when prospective customers needed reseller advice. However, Dell was about to make them into a source of weakness, as a result of a technically innovative approach to order taking.

Prospects placed their orders on Dell's website, specifying exactly the configuration they wanted and paid upfront. This new way of doing business offered major benefits for both customers and Dell, that IBM, Compaq, and HP could not match.

The first benefit for Dell's customers was the offer was made to order, thereby giving customers exactly what they wanted; whereas Dell's competition could only offer what their resellers had in stock, which might not really suit customers' needs.

The second benefit for the customer was Dell could incorporate the very latest components, literally based on what the knowledgeable customers had specified, whereas the competition had a 180-day disadvantage, consisting of ninety days of stock in the distribution pipeline and ninety days stock in their own warehouses. This at a time when 180 days was longer than the component product lifecycle. Using this model also gave Dell a better insight into what customers wanted, making its market segmentation more effective.

Dell benefitted from the fact they had negative working capital, allowing them to grow fast, without needing to go to the banks for more money and to set an 18–19% gross margin while their competitors needed 40%, allowing Dell to charge lower prices.[v]

IBM, HP, and Compaq were trapped; they could not go direct to compete with Dell because they would lose the goodwill of their resellers on whom they still relied. Dell had succeeded in turning their strength into a fundamental strategic weakness.

2. *New ways of solving existing needs*: Sometimes new ways of solving existing needs actually destroy existing ways of satisfying needs. Consider how the telex replaced the telegram. As a child, I can still remember my late mother, who was a journalist, writing her telegram by hand, taking it to the central post office in

Bombay (as it was then called), handing it over to a clerk who would then send it to the offices of the *Economist* or *Manchester Guardian* (as it was called in those days). Not a very convenient way of sending a message. This way of sending messages was replaced by the much more user-friendly telex. However, it could not be used easily for Japanese and Chinese messages, as these required the very complicated Chinese typewriter.[3] The fax had no such constraints. Even though the fax was invented by a Scot in 1843[vi] and commercialized in the West by Xerox in 1966, it was the Japanese who changed our habits by making faxes fast, light, and user friendly in the 1970s. By the late-1980s their faxes were desktop machines, so users no longer had to queue in the communal area to receive or send a fax—really inconvenient, if the message was confidential. Faxes were so successful they replaced telexes and became legally binding documents. However, except for Japan, where faxes still dominate office communications,[vii] faxes have been replaced by email and WhatsApp.

There are countless other examples of new solutions to existing problems rendering the incumbent obsolete; but few where the solution churn has been so dramatic.

Boards need to remember this, when allocating resources that can not be reallocated once committed, creating "stuckness," incurring write-offs damaging both the P&L and balance sheet.

3. *New ways of solving latent needs*: The best examples of this were Apple's inventions of iPods and smartphones: the first, to have ready access on the move to music libraries for a fee; the second, changing how we communicate and access information and entertainment, using a mobile phone platform.

Legal and Regulatory Developments

Directors need to answer five questions relating to regulations and the law. First, what is our philosophy regarding adherence to the law: are directors willing to break the law and pay the resulting fines, or do we expect adherence to the law as a minimum, or do we set ourselves standards that go beyond what is required by the regulations and the law?

Second, are we in fact obeying all the current laws and regulations that apply to our business covering environmental protection, employment terms and condi-

---

3 "Chinese typewriters look something like a cross between a deli-meat slicer and a small printing press. There are no keys, just thousands of little metal characters arranged in a grid system. Because Chinese has no alphabet and no alphabetical order, the operator must essentially memorize the location of each character —about 2,500 on a typical machine. They're heavy—roughly 30 to 40 pounds." Makinen, J. (2016), "Before the Computer, There Was Something Almost as Complex: The Chinese Typewriter," Los Angeles Times, September 3, 2016, http://www.latimes.com/world/asia/la-fg-chinese-typewriter-snap-story.html, accessed on July 13, 2018.

tions, consumer protection, contracts, intellectual property, listing requirements, and are our policies and procedures captured in our code of conduct and compliance mechanisms?

Third, do we understand the issues and trends that could affect legislation in the future relating to our industry? Do we really understand what is happening to public attitudes to our industry and company? Do we know where we stand regarding the public's view of our social "license to operate"? Are we up-to-date with the legislative agenda of the different political parties we have to deal with? Have we been tracking the bad actions and bad press of our competition as this may change how we are viewed, even if we ourselves have done nothing wrong?

Fourth, what is the status of litigation affecting our company and what is our philosophy regarding settling out of court? What cases are still outstanding and how much are they likely to cost, so we can make proper provisions for them? Is there a pattern in the cases being brought against us that either highlights a systemic problem or that could damage our reputation?

Finally, what risks are we facing from a regulatory or legislative perspective?

Environmental Trends

I still remember Sir Crispin Tickell, then the chief scientist to the UK government, saying at an environmental conference in Sarawak in 2005, "the economy is a subset of the ecology" and that we should never forget it.[viii] This was not a comment about climate change, but about the service nature provides humanity. At its most extreme, we would do well to remember that without oxygen, we survive for four minutes, and yet the oxygen-creating capacity of the oceans is being harmed by our actions.[ix]

The most important megatrends in environmental matters are climate change, conservation, and pollution, and now pollution with the problems of single-use plastics and their impact on our oceans:

1. *Climate change*: This now seems to be accepted as real,[4] despite the best efforts of climate change deniers in the United States, led by President Trump. Attempts to resurrect the coal industry in the United States are likely to fail because the economics of renewables are so much better than they were only fifteen years ago. More important, the awareness levels of potential customers are so much greater than when Al Gore launched *An Inconvenient Truth*. If the projections for electric cars are correct, and if the Chinese meet their targets, the demand for gasoline will be cut dramatically. As Sheikh Yamani said to his OPEC colleagues, when he was the Saudi oil minister in 2000:

---

[4] "Multiple studies published in peer-reviewed scientific journals show that 97 percent or more of actively publishing climate scientists agree: Climate-warming trends over the past century are extremely likely due to human activities." NASA, Global Climate Change, "Scientific Consensus: Earth's Climate Is Warming," https://climate.nasa.gov/scientific-consensus/, accessed on July 11, 2018.

> Thirty years from now there will be a huge amount of oil—and no buyers. Oil will be left in the ground. The Stone Age came to an end, not because we had a lack of stones, and the oil age will come to an end not because we have a lack of oil.[x]

Even though climate change requires global cooperation, individual companies can do their best, despite President Trump pulling the United States out of the Paris agreement,[5] to achieve the goals set on November 4, 2016 of whose central aim is to:

> Strengthen the global response to the threat of climate change by keeping a global temperature rise this century well below 2 degrees Celsius above pre-industrial levels and to pursue efforts to limit the temperature increase even further to 1.5 degrees Celsius.[xi]

2. *Conservation*: Businesses have long recognized the importance of the "Three R's"—reduce, reuse, and recycle—not just because of environmentalists interested in conservation, but also because it often makes good economic sense to practice the "Three R's."
3. *Pollution*: Until very recently the focus of business regarding pollution was mainly land-based: how to mitigate the damage done by mining, oil spills and effluents being discharged into rivers, like Love Canal in 1978[xii] or how to deal with air pollution caused by either industrial activity or by fires resulting from clearing tropical forests to plant oil palm. There were notable exceptions like the Minamata disease,[xiii] Torrey Canyon,[xiv], Exxon Valdez,[xv] or Deepwater Horizon[xvi] disasters polluting the sea. However, these were local events, whereas the latest focus on the pollution created by single-use plastics being dumped into the oceans is global and, on a scale, not understood only five years ago:

> One-third of fish caught in the UK are contaminated with microplastic. Oysters and mussels are contaminated. A recent study found 83 percent of drinking water samples around the world were contaminated. Contamination of sea water itself means there is microplastic in our table salt. Sea minerals and fish meal, the foundation of many agricultural fertilizers and feed for livestock and pets, are contaminated.

> We used science to create a material that lasts forever, and then we throw it away, all day, every day. That doesn't make any sense. And of course, there is no "away." Every single piece of plastic that has ever been created is still with us...

---

5 The CEOs of Apple, Bloomberg, Facebook, GE, Google, Mars, Microsoft, Salesforce, Shell Oil, SpaceX; the Governors of California, Connecticut, Massachusetts, New York, Washington; and Mayors of Boston, New York, Pittsburgh, disavowed President Trump's position immediately after his announcement. Jacobo, J. (2017), "Reactions Swift After Trump's Withdrawal from Paris Climate Accord," *ABC News*, July 1, 2017, https://abcnews.go.com/Politics/public-figures-react-trumps-decision-withdraw-paris/story?id=47767113, accessed on July 11, 2018.

...Getting new plastic bags every time, you buy groceries is ridiculous. Getting disposable plastic forks, plates, and bowls every time you eat a meal to-go is nuts. Using a plastic straw that will last forever for only a few seconds is crazy. And shipping water all over the world in little plastic bottles is totally absurd. People did just fine getting their food home from the store, eating outside their homes, and staying hydrated before all this plastic got involved.

With political will, a cultural shift, some scientific innovation, an eye to social justice, and by washing a few more dishes, we can work our way out of this enormous mess we humans have made.[xvii]

The challenge presented to boards of companies making or using single-use plastics is enormous; and it involves all forms of packaging which we were already overdoing[xviii] before plastics in the sea became an issue.

Analyzing Organizational Capabilities

There are several useful frameworks management employ to determine whether the existing business model used by the company is "fit for purpose." These models dig into operational detail and it is not really the role of directors to become actively involved in the use of the different models. Rather, it is the role of directors to be aware of their existence and to know what questions to ask of management regarding their assumptions; how they arrived at their conclusions; and what would happen in a range of different scenarios.

In my view, three models are useful (though there are many others). They are SWOT (or TOWS); "Five Forces," and the Business Canvas model.

SWOT

SWOT or TOWS examines the strengths, weaknesses, opportunities and threats faced by the company with which the board should familiarize itself. The best way to approach the exercise is shown in Figure 8.1.

		External factors	
		Threats (T)	**Opportunities (O)**
Internal factors	**Weaknesses (W)**	**WT strategic options:** Generate options that minimize impact of weaknesses and avoid threats	**WO strategic options:** Generate options taking advantage of external opportunities to overcome internal weaknesses
	Strengths (S)	**ST strategic options:** Generate options using internal strengths to avoid/ mitigate impact of external threats	**SO strategic options:** Generate options using internal strengths to take advantage of external opportunities

Figure 8.1: The TOWS matrix[xix]

The TOWS matrix offers a framework for options boards can consider. The responsibility of directors is to challenge management constructively by asking appropriately penetrating questions regarding threats, opportunities, weaknesses, and strengths (see Appendix 8.1 "Questions Regarding Threats and Opportunities"). Appendix 8.2 "Questions Regarding Weaknesses and Strengths" deals with the internally focused questions regarding both weaknesses and strengths. When assessing the organization's weaknesses and strengths, it is important to know how they compare with those of its competitors.

Asking these questions is a crucial part of the board's role in providing constructive challenge to management's assumptions of strategy and is fundamental, if directors are to assess which of the four generic options shown in Figure 8.1 are viable. Therefore, all of these questions must be answered when setting strategy. It is different when reviewing progress, and the best way to handle asking such questions will be covered in Chapter 9.

Five Forces

The key insight in Michael Porter's framework is companies have to worry about more sources of competition than just their head-head competitors at the center of the model. This is because the model looks at the market margin available in a given industry.

Competing for market margin

New entrants:
- New capacity
- Disruptive technology
- Exit/entry barriers

Supplier power:
- How many
- How strong

Head-head competitors:
- How many
- How strong
- How innovative

Buyer power:
- How many
- How strong

Alternatives/ substitutes:
- Existing capacity
- New capacity
- Exit/entry barriers

Competing for market margin

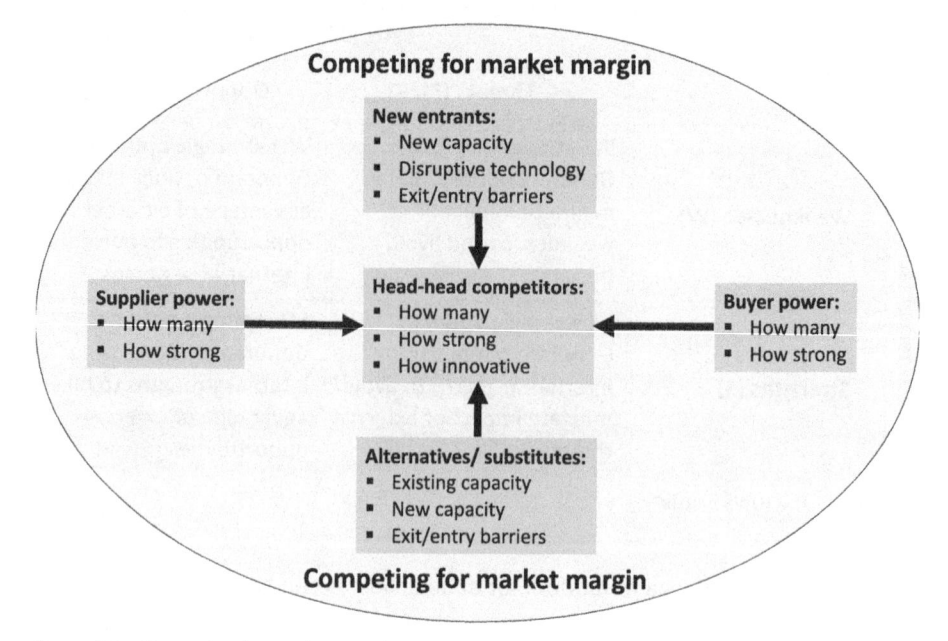

Figure 8.2: Competing for market margin[xx]

Figure 8.2 shows the amount of money a company can make from operating in a given product market is determined by five forces all competing for the market margin available in that product market.

Immediate Head-Head Competitors
Their strength and numbers determine how much market share the company can take. This lays the foundation for the amount of profit the company can make from a given product market, though that is immediately subject to two of the other four forces, namely:
1. *Supplier power:* whose relative strength compared to the company as the buyer of its products and services is affected by how many suppliers there are and how strongly they compete to get the company's business. This will decide how much margin they cede to the company and how much money it can make from them.
2. *Customer or buyer power:* whose relative strength as customers or clients is determined by how important they are as a percentage of the company's business and therefore how much the loss of any single one can hurt its bottom line.

The interaction between suppliers, the company, and its customers determines the attractiveness of the product market.

If the product market is too attractive because there is too much market margin (or money to be made), then other longer-term competitive forces come into play, namely:

a. *New entrants:* whose ability to enter the product market to capture some of the extra market margin will be determined by the ease/difficulty with which they can enter the market—the so-called barriers to entry. Low "barriers to entry" allow new entrants; high "barriers to entry" discourage them. New entrants will drive down prices and margins either as a result of their extra capacity fighting for the same business, or worse still, they introduce dramatically superior and disruptive technology providing better value at much lower prices, putting the company's existence at risk.

    The other side of the coin is once there are too many players in the market and there are high "barriers to exit," nobody can leave easily, because exiting costs too much and so the market becomes a competitive bloodbath. However, if the "barriers to exit" are low, it is easy to leave so market margin can be restored to more attractive levels.

b. *Alternatives and substitutes:* Their attractiveness to the company's existing customers will depend on relative price performance when compared with the original product or service. Alternatives replace the demand for the company's product with something different, satisfying the underlying need in a different way. Substitutes are less good solutions that become attractive only when the original becomes too expensive. Both place a ceiling on the amount of market margin any product market can command.

The interaction of these five forces determines whether a product market has "bad economics" or not.

It is absolutely essential boards appreciate the underlying economics of the product markets they wish to be in, when setting and overseeing strategy. This is why Warren Buffett was right to say it is more important to be in a good industry where even the least effective company can earn a good return, than to be the best competitor in a lousy industry where nobody makes a good return; and energy is better spent getting out of that industry rather than trying to improve it:

> Should you find yourself in a chronically leaking boat, energy devoted to changing vessels is likely to be more productive than energy devoted to patching leaks. [xxi]

> When a management with a reputation for brilliance tackles a business with a reputation for bad economics, it is the reputation of the business that remains intact."[xxii]

"Business Model Canvas"

Boards need to re-examine the assumptions on which the company business model is based and the "business model canvas" is as good a framework as any to help directors ask the right questions of management.[xxiii] This model looks at customer segments, customer relationships, channels, value propositions, key activities, key resources, and key partners to relate them to revenue streams on the one hand and the cost structure on the other. Appendix 8.3 "Questions Regarding Business Model Appropriateness" lists questions directors can ask regarding the appropriateness of the company's business model.

Deciding Where and How to Compete

The final set of issues directors must consider when setting strategy is deciding where and how the company can best compete. They are then faced with choices of whether or not to be or become a disruptor and whether to offer low cost leadership or differentiation.

Choosing Where and How to Compete

Companies have four possible development strategies they can follow, shown in Figure 8.3.

Competency

Products

Existing / New

Markets

Existing:
- **Protect/build**
  - Market penetration
  - Consolidation
  - Withdrawal
- **Develop product**
  - Existing competencies
  - New competencies

New:
- **Develop market**
  - New segments
  - New territories
  - New uses
- **Diversify**
  - Horizontally
  - Vertically
  - New line of business

Development strategies

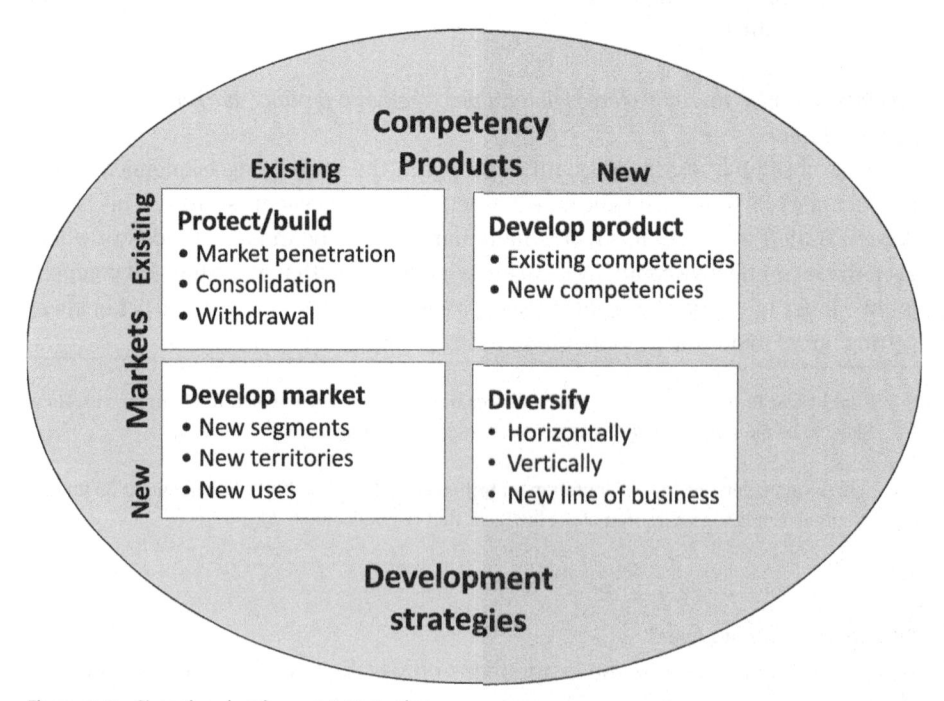

Figure 8.3: Choosing development strategies

Protect/Build Existing Products in Existing Markets

When considering the options, directors can choose to increase market penetration, if there is still scope to go for new customers; consolidate if the market is saturated and look to improve profits by cutting costs; or withdraw if the product market is in decline. This is the least risky set of choices because both the product and the competencies are in place and management understand the dynamics and demographics of the market.

Develop New Products and Competencies for Existing Markets

This makes sense if directors believe the existing market demographics are attractive and there are still good opportunities to be captured; and this is done with new products or with the development of new competencies (particularly for services). This choice is riskier than the first, because although the dynamics and demographics are understood, the company must create new products/services and/or develop new competencies—which run the risk of failing.

Develop New Markets for Existing Products

This makes sense if the directors are certain the products they already have can be taken to other markets. It is the basis on which many companies have chosen exporting from their domestic market without changing the offer. It is a risky choice, because although the company understands its products and has the necessary competencies in place domestically, they may not suit the new market because of different dynamics and demographics the company does not fully understand. For example, retail market leaders Walmart (United States), Carrefour (France), and Tesco (United Kingdom) have all found it very hard to export their retail concepts successfully.

Diversify

This is the riskiest choice of all—taking a risk of not having the right new products and competencies at the same time as not being entirely certain the company fully understands the dynamics and demographics of new markets.

In the past, conglomerates chose to diversify horizontally to remove head-head competitors and improve market profitability; or vertically along the value chain to capture all the market margin from raw material supply to final sale to end-users.

Horizontal diversification runs the risk of being regarded as monopolistic behavior, inviting regulatory interference. Vertical diversification runs the risk of requiring too many different competencies and cultures under one roof and has fallen out of fashion. For example, Unilever used to be in the oil palm plantation business to get the palm oil it needed to make soap and margarine. It had its own shipping line to take the fruit to its oil mills in Europe and the factories needed to make soap and margarine. It had its own logistics business to ship finished products to retail outlets (some of which it owned); and it had its own marketing companies and advertising agency (LINTAS) to capture all the market margin from tree to home. However, it realized the skills and cultures needed in these different businesses up and downstream were too different from each other. As a result, it divested its nonmarketing businesses to focus on what it does well—creating fast moving consumer good (FMCG) brands to serve households.

To Disrupt or Not?

Having decided which strategy development route makes the most sense for the company, directors have to consider whether or not to continue as incumbents or to become disruptors. Figure 8.4 shows the difference between the approach to strategy of incumbents and disruptors.

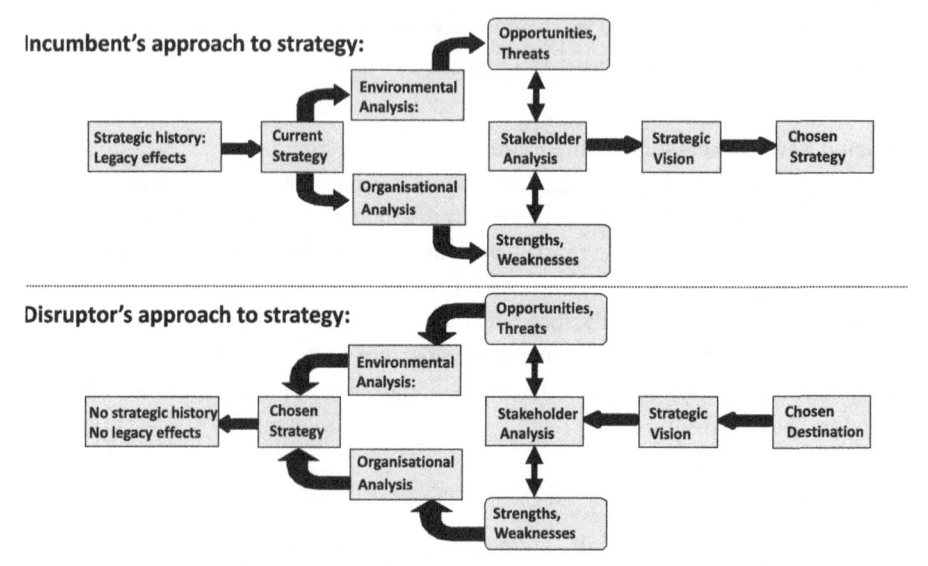

Figure 8.4: Two approaches to strategy[xxiv]

Incumbent's Approach

Incumbents are forced to begin with their strategic history and its associated "legacy effects." This may constrain them from innovating or recognizing threats to their business model because of vested interests in the organization and the unwillingness to write off prior investments.

Consequently, boards of incumbents are more likely to view strategic development as ways of "improving their game." They will tend to look at the resources they currently have (competencies, people, finance, and IP) and get their planners to evaluate where they can be deployed to achieve the best ROI. They take into account their environmental and organizational analyses, with the associated TOWS review and consideration of what their stakeholders need. Only then, they develop the strategic vision and adopt the chosen strategy. In other words, their chosen strategy reflects in large part their history and "how we got here."

The risk boards run when developing their strategic options in this manner is that they are trapped by the legacy effect: fear of change; fear of failure; concern "this is not who we are" if they have to change their culture and traditions; and how to deal with prior investments in R&D, processes, plant and equipment; and all the training employees have undergone. In other words, yesterday's successes make it difficult to think of any other way of doing business. I return to this issue in Chapter 16 when discussing innovation.

Disruptor's Approach
Disruptors, as latecomers to the game, are out instead to "change the rules of the game." They begin by choosing their destination, unencumbered by history, legacy effects or prior investments that must be justified or written off. Based on their chosen destination/destiny, they choose stakeholders with few vested interests to defend and get their buy-in before doing their environmental analysis, which then determines what kind of organization they will need. They may have no resources to deploy and, as a result, they are willing to leverage off the resources of others, instead of meticulously trying to work out the best way to deploy the resources they have.

Being "Close to the Customer" Is No Protection for the Incumbent[xxv]
Customer-centricity should be an advantage the incumbent has over the latecomer disruptor. Yet, it is not always so. When Data General and DEC, followed by IBM, lost out to PCs in the 1980s, their arrival was not seen to be a threat to "minis" sold by Data General and DEC, and later IBM's mainframes.

Their product planners were blindsided by the creation of the PC market on sound short-term business logic. No large customer of IBM, Data General or DEC was willing to use the new PCs. It took from 1977 to 1984 for the potential of PCs as tools for spreadsheets and word-processing for big business to be appreciated. Managers in big companies might like the benefits of distributed data processing, *but EDP departments[6] wanted to keep data processing centralized.*

IBM, Data General, and DEC were too close to the EDP community who wanted to maintain their control, power and authority over data processing. EDP departments created a mystique around their activities. Senior managers did not understand computing; did not think it was part of their job to do so; and were scared to question EDP

---

6 In the 1970s IT was called Electronic Data Processing (EDP) and was an arcane area boards and managers did not understand. EDP managers were treated like high priests of a religion its followers were not allowed to understand.

departments. EDP departments wanted faster and faster machines, which, in those days, meant bigger and more expensive "minis" and mainframes.

In 1975, planners in IBM, Data General and DEC were quite rational, as incumbents, to ignore PCs. They had huge investments in developing machines EDP departments wanted. They sold for over UD$100,000 each and had gross margins of around 45%. PCs, on the other hand, sold for US$2,000–3,000 with margins of 20–30%. Consequently, the logical reaction for IBM, Data General, and DEC was to continue to plow in resources to build ever faster, more expensive hardware with the potential to reach 60% gross margins to satisfy their customers—the EDP departments.

This blindness to PCs allowed Apple, Gateway, Compaq, and others to upgrade their products to the point where IBM recognized their potential, unlike Data General and DEC. IBM spotted the opportunity to make an end-run around the "mini" manufacturers. They set up their own PC division, as an independent operation in Boca Raton to prevent vested interests within IBM stopping the development of PCs. IBM subcontracted the chip to Intel and the operating system to Microsoft in their haste to disrupt their competition. IBM were successful in changing the PC's image into a key business tool for distributed data processing.

DEC resisted the change and ended up being taken over by Compaq, a PC upstart. However, even IBM failed to understand what they had done by subcontracting the chip to Intel and the operating system to Microsoft. IBM was sure they could make better chips than Intel and write a better operating system than MS-DOS. They were correct; but in the time, it took them to develop both, the network effects of the Wintel (Windows + Intel chip) approach overwhelmed IBM's offer when it was launched. The rest is history.

Low Cost Leadership or Differentiation?

In 1985, Michael Porter identified three possible routes a company could take to achieve long-term sustainable advantage, shown in Figure 8.5.

Cost Leadership
The company strives to be the lowest cost supplier in the sector to achieve and maintain superior profitability by achieving an above average price-cost margin. This can be done by matching the competition in an undifferentiated way while reducing costs through simplified processes; economies of scale and learning curve effects; and maximizing resource utilization so there is no unrecovered overhead from excess capacity. It is, however, a risky strategy to attempt because there can only be one low cost leader. The advantage may be short-lived if technology disrupts the market; imitation is easy; and customers can become less price sensitive over time.

1) Low cost leadership strategies
- Win price war in perfect markets
- Reduce and maintain margin
- Reduce costs (learning curves)

2) Differentiation strategies
- Differentiate
- Create imperfect markets
- Reinvest margin

Sustaining competitive advantage

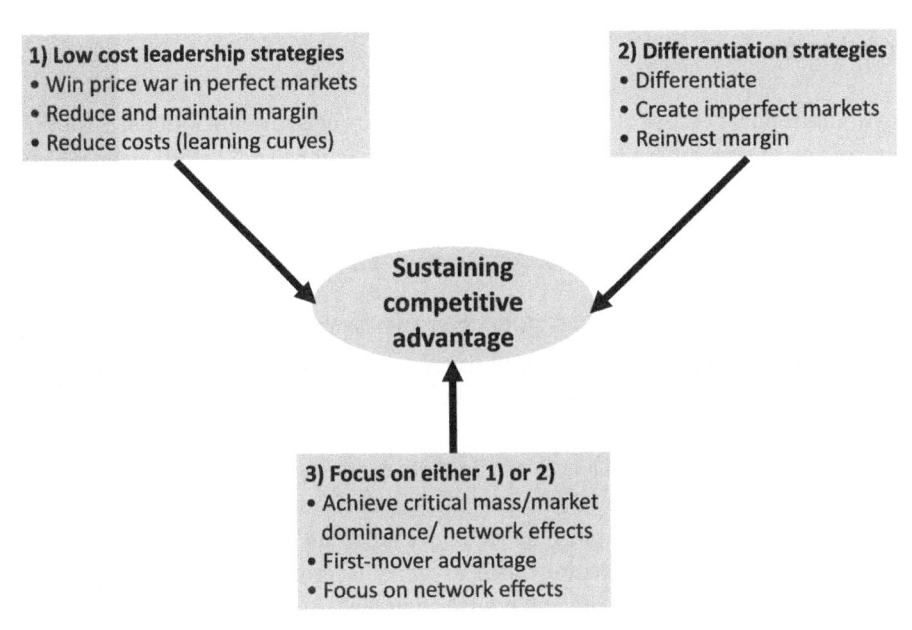

3) Focus on either 1) or 2)
- Achieve critical mass/market dominance/ network effects
- First-mover advantage
- Focus on network effects

Figure 8.5: Three routes to sustainable competitive advantage[xxvi]

Differentiation Strategy

The company can consider differentiation in markets where there are many ways to do this, provided customers are prepared to pay extra for differentiation because it increases costs of production. The risks in adopting this strategy are customers do not value the difference enough to pay extra. Competitors may be able to emulate the differentiation at lower cost; and maintaining distinctiveness requires continuous investment in updating the differentiation either through product enhancements or investments in advertising and promotion.

Differentiation can be product-based in terms of form or function, style or design, features and range, or affiliation—who the customers are and how they feel about being associated with the product. Differentiation can be nonproduct-based through serving customers based on the attitude, skills, and delivery of people involved; through distribution channels where the product is sold via vertical retail channels targeting unique segments; through the different purchase experience provided by exclusive, selective, or intensive distributors; after-sales service, support and advice; and financial packages

Focus Strategy

The company concentrates on a segment, applying either a low-cost leadership or a differentiation strategy to achieve market dominance through the network effects it has been able to achieve through being first or second to market.

Conclusion

Boards must plan because of the benefits the process brings to deliberations. However, directors must remember plans are not the same as actions and a strategy is only as good as its execution.

What matters in the process of planning are the assumptions underlying the strategy rather than the numbers. Any strategy must reflect the priorities of key stakeholders.

Setting strategy requires the board to first analyze the external environment and its impact on the company and its options going forward. To do this well, directors must question the assumptions regarding PESTLE environment in which the company operates.

Once the impact of PESTLE is clear, directors must examine the company's capabilities by ensuring a proper TOWS analysis is undertaken; the impact of the "Five Forces" on the ability to maximize its share of market margin is accounted for; and that appropriateness of the existing business model is tested. As part of this exercise, directors must also decide where and how to compete.

There are four possible options: to remain in the existing market with existing products, to take existing products into new markets, to launch new products in existing markets, or to diversify. Whichever is chosen, the board still needs to consider whether it will act as an incumbent seeking to "improve their game" or as a disruptor seeking to "change the rules of the game."

The board then has the option of low-cost leadership, differentiation, or focus as their chosen route as either incumbents or disruptors. When considering which of these three routes to take, they must remember to avoid getting "stuck"; with assets and a business model that does not allow them a way out, should circumstances change.

They must build flexibility into their allocation of resources. Companies undertaking massive centrally planned strategic approaches, "betting the shop" on the latest grand strategy tend to fail. Companies that experiment all the time without "betting the shop," learning quickly from failure and adapting accordingly, tend to survive, following what Tim Harford calls a biological approach to strategy:

> There are three essential steps to using the principles of adapting in business…First, try new things, expecting that some will fail. Second, make failure survivable: create safe spaces for failure or move forward in small steps… the trick here is finding the right scale in which to experiment: significant enough to make a difference, but not such a gamble that you're ruined if it fails. And third, make sure you know when you have failed, or you will never learn.[xxvii]

Appendix 8.1: Questions Regarding Threats and Opportunities

Questions regarding threats
1. *What are they?*
   a. Negative market trends
      i. Demographics?
      ii. Country economics?
      iii. Industry economics?
   b. Competition?
      i. New entrants?
      ii. New products?
      iii. New processes?
   c. Cost of finance?
      i. Debt?
      ii. Covenant cover?
   d. Hostile takeover?
   e. Weakness in supply chain?
   f. Legacy effects?
   g. Culture?
   h. Attrition of key people?
   i. Affect 'License to operate'?
      i. Political?
      ii. Legislative?
      iii. Regulatory?
      iv. "Civil Society"?

2. *How big are they?*
   a. Existential?
   b. Manageable

3. *How immediate?*
   a. Immediate?
   b. Within the next 12 months?
   c. Within 3–5 years?
   d. Within more than 5 years?
4. *What can we do to mitigate them?*

Questions regarding opportunities
1. *What are they?*
   a. Positive market trends
      i. Demographics?
      ii. Country economics?
      iii. Industry economics?
   b. Organic growth
      i. Enhanced portfolio
         1. New market?
         2. New product?
         3. Extend range?
      ii. New process?
      iii. New region?
      iv. New country?
   c. Growth via merger/acquisition?
      i. Vertical diversification?
         1. Upstream?
         2. Downstream?
      ii. Horizontal diversification?
      iii. Remove competitor?
      iv. Consolidate supply?
   d. Enhancing supply chain?
      i. Outsourcing?
      ii. Offshoring?
      iii. Insourcing?
      iv. Onshoring?
   e. Technology
      i. Continuous improvement?
      ii. Disruptive change?
      iii. Improved IT systems?

2. *How big are they?*
   a. Quantum jump?
   b. Incremental impact?
   c. No change, but prevent decline?

3. *How immediate?*
   a. Immediate?
   b. Within the next 12 months?
   c. Within 3–5 years?
   d. Within more than 5 years?
4. *What can we do to capture them?*

Appendix 8.2: Questions Regarding Weaknesses and Strengths

Questions regarding weaknesses and strengths and how they compare with competition

1. *What are they?*
   a. Research and development?
      i. Basic research?
      ii. Applied R&D?
      iii. Time to market?
   b. Technology?
      i. Product?
      ii. Process?
   c. Ability to innovate?
   d. Purchasing?
      i. Reliable, stable quality sourcing?
      ii. Stable supply chain?
      iii. Quality inputs?
      iv. Cost?
   e. Production?
      i. 'Lean manufacturing'?
      ii. Flexible?
      iii. Quality?
      iv. Cost?
   f. Product?
      i. Low cost leadership?
      ii. Differentiation?
      iii. Service?
   g. Value proposition?
      i. Prestige?
      ii. Premium?
      iii. Value for Money?
      iv. Low cost?
   h. People?
      i. Front line?
      ii. Back office?
      iii. After sales service?
      iv. Diversity?
   i. Marketing and Brands?
      i. Product development?
      ii. Corporate branding?
      iii. Product branding?
      iv. Sales?
   j. Distribution?
      i. Physical?
      ii. Virtual?
   k. Risk management?
      i. Risk appetite?
      ii. Risk management systems?
      iii. Compliance?
   l. Systems and processes?
      i. Aligned with Vision and Mission?
      ii. Reinforcing Purpose and Values
      iii. Recruitment, talent development, reward and recognition?
      iv. Succession planning?
      v. IT?
   m. Culture and Values?
      i. Clarity of Purpose?
      ii. "Way of doing things"?
   n. Ability to execute?
      i. Explicit knowledge?
      ii. Tacit knowledge?
   o. Finance/funding?
      i. Cost of capital?
      ii. Liquidity?
      iii. Leverage?
   p. Alliances/partnerships?
   q. Aligned shareholder expectations?
2. *How critical are they?*
3. *How can they be rectified?*
4. *When can they become strengths?*

Appendix 8.3: Questions Regarding Business Model Appropriateness

Revenue Streams
1. For what value are our customers willing to pay?
2. For what do they currently pay?
3. How are they currently paying?
4. How would they prefer to pay?
5. How much does each revenue stream contribute to the total?

Customer Segments
1. For whom are we creating value?
2. Who are our most important customers?
3. Which customers are profitable/ unprofitable?
    a. Mass market?
    b. Niche market?
    c. Segmented?
    d. Diversified?

Customer Relationships
1. What type of relationships do our customer segments expect of us?
    a. Personal assistance?
    b. Dedicated personal assistance?
    c. Self-service?
    d. Automated service?
    e. Communities?
    f. Co-creations?
2. Which ones have we established?
3. How are they integrated with the rest of our business model?
4. How much do they cost?

Value Propositions
1. What value do we deliver to the customer?
2. Which one of our customer's problems are we helping to solve?
3. What bundles of products and services are we offering to each customer?
4. Which customer needs are we satisfying?
    a. Innovation?
    b. Performance?
    c. Customization?
    d. "Getting the Job Done?"
    e. Design?
    f. Brand/Status?
    g. Price?
    h. Cost reduction?
    i. Risk reduction?
    j. Accessibility?
    k. Convenience/ease of use?

Key Activities
1. What key activities do our value propositions require?
2. How do we distribute our products?
3. What are our customer relationships?
4. Where do our revenue streams come from?

Key Partners
1. Who are our key partners?
2. Who are our key suppliers?
3. Which key resources are we acquiring from our partners?
4. Which key activities do our partners perform?

Key Resources
1. What key resources do our value propositions need?
2. What key resources do our channels need?
3. What key resources do our customer relationships need?
4. What key resources do our revenue streams need?
   a. Physical?
   b. Human?
   c. Financial?
   d. IP?

Channels
1. Which channels do our customers want to use?
2. How are we reaching them now?
3. How are our channels integrated?
4. Which ones work best?
5. Which ones are most cost effective?
6. How do they fit with our customer routines?
   a. How do we raise customer awareness of our products and services?
   b. How do we help them evaluate our customer value proposition?
   c. How do we help customers buy?
   d. How do we deliver our value proposition to the customer?
   e. How do we provide after-sales support?

Cost Structure
1. What are the most important costs inherent in the company's business model?
2. Which key features are most expensive?
3. Which key activities are most expensive?
4. Is the business more cost driven or value driven?
5. How important are the economies of scale/scope?

References

i Wallis, L. (2012), "A Life Below Stairs," *BBC News*, September 22, 2012, https://www.bbc.com/news/magazine-19544309, accessed on July 10, 2018.

ii The breakdown of the extended family means grandparents and unmarried aunts can not be so easily used as "unpaid babysitters." In Scandinavia and France, working women can take their children to crèches at or near work, thus creating a new service industry, while allowing mothers to go to work with clear consciences. Zinkin, J. (2003), *What CEOs Must Do to Succeed* (Petaling Jaya: Prentice Hall), 91.

iii World Travel and Tourism Council (2017), "Travel and Tourism Economic Impact 2017 World," https://www.wttc.org/-/media/files/reports/economic-impact-research/regions-2017/world2017.pdf, accessed on July 10, 2018.

iv Soonieus, R. (2017), "Should the Unilever Model of Capitalism be Protected?," *INSEAD Knowledge*, February 23, 2017, https://knowledge.insead.edu/blog/insead-blog/should-the-unilever-model-of-capitalism-be-protected-5301, accessed on July 10, 2018.

v Johnson, G. and Scholes, K. (2005), "Exploring Corporate Strategy, Seventh Edition" (Harlow, Essex: Prentice Hall), 6–8.

vi Higgins International, "History of the Fax Machine," https://www.faxswitch.com/fax_machine_history.html, accessed on July 13, 2018.

vii Fitzpatrick, M. (2015), "Why Is Hi-Tech Japan Using Cassette Tapes and Faxes?" *BBC News*, November 3, 2015, https://www.faxswitch.com/fax_machine_history.html, accessed on July 13, 2018.

viii Tickell, C. (2005), International Media Environment Summit, Kuching, Sarawak, November 30, 2005.

ix Nace, T. (2017), "Oceans Are Losing Oxygen, Just as They Did 94 Million Years Ago," *Forbes*, August 10, 2017.

x Fagan, M. (2000), "Sheikh Yamani Predicts Price Crash as Age of Oil Ends," *The Telegraph*, June 25, 2000, https://www.telegraph.co.uk/news/uknews/1344832/Sheikh-Yamani-predicts-price-crash-as-age-of-oil-ends.html, accessed on July 9, 2018.

xi United Nations Climate Change (2016), "The Paris Agreement", https://unfccc.int/process-and-meetings/the-paris-agreement/the-paris-agreement, accessed on July 11, 2018.

xii EPA (1979), "EPA scientists found 82 toxic chemicals in air, water, and soil samples near the dumps... The numerous toxic chemicals—a dozen of which are carcinogenic—discarded at Love Canal over the last 30 years have triggered several health problems, including miscarriages, among the area's residents, and have transformed whole sections of this once pleasant community into a ghost town... The relief being requested by the government [US$117,580,000 in clean-up costs and reimbursement for more than US$7million spent by Federal agencies in emergency measures] from these chemical companies represents one of the most significant and costly environmental remedies ever sought in a judicial action." "US sues Hooker Chemical at Niagara Falls, New York," *EPA press release*, December 20, 1979.

xiii "Minamata disease [caused by mercury poisoning from discharge into Minamata bay] came into being as a result of one chemical complex that was, at a certain point in time, positioned at the heart of a new and rapidly growing industry. Because of the company's pride in its own technological prowess, it was blinded to the dangers of the waste effluents that it allowed to enter the human environment..." http://www.unu.edu/unupress/unupbooks/uu35ie/uu35ie0e.htm, accessed on May 3, 2009.

xiv "Fifty years ago, the supertanker SS Torrey Canyon hit rocks off the coast off Cornwall, spilling more than 100,000 tonnes of crude oil into the English Channel. Beaches were left knee-deep in sludge and thousands of sea birds were killed in what remains the UK's worst environmental accident. It was the first major oil spill in British and European waters, causing enormous damage to marine life and the livelihoods of local people. It also led to changes in the way people viewed the environment," Bell, B. and Cacciotollo, M. (2017), "Torrey Canyon oil spill: The day the sea turned black," BBC News, March 17, 2017, https://www.bbc.com/news/uk-england-39223308, accessed on July 11, 2018.

xv "On March 24, 1989, the *Exxon Valdez* ran aground in northern Prince William Sound, spilling 42 million liters of crude oil and contaminating 1,990 kilometers of shoreline. Some 2,000 sea otters, 302 harbor seals and about 250,000 seabirds died in the days immediately following the spill. Now researchers writing in the journal *Science* caution that more than a decade later, a significant amount of oil still persists and the long-term impacts of oil spills may be more devastating than previously thought." Graham, S. (2003), Environmental Effects of *Exxon Valdez* Spill Still Being Felt." *Scientific American*, December 19, 2003, https://www.scientificamerican.com/article/environmental-effects-of/, accessed on July 11, 2018.

xvi "A sorry catalogue of technical, safety and regulatory failures all contributed to the Deepwater Horizon oil spill in the Gulf of Mexico, according to an interim independent report commissioned by the US Department of the Interior and published today. The oil spill began on 20 April when an uncontrolled release of oil and gas from an underwater well caused an explosion that engulfed the Deepwater Horizon rig, killing 11 crewmen on board. The leak continued until 15 July, releasing about 5 million barrels of oil into the Gulf, the largest accidental marine oil spill in history." Gupta, S. (2010), "Gulf Oil Spill Report Blames Industry and Regulators," *New Scientist*, November 17, 2010, https://www.newscientist.com/article/dn19739-gulf-oil-spill-report-blames-industry-and-regulators/, accessed on July 11, 2018.

xvii Johnson, A. E. (2017), "We Need to Kick our Addiction to Plastic," *Scientific American*, October 10, 2017, https://blogs.scientificamerican.com/observations/we-need-to-kick-our-addiction-to-plastic/, accessed on July 11, 2018.

xviii Othman, L. (2018), "Do Supermarkets in Singapore Use Excessive Packaging for Fresh Produce?" *Channel News Asia*, February 4, 2018, https://www.channelnewsasia.com/news/singapore/do-supermarkets-in-singapore-use-excessive-packaging-for-fresh-9926518, accessed on July 11, 2018.

xix Based on Johnson and Scholes (2005), op. cit., 347.

xx Based on Zinkin (2010), op. cit., 151.

xxi http://www.brainyquote.com/quotes/authors/w/warren_buffett_2.html#izWHsjmpYFlAKzVj.99, accessed on July 31, 2012.

xxii http://www.brainyquote.com/quotes/authors/w/warren_buffett_3.html#3lO4w81f3iXIbJxD.99, accessed on July 30, 2012.

xxiii Osterwalder, A. and Pigneur, Y. et al. (2010), *Business Model Generation* (Lausanne: Self-Published).

xxiv Based on Dobson, P., Starkey, K., and Richards, J. (2004), *Strategic Management: Issues and Cases* (Hoboken, NJ: Wiley Blackwell), cited in and based on Zinkin (2010), op. cit., 113–114.

xxv Zinkin (2003), op. cit., 118–119.

xxvi Johnson and Scholes (2005), op. cit., 253.

xxvii Harford, T. (2011), *Adapt: Why Success Always Starts with Failure* (London: Little Brown), 224.

Chapter 9
Reviewing Strategy

This chapter is presented in three parts: the first covers the process of review by the board, the second the appropriate metrics when reviewing progress, and the third using the "Five P" framework as a crosscheck.

This chapter focuses on the importance of measurement from both an oversight and management perspective. It recognizes the review process itself is a key signal to those being measured what they are doing matters to the board. It goes on to discuss financial and nonfinancial measures that matter when directors consider whether the strategy they have set is being executed properly. It concludes with the use of the "Five P" framework to check whether nonfinancial aspects have been given due weight.

Board's Strategy Review Process

Directors are helped if they have a formal review process for evaluating the effectiveness of strategy execution, having agreed on their desired strategy (preferably following the process outlined in Chapter 8). Figure 9.1 shows a five-step process for reviewing whether the chosen strategy still is appropriate in the current circumstances in which the company now finds itself:

The first step is to reevaluate the environment in which the company operates. This is best done at annual budget setting and then revisited either six or nine months after the budget has been agreed to see whether the company will be able to meet its budgeted targets. Directors should ask whether the actual performance to-date invalidates any of the key assumptions of the analysis they reviewed earlier in the year. If, during deliberations, it transpires there have been important changes, directors need to quickly check whether they are significant enough to lead to questioning whether the purpose, mission, and vision need modification. They will need to do this thoroughly each year, when resetting the strategic objectives for the coming year, particularly if they use "zero-based" budgeting.

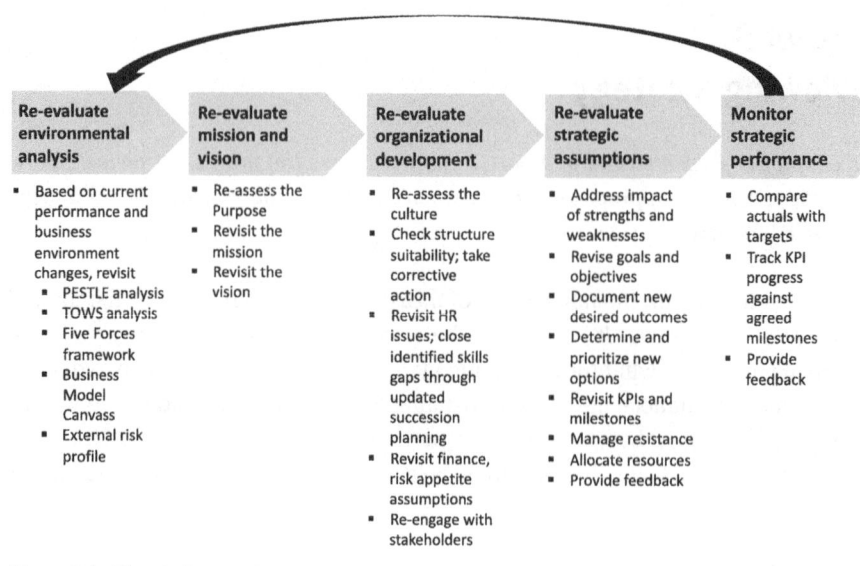

Figure 9.1: The strategy review process

Re-evaluate environmental analysis
- Based on current performance and business environment changes, revisit
  - PESTLE analysis
  - TOWS analysis
  - Five Forces framework
  - Business Model Canvass
- External risk profile

Re-evaluate mission and vision
- Re-assess the Purpose
- Revisit the mission
- Revisit the vision

Re-evaluate organizational development
- Re-assess the culture
- Check structure suitability; take corrective action
- Revisit HR issues; close identified skills gaps through updated succession planning
- Revisit finance, risk appetite assumptions
- Re-engage with stakeholders

Re-evaluate strategic assumptions
- Address impact of strengths and weaknesses
- Revise goals and objectives
- Document new desired outcomes
- Determine and prioritize new options
- Revisit KPIs and milestones
- Manage resistance
- Allocate resources
- Provide feedback

Monitor strategic performance
- Compare actuals with targets
- Track KPI progress against agreed milestones
- Provide feedback

Depending on the results of such deliberations, the board will have to review once more the organizational design of the company to see if it is still "fit for purpose." In doing this, they need a quick audit of the state of the culture and morale of the organization; they need to check if the structure still satisfies the demands of the strategy; they need to ensure they have the right people with the right skills and character to meet the agreed objectives.

If they do not, they either have to take rapid corrective action or modify the goals and objectives. Changing goals and objectives may require setting new priorities, allocating resources differently, and revisiting the key performance indicators (KPIs) and milestones. It will almost certainly require managing expectations and overcoming resistance from vested interests inside and outside the organization and explain why the changes are necessary.

Finally, at each board meeting, directors must spend time reviewing actual performance against agreed targets; track progress against KPIs and give feedback to management. Leading practice is not just to look at the financials alone, but also at the key elements underpinning the organization's ability to deliver desired results. This is best done by setting an annual calendar for review.[1] The scheduling of board meetings and when key topics will depend on when and how often the company declares interim financial results, if public listed. The board meeting to finalize the

---

[1] As an illustration, succession planning and talent management might be tabled for the first board meeting of the year; progress on IT issues at the second board meeting; capex and mid-year budget review at the third; and bonus and remuneration once the achievement of the budget is assured.

accounts and approve the directors' statement of internal controls (DSIC) must be done in line with when the company declares its full year results. The advantage of "calendarization" of key topics is management know months in advance when the subject will be discussed. This allows senior management to prepare thoroughly and present papers to the board early enough for directors to have ample time to read them and think about the issues they raise. It also makes it difficult for senior managers to claim they did not have enough time to prepare, helping the company secretary get papers on time to the board. However, given the much higher standards expected of directors since 2000, I do wonder whether four or six board meetings a year of two to three hours duration is still appropriate.

> Ten years ago, the definition of a good audit committee meeting was that it was short and had no surprises. The main focus was on hammering the auditor on fees and was relatively non-substantive. But now we're far more engaged, which has also led to higher expectations of our performance.[i]

If directors are now expected to "trust, but verify," can it really be done properly by reviewing twenty or so board papers for ten minutes each of discussion? In the case of Enron, the audit committee did meet regularly, but appear to have only spent 90 minutes reviewing a whole host of complex matters requiring in depth discussion, as they were flagged to the audit committee by Arthur Andersen for being high risk accounting treatments. They did so without understanding what they were agreeing to, in part because these treatments were new; in part because they were highly complex; and in part because the members of the committee did not devote enough time to ask probing questions because they were reassured by Arthur Andersen's apparent sign-off:

> When confronted by evidence of Enron's high risk accounting, all of the Board members interviewed by the Subcommittee pointed out that Enron's auditor, Andersen, had given the company a clean audit opinion each year. None recalled any occasion on which Andersen had expressed any objection to a particular transaction or accounting practice at Enron, despite evidence indicating that, internally at Andersen, concerns about Enron's accounting were commonplace. But *a failure by Andersen to object does not preclude a finding that the Enron Board, with Andersen's concurrence, knowingly allowed Enron to use high risk accounting and failed in its fiduciary duty to ensure the company engaged in responsible financial reporting.*[ii] [Emphasis mine]

Measures Matter

There are three sorts of boards: those who know the score and know they are winning, those who know the score and know they are losing, and those who do not know the score.

The simple act of measuring performance makes a difference because it provides feedback to the person being measured, known as the "Hawthorn effect."[2] How that feedback is created will affect whether the measurement process achieves the intended outcome or distorts behavior. It is important to think carefully why the measure is needed in the first place and whether it will distort behavior, leading to unintended results.

Unfortunately, companies also distort results to meet their annual budgets and satisfy the expectations of analysts. Directors need to remember the financial year-end is an accounting fiction. Customers still do business after the year-end: repeat business flows from one financial year into another; service contracts are multiyear annuity streams of income over the lifetime of the contracts.

Directors must remember if CEOs are rewarded too generously through stock options (as they are in the United States) whose value is the critical determinant of their remuneration, they will try to raise the share price and keep it high and massage the numbers when they do quarterly and yearend financial reporting. As long as CEOs and auditors respect the spirit as well as letter of financial reporting (the responsibility of the audit committee), this approach to remuneration is supposed to align the interests of management and shareholders. However, once CEOs find they can get away with creative accounting, aided and abetted by complaisant auditors and investment bankers, this focus on keeping the share price as high as possible no longer aligns behavior with the real interests of shareholders, witnessed by major accounting scandals this century, such as Enron,[iii] WorldCom,[iv] Xerox,[v] Qwest,[vi] in the United States, and Carillion[vii] in the United Kingdom.

So, if right behavior follows the adoption of correct metrics, what are the correct metrics? There are the quantifiable "hard" metrics and the much harder to quantify "soft" metrics that make the difference between success and failure. Financial failure is swift and unforgiving. Failure to do business in the right way, measured by the

---

[2] "Two groups of workers in [Western Electric's] Hawthorne factory were used as guinea pigs. One day the lighting in the work area for one group was improved dramatically while the other group's lighting remained unchanged. The researchers were surprised to find that the productivity of the more highly illuminated workers increased much more than that of the control group.

The employees' working conditions were changed in other ways too (their working hours, rest breaks and so on), and in all cases their productivity improved when a change was made. Indeed, their productivity even improved when the lights were dimmed again. By the time everything had been returned to the way it was before the changes had begun, productivity at the factory was at its highest level. Absenteeism had plummeted.

The experimenters concluded that it was not the changes in physical conditions that were affecting the workers' productivity. Rather, it was the fact that someone was actually concerned about their workplace, and the opportunities this gave them to discuss changes before they took place." "The Hawthorne Effect," *The Economist*, November 3, 2008, https://www.economist.com/news/2008/11/03/the-hawthorne-effect

"soft" metrics, will also end in disaster, but the collapse of the business will take much longer. So, we need both, recognizing:

> *Financial metrics focus on the past:* Although they provide an accurate view of the firm's financial "skeleton," they track past performance monthly, quarterly and at yearend; and are time-bound.
>
> *Financial metrics do not normally include the voice of the customer* in the budgeting process; and they should, because customers continue to do business with the company across the quarterly and yearend accounting boundaries.
>
> *"Soft" metrics focus management's attention on the present and future*—on what still needs to be done to remain successful.

I now look at how we should measure financials; include the "voice of the customer" and measure the "soft" KPIs.

Financial Metrics

Effective directors must be financially literate to appreciate the advantages and drawbacks of the different ways of evaluating the financial performance of their organization. Perhaps the best way of looking at financial metrics is to separate them into measurements for assessing whether or not to invest; for assessing the effectiveness of operations; and for their effect on the balance sheet.

Metrics for Investment

The most important considerations when making investments are the risk involved and whether the income stream generated by the investment exceeds the cost of capital associated with the investment. There are several ways of doing this:

1. *Payback*: This traditional method has gone out of favor, though it has some merit. Payback measures the time needed to get back the money invested in a project. It is simple but does not recognize the time value of money—that is, a dollar tomorrow is worth less than a dollar today, in part because of inflation, but more important because of the opportunity costs of money. Yet, payback is a good "quick and dirty" assessor of risk inherent in the assumptions regarding the investment. The longer a project takes, the greater the risk the assumptions regarding both revenues and costs will prove to be wrong. Some companies therefore use the length of the payback period as a time limit to frame the project. For example, if the intended project takes more than ten years to pay back, the board will not invest, even though other metrics suggest the project makes sense, because the board remains concerned the assumptions the later phases of the project may not be robust enough.

2. *Internal rate of return* (IRR): This establishes the discount rate to yield a net present value (NPV) of zero. It can then be compared with another project's IRR and, in principle, the project with the highest IRR wins because it has the highest rate of return. However, the problem with this approach is that a small, unimportant project may have a higher rate of return than a much larger, more important one. If the board were to act on IRR alone, they run the risk of choosing the wrong project.
3. *NPV*: This starts by assuming a given rate of return, typically the risk-adjusted cost of capital relating to the project being proposed as the discount rate or hurdle rate to be applied to the estimated cash stream from the project. If the resulting NPV is greater than zero, the project is worth investing in; if less than zero, it is not. The advantage of this approach over using IRR is it focuses attention on the absolute size of the NPV and therefore its material importance to the organization.

There are two issues with NPV calculations: the first is the further out in time the revenue and cost assumptions are projected, the less likely they are to be correct; the second is whether the correct cost of capital is being used as the discount/hurdle rate. Regarding the first issue, the temptation to recalibrate revenues upwards and the costs downwards and to allocate an unrealistically high terminal value to the assets at the end of the project's life to achieve a positive NPV is very real. This is not to suggest managers are being dishonest or fraudulent, but just to recognize the impact of their emotional commitment to projects.

As far as using the correct cost of capital is concerned, what must be used is the risk-adjusted weighted average cost of capital (WACC)[3] relating to the project and its risk profile, rather than the WACC of the organization. If the WACC is used without being risk-adjusted, then the board risks cross-subsidizing very risky projects by using too low a hurdle rate and of penalizing less risky projects by requiring too high a rate.

Metrics for Ongoing Operations

Ongoing businesses use two financial sets of measures to track the health of their operations: the income statement (P&L) resulting from their transactions and the balance sheet that shows their assets and liabilities and changes in them. Most

---

[3] "The WACC is a calculation of a firm's cost of capital in which each category of capital is proportionately weighted. All sources of capital, including common stock, preferred stocks and bonds and any other long-term debt. A firm's WACC increases as the beta and rate of return on equity increase, because an increase in the WACC denotes a decrease in valuation and an increase in risk.

WACC=E/V x Re + D/V x Rd x (1–Tc), where Re = cost of equity; Rd =cost of debt; E = market value of equity; D = market value of debt; V = E + D = total market value of firm's financing (equity + debt); E/V = percent of finance in equity; D/V = percent of finance in debt; Tc =corporate tax rate," Investopedia, "Weighted Average Cost of Capital (WACC)," https://www.investopedia.com/terms/w/wacc.asp, accessed on July 18, 2018.

people are very comfortable looking at the income statement to see how the business is doing, but many are less so when it comes to seeing how the balance sheet relates to everyday operations. The balance sheet matters because without assets and liabilities there can be no transactions. Companies must have fixed assets, cash, and working capital to do business.

Transactions take place every day, so some companies have become very sophisticated, measuring their revenues and margins and where they earn them on a daily basis, by geography, type of business, type of account and pack size.

The reason why it is harder to relate the balance sheet to everyday transactions is accounting systems find it more difficult to track changes in working capital on a daily basis and almost impossible to do this by client. As a result, CEOs often focus their board reports on revenue, margin and profit rather than what is happening to the capital intensity of the business, which is the best measure of effective resource allocation. This is reinforced by the way CEOs are remunerated with often an excessive emphasis on returns on equity—that is, on reported profits. Yet, the surprising fact is profits are only an accounting convention—they can be massaged depending on different approaches to depreciation and to recognizing income and expensing of costs. This can not be done to cash.

Directors should remember the only real thing in the financials is cash and focus their attention on what is happening to cash. Bills and salaries are paid in cash, not profits; as anybody who has ever studied what happens to profitable companies that overtrade and go bankrupt will know. *Every major fraud happened because of discrepancies between cash—the reality; and declared profits—the fraud.*

Rather than keeping the income statement and the balance sheet separate, as is normal accounting practice, I believe there is a better way of reporting both sets of financials to boards; to combine them using a modification of DuPont's return on net assets (RONA) "tree," first used in 1912.[viii]

The "tree" I propose is one designed to focus the attention of directors on the effective use of *average business assets—the assets used directly to do business*. The reason for doing this rather than sticking with the RONA tree is that sometimes a company's net assets reflect investments in fixed assets such as properties or financial assets that have nothing to do directly with daily business and how it is done.[4] The reason for suggesting *average* business assets is to avoid the temptation of window dressing at the end of each quarter or financial yearend to artificially make the numbers look better than they are, only to return to less good numbers after the audit closes.

---

4 For example, the UK's GEC had mountains of cash under Lord Weinstock before it became Marconi. Retailers may own a large property portfolio that could be sold and leased back. If companies hold cash or near equivalents as a hedge against a rainy day, they often become targets for asset strippers who can break up the business and use the cash to offset the cost of acquisition in order to "realize the value in unproductive assets."

Figure 9.3 shows the combined income statement and balance sheet in one "tree." The unshaded cells represent the elements of the income statement, whereas shaded cells represent the elements of the balance sheet, as follows:

1. Gross revenue is shown at the top on the right, attached to its two component elements—units sold times unit list price. Both are shown because a change in gross revenue can be caused by a change in the list price, or in the number of units sold, or as a result of change in the mix of business, or some combination of all these. Since each different combination needs a different corrective action to get back on track, it is important to show what is happening to the component parts.

2. Net revenue shows the actual amount paid to the firm, as a result of the different discounts the company has given to achieve its unit sales. By showing the different types of discount offered, the board can see whether there is price resistance or whether the discounts are part of increasing sales designed to hit higher targets.

   Net revenue is the denominator used in all calculations for tracking the profitability of the business. Discounts are tracked as a percent of net revenue, so are cost of goods, gross profit, commission (if any applies), gross profit after commission (GPAC), overheads, and finally, EBIT.

   Net revenue is also used as the denominator in all calculations for assessing asset intensity—that is, how efficiently the resources are used. Total assets are tracked as a percent of net revenue;[5] so are its component parts: fixed business assets, cash, debtors, stock, and creditors.

   Fixed business assets include plant, equipment and machinery to create products as well fixtures and fittings in factories, warehouses and offices and the buildings themselves, if they contribute to daily activities, as opposed to passive investments. Vehicles are included, if owned; excluded if leased—the leasing costs go into the income statement.

   Cash is included even though it is the difference between working capital assets and liabilities plus any loans. Although cash by itself does not create business since credit can take its place, cash should be viewed as a safety margin should debtors fail to pay on time, inventory be unsold and creditors demand payment. A company with no cash reserves is dangerously exposed in the event of a liquidity crunch.

   Debtors are a serious policy issue for the board to consider as part of its risk management. The decision to grant credit and the credit limits are often taken

---

[5] A lower percentage reflects a lower asset intensity and a more efficient use of funds: a higher percentage reflects a higher asset intensity and a less efficient use of funds. For example, if the total assets are 10% of net revenue, this means they generate ten times their value in a year. An increase in the percentage to 20%, would indicate increased asset intensity, because the total assets can only generate five times their value in a year; a decrease in the percentage to 5%, means they can generate twenty times their value in a year.

without giving sufficient thought to the impact on the company's working capital cash-cash cycle. This affects the company's ability to grow and/or undercut its competitors, shown by the rise of Dell, discussed in Chapter 8.

It is ironic positive working capital is regarded as a strength on the balance sheet because debtors and inventory (assets) are greater than creditors (liabilities), when it can cause a company to go bankrupt or become ever more beholden to banks. The faster a company grows if it has positive working capital, the more it consumes cash and ends up working for its banks rather than the shareholders. However, if the company has negative working capital, that is, the balance sheet shows creditors (liabilities) exceeding debtors plus inventory (assets), the faster it grows, the more cash it generates, the less it depends on banks and the more money it must invest or for the shareholders.

Debtors are only assets if they are paid promptly. Keeping debtors for a long time may reflect agreed credit terms or else their inability to pay on time. This creates the risk of default at which point they become a painful liability. This explains in part why so many telco suppliers lost money during the 2000 dotcom boom, where leading companies offered customers vendor finance to allow them to buy product in the boom years. Once the boom was over, the vendor finance crystalized into losses going straight to the bottom line.

Inventory (stock) is also treated as an asset, until it can not be sold. Obsolete inventory has to be cleared at deep discounts, damaging the brand; and sales forces are encouraged to stuff the channels with product their distributors do not really want. In hi-tech, obsolete stock has almost no value, so the hit is even greater. A natural response to this risk is to outsource the holding of inventory to suppliers. However, the experience of the telco's and telco suppliers in 2001 is a salutary lesson in the costs of losing control of inventory in the supply chain:

> OEMs and CEMs[6] run their businesses with different sets of goals and different methods for achieving them. OEMs, with more comfortable margins, focus on early penetration and rapid market share growth to generate profits. CEMs, operating with razor-thin profit margins, need to maintain an aggressive focus on cost... OEMs, to achieve their goals, need flexibility—the kind of agility that allows them to divert resources to a given product as it becomes a hit. CEMs, on the other hand, need predictability—they want to make commitments in advance to reap benefits like big-lot purchases and decreased overtime. The OEMs' tactics, therefore, keep them from making the firm commitments the CEMs need to keep their costs down. Indeed, *when OEMs begin to engage in the sort of longer-term commitments that CEMs need, their flexibility is reduced almost immediately. When times go bad, their different techniques for fixing problems are incompatible.*[ix] [Emphasis mine]

---

6 OEM = original equipment manufacturer; CEM = contract equipment manufacturer.

Creditors are an area where the accountants will always argue they should be paid as late as possible to improve working capital. Governments and large companies do this to small suppliers. It is a naked power play of the kind identified in the "five forces" framework. However, it does strain the goodwill of suppliers and this may mean at a later date when their goodwill is needed, it is not forthcoming. Additionally, if credit terms are too attractive, the company may take excess inventory and regret it later, if it becomes obsolete.

Figure 9.2 shows the income statement and balance sheet with all the items discussed above.

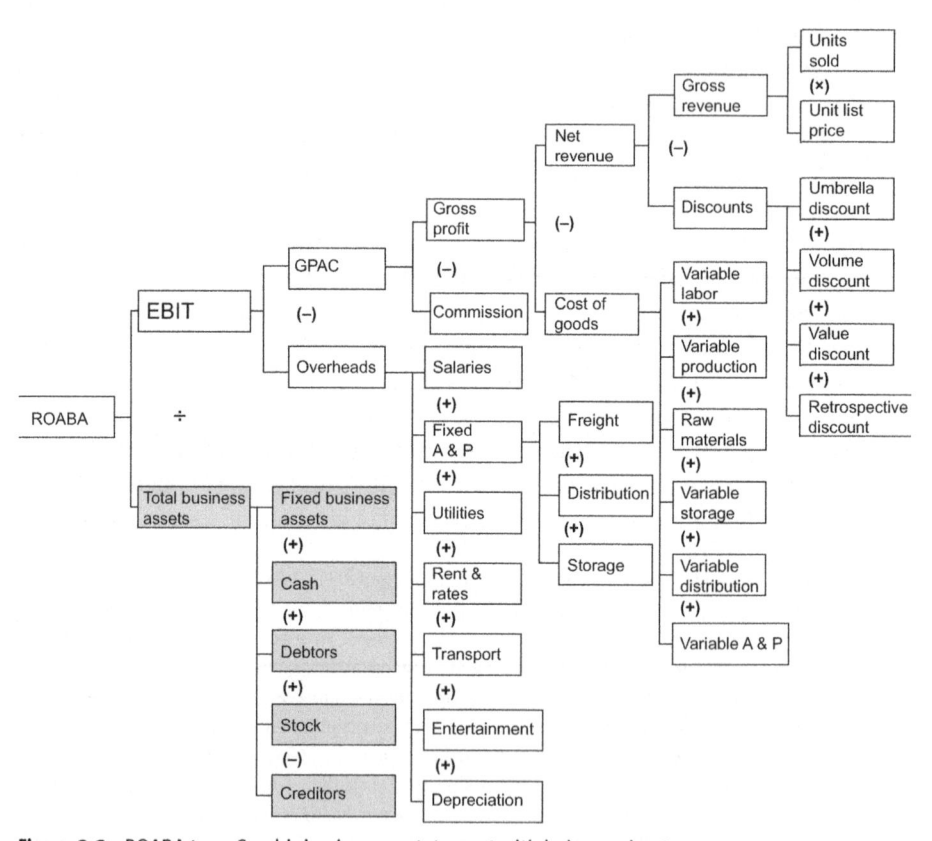

Figure 9.2: ROABA tree: Combining income statement with balance sheet

The best way to use the return on average business assets (ROABA) "tree" is to track changes in each cell dynamically as a percentage of net revenue. This is done by tracking actuals against budget by quarter. The advantage of using a tree like this is it becomes immediately obvious which numbers are material and which variances against budget are both large and material. The best benefit of the tree is directors can see at a glance how the balance sheet and the income statement connect. Variations on ROABA can be used such as: ROE (Return on Equity) where the total business assets are split into those funded by debt and those funded by equity shown in their respective shaded cells; or RONA (Return on Net Assets) where the nonbusiness assets are added in an extra cell; or ROCE (Return on Capital Employed) where the total of debt and equity are added to the balance sheet shaded cells.[7]

Financial objectives vary depending on the three "lifestages" of the company or its business units: growth, maturity, or harvesting. For each of these there are three financial foci driving the strategy: revenue growth and mix, cost reduction and productivity improvement, and asset utilization and investment. Table 9.1 shows how these themes fit with business unit strategies.

Table 9.1: Financial themes by business unit strategy[x]

Business unit lifestage strategy	Growing revenue, changing mix	Reducing cost, improving productivity
Growth	1. Grow sales by segment 2. Increase percent revenue from new product or service and new customers	1. Increase revenue per employee 2. Aim for economies of scale and scope 3. Control fixed cost growth as revenues grow
Maturity	1. Maintain market share of targeted product market, key accounts and customers 2. Track customer and product line profitability (using activity-based costing) 3. Eliminate cross-subsidies 4. Maintain targeted percentage of net revenue from new products	1. Capture economies of scale and scope 2. Benchmark cost against competition 3. Aim for continuous cost improvement, setting cost reduction targets, without risking quality or safety 4. Optimize indirect costs as percent of net revenue
Decline/harvesting	1. Focus on maximizing customer and product line profitability, using activity-based costing 2. Prune unprofitable products and customers 3. Eliminate cross-subsidies	1. Focus on cost reduction per unit of output 2. Focus on reducing transaction costs 3. Cut overheads 4. Do not put quality or safety at risk

---

[7] One caveat should be mentioned. When assets are revalued upwards or downwards, it distorts the percentage relationship to net revenue; and management and the board need to take this possibility into account when there appears to be an unexplained jump or fall in asset intensity.

Including the "Voice of the Customer"

The "voice of the customer" begins with market share. Market share needs first to be disaggregated into its component parts: geography (national, regional, local, rural urban); trade class; customer size and type; customer brand usage ("never," "hardly ever," "sometimes," "often," "always").

It is important to define which of four market segment archetypes the company is choosing to target. Although there are five ways of splitting a market according to pricing: these can be simplified into four segments. The five ways of pricing are:
1. *Bespoke:* clients pay "whatever it takes" to design a unique solution for their needs to get ahead and stay ahead
2. *Luxury/prestige:* customers pay exclusive prices for superior quality and "bragging rights"
3. *Premium:* customers pay for quality and brand name reassurance
4. *Value for money:* customers pay based on calculations of price-performance, including estimating lifetime costs of ownership
5. *Affordable:* customers are constrained by budgets regarding what they can pay for acceptable performance

Segments 2 and 3 can be merged into one, creating the four segment archetypes shown in Figure 9.3, which are explained in detail in the following paragraphs.

Impact of Maslow's hierarchy of needs:
Four segments created by customers' rational (Know/Don't Know) and emotional (Care/Don't Care) product evaluation

Impact on the offer:
Four different offers, each with their own business model and different pricing strategies, needed to satisfy customers in each segment

	Know	Don't Know
Care	Segment 1: 'Self-actualizers' • Innovators • Control of own destiny • Buyer interested in the specification	Segment 2/3: 'Belongers' • Popularity and opinion of other people matter • Buyers not interested in specification
Don't Care	Segment 4: 'Safety seekers' • "What have you done for me today?" • Experienced buyer interested in specification	Segment 5 'Survivors' • Financially constrained • Indifferent, uninvolved • Easy decisions

	Know	Don't Know
Care	Segment 1 Bespoke solution • 'Pay whatever it takes' • Breakthrough technology to solve unique needs • Partnership with client	Segment 2/3 Generic bundled solutions • Prestige/Premium pricing • Quality essential • Technology follower
Don't Care	Segment 4 Value engineering • Value for money • Unbundled component approach to systems • Range extensions	Segment 5 Undifferentiated product • Sold on price • Acceptable quality • Easy availability

Figure 9.3: Four segment archetypes based on Maslow's hierarchy of needs

Figure 9.3 shows how Maslow's hierarchy of needs creates four segments, each with their own characteristics in terms of what drives them when they buy.

Segment 1: The buying process is both rational and emotional because customers in this segment seek to do things differently to be in control of their destinies, so they are driven by what ownership both does for them and says about them. As a result, the offer is a bespoke solution, designed in partnership selling mode to solve unique needs, recognizing the client will pay "whatever it takes" to get ahead and stay ahead.

Segment 2: Customers or clients in this segment are driven primarily by emotional considerations, so they are not really interested in how the product or service is made. What matters to them are either "bragging rights" offered by owning a luxury product (Hermes, Chanel, etc.) or brand name reassurance of quality if it is a premium product (BMW or Mercedes). As a result, the offer is often a generic bundled solution relying on the brand name; for example, for smartphones and accessories (Apple) or hi-fi (Bose, Bang & Olufsen).

Segment 3: These buyers are primarily interested in rational assessment of what the product or service has to offer. Emotions hardly come into the decision. Such people are typically experienced, frequent buyers of the product or service (often professional business buyers) who will look at the lifetime costs of ownership, including trade-in value when they look to replace the product. They do not need brand name reassurance because they know enough about the specifications to assess whether the offer represents good value for money. As a result, they look for range extensions and are willing to create their own bundled solutions from more than one supplier, rather than relying on one supplier's bundled products.

Segment 4: Buyers in this segment look at price only. They have little emotional or rational interest in what the product does other than that it should be affordable, easily available and of an acceptable quality. As a result, the offer must focus on price, adequate quality and maximum distribution to make it as easy as possible for the customer to buy.

Once the company has decided which segment it serves and has adopted the appropriate business model to serve it well, directors should resist the temptation to stray into another segment looking to expand the franchise because the business models are different and their associated cultures and cost structures are difficult to integrate into one organization: This is demonstrated by the difficulty full service airlines faced when attempting to compete with low cost carriers everywhere in the world. Nevertheless, having committed the company to a given segment, what matters is the market share it commands in its segment of choice.

However, looking at market share by itself misses the fact it is an outcome of four factors: relative penetration, relative frequency of purchase, relative volume purchased and relative value purchased.

Penetration
This is defined as the proportion of those people interested in the category buying the brand. It recognizes not all people are interested in the category and of those who are

interested in the category, not all are interested in buying the brand. When defining market share, it is the relationship between the category penetration and the brand penetration that matters—the percentage of those who are interested in the category who buy the brand.

Frequency of Purchase

This measures the number of times in a period the brand is purchased by those who are interested in buying the brand. This is then compared with the frequency of purchase of those who are interested in buying the category to establish the relative popularity of the brand—in a sense the number of times buyers vote for the brand by buying it, compared with the number of times the targeted population votes by buying products belonging to the category. The relative differences could be a function of different usage levels; they could also be the result of different pack sizes and special offers leading people to buy more at one time but less often than the population as a whole.

Volume Purchased

This measures the amount buyers of the brand buy each time they make a purchase and compares it with the amount other people who are interested in the category buy when they make their purchase. The relative differences could be a function of usage, pack sizes, or special offers.

Value Purchased

This measures the amount buyers of the brand pay when they make a purchase and compares it with the amount other people who are interested in the category pay when they make a purchase. The relative difference could be a function of the price positioning of the products being compared; special offers or differences in volumes purchased.

These four factors, combined, determine the health and strength of the brand. Appendix 9.1 compares four brands, each with 20% market share, showing how the first three of the four factors lead to each brand reaching 20% share of volume, but with very different profiles, requiring different strategies as a result.

Voice of the Customer

Traditional accounting does not take the "voice of the customer" or the lifetime value a customer brings to a company into account. For a company to achieve long-term success, it must create sustainably profitable customer relationships. To do this, it must go much further than merely measuring customer satisfaction, though it is a start. Appendix 9.2 shows the four factors impacting customer satisfaction: account development and the customer acquisition process, quality of operations, after sales service, and so-called moments of truth when dealing with the organization. More important than customer satisfaction, the company must track the cost of acquiring and of retaining a customer by channel; the profitability of a customer through his or her lifetime; and the loyalty of that customer.

Directors do not always appreciate the way customers can affect the profitability drivers of the business. There is an unfair asymmetry between the impact satisfied and dissatisfied customers have on the business: satisfied customers only tell three to five other people, whereas dissatisfied customers will complain to thirteen other people. Acquiring a new customer can cost ten times more than selling additional items to a customer the company retains.

The effort and cost of selling to a customer is a function of the odds of getting a sale. With an existing customer, the odds are 50%; with a lapsed customer 10–15%; and with a new customer 5–10%. A 5% increase in customer retention can improve profits by more than 60%. Over time, the frequency of purchase by the retained customer rises, as does the value of those purchases.[xi] This is why retailers, credit card companies, and airlines spend so much time and ingenuity on loyalty programs and financial institutions focus on maximizing customer "stickiness."

Perhaps the most important metric not recorded by the finance function is customer lifetime value (CLV).[xii] This considers the potential lifetime of margin customers can generate for the company after allowing for estimated attrition. This yields the retention rate; and allowance then needs to be made for the cost of acquisition. Once this is done, the expected income stream over the estimated lifetime of the customer is discounted to get its NPV. This allows management to calculate the cost of losing customers when they defect. Appendix 9.3 shows how to calculate CLV. However, it should be noted it is essential to use activity-based costing (ABC) to be able to do this accurately.

Soft Metrics and KPIs

These must be divided into KPIs promoting innovation; those measuring process quality of operations; and employee satisfaction, retention and productivity.

Innovation
The key measures for innovation are:
1. Targeted percentage of revenue derived from new products that did not exist three years earlier (used by 3M)
2. Targeted percentage of revenue derived from proprietary products to measure the commercialization of IP

3. Comparing rate of introduction of new products against competition and against plan
4. Time needed to develop new products, and more important, to get them to market
5. Time needed to reach breakeven (HP's BET measure[xiii]). The merit of this measure is it focuses on time, cost and profitability—all key measures of effective innovation

Process Quality Measures
These refer primarily to process quality initiatives and track:
1. Manufacturing cycle effectiveness that measures throughput time: the sum of processing; inspection; movement and storage time taken; from when a customer order is received; scheduled for production; appropriate raw materials ordered and received; production initiated and completed; and the order is shipped and received by the customer[xiv]
2. Process parts per million defect rates (Motorola's and GE's Six Σ being the most famous example)
3. Yields
4. Waste and scrap
5. Reworking—number of items and time taken
6. Returns
7. Percent of processes under statistical process control
8. Waiting times for customers
9. Inaccurate information provided to customers
10. Access denied to customers[xv]

Employee Satisfaction, Retention, and Productivity
Employee morale is important, and even more so, in service businesses where often the least well paid and lowest skill employees interface the most with customers. Employee satisfaction surveys are an important tool to guide the board regarding the ability of the organization to do what it needs with its people to achieve alignment with its mission and vision. Typical elements in an employee satisfaction survey are:
1. How involved do they feel they are in decision making?
2. Are they recognized for doing a good job well?
3. Do they have access to all the information they need to do their job well?
4. Are they actively encouraged to be creative and show initiative?
5. Do they get proper support from staff functions?
6. Would they recommend the company to their friends?

Employee retention is critical provided the right employees are being retained. Long-term loyal employees carry the values of the organization; understand how things are done and should be good at anticipating customer needs because of their experience. The normal measure of retention is staff turnover as a percentage of total headcount.

As far as productivity per employee is concerned, the key measures are revenue; gross and net margin per capita; and the more complex value added per capita. However, these particular measures can be abused to achieve short-term but unsustainable long-term gains.

Using "Five Ps" to Crosscheck

Directors have a huge number of questions they could ask management when setting strategy (covered in Chapter 8) and reviewing the effectiveness of strategy, covered in this chapter. The "Five P" framework can be used as an effective way to group them under the headings of "purpose," "principles," "power," "people," and "processes," using a calendarized approach to discuss the issues under each of these headings. For example, "purpose," "principles," and "power" could be used as a framework for discussion when setting the annual budget and again at mid-year review to check what is being proposed does not deviate from what has been agreed under these three headings. "Processes" could be used as a framework for reviewing risk management, succession planning, remuneration, internal controls, and systems discussions, as well as how to improve productivity and asset utilization. "People" and "power" for discussing talent management and organization design to ensure the organization can still achieve its mission and vision. Finally, "purpose" is essential when considering stakeholder engagement.

Conclusion

The board must have an effective strategy review process consisting of five steps: reviewing the environmental analysis and its assumptions, being prepared to revisit the mission and vision if needed, revisiting the relevance of the agreed organizational design, challenging and reviewing the strategic assumptions, and then monitoring agreed execution on a continuous basis.

As far as the financials are concerned, the board has tools to assess the value of investments: payback, IRR, and NPV using the appropriate risk-adjusted WACC as the discount or hurdle rate. Each of these tools has advantages and drawbacks: payback is simple but ignores the time value of money; IRR does not consider the materiality of the project when used for comparison purposes; NPV can be fudged by assuming optimistic revenues; conservative costs and too high a terminal value.

From an operational perspective the board must look at both the income statement and the balance sheet, remembering the critical importance of the working capital cash-cash cycle. Positive working capital appears on the balance sheet as an asset, but the faster the organization grows, the more cash it consumes to finance the positive working capital— making it beholden to the banks or else going bust if it overtrades. Negative working capital appears as a liability on the balance sheet, but by throwing off cash, it allows the organization to grow. Directors often find it difficult to connect the balance sheet to the income statement and the ROABA tree is proposed as a good way of doing this.

The appropriate financial focus depends on three business unit lifestages: growth, maturity, and decline. Directors also need to remember traditional financials ignore the "voice of the customer" and the elements affecting the "voice of the customer" need to be tracked as well as the financials to evaluate the effectiveness of strategy execution.

Each of the four customer segment archetypes have distinct characteristics affecting the business models and cost structures suited to serving them. Therefore, directors should not be tempted to stray from one into another in the search for additional market share. Market share matters, as does how it is achieved; and so does CLV. Finally, there are the soft metrics and KPIs to be considered as they affect innovation, process quality, and employee satisfaction.

A useful way of reviewing these issues is the "Five P" framework.

Appendix 9.1: Four Brands' Volume Market Shares Compared

1. Relative penetration as percent of population:
    a. Category = 50%
    b. Brand A = 50% = 50/50 = 1 times the target population
    c. Brand B = 10% = 10/50 = 0.2 times target population
    d. Brand C = 20% = 20/50 = 0.4 times target population
    e. Brand D = 25% = 25/50 = 0.5 target population
2. Relative frequency of purchase per year:
    a. Category = 10 = 100% of the target population frequency
    b. Brand A = 2 = 2/10 = 0.2 times target frequency
    c. Brand B = 40 = 40/10 = 4.0 times target frequency
    d. Brand C = 2 = 2/10 = 0.2 times frequency
    e. Brand D = 10 = 10/10 = 1.0 times frequency
3. Relative units purchased at each purchase occasion:
    a. Category = 1 = 100% of the target population volume
    b. Brand A = 1 = 1/1 = 1 times the target volume
    c. Brand B = 25 = 25/10 = 2.5 times target frequency
    d. Brand C = 20 = 20/10 = 2 times target frequency
    e. Brand D = 10 = 10/10 = target frequency

Calculating Market Share

Market share = P x F x V as a percentage:
where P = relative penetration; F = relative frequency of purchase; V = relative volume purchased at each purchase occasion.

Below are four brands, each with 20% market share. However, how that share is achieved and what the brand owners need to do to improve their brand positions are quite different:

1. Brand A is bought by 100% of the people interested in the category but only 20% of the time and purchasers buy one unit in line with the category as a whole. The problem with brand A is that it has very low loyalty; people try it but do not seem to want to come back to it. Brand A's owner must work on improving the brand's attributes to increase frequency of purchase.
2. Brand B is bought by only 20% of the people who are interested in the category. Loyalty seems high since they buy four times more often than the rest of the target market, but they only buy 25% of the volume when they buy. This suggests these people may be budget constrained and are buying small pack sizes because they can not afford to buy larger ones. Brand B's owner must work on increasing trial amongst non-users interested in the category and think about how to get existing buyers to buy more each time they buy.
3. Brand C is only bought by 40% of the people interested in the category. They buy only 20% of the time the others do, but they buy 2.5 times more each time they buy. Here the owner of brand C needs to think about getting buyers to buy more often, perhaps through loyalty programs.
4. Brand D is only bought by 50% of the people who are interested in the category who buy in line with the category as whole, but only buy 40% of the volume when they buy. The owner of brand D needs to work on getting the buyers to buy more each time they buy, perhaps through special offers.

Brand	Times category penetration (P)	Times category frequency (F)	Times category volume (V)	Market share = P x F x V as %
Brand A	1.0	0.2	1	1.0 x 0.2 x 1.00 = 0.2 = 20%
Brand B	0.2	4.0	0.25	0.2 x 4.0 x 0.25 = 0.2 = 20%
Brand C	0.4	0.2	2.5	0.4 x 0.2 x 2.50 = 0.2 = 20%
Brand D	0.5	1.0	0.4	0.5 x 1.0 x 0.40 = 0.2 = 20%

Appendix 9.2: Measuring Customer Satisfaction

There are four factors impacting customer satisfaction: account development and the customer acquisition process, quality of operations, after sales service, and so-called "moments of truth" when dealing with the organization as a whole:

1. *Account development and management relationship audit:*
    a. Quality of salesmanship and attitude of sales people
    b. Continuity of representation
    c. Understanding of customer needs
    d. Quality of recommendations
    e. Trust
2. *Operations:*
    a. Order turnaround times
    b. Order fulfilment (back order, partial deliveries)
    c. On-time delivery
    d. Professionalism and attitude of delivery personnel
    e. Easy to use, quality product documentation
3. *After sales:*
    a. Invoice accuracy and timeliness
    b. Lifetime costs of ownership
    c. Warranties and defective performance tracking
    d. Product reliability, for example:
        i. Number of faults/units
        ii. Miles between services for vehicles
        iii. Washes between calls for washing machines/dishwashers
        iv. Copies between breakdowns for copiers
        v. Dropped calls and coverage for mobile phones
    e. Product serviceability, for example:
        i. Mean time to repair
        ii. Mean time between call outs
        iii. Number of calls to connect and time taken to connect for ISPs
    f. Attitude of engineers on call
    g. Attitude of service department on the phone
    h. Time taken to answer call
    i. Time spent on call
    j. Percentage of "first pass" calls
    k. Telephone skills
4. *"Moments of truth":*
    a. Quality and ease of use of documentation
    b. Speed of negotiation and settlement in claims handing and settlement
    c. Accuracy in invoicing
    d. Ease in doing business:

i. Complaints handling procedures and access to senior management
ii. Credit limits
iii. Payment terms
iv. Returns policy
v. Flexible order placement
vi. Cancellation clauses
vii. Delivery time windows
viii. Speed of delivery
ix. Condition of premises and infrastructure

Appendix 9.3: Calculating Customer Lifetime Value

Four equations are needed to calculate value of the individual acquired customer:
1. *Customer lifetime margin:*
   $M = \Sigma_t m/(1+i)^t$, where t = time, m = annual margin, i = interest
2. *Retained customer margin:*
   $R = \Sigma_t mr^t/(1+i)t$, where t = time, m = annual margin, r = annual retention rate, i = interest
3. *Value of acquired customers:*
   $V = n\Sigma_t mr^t/(1+i)t - a$, where n = number of customers, t = time, m = annual margin, r = annual retention rate, i = interest, a = acquisition costs
4. *Value of individual acquired customer:*
   $V = (n\Sigma_t mr^t/(1+i)^t - a)/n$, where n=number of customers, t=time, m=annual margin, r=annual retention rate, i=interest, a=acquisition costs

Example of calculation of value of individual acquired customer
1. The value of 1,000 customers with an average margin (m) of $ 100
2. Acquired as a cohort at a cost (a) of $ 8,000
3. With a 70% retention rate (r)
4. Discount rate of 10% (i)
5. Over three years is:

Year 1 = 1,000 x (100x0.7¹)/1.1¹ = 63,636
Year 2 = 1,000 x (100x0.7²)/1.1² = 40,500
Year 3 = 1,000 x (100x0.7³)/1.1³ = 25,770
                                      Total = 129,906
Less acquisition cost   8,000
COHORT VALUE   121,906
Divided by original number of customers (1,000)
CUSTOMER LIFETIME VALUE = 121.91

References

i Tapestry Networks Inc. (2007), "Four Lessons for Audit Committees from High-Profile Accounting Scandals," *Viewpoints from the Audit Committee Leadership Summit*, Issue 2, April 6, 2007, http://www.tapestrynetworks.com/documents/Tapestry_EY_Summit_View2_Apr07.PDF, accessed on July 17, 2018.

ii Permanent Subcommittee On Investigations Of The Committee On Governmental Affairs, United States Senate (2002), *The Role of the Board of Directors in Enron's Collapse*, 22–23, file:///D:/BGAB%20Enron%20Congressional%20Report.pdf, accessed on July 17, 2018.

iii Segal, T. (2017), "Enron Scandal: The Fall of a Wall Street Darling," *Investopedia*, September 20, 2018, https://www.investopedia.com/updates/enron-scandal-summary/, accessed on November 25, 2018.

iv Breeden, R. (2003), "Restoring Trust: Report to the Hon. Jed S Rakoff, The United States District Court of New York on Corporate Governance for the Future of MCI," *SEC*, August 2003, https://www.sec.gov/spotlight/worldcom/wcomreport0803.pdf, accessed on November 25, 2018.

v Pratley, N. and Treanor, J. (2002), "Xerox in $2bn Scandal," *The Guardian*, June 29, 2002, https://www.theguardian.com/business/2002/jun/29/, accessed on November 25, 2018.

vi SEC (2004), "SEC Charges Qwest Communications International Inc. with Multi-Faceted Accounting and Financial Reporting Fraud," October 21, 2004, https://www.sec.gov/news/press/2004-148.htm, accessed on November 25, 2018.

vii Hughes, S. (2018), "The Carillion Scandal Is Proof that Big Business Should Not Run Government Services," *Vice*, https://www.vice.com/en_uk/article/bjybmq/the-carillion-scandal-is-proof-that-big-business-should-not-run-government-services, accessed on November 25, 2018.

viii Phillips, M. (2015), "Beyond Teflon: The DuPont Invention that Forever Changed How Things Work in the Corporate World," *Quartz*, December 9, 2015, https://qz.com/569738/the-dupont-invention-that-forever-changed-how-things-work-in-the-corporate-world/, accessed on July 18, 2018.

ix Lakenan, B., Boyd, D., and Frey, E. (2001), "Why Cisco Fell: Outsourcing and its Perils," *Strategy + Business*, Third Quarter 2001, Issue 24, https://www.strategy-business.com/article/19984?gko=e4f2f, accessed on July 18, 2018.

x Based on Kaplan, R. S. and Norton, D. P. (1996), *Translating Strategy into Action: The Balanced Scorecard*, (Boston, MA: Harvard Business School Press), 52.

xi Wreden, N. (2005), *ProfitBrand* (London: Kogan Page).

xii Zinkin, J. (2007), "Budgeting to Reflect the Voice of the Customer," ACCA workshop, J.W. Marriott Hotel, Kuala Lumpur, February, 6, 2007.

xiii Kaplan and Norton (1996), op. cit., 103.

xiv Ibid., 116–117.

xv Ibid., 119–120.

Chapter 10
Managing Risk

This chapter is presented in six parts: the first discusses the role of the board, the second explores the "cultural" risks rarely discussed by boards, the third briefly reviews the strategic risks faced by companies, the fourth is a brief review of "traditional" risks boards must consider, the fifth discusses briefly the shared responsibility boards and management have regarding "earnings driver' risks,"[i] and the sixth concludes with using the "Five P" framework's "purpose" lens as a quick check everything material has been covered.

Role of the Board

When discussing the role of boards in managing risk, it is worth remembering boards are being asked to take informed and manageable risks; businesses must take risks if they are to make a profit. Directors need a real understanding of the drivers of risk; a fairly high level of technical understanding of the components of risks; and an ability to set the required risk appetite for the company overall, while at the same time ensuring it matches the risk appetite of the owners of the company. Finally, boards are accountable for ensuring there is a proper enterprise risk management process in place and that it really is being adhered to (this and the role of COSO are discussed in more detail in Chapter 12).

Perhaps it is helpful to define what is meant by risk:

> A probability or threat of a damage, injury, liability, loss, or other negative occurrence that is caused by external or internal vulnerabilities, and that may be neutralized through pre-emptive action.[ii]

> The probability of loss inherent in an organization's operations and environment (such as competition and adverse economic conditions) that may impair its ability to provide returns on investment. Business risk plus the financial risk arising from use of debt (borrowed capital and/or trade credit) equal total corporate risk.[iii]

> Risk is defined by ISO31000 as "the effect of uncertainty on objectives"[iv]

The UK CG Code states:

> The Board is responsible for determining the nature and extent of the principal risks it is willing to take in achieving its strategic objectives. The board should maintain sound risk management and internal controls systems.[v]

Not all boards have established a risk management committee (RMC) to do what is required, leaving it to the audit committee (AC) instead or failing to appoint a specific risk committee altogether, shown in Table 10.1.

Table 10.1: Incidence of board risk committees (%)[vi]

Country	Separate RMC	Risk dealt with by another committee	No specific risk committee
Australia	22	54	24
Brazil	26	18	56
China	30	18	52
Mexico	18	0	82
Netherlands	8	4	88
Singapore	42	10	48
UK	20	18	62
US	8	6	86

It is surprising how little attention appears to be given to dealing with risk specifically (with the exception of Australia), given the board's role is to:
1. Understand how the organization has implemented risk management processes
2. Ensure the risk discussion is built into strategic planning using SWOT and PESTLE, as well as considering systemic, key performance indicator (KPI), CEO and reputation risk and the impact on the risk profile when strategy changes and vice versa
3. Review and approve the enterprise risk management (ERM) policy and framework, risk criteria, and risk tolerances
4. Review and discuss the risk profiles, understanding how they have been derived, how far down the organization they have been workshopped, and how often reviewed
5. Ensure risks are evaluated as part of all major capex approvals and during implementing critical projects
6. Ensure the ERM process is robust and that the chief risk officer (CRO) and head of internal audit (IA) have the stature, skills, access, and resources to do their jobs effectively[vii]
7. Practice sound "insurance" principles when dealing with identified potential risks: namely eliminate them through effective risk-based preventive actions; failing that, mitigate them to reduce their impact; and if that is impossible, either "pay them off" through insurance or accept them and, in effect, self-insure, provided they are not catastrophic in nature
8. Ensure the agreed risk appetite matches the risk-reward expectations of investors and analysts

Still thinking about risk in general terms, boards have two options when allocating resources to reduce risks, illustrated in Table 10.2.

Table 10.2: Alternative ways of reducing risk[viii]

Project	Risk score for safety	Risk score for finance	Risk score for customers	Total risk score	Cost to implement	Cost of unit of risk reduction for dollars spent
A	7	2	3	12	$180,000	$15,000
B	3	8	6	17	$306,000	$18,000

It is up to the board to choose to either reduce the higher total risk score (B) or go with the most cost-effective option (A). When scoring, boards should consider key risk indicators and the possibility of "Black Swans" by thinking through pre-mortem disaster scenarios and what can be done to mitigate them, however unlikely. They should use risk mapping, measuring the magnitude of impact against probability of the event, as shown in Figure 10.1.

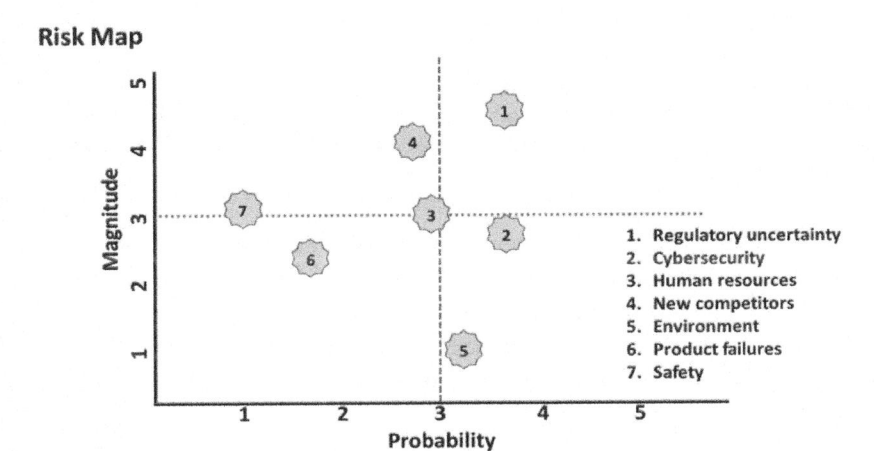

Risk Map

1. Regulatory uncertainty
2. Cybersecurity
3. Human resources
4. New competitors
5. Environment
6. Product failures
7. Safety

Figure 10.1: Risk map ranking of risks[ix]

Once this is done, the likely magnitude of the impact can be scored as follows:
    5 = Worst case   = Extended negative international press coverage
    4 = Major   = Extended negative national press coverage
    3 = Moderate   = Extended negative local press
    2 = Minor   = Letter of complaint from important person/government to chair
    1 = Insignificant = Complaint letter that can be expedited

In 2004, Booz Allen and Hamilton divided the risks faced by companies into three families: "traditional," "earnings driver," and "cultural" risks.[x] They found boards hardly considered "cultural" risks, focusing instead on "traditional" risks and working with management on "earnings driver" risks.

"Cultural" Risks

My reason for prioritizing culture and the risks it poses to strategy over "traditional" and "earnings driver" risks is Peter Drucker's alleged comment:

> Culture eats strategy for breakfast.[xi]

This statement has been accepted as critically important for effective execution of strategy by consultants and boards. However, it would seem that this acceptance is really more lip service than applied practice:

> *Despite culture being in the top three priorities for company boards, only 20% of 450 London-based directors and board members reported spending the time required to manage and improve it.*
>
> Some 62% of survey respondents felt that they were primarily responsible for setting culture from the top of an organisation.
>
> However, a similar proportion *(63%) either did not consider culture as part of their formal risk assessment or failed to routinely consider the risk associated with their corporate culture.*[xii] [Emphases mine]

This failure by directors in 2017 still to consider culture as a crucial risk is all the more extraordinary, given it was highlighted 13 years earlier in 2004[xiii] and features prominently in Warren Buffet's thinking about his success in running Berkshire Hathaway. Warren Buffett, time and again, emphasizes the importance of instilling the right culture to create wealth. His model of how to run his incredibly successful business at arms' length is based on a simple equation:

$$\text{Culture + Leadership + Trust = Wealth}^{\text{xiv}}$$

If this equation is correct, risks to wealth creation and preservation clearly come from the wrong type of culture; failures of leadership; and the erosion of trust. Three areas directors apparently do not spend enough time assessing, all of which come under the heading of "cultural" risks.

Maybe one of the reasons why so few boards report assessing "cultural" risks specifically, is they may already be addressing some of these risks without realizing it. So, what are the areas where "cultural" risks matter? Some are obviously defined as "cultural" and others are called by different names, though their impact affects the culture of the organization. It helps to define "culture":

> "Culture" is difficult to define, I think it's even more difficult to mandate—but for me *the evidence of culture is how people behave when no-one is watching.*[xv] [Emphasis mine]

It is ironic the definition of "culture" I like best is Bob Diamond's quote above, when he was CEO of Barclays; yet he was the person most responsible for the destruction of three hundred years of its Quaker culture and values during his tenure. "Cultural" risks are the result of:

Ethics Conflicts

These arise when the culture demands success regardless of how it is achieved; when senior management only want to hear good news and punish failure and rule in a climate of fear. In Chapter 3, I discussed how successful "imperial CEOs" who brooked no disagreement from management and were not challenged by their boards in three financial institutions led them into bankruptcy. Such CEOs are themselves a major source of risk (covered further in Chapter 11).

Similar conditions led Volkswagen (VW) to commit fraud with disastrous results not just for the company but also for the reputation of German automotive engineering. A study by Professor Lynch of the Darden School of Business[xvi] into what happened explains why:

1. *Simple, overambitious goals:* When Martin Winterkorn took over from Ferdinand Piëch as CEO in 2007, he set the goal to overtake Toyota to become the world's largest car manufacturer by selling 10 million cars a year. The justification for this ambition was it would help the German economy in the aftermath of the Global Financial Crisis. The U.S. market presented a great opportunity if VW could triple its sales there by introducing powerful diesel cars, with better CO_2 emissions performance than petrol engine cars and much greater fuel economy, replicating the success of diesel in Europe.

    VW had to meet the much more stringent U.S. emissions standards fast; and they had to do it on their own because Winterkorn did not want to use Daimler Benz's technology for neutralizing NO_x emissions.

2. *Autocratic, fear-based leadership:* Winterkorn was not interested in reasons why his objective could not be met. He and his predecessor Piëch had created a toxic but successful culture:

    > The company had known success under the autocratic leadership of Winterkorn and his mentor, Ferdinand Piëch, both of whom kept VW under tight control. The company's leadership set aggressive goals, and senior executives involved themselves in even minor deci-

sions. Former employees described a workplace in which subordinates were afraid to admit failure or contradict superiors. Company leaders bullied employees. Piëch bragged that he forced superior performance by "terrifying his engineers" and at times fired engineers or executives who displeased him.[xvii]

3. *The Fraud triad:* VW's engineers solved their problem by installing emissions device defeating software to pass the U.S. tests. This defeat software meant the emissions testing devices recorded thirty-five times less emissions in the regulatory laboratories than occurred when the cars were driven on roads. This cheating was discovered by accident in 2014 by a nongovernmental organization (NGO) interested in understanding why the cars seemed to perform so much better in the United States than in Europe.

   What VW's engineers did, was to prove disastrous for VW's reputation and the reputation of diesel cars not just in the United States but in Europe and Asia as well,[1] costing Winterkorn his job. Diesel's peak market share in Europe was 55.5% in 2011; by 2017 it had fallen to 43.7%.[xviii] Why did they do it? Three reasons:
   - Pressure:

     The pressure from the top was intense. VW's 25-page *Code of Conduct*, on which every employee was ostensibly trained in ethics, seemed irrelevant when contrasted with management's autocratic leadership style and single-minded goal to succeed at any cost. What's more, the company's engineering reputation was at stake, and the consequence of failure for the German economy and reputation around design and manufacturing would be substantial.[xix] [Emphasis mine]

   - Opportunity:

     Coinciding with the directive the engineers received to come up with a new solution, Bosch sold VW the diesel-engine-management software that could detect when a vehicle was being tested and turn on emission-controlling devices—*on the understanding that it would be used for internal testing, as use was illegal in vehicles sold to the public*. And modern cars operate with about 100 million lines of software code, making it easy to hide cheating software code amidst the complexity.[xx] [Emphasis mine]

---

[1] Phase out timelines: Toyota by end of 2018; Nissan and Fiat Chrysler will phase out diesel passenger cars by 2021. Copenhagen, Beijing, Hamburg, Helsinki, London, Madrid, Oslo, Paris, Rome, and Shanghai all have plans to phase out diesel passenger cars and Norway plans to phase them out by 2025. "Other countries, including France, Germany, India, and China, have said they would follow suit, although some have not yet established firm timelines. France has committed to a ban by 2040. India's government has said it plans to ban sales of new cars powered by internal combustion engines by 2030. India's future is electric, and so is China's. With those two behemoths paving the way, the rest of the world is likely to follow." Zimmermann, N. (2018), "Move Is on to Ban Diesel Cars from Cities," *Deutsche Welle*, February 26, 2018, https://www.dw.com/en/move-is-on-to-ban-diesel-cars-from-cities/a-42747043, accessed on July 28, 2018.

- Rationalization:

    The engineers knew that in the 1970s, VW engineers had installed in Volkswagens "defeat devices" that allowed the company to cheat on newly enacted emission standards. *The consequence then was minimal—a mere $120,000 fine. Even if they cheated, the punishment would be light, they may have rationalized.* How else might they have rationalized such a feat? Perhaps they thought it was in the best interest of the company and, as a result, management would approve.[xxi] [Emphasis mine]

The cost to VW of this failure of ethics was not just reputation damage that will take years to recover from. It was also financial. In the United States alone, VW had to pay US$ 30 billion for "Dieselgate," including the costs of withdrawing 500,000 cars from the U.S. market:

    The ruling now brings to around $30 billion the costs VW will incur after being caught rigging two of its diesel engines to pass U.S. emissions tests—a figure that includes the price of buying back almost 500,000 vehicles sold in the country. Meanwhile, seven current and former Volkswagen employees have been charged with crimes connected to the scandal, while an investigation continues in Germany.[xxii]

In the European Union (EU), VW had to pay another €1 billion to settle with the regulators. These fines do not include the costs of any civil class actions brought against VW by customers who have incurred losses as a result of the damage to the value of their cars. Audi has also had to pay an additional € 800 million to settle with regulators its part in the scandal.[xxiii]

The industry's reputation in the EU is also damaged and the EU will fine car makers €30,000 per car to prevent a repeat of "dieselgate."[xxiv]

Misaligned Incentives and Strategy

Misalignment occurs between companies and investors, different entities working together, different strategic business units (SBUs) and departments, caused by different KPIs.

Companies and Investors

Good CG requires boards to reconcile the need to satisfy shareholder expectations with the creation of sustainable long-term value. This has often proved to be difficult for two reasons. First, there is increasing divergence between time horizons as shareholders behave more and more like short-term speculators,[xxv] as opposed to owners who are interested in long-term sustainable value. Second, the unreasonable expected returns demanded by investors as a result of Milton Friedman's idea that the purpose of business is to *maximize* shareholder value. Before he popularized this idea in 1970,[xxvi] investors were comfortable with a 3–5% premium on the so-called risk-free rate represented by U.S. treasury bills or the UK "gilts"—that is, a fair return. This meant expected return on equity (ROE) on average was around 8–9%.

The result of investors expecting a *maximum* return was pension fund managers and investors were encouraged by asset managers to switch in and out of stocks in the search for maximum returns in the financial markets. These markets worked twenty-four hours a day because money could be moved from Tokyo or Hong Kong to London and then to New York to capture the benefits of three overlapping time zones creating a twenty-four-hour investment cycle.

As a result, investors gradually ceased to behave as owners of the business in which they were invested, with a long-term view, and became more like speculators interested in maximizing yield through day trading and later high-speed algorithmic trading. Boards and management were increasingly pressurized to achieve double-digit growth rates and ROE in the high teens, leading companies to either take unreasonable risks or else to buy back shares to maintain short-term ROE, instead of investing in the future of the business.

Entities that Work Together

This applies to companies seeking to merge or acquire other companies. Work done by McKinsey showed nearly 70% of mergers and acquisitions destroyed shareholder value.[xxvii] The reason for this was estimated synergies justifying the large premiums paid by the acquiring company failed to materialize, largely because of the resistance of vested interests in both acquirer and acquired to realize the transformation promise—the result of different cultures.

Different SBUs

Perhaps the clearest indication of the challenge presented by trying to create a unifying culture out of disparate SBUs is best demonstrated by the difficulties experienced by Antony Jenkins, an English retail banker by background, to rebuild Barclays' culture after he replaced Bob Diamond, an American investment banker by background as CEO.[xxviii] After three years of trying[xxix] and failing, he was replaced by Jess Staley,[xxx] another American investment banker.

The reason for the difficulties is "universal banks" like Barclays have three "tribes" of employees operating within them: traditional retail bankers who live in a long-term "win-win" world recognizing they prosper when their clients prosper; investment bankers who are only interested in doing the deal, walking away after it is done; and traders who by definition live in a "win-lose" world. Their differences in assumptions about how they operate are only accentuated by the differences in the way they are remunerated and differences in personality and values.

One of the reasons why Unilever chose to divest its traditional operations discussed later in this chapter was the incompatibility of cultures in its plantation, shipping and logistics, advertising, consumer goods marketing companies, retailing operations, and its industrial divisions.

GE (U.S.), Sime Darby (Malaysia) and other conglomerates all suffered from the so-called conglomerate discount, which sets a price on the problems of cultural incompatibility; ultimately leading to their break up to release shareholder value.

Different Departments
The existence of so-called silo management reflects the reality different departments within a single organization have distinctive ways of doing things; different emotional dynamics and rationales for what they do. The culture of a direct selling sales force is totally different from the culture of manufacturing, after-sales service, administration, or of internal audit and compliance in the same company.

Inappropriate KPIs
Take for example, BP and the Deepwater Horizon disaster. It has been argued BP made decisions that favored speed over safety, and the company had a reputation for being particularly hard-driving. For a long time, BP had been very successful in pushing the exploration envelope working with its subcontractors even though the risks of disaster were growing. Their success encouraged their crews to ignore the fact they were getting closer to disaster, as were the Transocean crew; also involved in the dubious decision making. And the federal regulators who supervised drilling in the Gulf of Mexico signed off on their plans at every stage because they believed BP's track record. The essential errors leading to the disaster were BP's focus on speed and cost, combined with the belief they were not pushing the envelope too far and fast because each incremental step had worked, anaesthetizing them to the fear of cumulatively small errors leading to catastrophic failure through a process called the "normalization of deviance," experienced by NASA in the *Challenger* disaster:[xxxi]

> Vaughan and other researchers argue that most high-risk industries are prone to normalizing deviance. We've all seen this, even in businesses that don't involve life-and-death decisions: Managers focus on positive data about their operations and tune out small signs of trouble, safety margins get shaved in the name of efficiency, and small deviations from procedural rules are tolerated. But disaster researchers have also developed strategies to help counteract the tendency: tools to help managers be more aware of "weak signals" hinting at trouble, for example, and policies that empower whistleblowers.[xxxii]

Inappropriate Rewards

As a result of the Global Financial Crisis, executive compensation in banks has become a flashpoint for boards to consider. Remuneration for CEOs in the United States and the United Kingdom has caused adverse comment regarding the absolute levels bank and investment bank CEOs were getting paid; the fact that there does not seem to be any clear link between performance and pay; and that CEOs have been able to walk away with enormous packages when they have been terminated. This has led to a serious deterioration in the climate of opinion regarding banks, and in the case of Bob Diamond's package, before he was asked to resign, to a shareholder revolt and ultimately to the resignation of Alison Carnwath, the board member chairing Barclays Remuneration Committee.[xxxiii]

Directors may regard paying attention to reward and remuneration as being something different from "cultural" risks. They would be wrong to separate how people are paid and what they are paid for from "culture," particularly if they are rewarded for short-term performance where they bear no risk for the long-term consequences of their actions. The Global Financial Crisis highlighted the problem of inappropriate rewards: from the way mortgage brokers were incentivized; credit rating agencies were paid; investment bankers received bonuses for highly risky short-term behavior that ignored long tail impacts on the viability of the business; to CEOs being measured on ROE.

> We know banks can be ruthless when pursuing profits. But bank lawyers are not supposed to think like bankers. Decades ago, the general counsel of a bank thought more about ethics than efficiency. But today's in-house counsel are often profit centres, fonts of wisdom on how to avoid accounting rules, cut taxes and maintain the secrecy of dubious practices. One reason for the recent wave of abuses at big banks is that their in-house lawyers have been more focused on speed and profit than on right and wrong.
>
> ...As recent debacles at Barclays, HSBC and now Standard Chartered demonstrate, employees of big global banks increasingly lack a moral compass. Some general counsels and compliance officers do provide ethical guidance. But many are facilitators or loophole instructors there to show employees the best way to avoid the law. Not even mafia lawyers go that far; unlike many bankers, mobsters understand the value of an impartial *consigliere* who will tell them when to stop.[xxxiv]

Differences of Social Culture

Organizational culture incorporates values, codes of conduct, the essence of "who we are, what we do, and how we do it" discussed in Chapter 2. Boards must also recognize there will inevitably be sociocultural differences based on nationality, religion, and ethnicity; age; profession, education, and income. Each group has its own set of axioms, beliefs and way of doing things. Boards must therefore ensure any strategy or change considers these differences so people can work together effectively: taking the same things for granted; able to trust each other and rely on each other to get things done according to the company's agreed values.

Systemic Risks

Systemic risks are a relatively new area for boards to consider and have only become a priority since the Global Financial Crisis began in August 2007.[xxxv] Since then, financial regulators have been looking at what they call "macroprudential" risks as much as at "microprudential" risks. Macroprudential risks affect the entire industry or economic system, whereas "microprudential" risks affect only the individual organization.

Regulators came to understand decisions taken by the individual organization may seem to be risk-free for the organization but become a threat to the entire industry or system if every organization takes the same sensible risk at the same time.[2] For example, an individual bank manager may regard a mortgage as a safe loan; it is backed by collateral—the house. The act of providing a loan takes a house off the market and should therefore contribute to rising house prices, making the loan even safer. However, if every bank manager does the same thing, it creates a housing bubble; leading to the inevitable crash when the bubble bursts; spectacularly so, in the case of the U.S. subprime crisis in 2008. When only a few companies were selling subprime mortgage backed securities they made a great deal of money, because the system could stand the relatively high-quality risks, but when everybody got into the act, the quality of the risks deteriorated dramatically and the resulting defaults brought the system to its knees.

There are several reasons why companies regularly put the system at risk.

Herding Behavior

The madness of crowds, beginning with Dutch tulipomania, is a well-documented phenomenon,[xxxvi] yet companies regularly fall into the trap of "following the herd." For example, this happened when boards of banks or insurance companies saw their competitors getting into apparently profitable subprime lines of business that were inherently much riskier over the long term.[3] As a result, when analysts and inves-

---

2 The "tragedy of the commons" occurs when an action that makes sense for one individual leads to all individuals taking this action and as a result destroying what they have in common. Thus, if there is common land for sheep to graze on, it always makes sense for each individual farmer to put one more sheep on the grass when he only considers his own economic gain. However, if all the farmers do the same thing, the commons are destroyed and all the grass is eaten, resulting in every farmer being worse off.

3 "When the music stops, in terms of liquidity, things will be complicated," Prince said. "But as long as the music is playing, you've got to get up and dance." Chuck Prince, CEO of Citi in 2007, quoted in Nakamoto, M. and Wighton, D., "Citigroup Stays Bullish on Buy-Outs," *Financial Times*, July 10, 2007.

tors put pressure on them to match the competition[4] or get into the supposedly more profitable lines of business their competition was in, it was very difficult for boards to resist.

The pressure may also come from consultants who present comparisons of business portfolios without understanding the differences in the risk profiles of the various businesses, suggesting to the board it is sensible to do what others are doing. This contributed to UBS entering investment banking—done without appreciating the difference in risks between its traditional lines of business and investment banking; and the need for different risk management systems UBS failed to put in place.[xxxvii]

Failure of Systemic Integrity

This occurs typically when there is a disaggregation of the value chain. This results in nobody taking responsibility for the integrity of the entire system, preferring instead to pass the problem on to the next participant in the value chain, passing the buck to another organization so it becomes their problem. Subprime was a classic example of this, as was the melamine milk scandal in China and BP's "Deepwater Horizon" disaster in the Gulf of Mexico. Participants in the value chain *ignored their responsibility to behave with integrity to protect the system as a whole* to get an unfair advantage at the expense of their value chain partners.

This is a relatively new problem boards have to consider as companies have chosen, like Unilever, to abandon a strategy of vertical integration to capture market margin across the supply chain. They have chosen to focus instead on core competencies as a source of long-term competitive advantage, relying on their supply chain members to fulfill their roles with equal dedication. However financially attractive jettisoning noncore activities may be, the costs to the company of mistakes/failures in the value chain, caused by no one company being accountable for the systemic integrity of the entire value chain, can be devastating; demonstrated by Sanlu's melamine-in-milk scandal in China:

---

[4] The pressure analysts can bring to bear is illustrated by Michael Armstrong's departure as CEO from AT&T for allowing the share price to fall. One of the key reasons for the difference in performance was AT&T's numbers were true, whereas MCI's were false:
> Part of AT&T's revenue shortfall was caused by aggressive price-cutting to stay competitive with MCI, which was reporting mystifyingly better financials. Little did AT&T or anyone else outside of MCI management know that MCI was cooking the books.
>
> "Believing MCI's numbers was a terrible mistake," Cauley says. "But how can you say a major Fortune 50 company is lying through their teeth? You don't expect that. *An innocent mistake but a fatal mistake.*" [Emphasis mine]

Duffy, J. and Pappalardo, D. (2005), "AT&T: Fall of an Icon," Network World, October 31, 2005, https://www.networkworld.com/article/2315434/lan-wan/lan-wan-at-t-fall-of-an-icon.htm, accessed on July 25, 2018.

> The problems in China's dairy industry were a result of rapid growth fueled by large investments from multinational dairy firms, development of a highly modern and concentrated processing sector that obtained its raw materials from millions of small, poor and uneducated traditional farmers and government support and encouragement for growth but *with little emphasis on inspection and safety issues*.[xxxviii] [Emphasis mine]

or BP's "Deepwater Horizon" disaster:

> Though representatives of BP conceded that the company was responsible for some of the factors contributing to the spill, they stressed that their partner companies were also to blame. Halliburton and Transocean similarly pointed to failures on the part of the other parties involved. [xxxix]

Moral Hazard

Does the fact the organization is deemed to be "too big to fail" encourage unreasonable ambition and systemically dangerous risk taking? When considering "too big to fail," most people will immediately think of banks like Citi, bailed out three times because of the threat to the U.S. financial system, were Citi to fail.

There have been cases in other industries too. For example, in 1971, Rolls-Royce went bankrupt because of risks it took developing the RB211 jet engine for McDonell Douglas's DC10 and Lockheed's Tristar. At the outset, both plane makers wanted the RB211, but Congressional pressure to "buy American" meant the RB211 could only be chosen by one. Unfortunately for Rolls-Royce, Lockheed chose first and so Rolls-Royce was left with the smaller opportunity and with a *fixed price contract they knew would lose them US$264,000 on every engine sold.*[xl]

At a presentation to the 1971 MSc class of the London Business School by the then sales director of Rolls-Royce, he explained the company had no choice but to bet on the RB211 if it was to have a future in civil aviation; even if it meant incurring terrible losses. The board gambled the British government would bail the company out because it was "too big to fail"; 40% of friendly air force planes in 1971 flew with Rolls-Royce engines. The board was correct, but the reaction of the British government was not what they expected. It let the company fail and reconstituted it as Rolls-Royce (1971), with a new board and sold off the iconic automotive business. The RB211 went on to become a great success and the foundation of Roll-Royce's (1971) current aero engine business.

"Traditional" Risks

Traditional risks reflect what can be managed through sensible policies, mitigated through careful monitoring, with the resulting residual risks being insured.

Financial Risk and Credit Risk

These reflect what happens to the company's cash flows and its subsequent ability to finance its operations. This can be easily quantified, if the assumptions about the probabilities of occurrence are correct and no "Black Swans" materialize.

Market risk represents the risk the company's portfolio of investments will be affected by changes in market sentiment—whether this is regarding equities or bonds. These can be mitigated through sensible diversification policies, as long as assumptions about the lack of correlation between different asset classes hold true.

> We rediscovered, however, in the 2008 Global Financial Crisis asset class values tend to become highly correlated, nullifying the assumptions underlying Value at Risk (VAR). This happens when there is a liquidity crunch, panicking asset owners into selling more than one asset class at the same time to pay off their debts, creating a contagion effect from one asset class into the next. I say "rediscovered" because this had been foreseen by Hyman Minsky's "Minsky moment" explanation of why credit booms and debt busts occur.[5]

Natural Hazards

These represent the risk of natural events disrupting either the company supply chain (e.g., the Thai floods of 2011) or damage to the company's own physical assets (as in the Fukushima nuclear plant disaster in Japan). The company is hostage to fortune and mitigation and insurance are the only options available, once the board has decided where to locate fixed assets.

Physical Security

This represents the risks of all the things that can go wrong in health and safety, and more recently the addition of terrorist events (e.g., 9/11, plane hijacking and piracy). There are risk mitigation policies such as not allowing the whole senior management team to fly on the same plane or making sure there are good security arrangements to protect plant and other assets. This is particularly important in failed state environments or where there is civil strife.

---

[5] "Time when a flourishing market and a prospering economy lead consumers to be overly optimistic and borrow beyond their means. The upswing in the market is followed by spiraling debt and consumers who have borrowed too much must sell their good assets to pay their loans or default if they have no assets available to meet their debts," http://www.businessdictionary.com/definition/Minsky-moment.html, accessed on July 23, 2018.

Legal/Regulatory

This risk reflects the possibility the political climate of opinion will change to the disadvantage of the company, leading to restrictions on its social "license to operate" and to regulations making it costlier to do business.

Compliance and Fraud

These represent a different kind of risk, namely things inside the company are not working as they ought to. In the case of compliance failures, it is the board's responsibility to ensure the compliance function has the authority, skills, and power to enforce compliance and to check policies are in fact being adhered to.

The case of fraud is more difficult to deal with as it involves people acting in deliberately misleading ways. The only defense directors can have against fraud is to watch for "red flags" and follow them up, however insignificant they seem, and start digging into the numbers (see Appendix 10.1).

IT and Cybersecurity Risks

This is an area that has existed ever since computerization, hence it is grouped with other "traditional" risks. It is a subject that boards do not really understand, and many boards have not given it the attention it deserves.

First, there are *external* risks that could be regarded as being systemic or specific to the organization. They are systemic when "bad actors" target the system as a whole; for example, hostile governments trying to bring down national interconnected infrastructure (e.g., power grids);[xli] government data hacks[xlii] or where social media like Facebook and twitter are abused by trolls whose purpose is to sow dissension, division and conflict between different political and demographic groups,[xliii] leaving organizations caught in the crossfire. There are organization-specific events, such as Target's expensive data breach, costing $18.5 million to settle[xliv] and Sony's data hack, creating huge embarrassment and costing $8 million to settle.[xlv] Finally, there are hybrid events where several organizations are caught by a zero-day malware attack across the entire internet. The consequences of each type of event differ:

> A zero-day attack on a wide range of targets is systemic, and any one target is unlikely to stand out and be held to account. Whereas, an institution specific attack could well be costly and reputationally damaging. But in either case, adequate insurance coverage should mitigate the financial impact. Additionally, as we have learnt in recent instances, there is a hybrid, which is a large number of targets being infected with previously used malware, for which corrective patches were created but which they did not bother to install. To me, this is the most damaging one, as it shows that the targets were lackadaisical about shoring up their defenses and were

careless. Also, from a financial point of view, such an event might well lead the insurers to reject the claims, arguing negligence on the part of the target.[xlvi]

Second, are problems created *internally* either through bad practice and carelessness for which directors are entirely responsible:

> Some of the biggest and most significant government data breaches come down to human error: from lost hard drives, misconfigured databases, and physical device theft to simple mistakes that lead to millions upon millions of leaked Social Security numbers, names, addresses, voting affiliations, and other sensitive data.[xlvii]

Third, are *internal* problems caused by ageing or incompatible IT system breakdowns, like the IT meltdown experienced by Royal Bank of Scotland's customers in the United Kingdom for which, once again, directors are responsible:

> RBS has promised that there will be no repeat of the June 2012 IT meltdown that left 6.5 million customers locked out their accounts for days and led to Thursday's £56m fine. The bank, which is 81% owned by the taxpayer, also issued an apology and said it had docked £6m in bonuses from staff after the collapse of the IT systems which affected customers at RBS, NatWest and Ulster Bank.

> Regulators pointed out that the 6.5 million people affected represented 10% of the population, while RBS insisted it was spending £750m to ensure it would not happen again.

> In the latest hit to RBS's reputation, just eight days after it was fined £400m for allowing foreign exchange markets to be rigged, regulators said the bank had suffered from failures at many levels and failed to keep its computer systems up to date, despite spending £1bn a year on technology. [xlviii]

"Earnings Driver" Risks

These operational risks affect margin and the company's ability to remain profitable. There is not much boards can do about these risks other than to understand their impact on the income statement (P&L) and to encourage management to take corrective or remedial action; failing which, to be realistic about how to manage the resulting decline in profitability.

Product Innovation

Technological improvements may improve company margins or create entirely new ways of doing business. This also applies to the competition. Boards must therefore keep track of innovations in their industry and of their company's ability to innovate as rapidly as or quicker than their rivals. Directors must remember the risk the lifespan of their company may be shorter than they expected, given the lifecycles of companies have become dramatically shorter. The lifespan of an average S&P company has dropped from 60 years in the 1950s to a forecast 12 by 2027.[xlix] Given the interest analysts show in the company's relative ability to innovate, the board must highlight to management the need for successful innovation.

Brand Impairment

Strong product brands command superior margins; weak brands have lower margins. Managing product brands is the responsibility of management, though boards should keep an eye on the overall health of the brand portfolio. The corporate brand, however, is the direct responsibility of the board because of the effect brand impairment has on overall reputation and as a result on market capitalization.

Pricing Pressure

Pricing issues are really operational matters best left to management, though boards need to be aware of any pricing issues that could affect the company's reputation and brand.

Supplier Relationships

Supplier relationships are operational matters. They are only the concern of the board when they affect corporate reputation through violations of environmental, health and safety regulations or create undue NGO and media interest in how the company operates abroad.

Good examples of such problems were Nike's employment of children making footballs in Pakistan[l] after they had already suffered serious reputation problems in the 1990s affecting their business model and brand,[6] or Apple's problems with

---

6 When Phil Knight and the rest of the top officials at Nike were given the 1997 reports regarding the human rights and labor violations being committed in their Asian factories, it was very clear that they were going to have to take swift action to remedy the situation. The fact was that "shoes and clothing are only the secondary products of the fashion industry. What [Nike] primarily sells is image. For Nike to have its image associated with sweatshops in Asia was more than an embarrassment; the revelations threatened sales" (Sweatshop Agreement, Part 1). The shoe and apparel producer could not afford to continue to see its name dragged through the mud. Sales were dropping and Nike was being portrayed in the media as a company who was willing to exploit workers and deprive them of the basic wage needed to sustain themselves in an effort to expand profits.
Wilsey, M. and Lichtig, S., "The Nike Controversy," https://web.stanford.edu/class/e297c/trade_environment/wheeling/hnike.html, accessed on July 23, 2018.

working conditions at their supplier, Foxconn's[li] plants in China. Boards must therefore reassure themselves no such problem could arise.

Distribution Channels

Typically, these risks are operational, unless the business model itself envisages a totally different way of using or not using distribution channels—for example, Dell (discussed in Chapter 8), or the impact of Amazon on traditional bricks and mortar retailers by introducing customers to a nearly frictionless shopping process with almost immediate results.[lii]

Alternative Technologies

These are the risks that can put a company out of business. Although they are operational in nature, boards need to be aware of their existence and potential impact on the long-term viability of the company. Amazon's impact on traditional bricks and mortar retailers is the result of Amazon's investment in internet-enabled logistics. Amazon has also had a major impact on traditional IT companies through its leadership investments and dominance in cloud-based computing. Fintech and the blockchain are other examples of such a threat to financial institutions.

Customer Churn

Customer loyalty is now recognized as being more important than customer satisfaction[liii] as an indicator of the health of customer relationships (discussed in Chapter 9). This is primarily an operational matter and only a cause for board concern as a leading indicator of problems.

Using the "Five P" Framework to Cross Check

Reputation risk is the sum of "cultural," systemic, "traditional," and "earnings driver" risks. The best way of ensuring it is properly considered is to use the "Five P" framework when looking at each of these four component parts of reputation risk by checking whether it has been covered properly as follows:

Purpose

The board must check whether the organization is still being true to its purpose from a cultural perspective. It needs to consider whether its purpose is in some way creating or making systemic risks worse and what can be done to minimize the systemic risks identified with continuing its purpose, particularly if management is suggesting a change. This applies equally to the "traditional" and "earnings driver" risks. This is best done by getting answers to the questions in Appendix 10.2.

Principles

The board must check whether the principles or values they have agreed are still compatible with the "cultural" risks they have identified, and if they are not, how to reconcile them. Next the board must consider the impact of the organization's principles on systemic risks and vice versa and how to reconcile them if there is a divergence. Finally, the board must ensure the agreed principles are respected when dealing with "traditional" and "earnings driver" risks to ensure adherence to ethical practices.

Power

The board must consider whether the agreed organizational design can deal with the "cultural," systemic, "traditional," and "earnings driver" risks and if it is not, how it should be changed to mitigate the challenges presented to the long-term viability of the business.

People

The board must consider whether the organization has enough people to fulfil the identified roles and responsibilities, ensuring the appropriate competencies now and into the future required in light of the "cultural," systemic, "traditional," and "earnings driver" risks. It is particularly important this review does not just focus on job evaluations and competencies but includes character as well, to ensure ethical practices are adhered to. This is covered in Chapter 11.

Processes

Finally, the board must ensure the processes meet the requirements and challenges presented by the interaction of "cultural," systemic, "traditional," and "earnings" driver risks so the risk management processes provide assurance the right risks are being taken in an informed way and the right processes are in place to mitigate their impact on the business and protect its reputation.

Conclusion

Boards must take risks; without risks, there can be no profits. Given the importance of taking well-informed decisions, taking risk into account, it is sensible leading practice to appoint a risk management committee to do this, rather than having no committee designated to look after risk or leaving it to the audit committee. Risks can be grouped into four families: "cultural," systemic, "traditional," and "earnings driver" risks. The first three are primarily issues of policy, while "earnings driver" risks are operational in nature and the responsibility of management.

Given Warren Buffett's explanation for his success that "culture + leadership + trust = wealth," this chapter argues the "cultural" components of risk are the most important. Most boards recognize this, but in practice only pay lip service to the idea they are responsible for it. "Cultural" risks are created by ethical conflicts often caused by "imperial CEOs" with simple, overambitious goals, autocratic leadership and a top-down fear-based style of management; misaligned incentives and strategy and inappropriate KPIs; inappropriate rewards and remuneration; and differences in social culture.

Systemic risks are an area where boards have tended to pay insufficient attention; yet as the subprime crisis in the US demonstrated their impact can be global. The reasons why directors allow their companies to ignore systemic risks, apart from ignorance, are herding behavior; failures of systemic integrity; moral hazard and the belief the company is "too big to fail" leading to excessive risk-taking.

Boards deal with the "traditional" risks reasonably well from a policy perspective, though they may need to pay more attention to the "Minsky moment." "Traditional" risks cover financial and credit risk; market risk; natural hazards, physical security; legal/regulatory risk; compliance and fraud risks; and IT and cybersecurity risks, to which boards will need to pay *much, much more attention in future*.

Working with management, boards need to be briefed on operational issues occurring in "earnings driver" risks. These are failure to innovate, brand impairment, pricing pressure, changes in supplier relationships; changes in distribution channels, the impact of alternative technologies on either revenues or methods of distribution, and customer churn.

The "Five P" framework's "purpose" lens provides a useful checklist of questions and issues for directors to evaluate the impact of these four families of risk on the business purpose.

Appendix 10.1: Fraud Red Flags

The topics divide into "red flags" in general, issues of governance, strategy, and financing:

1. "Red flags" in general:
    a. Duties are not segregated; or even if segregated, employees have moved from one department to another and know how to exploit weaknesses in the system to hide bad trades (e.g., Nick Leeson at Barings)
    b. Revaluations are not independent
    c. No independent production and verification of management reports
    d. No check on the profitability of lines of business and of customers
    e. Unclear process for setting and reviewing risk limits
    f. High turnover of key people
    g. Executives selling down shares
    h. Involvement in legal disputes significantly greater than peers
    i. Excessive use of nominees;
2. Governance
    a. Dominant CEO
    b. Unbalanced board—insufficient independents
    c. Inexperienced/ineffective Board/Audit Committee, which principally rubber stamps management decisions with
        i. Executives on the Audit Committee
        ii. No accountant
    d. Management compensation excessive or poorly aligned with the interests of stakeholders
    e. Frequent changes in legal advisors and auditors
    f. Weak finance team
3. Strategy
    a. Business strategy not clear and not agreed by the board
    b. Strategy unsustainable
    c. Aggressive business model—growing through large acquisitions or expansion into unproven markets
    d. Fast track revenue generation overseas or revenue growth not creating corresponding cash flow increases
    e. Significant related party transactions
    f. History of frequent retrenchment and restructuring
    g. Unnecessarily complex structure involving unusual legal entities or managerial lines of authority with:
        i. Special Purpose Entities
        ii. Significant bank accounts or subsidiary or branch operations in tax-haven jurisdictions

4. Financial
    a. Performance ratios differ significantly from industry trends
    b. Business consumes cash
    c. Financial ratios do not make sense as % net revenue for:
        i. Working capital cycle (receivables, inventory, payables)
        ii. Operating Expenses
    d. Changing asset intensity changing with the entity's cash flow coming primarily from disposal of assets
    e. Auditor's request to make final adjustments to draft accounts presented by management after the audit review—if the difference is greater than 2%, this could lead to massive fines by the stock exchange
    f. Funding unsustainable
        i. Debt/equity ratios high
        ii. Interest cover inadequate
        iii. Punitive banking covenants
        iv. High cost of capital
        v. Failure to match assets and liabilities, both short and long term;
    g. Creative accounting mindset suggested by:
        i. Aggressive application of accounting standards, or opaque financial reporting
        ii. Significant related party transactions
        iii. Consistent/rapid earnings growth without corresponding cash flow increases
        iv. Business managing numbers to meet analysts' growth expectations
        v. Majority of income coming from one off items
        vi. Messy accounting systems (journals/suspense accounts)
        vii. Long-standing nonreconciled accounts
        viii. Debtors written off without serious collection efforts
        ix. Net income or profits reported consistently greater than actual operating cash flows generated
        x. Last minute adjustments to the trial balance before the audited accounts resulting from top-side adjustments
        xi. Need to get auditors to explain why they intend to report "Key Audit Matters"
    h. Weak internal auditing
        i. Weak staffing with poor access and little authority
        ii. Audit coverage not comprehensive—too long a cycle
        iii. Internal audit outsourced and/or under-resourced
        iv. Internal audit has never waved a red flag
    i. Weak external auditing
        i. External audit does not understand the business—poor industry knowledge

ii. Weak staffing (lead partner, manager)
iii. Insufficient time and support
iv. Unrealistic expectations

Appendix 10.2: "Purpose" Checklist of Questions and Issues

The questions directors ask divide into those concerned with policy issues, which are their responsibility and operational issues, which are the responsibility of management. As far as operational issues are concerned, directors need to be kept informed of trends and how competitors perform on a comparative basis, but do not need to go into the same level of detail as on policy issues. Policy issues cover "cultural," systemic and "traditional risks," whereas "earnings driver" risks are operational:

1. "Cultural" risks
    a. *Ethics conflicts:* Does our business purpose create ethics conflicts by:
        i. Having simple, overambitious goals?
        ii. Discouraging "telling truth to power" because of autocratic, fear-based leadership?
        iii. Creating the "fraud triad":
            1. Excessive pressure?
            2. Creating the opportunity?
            3. Providing basis for rationalization?
    b. *Misaligned incentives:* Does our purpose reconcile incentives between our:
        i. Organization and its investors?
        ii. Partners or acquisition targets?
        iii. SBUs?
        iv. Departments?
    c. *Inappropriate KPIs*: Is our purpose reinforced or undermined by the KPIs we set?
    d. *Differences in social culture*: Do they lead to misunderstandings based on:
        i. Nationality, religious, and ethnicity?
        ii. Demographics:
            1. Age?
            2. Education?
            3. Income?
            4. Rural versus urban?
2. Systemic risks
    a. How vulnerable is our purpose to risks posed by disaggregation of the value chain?
    b. Is our purpose affected by herding behavior or are we successful contrarians?
    c. How vulnerable is our purpose to the "tragedy of the commons"?
    d. How vulnerable is our purpose to potential failures of systemic integrity?

e. *Does our purpose assume we are "too big to fail," leading to excessive risk taking?*
3. "Traditional risks"
   a. *Financial and credit risk:*
      i. How vulnerable is our purpose to problems of cash flow and liquidity crunches; what stress testing have we done under scenarios?
      ii. What assumptions are we using about VAR?
      iii. Have we made enough allowance for "Black Swans"?
   b. *Market risk:*
      i. How vulnerable is our purpose to changes in market sentiment affecting bonds and equity?
      ii. How vulnerable is our purpose to changes in interest rate and exchange rate risk?
      iii. What impact would a 'Minsky moment' or the 'Kondratieff Wave' have on our purpose?
   c. *Natural hazards:* How vulnerable is our purpose to natural hazards (fire, flood, and earthquakes):
      i. Are our physical assets located in safe places? If not, can they be relocated or backed up to minimize the risk of business interruption?
      ii. Do we have proper business interruption procedures in place to protect our purpose?
      iii. Do we have appropriate insurance and reinsurance policies?
      iv. Do we have a tested crisis communications plan?
   d. *Physical safety risks:*
      i. Is our business conducted in line with relevant occupational health and safety regulations?
      ii. How safe are our locations; and if there are any safety risks, what is being done to protect employees and the assets?
   e. *Regulatory/legal risks:*
      i. Does the regulatory environment present a risk currently?
      ii. What trends could affect the legal and regulatory impact on our social "license to operate"?
      iii. What are we doing to maximize our strategic degrees of freedom to continue doing the business?
      iv. What litigation is the business involved in and what are the likely judgments?
   f. *Compliance and fraud risks:*
      i. How effective are our compliance policy and procedures?
      ii. Does compliance have the necessary resources and standing to do its job?
      iii. How effective is internal audit?

iv. Does internal audit have the necessary resources and standing to do it job?
v. How effective is our whistle-blower policy?
vi. Does our "culture" make fraud more likely through:
1. Excessive pressure to achieve results regardless of how it is done?
2. Shooting the messenger?
3. High power distance?

4. "Earnings driver" risks:
As far as these risks are concerned, they are operational where directors need to be kept up to date on trends, comparative competitive performance and progress against agreed goals regarding:
   a. *Product innovation:* Directors need to be updated on the targeted rate of innovation; the percentage of revenue in new product and services; the time to take new products to market and how this compares with key competitors; and what action is being taken to get back on track.
   b. *Brand impairment:* Directors need to understand what, if anything, is affecting the value of the company's brands and brand portfolio; the changing brand mix and its impact on revenues and margins; the reasons for impairment and what is being done to improve the position in terms of R&D investment or increased A&P support.
   c. *Pricing pressure:* Directors need to understand the impact of pricing pressure on the company's financial position, the causes of pressure; whether the brands are price leaders or price takers and what is being done to restore their position; failing which, what is being done to protect margins.
   d. *Supplier relationships:* Directors should be aware of who the key suppliers to the company are; what percentage of the company's purchases they represent; how much power they have to set prices; whether they are financially robust; who else they supply; whether they could become competitors over time.
   e. *Distribution channels:* Directors need to understand which channels matter; whether they are changing and, if threatened by internet-enabled competition what can be done to mitigate the threat; how much margin is ceded to channel members; the advantages of exclusive, selective and intensive distribution or franchising.
   f. *Alternative technologies:* Directors must be briefed on developments in alternative technologies that could put at risk sources of supply; company revenues; channels of distribution; and customers.
   g. *Customer churn:* Directors need to understand who the key customers are; which are growing/declining as a percent of the business; what percent of their business the company is winning; and customer loyalty.

References

i Booz Allen & Hamilton (2004), "Too Much SOX Can Kill You: Resolving the Compliance Paradox."
ii http://www.businessdictionary.com/definition/risk.html#ixzz22azPiKXD visited on August 5, 2012.
iii http://www.businessdictionary.com/definition/business-risk.html#ixzz22b2MK5uF visited on August 5, 2012.
iv Fraser, J. R. S. (2016), "The Role of the Board in Risk Management Oversight," quoted in *The Handbook of Corporate Governance*, edited by Richard Leblanc (Hoboken, NJ: John Wiley & Sons), 288.
v Ibid., 285.
vi Deloitte Touche Tohmatsu Limited (2014), "As Risks Rise, Boards Respond. A Global View of Risk Committees," quoted in *The Handbook of Corporate Governance*, edited by Richard Leblanc (Hoboken, NJ: John Wiley & Sons), 301.
vii Fraser (2016), op. cit., 303.
viii Ibid., 297–299.
ix Ibid., 296.
x Booz Allen & Hamilton (2004), op. cit.
xi Cave, A. (2017), "Culture Eats Strategy for Breakfast. So, What's for Lunch?" *Forbes*, November 9, 2017, https://www.forbes.com/sites/andrewcave/2017/11/09/culture-eats-strategy-for-breakfast-so-whats-for-lunch/#738149a47e0f, accessed on July 23, 2018.
xii Ibid.
xiii Booz Allen & Hamilton (2004), op. cit.
xiv Rittenhouse, L. (2015), "Warren Buffett's Two Tips on Building Successful Businesses–Pass them Along," *Forbes*, March 4, 2015, https://www.forbes.com/sites/laurarittenhouse/2015/03/04/warren-buffetts-two-tips-on-building-successful-businesses-pass-them-along/#1c933c9b46e1, accessed on July 23, 2018.
xv Diamond, R. (2011), "Today Business Lecture," *BBC Radio 4*, http://news.bbc.co.uk/today/hi/today/newsid_9630000/9630673.stm, accessed on July 23, 2018.
xvi Lynch, L. and Santos, C. (2016), "VW Emissions And the 3 Factors That Drive Ethical Breakdown," *Darden Ideas to Action*, (University of Virginia, Darden School of Business), October 17, 2016, https://ideas.darden.virginia.edu/2016/10/vw-emissions-and-the-3-factors-that-drive-ethical-breakdown/, accessed on July 26, 2018.
xvii Ibid.
xviii Winton, N. (2018), "Diesel Sales In Europe Slide In 2017, And Dive In December," *Forbes*, January 29, 2018, https://www.forbes.com/sites/neilwinton/2018/01/29/diesel-sales-in-europe-slide-in-2017-and-dive-in-december/#6f4a54a942fb, accessed on July 30, 2018.
xix Ibid.
xx Ibid.
xxi Ibid.
xxii Eisenstein, P. A. (2017), "Volkswagen Slapped With the Largest Ever Fine for Automakers," *NBC News*, April 22, 2017, https://www.nbcnews.com/business/autos/judge-approves-largest-fine-u-s-history-volkswagen-n749406, accessed on July 26, 2018.
xxiii Reuters (2018), "German Prosecutors Fine Audi 800 Million Euros for Diesel Violations," October 16, 2018, https://uk.reuters.com/article/us-volkswagen-emissions-audi/german-prosecutors-fine-audi-800-million-euros-for-diesel-violations-idUKKCN1MQ12Z, accessed on October 18, 2018.
xxiv Carrington, D. (2017), "Diesel Vehicles Will Disappear Sooner than Expected, Says EU Industry Chief," *The Guardian*, April 4, 2017, https://www.theguardian.com/environment/2017/apr/04/diesel-vehicles-will-disappear-sooner-than-expected-says-eu-industry-chief, accessed on July 26, 2018.
xxv Bogle, J. C. (2008), *Enough: True Measures of Money, Business and Life* (Hoboken, NJ: John Wiley & Sons).
xxvi Friedman, M. (1970), "The Social Responsibility of Business is to Increase its Profits," *The New

York Times, September 13, 1970, https://www.nytimes.com/1970/09/13/archives/article-15-no-title.html, accessed on July 26, 2018.

xxvii Christofferson, S. A., McNish, R. S., and Sias, D. L. (2004), "Where Mergers Go Wrong," *McKinsey Quarterly*, May 2004.

xxviii Brinded, L. (2012), "Barclays Retail Chief Antony Jenkins Replaces Bob Diamond as CEO," *International Business Times*, August 30, 2012, https://www.ibtimes.co.uk/barclays-new-ceo-anthony-jenkins-bob-diamond-378848, accessed on July 26, 2018.

xxix Moore, J. (2013), "Can Antony Jenkins Get Rid of Bob Diamond's Legacy at Barclays?" *Independent*, January 18, 2013, https://www.independent.co.uk/news/business/analysis-and-features/can-antony-jenkins-get-rid-of-bob-diamonds-legacy-at-barclays-8456614.html, accessed on July 26, 2018.

xxx Treanor, J. (2015), "Barclays Fires Chief Executive Antony Jenkins," *The Guardian*, July 8, 2015, https://www.theguardian.com/business/2015/jul/08/barclays-fires-chief-executive-antony-jenkins, accessed on July 26, 2018.

xxxi Meigs, J. B. (2016), "Blame BP for Deepwater Horizon. But Direct Your Outrage to the Actual Mistake," *Slate*, September 30, 2016, http://www.slate.com/articles/health_and_science/science/2016/09/bp_is_to_blame_for_deepwater_horizon_but_its_mistake_was_actually_years.html, accessed on July 26, 2018.

xxxii Ibid.

xxxiii Treanor, J. (2012), "Barclays Pay Chair Alison Carnwath Quits," *The Guardian*, July 25, 2012, http://www.guardian.co.uk/business/2012/jul/25/alison-carnwath-barclays-bob-diamond-pay visited on January 30, 2013.

xxxiv Partnoy, F. (2012), "Who Are the True Villains of the Stanchart Tragedy?" *The Financial Times*, August 9, 2012, http://www.ft.com/intl/cms/s/0/7509156e-e143-11e1-9c72-00144feab49a.html#axzz-2JRCBVCGV accessed on August 18, 2012.

xxxv Boyd, S. (2007), "BNP Paribas Freezes Funds as Loan Losses Roil Markets," *Bloomberg*, August 9, 2007, http://www.bloomberg.com/apps/news?pid=newsarchive&sid=aW1wj5i.vyOg, accessed on August 18, 2012.

xxxvi Mackay, C. (1841), "Extraordinary Popular Delusions and the Madness of Crowds," Pantianos Classics.

xxxvii Reuters staff (2011), "Timeline: UBS Investment Bank Mishaps," *Reuters*, September 15, 2011, https://www.reuters.com/article/us-ubs-timeline/timeline-ubs-investment-bank-mishaps-and-upheavals-idUSTRE78E2FM20110915, accessed on July 25, 2018.

xxxviii Xiu, C. and Klein, K. K. (2010), "Melamine in Milk Products in China: Examining the Factors that Led to Deliberate Use of the Contaminant," *Food Policy*, Volume 35, Issue 5, October 2010, 463.

xxxix Pallardy, R., "Deepwater Horizon Oil Spill of 2010," *Encyclopaedia Britannica*, https://www.britannica.com/event/Deepwater-Horizon-oil-spill-of-2010, accessed on July 25, 2018.

xl Lee, J. M. (1971), "Rolls-Royce is Bankrupt: Blames Lockheed Project," *The New York Times*, February 5, 1971, https://www.nytimes.com/1971/02/05/archives/rollsroyce-is-bankrupt-blames-lockheed-project-rollsroyce-enters.html, accessed on July 25, 2018.

xli Greenberg, A. (2017), "How An Entire Nation Became Russia's Test Lab For Cyberwar," *Wired*, June 20, 2017, https://www.wired.com/story/russian-hackers-attack-ukraine/, accessed on August 2, 2018.

xlii Lord, N. (2017), "Top 10 Biggest Government Hacks Of All Time In the US," *Digital Guardian*, April 11, 2017, https://digitalguardian.com/blog/top-10-biggest-us-government-data-breaches-all-time, accessed on August 2, 2018.

xliii Earle, S. (2017), "Trolls, Bots and Fake News: The Mysterious World of Media Manipulation," *Newsweek*, October 14, 2017, https://www.newsweek.com/trolls-bots-and-fake-news-dark-and-mysterious-world-social-media-manipulation-682155, accessed on August 2, 2018.

xliv Reuter (2017), "Target Settles 2013 Hacked Customer Data Breach for $18.5 Million," *NBC News*, May 24, 2017, https://www.nbcnews.com/business/business-news/target-settles-2013-hacked-customer-data-breach-18-5-million-n764031, accessed on August 2, 2018.

xlv "Sony Pays Up to $8 Million to Settle," *BBC News*, October 21, 2015, https://www.bbc.com/news/business-34589710, accessed on August 2, 2018.

xlvi Nasr, Y. (2018), in an email to the author, dated July 30, 2018.

xlvii Lord (2017), op. cit.

xlviii Treanor, J. (2014), "RBS Fined £56 Million for IT Breakdown," *The Guardian*, November 20, 2014, https://www.theguardian.com/business/2014/nov/20/royal-bank-of-scotland-it-breakdown-56m-pounds-fine, accessed on August 2, 2018.

xlix Anthony, S. D. et al. (2018), "2018 Corporate Longevity Forecast: Creative Destruction is Accelerating," *Innosight*, https://www.innosight.com/insight/creative-destruction/, accessed on August 23, 2018.

l Clark, A. (2006), "Nike sacks Pakistani supplier over Child Labour Row," *The Guardian*, November 20, 2006, https://www.theguardian.com/business/2006/nov/20/2, accessed on July 23, 2018.

li Vega, N. (2017), "Apple Has Been Using Teen Labor to Assemble the iPhone X," *New York Post*, November 21, 2017, https://nypost.com/2017/11/21/apple-has-been-using-teen-labor-to-assemble-the-iphone-x/ , accessed on July 23, 2018.

lii Grosman, L. (2018), "What the Amazon Effect Means for Retailers," *Forbes*, February 22, 2018, https://www.forbes.com/sites/forbescommunicationscouncil/2018/02/22/what-the-amazon-effect-means-for-retailers/#74020b112ded, accessed on July 23. 2018.

liii Reichheld, W. (1996), *The Loyalty Effect* (Boston: Harvard Business School Press).

Chapter 11
Planning Succession; Managing Talent

This chapter is presented in five parts: the first deals with succession planning for the board and the desired attributes of directors; the second with CEO succession; the third deals with the issues of CEO remuneration and performance measurement; the fourth deals with the board's responsibility for effective talent management; and the fifth concludes with the "Five P" framework's "purpose," "principles," and "processes" lenses to check everything material has been covered.

I am always surprised by two contradictory answers from the same directors to my questions regarding the importance of people:

> People are our most important asset.

> The board spends less than 10% of its time thinking about succession planning and talent management.

In some cases, directors have even admitted the board spends almost no time on HR issues. This suggests boards by and large only pay lip service to the importance of people as an asset and reinforces the perception people are a cost to be cut whenever possible. This makes little sense if people are the company's most important asset; it is a clear failure by the board to fulfil one of its core responsibilities and of shareholders to understand that without the right people in the right jobs at the right time, the company will fail.

Succession Planning for the Board

Malaysia's Securities Commission and Stock Exchange, for example, mandate the existence of a nomination and remuneration committee (NRC).[1] The 2017 revised Malaysian CG code goes further. It expects the board to appoint directors and senior management based on objective criteria, merit, and with due regard for diversity of skills, experience, age, cultural background, and gender;[2] to disclose in its annual report the policies on gender diversity, its targets, and the policies to meet those targets;[3] to use independent sources to identify suitably qualified candidates rather than relying solely on recommendations from existing board members, management, or shareholders; limiting INED tenure to nine years, though there is a process for extending it to twelve years (see Appendix 11.1).

So, what are the criteria for appointing effective INEDs? First, a candidate for director should be able to demonstrate the following abilities: thinking strategically, understanding strategic and operational issues; collaborating with other directors and managers in delivering the agreed strategy; adding intellectual and experiential diversity to guide the business purpose, its strategy and execution; willingness to stand up and be counted, demonstrating the "courage to speak truth to power"; adding value not just to the boardroom but to the C-suite as well.[i] Second, a candidate should be able to provide an external perspective on strategy and control; an independent and objective point of view when challenging management; a neutral point of view whenever there are conflicts of interests; and business connections and contacts.[ii] It is important, however, to remember:

> Experience does not equal competence.[iii]

---

1 The Malaysian Code on Corporate Governance 2012, Recommendation 2.2, 2–1, 2–2 states: "The Nominating Committee's responsibilities include assessing and recommending to the board the candidature of directors, appointment of directors to board committees, review of board's succession plans and training programmes for the board. In assessing suitability of candidates, considerations should be given to the competencies, commitment, contribution and performance. The Nominating Committee should facilitate board induction and training programmes. The nomination and election process of board members should be disclosed in the annual report."

"The board should establish a policy formalising its approach to boardroom diversity. The board through its Nominating Committee should take steps to ensure that women candidates are sought as part of its recruitment exercise. The board should explicitly disclose in the annual report its gender diversity policies and targets and the measures taken to meet those targets."

2 Leading companies have specific diversity and inclusion targets and appoint a senior manager whose responsibility is to make sure those targets are met.

3 For large companies the board must have at least 30% women directors; MCCG 2017 recognizes SMEs may have difficulty adopting all its recommendations and therefore draws a distinction between large public listed entities and SMEs.

Competence in the boardroom is about the ability to do all the things already mentioned and, above all, it is about appropriate boardroom behavior—evaluated annually in the board effectiveness assessment; the results of which feature in the annual report. There are different approaches to identifying desired behavioral attributes, but they share common elements, shown in Table 11.1.

Table 11.1: Two sets of desired INED attributes

Australian Institute of Company Directors (AICD) 10 attributes[iv]	Professor Richard Leblanc's 10 attributes[v]
1. Integrity	1. Independent judgment
2. Leadership	2. Integrity
3. Competence	3. Loyalty
4. Enterprise	4. Commitment
5. Fairness	5. Capacity to challenge
6. Commitment	6. Willingness to act
7. Confidence	7. Conceptual thinking skills
8. Respect	8. Communication skills
9. Accountability	9. Teamwork skills
10. Transparency	10. Influence skill
See Appendix 11.2 for details	

Board effectiveness evaluations, undertaken by the chair and NRC, are an essential part of succession planning. To be done properly, from my experience, they must consider the following eleven attributes with answers to the questions shown in Table 11.2.

Table 11.2: Directors' gap analysis[vi]

Knowledge and performance areas	Questions to ask to establish board performance gaps
1. Ability to perform well within the board and with stakeholders	Is there sufficient diversity of thought in the board? Do directors have collective experience and expertise to understand and address the key risks and opportunities facing the organization, including those created by digital disruption and increased global competition? Does the board function effectively as a team? Is there a sense of trust among directors and between the board and management?

Table 11.2 (continued)

Knowledge and performance areas	Questions to ask to establish board performance gaps
2. Understanding director's fiduciary duties	Do directors understand their roles and responsibilities? Are directors aware of and acting in line with their fiduciary duties? Are directors familiar with common offences committed by directors under the relevant companies act?
3. Understanding how the board can improve financial performance	Are directors financially literate—do they understand income statements, balance sheets, cash flows, sources, and uses of funds and key ratios? Do directors regularly compare financial actuals with budgets? How do directors ensure differences between budget and actuals are addressed and corrective action is tracked?
4. Understanding governance and ethics issues	What is the chair's role in building an effective board?[4] What is the chair's role in board evaluation and feedback? How does the chair deal with a director who is not performing or not interacting effectively with other directors? How can the chair and company secretary help the board keep its mandates, policies, and practices up-to-date?
5. Understanding board's role in strategy and risk management	Do directors have a common understanding of their strategy? Can they articulate the company's values and goals? How are directors engaged in strategy development or are they rubber stamps? Do they understand the investors' risk appetite? Can directors assess the "cultural," systemic, "traditional," and "earnings driver" risks the board faces (discussed in Chapter 10)? What do directors know about countries and industries in which the company operates? Do directors understand how strategy affects the company's skills and resources, now and in the future? Are directors prepared for events putting them on the front line of high-stakes strategic decisions? Can directors justify measures and targets used to judge progress in achieving vision, mission and values? Can directors explain how the objectives reflect and support the agreed strategy and the choice of product markets and activities?

---

4 If there is a governance committee, it has the responsibility for doing what is allocated to the chair in Table 11.2.

Table 11.2 (continued)

Knowledge and performance areas	Questions to ask to establish board performance gaps
6. Understanding human capital as strategic tool	How much time does the board spend on succession planning and talent management? How well do directors understand key human resource trends and their impact on the company and its ability to deliver its goals? Can directors explain the approach to succession planning and the philosophy of talent management? How often do directors review replacement charts and competency dictionaries to ensure they are up-to-date? Are directors involved in evaluating the cost-effectiveness of talent management?
7. Ability to innovate and sustain organizational growth	Does the board regard innovation as a core responsibility? Does the board encourage and support idea generation, sharing of ideas, experimentation, controlled failure, innovative action, and learning? Do directors encourage the concept of success beginning with failure or do they foster a climate of fear of failure? Do directors understand how management approaches innovation? Do directors hear a range of ideas before management invest in business cases? Is innovation regarded as an essential skillset for the board to have?
8. Providing input for mergers and acquisitions	Do the directors have the analytical skills and experience to evaluate the barriers to and enablers for successful mergers, acquisitions or divestments in the areas of: 1. Promised synergies 2. Cultural compatibility 3. Funding and costs of capital 4. Logistics and supply chain 5. Technological infrastructure compatibility 6. Talent

Table 11.2 (continued)

Knowledge and performance areas	Questions to ask to establish board performance gaps
9. Providing input to IT strategy and implementation	How well do directors understand the role of IT in creating and capturing value, as well as reducing cost? Do directors understand the importance of IT to achieve company objectives? Do directors appreciate the potential for IT developments to destroy the company business model? Do directors appreciate IT and cybersecurity risks? Are directors up-to-date with the latest thinking on cybersecurity and what plans have they put in place? Do directors know what the business interruption plans are and have they checked their robustness? Has the board developed a succession plan for IT personnel?
10. Ability to provide industry and business leadership	Are directors up-to-date with regulations as they might affect the company? Are directors capable of acting as spokespersons for the company and industry? Do directors work with peers and others in industry to ensure effective collective advocacy to minimize the adverse impact of new regulations on the industry and company?
11. Reconciling stakeholder interests with shareholder value	How well do directors understand the financial and reputation risks associated with subsidiaries, and how are those risks being mitigated? How well do directors understand local regulatory requirements applicable to subsidiaries? How much time do directors spend on issues associated with subsidiaries? Is there a governance framework clearly setting out roles and responsibilities of parent and subsidiary boards? 1. Does it clearly indicate matters that must be reviewed and approved by the parent board? 2. With clear and open communications between the parent and subsidiary boards? Do some directors sit on both subsidiary and parent boards and how do they reconcile conflicts of interest between parent and subsidiary if they arise?

Only by answering these questions can the chair and NRC know what skills and experience are missing in the board as a whole, and the level of competence of each individual director. Based on this analysis, the chair and NRC can plan succession for the board and tailor-make training and development programs for each director, as they assess existing needs and think about future needs.

Applying this process properly to succession planning for directors and the top management team is time-consuming. Moreover, it can be seriously undermined when dealing with either the founding family and its ambitions for its members or a change of government, if the organization is either a government or government linked entity where external political considerations and changes of direction require a wholesale replacement of key personnel.[5]

CEO Succession

> CEO succession planning is a core responsibility of the board… the evidence suggests that boards. are not uniformly effective in carrying out this function… the skill and care with which a board plans for a CEO departure and identifies a qualified successor can provide important insights into the general care with which they exercise their oversight responsibilities and the overall quality of governance at the firm.[vii]

Planning CEO succession often proves very difficult and sometimes can lead to embarrassing failure, as happened with HP with three departing CEOs in a row—Carly Fiorina[viii] followed by Mark Hurd[ix] and then Leo Apotheker.[x]

Recruiting a CEO can be done in three ways:[xi] First, rationally, relying on a succession planning process with replacement charts, redundancy in bench strength and depth, formal assessment methods and transition planning. This approach is expensive and often causes talented candidates who did not get chosen to leave the company. Second, politically, more like a horse race depending on competing board factions and vested stakeholder interests. This approach can be highly divisive and may not lead to the best candidate getting the job. Third, emotionally, depending on the current CEO's attitude to recruiting a replacement and the relationship with the CEO and the senior management team. This approach can lead to problems when what is needed is a different type of CEO from the incumbent who is likely to look for a clone. It is also important to remember there are ten reasons why CEO succession plans fail,[xii] shown in Appendix 11.3.

---

5 For example, the opposition victory in Malaysia's 14th general election in May 2018 resulted in a change of government policy and direction affecting all government linked entities and third-party contractors to government projects. This led to the resignation of the entire board of Khazanah—the state sovereign wealth fund—to "clear the deck to allow the government to restructure it" on July 27, 2018, replaced by a completely new board on July 30, 2018 with a new CEO from August 20, 2018. The impact of this change of direction will affect succession planning and talent management not only at Khazanah, but also at all its subsidiary boards as well.

In any event, successful CEO succession planning requires hard conversations based on courage, candor and common sense:

> At the end of the day, courage, candor and common sense lie at the heart of effective CEO succession. Planning is critical, tools and methodologies are important, but in the final analysis, successful transitions rest upon the ability of proud and powerful business professionals to have these essential, hard conversations each step of the way.[xiii]

What should the chair and NRC look for when appointing a CEO? Based on a five-year project for INSEAD,[xiv] the authors found effective CEOs were no longer "commanders in chief," but "chief enabling officers" instead:

> The contemporary CEO cannot pretend he or she knows more than other members of the organisation, has access to data and information they don't and sees further ahead than anyone else. Today's knowledge workers have superior technical skills, and technology has made information accessible to all. In management, as in other fields, collaboration has long since replaced individual genius as the principal source of creativity. Trying to apply the old model of determining strategy in the corner office and issuing orders is simply ineffective and inefficient today. From "Commander-in-Chief", the CEO has become "Chief Enabler of the Organisation". His or her role is to *enable* other employees to perform.[xv]

The conclusions of the twenty CEOs in the study from around the world were that such enabling CEOs:

1. *Reduce uncertainty:* In times of increasing complexity, this is a core practice of effective CEOs. They have only a few priorities, described simply and in quantitative terms. They distribute leadership, recognizing leaders exist at all levels in the organization. They streamline structure and governance with as few rules as possible—creating new rules, policies, and procedures only when necessary and culling outdated ones on a regular basis. They use simple language, mentoring people to simplify rather than complicate things, holding people accountable for creating unnecessary complexity. They promote clarity and transparency at all times, making information and data accessible and understandable to all members of the organization; recognizing transparency eliminates distrust and the frictions it creates.
2. *Encourage collaboration, removing organizational barriers:* Good CEOs promote horizontal, vertical, and diagonal collaboration by setting expectations, allocating time, establishing platforms and formats for collaborative work, and rewarding collaborative behavior. They recognize collaboration does not come naturally—modern organizations are full of barriers, such as asymmetrical knowledge, geographical distance, organizational hierarchy, and even office design. They spot these barriers and remove them. Most importantly, they set an example of openness and proactivity in fostering collaboration.
3. *Create autonomy for employees:* As Peter Drucker pointed out, knowledge workers need autonomy to work out for themselves the best ways of doing things; man-

agers should get out of their way and let them get on with their jobs.[xvi] Effective CEOs should make as few decisions as possible, giving the opportunity to others in the organization.[6]

4. *Support but challenge:* Good CEOs believe in the ability of their people and, if they prove effective, give them complete support. They challenge colleagues by questioning assumptions, encouraging alternative thinking, negotiating higher targets and provoking unorthodox approaches. They energize staff with ambitious goals, tough benchmarks and examples of superior performance—along with stories of hubris that led to disaster.

5. *Educate:* Effective CEOs make learning one of the company's values. They build it into every job and create training programs or corporate universities, rotating people across positions, functions and geographies to broaden their horizons. Investment in employee development is the most protected line of the budget. The CEOs themselves are educators, mentors and coaches and expect subordinates to do the same. *"Leaders teaching future leaders"* becomes an organization-wide value.

6. *Stay in touch with business and the outside world:* Good CEOs monitor the "big picture" by constantly reviewing performance indicators, but most importantly proactively speaking with colleagues, consultants, experts, analysts, investors, academics, and politicians.

7. *Are role models:* This provides a behavioral benchmark for the CEO's subordinates and legitimacy to the CEO if he or she "walks the walk and talks the talk."

In summary:

> *The enabling CEO tries to keep things simple and fight organisational complexity in all its forms. He or she makes as few decisions as possible, doesn't meddle in office politics or power struggles and challenges staff, by setting high standards and asking tough questions. Such leaders support their followers with resources, attention and mentoring—energising the whole organization.*[xvii] [Emphasis mine]

There is another attribute the study identified when appointing a CEO—the ability to be a "crisis CEO." When a crisis hits, normal decision making breaks down; entirely new answers are needed fast. The CEO must make sure the company finds these solutions before it is too late.[xviii] The advice offered on how to be an effective "crisis CEO" is:

1. *Accept crises happen and be prepared:* Good CEOs know crises will happen on their watch and so must be prepared for the day when a crisis strikes. Preparation means working out scenarios for organizational response, studying what other companies have done, training people, and accumulating resources critical

---

6 This advice may seem obvious to people who live in "low power distance" cultures; it goes against everything people who live in "high power distance" cultures believe about leadership.

for business survival. Yet even good CEOs do not know *when* a crisis will strike. However, assuming it will happen, talking openly about it; and preparing for it, reduce its abnormality, make it feel it belongs among "normal" events, making it easier for everyone to cope when the worst happens.

2. *Mitigate risks:* The best way to manage a crisis is to avoid one in the first place. Good CEOs develop a comprehensive system of risk identification and mitigation, which combines mathematical tools, big data, diverse human expertise and leadership judgment grounded in experience, knowledge and intelligence.

3. *Stay calm:* Good CEOs keep a cool head and continue to work rationally, relying particularly on their ability to think systemically.

4. *Act quickly:* Flexibility, rapid response to initial feedback and swift adjustments in the course of action: short feedback loops, experimentation, adjustments, learning from mistakes—these are all ingredients of effective crisis management.

5. *Organize "teaming": collaboration:* Although the CEO takes on the responsibility for crisis management, it is even more important when uncertainty prevails, to draw on the intelligence and experience of many people. Effective CEOs organize "teaming": collaboration, cutting across formal organizational boundaries. "Teaming" mobilizes the creative energy of people from different parts of the company to not only to overcome the crisis but also to come out of it stronger than before.

6. *Pay attention to people:* In a crisis, CEOs must become even more attentive to the ideas and *feelings* of their employees. Through "teaming," they seek out and test solutions. In return, they provide the direction and authority sought by their staff. But they also need to supply empathy and sympathy, recognizing the unprecedented nature of the challenge and stressful working conditions. They make themselves more available to provide support and advice where needed, communicating with warmth and humor, exhibiting a confidence and optimism they may not feel at the time that the crisis can be tamed by working together:

> The CEOs we interviewed don't make a drama out of crisis. They accept that risk-taking is an indispensable part of their jobs, but are prepared mentally and physically for the moment crisis strikes. Being ready to move when it's least expected and adopting a different behaviour pattern at short notice stands them in good stead for the day when unforeseen circumstances arise.[xix]

Perhaps one of the reasons why CEOs promoted from within do better than CEOs hired from outside in seven out of ten cases,[xx] is because the chair and NRC have the necessary information to assess whether the candidate is a good "enabling" and good "crisis" CEO, whereas when hiring from outside, they have to take it on faith from headhunters with a vested interest in closing the sale.

Remuneration and Performance Measurement

Assuming the board has an effective process for appointing a good CEO, what should the chair and NRC consider? First it is worth remembering boards give underperforming CEOs more latitude than might be expected.[xxi] This is because turnover of CEOs is a function of board oversight, shareholder oversight and financial restatements[xxii] and CEO evaluations are not rigorous—only 16% of directors believe CEO evaluations are rigorous.[xxiii]

Second, CEOs (at least in the United States and United Kingdom), are grossly overpaid for what they do; particularly if we consider modern CEOs are no longer commanders in chief who "alone can fix it," but "enablers" relying on distributed leadership across and down the organization. In 1965, Peter Drucker argued CEOs should be paid twenty times the average American workers salary.[xxiv] He has been ignored:

> As things stand now, many CEOs earn more in a single workday than the average worker makes in an entire year.
>
> In many respects, extremely large CEO compensation packages are problematic. The practice over-emphasizes the impact of a single individual and undervalues the contributions of other employees to the success of a company. *What make these ratios even more troublesome are studies that show that companies with high CEO-to-worker pay ratios have lower shareholder returns*[xxv]*than companies with lower ratios.*[xxvi] [Emphasis mine]

Fourth, Equilar research showed external CEOs cost between $1–2.5 million more than internal CEOs for three reasons: a) they already have CEO experience and internal candidates do not, b) they must be compensated for incentives they forego to join, and c) underperforming companies must pay a risk premium.[xxvii]

Equilar's research would, however, seem to contradict other findings, if the comparison between myth and reality shown in Table 11.3 is correct.

Table 11.3: CEO compensation myths and reality[xxviii]

Myths	Reality
1. CEOs need high pay to motivate them to exceptional performance.	High achieving CEOs will work hard whatever they are paid. Given human motivation, people interested in being CEOs come in this category: "From my experience working with these people, *they will work hard regardless of salary.*"
2. Large CEO salaries reflect market demands for a CEO's unique skills and contribution to the bottom line.	CEOs are not that exceptional and it's almost impossible to measure their singular contribution to the bottom line. "No matter how talented, CEOs cannot run their companies alone. Other qualified people are needed to make it happen. Given economic upswings and downswings, it's very hard to determine the exact value a single CEO creates or destroys. A company's success is always the result of a team effort."
3. The market provides effective signals regarding remuneration through benchmarking	The market is imperfect providing weak signals of appropriate levels of remuneration "At any given time, there are few jobs available and not many candidates with the skills and attributes sought. – Not all firms have the same objectives, for example, government-linked companies and state-owned enterprises, often have—legitimately—different objectives from family-controlled firms, and from firms with widely dispersed ownership. – Even firms with similar ownership structures and objectives may pursue significantly different business strategies and, consequently, seek different skill sets from senior executives. – Remuneration data is not easily available, and its quality is generally not high. – The few candidates for the posts available offer significantly different skill sets."[xxix]

The reason for this difference is the greed spiral affecting CEO compensation, which NRC's seem powerless to break and which seems to be disconnected from performance. It is the result of the fear good CEOs will be poached if they are not paid in the top quartile; the "above average effect" where CEO recruits are paid above average on the presumption promoted by headhunters they are "above average" performers;[xxx] of the stock options granted since 1993, whose deleterious economic and social impact has been made worse by share buybacks,[xxxi] which have nothing to do with value creation and everything to do with maximizing the value of the options granted to the CEO:

> In 1993, US Congress amended the tax code to tie executive pay closer to performance by allowing stock options. As a result, the percentage of CEO in options went from 35% in 1994 to more than 85% in 2001 and *average pay went from 140 times that of average employees in 1991 to 500 times in 2003.*[xxxii] [Emphasis mine]

So, what are the best performance metrics for CEOs if boards are to optimize long-term value creation? Measurement candidates are total shareholder return (TSR), economic profit (EP), and innovation and future value creation (FV).

For TSR to be a valuable measure, it must be broken down into its component parts, shown in Figure 11.1. Current value (CV) reflects the mix of growth, profit, and operating return metrics and their performance can explain close to 50% of shareholder returns. The other 30–50%, depending on the company, can be explained by the expectation of growth, innovation and FV based on what management states its strategy to be. FV can be inferred from taking enterprise value (EV) minus CV and is based on discounted cash flows (DCF), providing insight into the level of expected growth beyond current earnings and cash flows from current operations.[xxxiii]

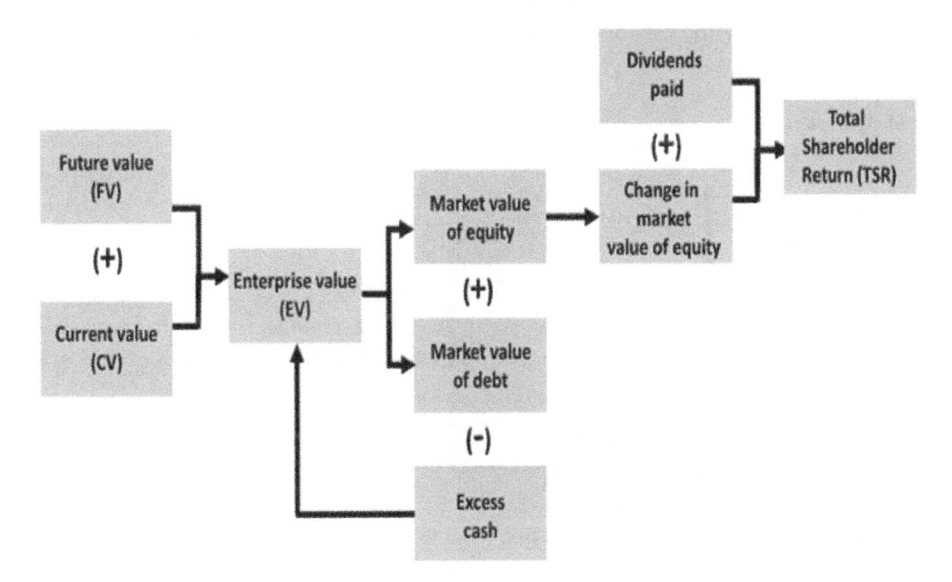

Figure 11.1: Components of TSR[xxxiv]

There are two problems with TSR. The first is that it easily gamed by CEOs:

> Research into CEO pay shows that total shareholder return (TSR) is, by far, the most dominant performance metric...Yet, increased TSR often has little to do with CEO effort or actually growing a business for the long term...TSR is easily gamed through cost-cutting measures..., reducing R&D, stock buybacks, or financial engineering. In contrast, developing new products, training staff, and increasing sales take more creativity and may take years to bear fruit. *Researchers found that economic performance explains only 12 percent of variance in CEO pay, whereas more than 60 percent is explained by company size, industry, and existing company pay policy. None of those other measures are performance driven.*[xxxv] [Emphasis mine]

The second problem with TSR is it is based on what Jack Welch called "the dumbest idea in the world"—maximizing shareholder value rather than focusing on creating long-term value through creating loyal customers through investing in people, innovative products and processes and maximizing the social "license to operate."[xxxvi] TSR has not been the driver behind the staggering growth of Apple, Facebook, Amazon, or Alphabet in the United States; and certainly not behind the rise of the Chinese giants, Alibaba, TenCent, Huawei, and Baidu. In the words of Jack Ma, founder CEO of Alibaba:

> We believe customers are number one. Employees number two. Shareholders number three.[xxxvii]

EP at least uses the cost of capital as a way of assessing whether the value created exceeds the WACC—the cost of capital of the enterprise, shown in Figure 11.2.

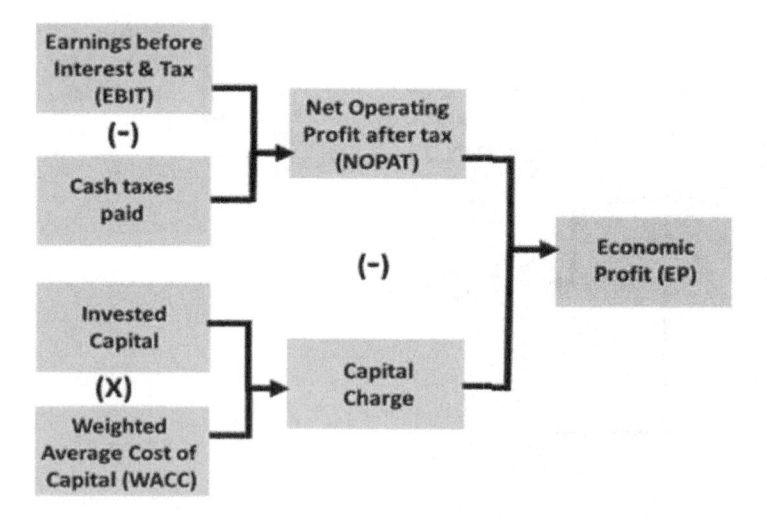

Figure 11.2: Economic profit value driver tree[xxxviii]

In theory, the EP approach is a good one. However, in practice it does not seem to have worked out as intended. Over the period 2003–2012, more than 43% of the S&P 500 was achieving a cumulative five-year return on invested capital (ROIC) less than their WACC, destroying value for their shareholders. There were other problems as well. The EP approach only correlated 38% with TSR; it did not measure capital efficiency (ROA/ROABA) or quality of earnings which creates long-term value. Most seriously, the emphasis on short-term EPS can lead to reduced investment in R&D, capex and innovation to meet short-term targets at the expense of long-term sustainability. *Finally, it is subject to earnings manipulation through share buybacks which create no added value but raise the value of CEOs' stock options artificially.*[xxxix]

A better approach to measuring the performance of the CEO would be to provide a "line of sight" to future value creation, with remuneration based on how well this is done. This forces the CEO and senior management to consider investing in process innovation, developing breakthrough new products, entering brand new markets; creating new business models, working in new industries and ecosystems, and investing new sources of capital (rather than buying back shares to improve the value of options). This is shown in Figure 11.3.

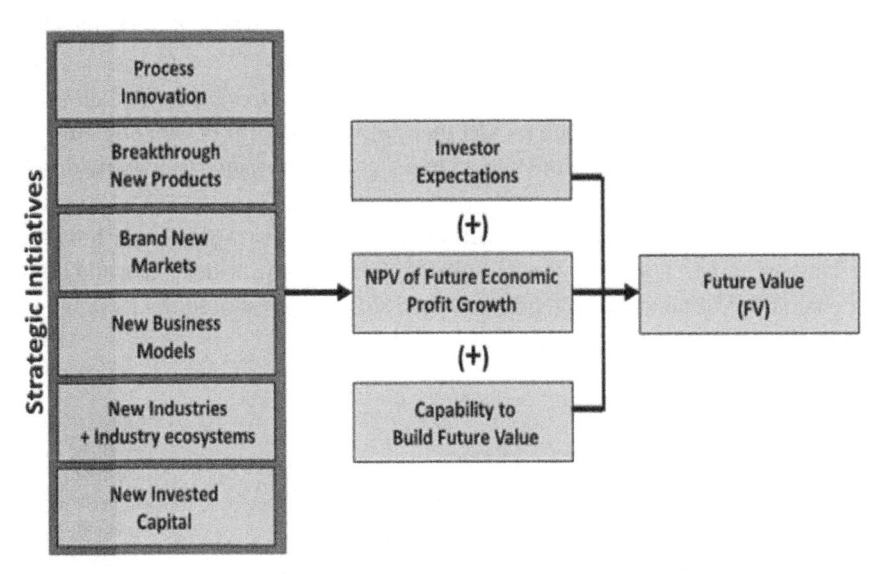

Figure 11.3: Future value tree[xl]

Including input key performance indicators (KPIs), demonstrating how the net present value (NPV) of future growth will be achieved, matching it to investor expectations and highlighting the increased capability to build future value provides a "line of sight" to long-term value creation instead of financial engineering designed to increase the share price in the short term.

This can be broken down into targeted levels of CEO performance for the board to evaluate in terms of creating CV and FV. CV creation consists of everyday "situational work" measuring improvement in revenue, margins, costs, TQM and manufacturing efficiencies on a quarterly and annual basis. CV creation also includes medium-term "systemic work" measuring improvements year on year from *existing customers* in revenue and margin growth, NOPAT and EP improvements achieved through strategic initiatives in innovation (shown in Figure 11.3) as part of the annual budgeting process.

FV creation provides the metrics of long-term value creation, divided into three different time horizons:
1. *First, 3–5 years, measuring progress made in "breakthrough work,"* which covers the portfolio of products and services and improvements in 3–5-year revenue, margin, EBIT and ROIC arising from new products, markets, technologies and channels from *new customers.*
2. *Second, a five-year evaluation "transformational work" on the business model,* which reviews the five-year growth in revenue, ROIC exceeding 8% and how relative P/E has performed, as a result of the long-range strategy and the implementation of innovation.
3. *Third, the seven-year perspective for "global transformation work,"* covering *changes in the business portfolio,* and their impact on portfolio revenue growth, ROIC, CV, and FV growth in the light of industry and ecosystem transformation.[xli]

Figure 11.4 shows how CV and FV creation are linked by strategies and how the long-range goals cascade down to quarterly results to provide a short-term and long-term evaluation framework for the CEO, which still applies should the CEO depart unexpectedly.

FV creation

CEO Work Level 5	'Global transformational work' on business portfolio measuring: 7 year change in portfolio revenue growth, ROIC, P/E, CV/FV $ growth, business portfolio, industry structure and ecosystem transformation	Goal-setting cascade linking long-term plans to quarterly results
CEO Work Level 4	'Transformational work' on business model measuring: Relative 5 year revenue growth, ROIC>8% and relative P/E through business strategy and new business model innovation	
CEO Work Level 3	'Breakthrough work' on product/service portfolio measuring: 3-5 year revenue growth, EBIT, margin, NOPAT, ROIC growth from *new* products, markets, technologies, channels and product portfolio strategy	

CV creation

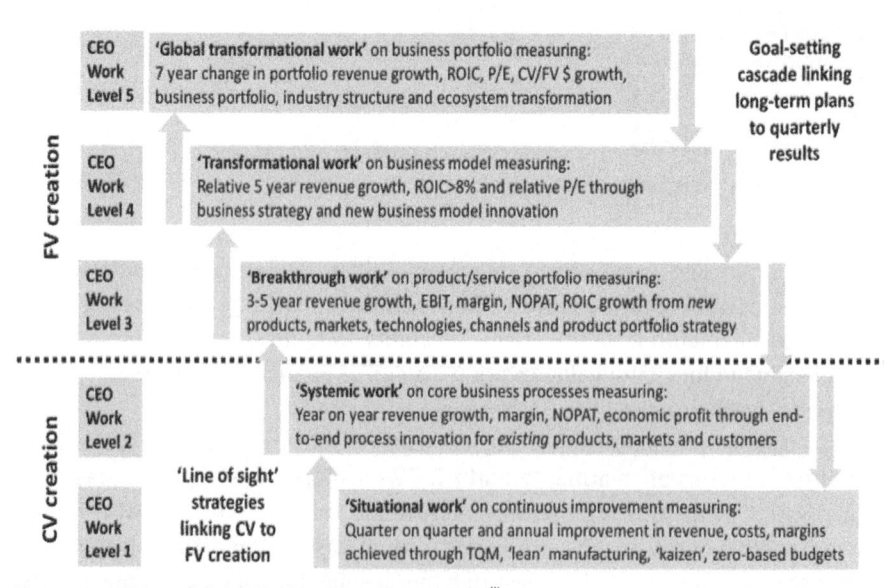

CEO Work Level 2	'Systemic work' on core business processes measuring: Year on year revenue growth, margin, NOPAT, economic profit through end-to-end process innovation for *existing* products, markets and customers	
CEO Work Level 1	'Line of sight' strategies linking CV to FV creation	'Situational work' on continuous improvement measuring: Quarter on quarter and annual improvement in revenue, costs, margins achieved through TQM, 'lean' manufacturing, 'kaizen', zero-based budgets

Figure 11.4: "Line of sight" linking CV and FV creation[xlii]

Applying a framework of this type to CEO remuneration would go a long way to reducing the increasing unhappiness of shareholders with the excessive levels of CEO remuneration that do not seem to be clearly connected with value creation, as opposed to financial engineering to maximize the short-term share price.

This assumes a CEO will be in the job for the seven-year period indicated. The NRC needs to consider the long-tail consequences of decisions taken by the CEO after the CEO's contract ends. A solution to this problem is to hold the variable (bonus) element of the CEO's remuneration in escrow until the time elapsed is sufficient to take account of the consequences of the decision. If all goes well, the money is released; if there is a problem, the money is clawed back.

Another consideration regarding CEO remuneration and its role in creating long-term value is whether their payouts can be justified:

> Too many golden parachutes and too many retirement packages are of a size that clearly seems only in the interest of the departing executive...It would seem that compensation committees have lost sight of the original principles, resulting in little or no value for shareholders despite excessive compensation.
>
> Directors who approve such awards for an incoming CEO or allow them to continue in place for existing CEOs may be held accountable when CEOs receive tens of millions after a short or unproductive tenure. *They may also be held accountable if CEOs are paid twice for their successes.*[xliii] [Emphasis mine]

That said, directors must recognize particular circumstances of the company, the credibility of its CEO as a long-term creator of value and the track record of sustained performance all affect how the market will view the remuneration of the CEO:

> Of course, sustainable value added is the best measure of a CEO's performance. And the weaknesses pointed out in TSR, EPS etc., are all true. But in the real world, especially for listed companies, *those shorter term and manipulation prone numbers take on extreme or even existential importance if they attract the attention of aggressive short-term investors like hedge and vulture funds, activists etc., should they consider them sub-par.* And dealing with this is not only distracting but might also force the company to take measures which impede longer term value-added initiatives. So, I believe, despite all the good arguments against TSR, EPS etc., they should nevertheless feature in a CEO's performance targets. The weighting they carry depends on the company's current circumstances. Take GE for example, and Jack Welch. At his time, I would have assigned a relatively low weighting to such measures because he had great credibility as a sustainable value creator. But right now, with the share price under pressure; years of underperformance under Immelt; intolerant markets; and a new CEO, Flannery's targets should contain a heavy dose of TSR, EPS etc.[xliv] [Emphases mine]

The market seems indeed to have been intolerant of Flannery's plans and the GE board terminated him after only fourteen months.[xlv] Previously GE had only six CEOs in 120 years.

Company Succession and Talent Management

Regulators do not specifically mention talent management, only mentioning succession planning. This is because talent management covers all levels of the organization, whereas the presumption is boards need only concern themselves with the senior positions, given the limited amount of time they can give to the subject. In the past, regulators viewed talent management as an operational matter best left to executive management and HR. The modern view appreciates the importance of the board working with management and HR, shown in Table 11.4.

Table 11.4: Four steps in talent management[xlvi]

Steps in the Process	Board's role	CEO's role	HR's role
Step 1: Develop talent strategy and define who the talent is	Ensure strategy satisfies *agreed* business strategy, vision, values, and culture Challenge strategy presented by management to the board Agree optimum philosophy	Agree with board impact of business strategy on talent needs Align strategy to satisfy business strategy, vision, values, and culture Identify current and *future* needs	Develop future focused strategy with CEO Agree *future* roles and responsibilities and their impact on talent with CEO
Step 2: Identify pivotal positions and competencies	Approve pivotal positions identified by CEO Ensure competency models deliver business strategy, vision, values, and culture	Determine number of pivotal positions Agree key current and future competencies to satisfy business strategy, values, and culture	Identify future pivotal positions Update competency models to reflect future business needs
Step 3: Identify and develop talent pipeline	Get to know each high potential candidate personally; Assess external options for leadership if internal pipeline is inadequate.	Agree talent pipeline based on individual appraisals; Provide career enhancing opportunities for high potential candidates; Agree individual talent development plans; Provide performance feedback and progress reviews to identified talent	Develop up-to-date training needs analysis; Reflect strategy in recruiting. Recruit and develop external talent when needed; Agree replacement chart with CEO and top management.

Table 11.4 (continued)

Steps in the Process	Board's role	CEO's role	HR's role
Step 4: Monitor and evaluate	Ensure succession planning, talent management, and competency modeling are regular board items. Require high potential candidates to present to board meetings	Evaluate effectiveness of talent management and leadership development activities. Report regularly to board on progress. Take part in evaluating individuals' progress	Update talent management, leadership development, and succession planning progress annually. Review high potentials and their readiness to move to next role. Report on program status and individuals' progress

Perhaps the most important factor for the board to check is whether the agreed business strategy is vulnerable to failures in closing gaps between current and future organization design and current and future talent.

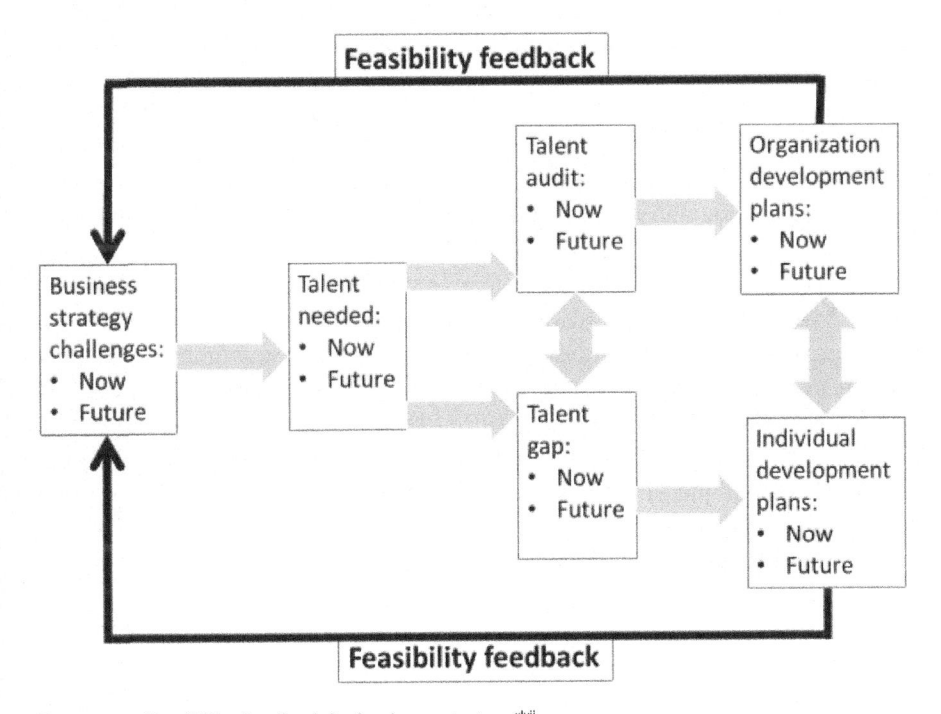

Figure 11.5: Feasibility feedback for business strategy[xlvii]

To minimize the risk of strategic failure, *it is essential to undertake regular "feedback loop" reviews*, shown in Figure 11.5 and *change the business strategy if the gaps prove to be serious*, rather than sticking with it and hoping all will be well.

Using the "Five P" Framework to Cross Check

It may help directors to use the "Five Ps," "purpose," "principles," and "processes" as lenses through which to view proposals on succession planning and talent management as a cross check that nothing important has been forgotten.

Purpose

Succession planning and talent management are driven by the business strategy; itself a reflection of the business purpose. In these circumstances, it is only appropriate that the chair and NRC should evaluate current and future members of the board based on their ability to contribute to developing, challenging, and advising on the best way to achieve the business purpose. Equally, it makes sense to check whether the background of future CEOs suits them to run the business, lest the board find itself in the same position as HP did with Carly Fiorina and Leo Apotheker.

Principles

Succession planning and talent management too often look only at the number of jobs needed to ensure the organizational design is still fit for purpose, with an understandable focus on the technical competencies required to do the jobs. However, this ignores "principles"—the agreed values determining with whom the company will do business; and how it will transact such activities. *Hiring and promoting very talented and skilled people who do not share the agreed values is a recipe for reputational disaster. The more talented, the more skilled, the more charismatic such people are, the greater the harm they can do.* The NRC must ensure the people they choose fit with and believe in the agreed values of the business; otherwise they run the risk of destroying the "tone at the top"; the company's social "license to operate"; alienating their own best people and the regulators.

Processes

Finally, it is critical to make sure the "processes" of recruitment, promotion and remuneration of pivotal people do not undermine the "principles" of the business, by hiring inappropriate role models and rewarding inappropriate behavior. It is particularly important remuneration of the CEO and the top team provides a clear "line of sight" linking CV to FV creation.

Conclusion

Boards are responsible for both succession planning and talent management, even though they spend so little time on them, despite asserting "people are our most important asset." When choosing directors, it is important to recognize experience is not enough. Directors should be able to think strategically; work with their colleagues; be willing to "speak truth to power" and bring an independent, objective perspective to deliberations. When evaluated in annual board assessments, there are eleven attributes to be covered.

CEO succession is perhaps the most important responsibility of the board and it is typically undertaken rationally, politically, or emotionally. Whichever route is chosen, directors should remember there are ten possible reasons for failure, which may explain why the process outcomes are often unsatisfactory. That said, it is critical to recognize effective CEOs are no longer "commanders in chief," running a top-down command and control type of organization. Instead they are "enablers," relying on distributed leadership across and down the organization to create collaborative "teaming," bringing together relevant skills from across the organization to solve problems.

Clearly the focus on TSR alone and shareholder value maximization does not work well, as it allows CEOs to indulge in financial engineering to maximize the value of their stock options in the name of shareholder value. Instead, they should be remunerated through a system providing a clear "line of sight" linking CV to FV creation, encouraging them to build sustainable value by investing in the future, rather than focusing on short-term EPS.

Working with the CEO, the NRC process for managing talent involves four steps: developing the strategy and defining who the talent is, agreeing current and future pivotal positions with their associated competencies with the CEO, identifying and developing the talent pipeline, and monitoring and evaluating its effectiveness.

The NRC must check whether the agreed business strategy is still feasible by examining the suitability of organizational design and individual talent. If these prove to be too unsuitable, use the feasibility feedback loops to revisit the agreed business strategy and modify it, acknowledging their implications on the feasibility of the agreed strategy, rather than sticking with it in the vain hope all will be well.

Finally, the "purpose," "principles," and "processes" lenses of the "Five P" framework are useful cross checks nothing material has been omitted.

Appendix 11.1: MCCG 2017 Guidance Regarding INED Tenure

1. When assessing a director's independence, it is critical to evaluate whether the director can act independently of management as well as whether the director satisfies the criteria of independence in the Malaysian Companies Act 2016
2. Long exposure to the company's management and its strategy may undermine the ability of directors to remain objective
3. INEDs may also become "dependent" as a result of remuneration packages and benefits
4. At least 50% of the board comprises INEDs; for *large companies,* INEDs must be the majority
5. INED tenure should not exceed a term of nine (9) cumulative years. After nine years the INED may continue to serve as:
   a. Nonindependent director
   b. INED, if and only if the board has sought, justified the request and obtained annual shareholder approval for a further three (3) years
   c. After twelve (12) years, if the board wishes to retain the INED, it must do so via annual shareholders' approval through a two-tier voting process
   d. *Step Up: The board has a policy to limit the tenure of INEDs to nine (9) years*
   e. *Large companies* are not encouraged to retain an INED for more than nine (9) years
   f. If companies wish to retain INEDs beyond twelve (12) years, they must use the following two-tier process:
      i. Shareholders votes will be cast as follows in the same shareholders' meeting:
         1. Tier 1: only *large shareholders* of the company vote
         2. Tier 2: shareholders other than *large shareholders* vote
      ii. Large shareholder is defined as:
         1. Person entitled to exercise or control the exercise of not less than 33% of the voting shares
         2. Largest shareholder of voting shares
         3. Person with power to appoint or cause to be appointed a majority of the directors or to make or cause to be made, decisions affecting the business or administration of the company
      iii. Decision for retaining the INED is based on the vote of Tier 1 and a simple majority of Tier 2. If more than one large shareholder in Tier 1, a simple majority in Tier 1 determines outcome of Tier 1 vote
      iv. The resolution passes if both Tier 1 and Tier 2 votes support it. The resolution is defeated if there is a difference between Tier 1 and Tier 2 or if Tier 1 voters abstain

MCCG 2017, pp. 24, 25

Appendix 11.2: AICD's 10 Core Director Attributes

1. Integrity	Expected behavior
"Being honest in all things and true to the role and duties entrusted to you and the board" AICD (2010), *Guide for Directors and Boards—Delivering Good Corporate Governance*, 6	1. Act honestly and in good faith 2. Act with integrity and in keeping with your fiduciary duty 3. Exercise powers for proper purposes only and for the benefit of the organization 4. When acting, consider all relevant laws and regulations 5. Respect confidentiality and do not disclose improperly or misuse information or take advantage of a corporate opportunity received in your capacity as a director
2. Leadership	
"Providing a strong and positive example of appropriate decision making, attitude and behaviour on behalf of the organisation" Ibid., 7	1. Provide effective leadership to make wise decisions and be a role model of the values and principles of the organization for the benefit of all stakeholders 2. Contribute to sound judgments and decision regarding strategic focus and the circumstances at the time 3. Apply your experience and unique perspective for the benefit of the organization
3. Competence	
"Developing and fostering the existence, maintenance, development and application of appropriate skills, knowledge, personal aptitudes and acumen required for a director and the board" Ibid., 8	1. Foster the presence of appropriate personal skills, knowledge, aptitude, and acumen for directors given the context of the company on whose board they sit 2. Continuously develop and update these skills and knowledge to enhance the aptitudes and acumen of directors through formal and informal education, training, and development 3. Develop, review and evaluate on a regular basis appropriate governance policies, systems and processes for the company, the board and the directors

4. Enterprise	Expected behavior
"Guiding the organisation towards fulfilment of its organisational objectives or purpose by: setting appropriate strategic direction and appetite for risk, fostering entrepreneurial approaches and assessing whether the organisation's resources and organisational culture are aligned to achieve those objectives or that purpose" Ibid., 9	1. In the board contribute collaboratively to setting the mission, vision and values as well as strategy and monitoring their implementation 2. In an informed and deliberative manner balance the potential business upsides with the associated risks and potential downsides and ensure they are within the agreed risk appetite 3. Identify risk and ensure that they are analyzed appropriately using a suitable risk management framework
5. Fairness	
"Behaving fairly and equitably, in the interest of the organisation, with proper regard to the legitimate interests of relevant stakeholders" Ibid., 10	1. Respect the rights of shareholders, and the relevant interests of minority shareholders or members 2. Have regard to the interests of all stakeholders with fairness and equity
6. Commitment	
"Dedicating adequate engagement by giving the necessary time, thought, care and diligence so that the interests of the organisation are appropriately served" Ibid., 11	1. Exercise care and diligence in discharging the functions and responsibilities of directors 2. Act conscientiously 3. Be available and attentive when needed 4. Be contactable and in touch with the organization between board meetings 5. Be mindful of the checks and balances needed in quality decision making
7. Confidence	
"Honouring and upholding the confidence that others place in the board and its directors, and the confidentiality of office of a director" Ibid., 12	1. Honor confidence and strengthen the reputation for integrity of the organization, its directors and the board 2. Address any potential conflict of interest including by promptly acknowledging, disclosing and managing the conflict according to relevant laws, regulation and governance protocols 3. Be conscious that public perceptions of potential conflicts, whether justified or not, can damage individual and organizational confidence and reputations 4. Deal with conflicts of interest appropriately in the boardroom

8. Respect	**Expected behavior**
"Behaving respectfully to others whether or not you agree with their input" Ibid., 13	1. Behave respectfully to others and to the physical and social environment in which the organization operates 2. Have due regard to the sustainable position of the organization as a member of the community and the environment (physical and social) in which it operates to maximize the long term "license to operate" 3. Be sensitive to cultural and religious differences and respect and value diversity 4. Appreciate that mutual respect is essential if a board is to be effective 5. Treat fellow directors and executives with respect
9. Accountability "Accepting responsibility for the proper discharge of the roles and responsibilities of the board and giving account to those to whom the responsibility is owed" Ibid., 14	1. The board should require the organization to engage actively with its stakeholders to account for its performance in discharging its duties and that of the organization in meeting its obligations
10. Transparency "Within reasonable commercial and confidentiality constraints, being frank, open and without pretext in the manner the board accounts to shareholders and stakeholders" Ibid., 15	1. The board should require its governance policies, systems, and processes to be published and disclosed 2. The behavior, deliberations, and decisions of a board and its directors should be consistent with, and defensible in terms of, its governance policies, systems, and processes

Appendix 11.3: Ten Reasons for CEO Succession Failure[xlviii]

1. *Talent disconnect*—the problem faced by HP with Carly Fiorina and Leo Apotheker
2. *Reluctant retirees and their four excuses*:
   a. The founder cannot imagine anybody else in the role
   b. The CEO can not accept mortality in absence of mandatory limits
   c. Work is so important the CEO does not have time to think about succession
   d. The CEO wants to avoid a horse race between internal candidates that could lead to factionalism below
3. *Absence of strategic HR input*:
   a. Only 31% of NACD respondents in 2014 said their chief HR officer had "a good or deal of influence"
   b. Nearly 25% said they had none
4. *Assessment tool obsession*:
   a. 75% of respondents favor multiple sources of data (past performance; 360s for internal candidates; reference checks for external)
   b. 19% rate behavioral interviews; 11% rate cognitive tests and 5% rate business simulations[xlix]
5. *Irrelevant criteria*:
   a. Cloning exercise
   b. Unfair comparisons (non-CEOs compared with CEOs) leading to difficult comparisons between performance and potential
   c. Not ready yet
   d. Personal preferences reflecting irrelevant bias (candidate is fat, candidate's wife's behavior)
   e. Prejudices re insiders or outsiders
6. *Cultural problems*: for example, Carly Fiorina at HP; Bob Diamond at Barclays
7. *Mysterious talent pool*: The directors do not know who the talent is. Most directors only meet them in the boardroom (97% according to Spencer Stuart). Only 31% had regular meetings outside the boardroom with C-1 and only 26% regularly did site visits where they could interact with candidates in their natural environments
8. *Never-ending transition*
9. *The "forever" CEO*: 39% remain as chair for at least one year; 26% for at least three, acting as shadow emperors. Spencer Stuart found 45% of departing CEOs remained as chair of the board for a while and the Conference Board found 36% were there for two years with 26% staying on for more than five years. It is a bigger problem in small companies than large ones in the US where 30% of companies with revenues greater than US$20 billion have policies preventing departing CEOs from staying on, while only 4.5% of companies with revenues less than US$500 million do so
10. *It is just for the big firms*: Small firms can not afford the redundancy required for bench strength and depth of the kind multinationals have

References

[i] Pierce, C. (2016), "Trends in Corporate Governance," quoted in *The Handbook of Corporate Governance*, edited by Richard Leblanc (Hoboken, NJ: John Wiley and Sons), 41.
[ii] Ibid., 50.
[iii] Leblanc, R. (2016), "Director Independence, Competency and Behavior," quoted in *The Handbook of Corporate Governance*, 171.
[iv] AICD (2010), *Guide for Directors and Boards—Delivering Good Corporate Governance*, 6–15.
[v] Leblanc (2016), op. cit., 177–178.
[vi] Based on Behan, B. (2011), *Great Companies Deserve Great Boards: A CEO's Guide to the Boardroom* (New York: Palgrave Macmillan).
[vii] Larcker, D. P. and Tayan, B. (2016), "CEO Succession Planning," quoted in *The Handbook of Corporate Governance*, op. cit., 155.
[viii] La Monica, P. (2005), "Fiorina Out, HP Stock Soars," *CNN Money*, February 10, 2005, https://money.cnn.com/2005/02/09/technology/hp_fiorina/, accessed on July 31, 2018.
[ix] Worthen, B. and Wing-Tan, P. (2010), "H-P Chief Quits in Scandal," *Wall Street Journal*, August 7, 2010, https://www.wsj.com/articles/SB10001424052748703309704575413663370670900, accessed on July 31, 2018.
[x] Goldman, D. (2011), HP CEO Apotheker Fired, Replaced by Meg Whitman," *CNN Money*, September 22, 2011, https://money.cnn.com/2011/09/22/technology/hp_ceo_fired/index.htm, accessed on July 31, 2018.
[xi] Nadler, M. (2016), "CEO Succession: An Owner's Guide for Directors," cited in *The Handbook of Corporate Governance*, op. cit., 121.
[xii] Ibid., 123–140.
[xiii] Ibid., 140.
[xiv] Shekshnia, S., Kravchenko, K., and Williams, E. (2018), *CEO School: Insights from 20 Global Leaders*, quoted in *INSEAD Knowledge: Leadership and Organisations*, May 9, 2018, https://knowledge.insead.edu/sites/all/themes/knowledge2015/, accessed on July 31, 2018.
[xv] Ibid,
[xvi] Drucker, P. (1992), *Management Challenges for the 21st Century* (Oxford: Butterworth Heinemann), 142.
[xvii] Shekshnia, Kravchenko, and Williams (2018), op. cit.
[xviii] Ibid.
[xix] Ibid.
[xx] Karlsson, P. O., Neilson, G. I., and Webster, J. C. (2016) "CEO Succession 2008: The Performance Paradox," *strategy+business* 51 (2008), quoted in *The Handbook of Corporate Governance*, op. cit., 148–149.
[xxi] Ibid., 146.
[xxii] Ibid., 147.
[xxiii] Research undertaken in 2013 by Stanford University and the Miles Group, cited in ibid., 147–148.
[xxiv] Kets de Vries, M. F. R. (2018), "Do CEOs Deserve their Pay?" *INSEAD Knowledge, Leadership and Organisations*, February 7, 2018, https://knowledge.insead.edu/sites/all/themes/knowledge2015/img/, accessed on July 21, 2018.
[xxv] Kets de Vries (2018), op. cit.
[xxvi] Ibid.
[xxvii] Equilar Inc., "Paying the New Boss: Compensation Analysis for Newly Hired CEOs," June 2013, cited by Karlsson, Neilson, and Webster (2016), op. cit., 149.
[xxviii] Kets de Vries (2016), op. cit.
[xxix] Bennett, C. (2018), "Benchmarking as a Tool for Determining Pay," *Singapore Business Times*, January 17, 2018, https://www.businesstimes.com.sg/opinion/benchmarking-as-a-tool-for-determining-pay, accessed on October 6, 2018.

xxx Ibid.
xxxi Lowrey, A. (2018), "Are Stock Buybacks Starving the Economy?" *The Atlantic,* July 31, 2018, https://www.theatlantic.com/business/archive/2018/07/are-stock-buybacks-starving-the-economy/566387/, accessed on August 4, 2018.
xxxii McRitchie, J. (2016), "The Individual's Role in Driving Corporate Governance," quoted in *The Handbook of Corporate Governance,* op. cit., 433.
xxxiii Ibid., 522.
xxxiv Van Clieaf, M. (2016), "Designing Performance for Long-Term Value," quoted in *The Handbook of Corporate Governance,* op. cit., 521.
xxxv McRitchie (2016), op. cit., 433.
xxxvi Denning, S. (2014), JP Morgan Embraces "The World's Dumbest Idea," *Forbes,* December 26, 2014, https://www.forbes.com/sites/stevedenning/2014/12/26/jp-morgan-embraces-the-worlds-dumbest-idea/#635de23ad098, accessed on August 4, 2018.
xxxvii Van Clieaf, M. (2016), "Designing Performance for Long-Term Value," quoted in *The Handbook of Corporate Governance,* op. cit., 520.
xxxviii Ibid., 517.
xxxix Ibid., 518.
xl Ibid., 520.
xli Ibid., 527.
xlii Based on ibid., 527.
xliii Hodgson, P. (2012), "Twenty-One U.S. CEOs with Golden Parachutes of More Than $100 Million," *GMI,* January 2012, quoted in Zinkin, J. (2014), *Rebuilding Trust in Banks: The Role of Leadership and Governance* (Singapore: John Wiley & Sons), 181–182.
xliv Nasr, Y. (2012), in an email to the author in answer to a question on the topic of CEO remuneration, August 12, 2018.
xlv Melin, A. and Ritcey, A. (2018), "GE's John Flannery May Get Nothing After 14-Month Tenure As CEO," *Bloomberg,* October 2, 2018, https://www.bloomberg.com/news/articles/2018-10-01/ge-s-john-flannery-may-get-nothing-after-14-month-tenure-as-ceo, accessed on October 2, 2018.
xlvi Based on Zinkin (2014), op. cit., 188–189.
xlvii Ibid., 186.
xlviii Nadler, M. (2016), "CEO Succession: An Owner's Guide for Directors," cited in The Handbook of Corporate Governance, op. cit., 123–137.
xlix Ibid., 128.

Chapter 12
Ensuring Internal Controls

This chapter is presented in five parts: the first explores the relative merits of three lines of defense and five lines of assurance; the second deals with "minding the numbers"; the third deals with compliance; the fourth briefly introduces the COSO enterprise risk management framework; and the fifth uses the "purpose" and "principles" lenses of the "Five P" framework to cross check everything material is covered.

Three Lines of Defense Versus Five Lines of Assurance

Traditionally, boards have relied on internal audit reporting to the audit committee to ensure the integrity of internal controls, using the so-called three lines of defense (TLOD). This approach has been promoted by the Institute of Internal Auditors (IIA). More recently, regulators have encouraged boards to adopt the so-called five lines of assurance (FLOA) approach because it involves the board and the CEO directly in the process of ensuring the integrity of the control processes. Table 12.1 compares the two approaches.

Table 12.1: "Lines of defense" approaches compared

TLOD[i]	FLOA[ii]
Reporting to management: 1. *First line of defense:* Management controls and internal control measures 2. *Second line of defense:* Compliance, inspection, quality risk management, security, and role and responsibility of the finance function **Reporting to audit committee:** 3. *Third line of defense:* Internal audit	**Reporting to management:** 1. *First line of assurance:* Management controls and internal control measures 2. *Second line of assurance:* Compliance, inspection, quality risk management, security and role and responsibility of the finance function **Reporting to audit committee:** 3. *Third line of assurance:* Internal audit 4. *Fourth line of assurance:* CEO actively responsible for reporting on residual risk; **Board collectively responsible for Directors Statement of Internal Control (DSIC):** 5. *Fifth line of assurance:* Board's collective liability

The key difference in the two approaches is in the TLOD approach where the IIA sees boards as overseers rather than active participants in defending the company, with external auditors and the regulator acting as last resorts.[iii] For example, the European

Confederation of Institutes of Internal Auditors (ECIIA) explains the TLOD approach as follows:

- As a first line of defense, the organization's operational management has ownership responsibility, and accountability for assessing, controlling, and mitigating risks.

- As a second line of defense, the risk management function (and also other supporting functions like compliance and quality) facilitates and monitors the implementation of effective risk management practices by operational management and assists the risk owners in reporting adequate risk related information up and down the organization.

- As a third line of defense, the internal auditing function will, through a [risk-based] approach, provide assurance to the organization's board and senior management, on how effective[ly] the organization assesses and manages its risks, including the manner in which the first and second lines of defense operate. This assurance task covers all elements of an organization's risk management framework: i.e. from risk identification, risk assessment and—response to communication of risk related information.[iv]

The IIA's model does not include the board of directors and equivalent governing bodies or senior management among the lines of defense. Instead, they are considered stakeholders served by the three lines. However, because they are responsible for setting organisational objectives and establishing structures to manage any risks arising in the pursuit of those objectives, they play an important role in risk and control.[v]

The TLOD approach is probably satisfactory in jurisdictions where class actions against directors by investors against directors do not happen. In litigious regimes, where class actions, based on contingency fees, are a regular feature of life, it may make more sense for directors to opt for the FLOA approach which involves the CEO and the board from the outset, given even the IIA recognizes directors and senior management "play an important role in risk and control," resulting from the organizational objectives they have agreed.

There are important advantages in adopting the FLOA approach.[vi] The board is actively engaged in ensuring the CEO and CFO operate within limits set by the risk appetite and tolerances agreed with the board to reflect the risk-reward profile of the company's investors. CEOs are directly responsible for reporting the treatment of residual risk to the board. Unlike the TLOD approach which focuses on avoiding shareholder value destruction, the FLOA approach has room for shareholder value creation as well.[vii] The status of internal audit is raised and there is a clearly defined role for risk specialists, allowing risk control to develop into risk treatment over time. Perhaps the most important advantage of the FLOA approach is the clear signal sent by regulators to boards and CEOs they must play a key role in risk governance.

"Minding the Numbers"

Audit committees need strong charters to fulfil their role. They also need directors who have the time, financial expertise, and professional skepticism to oversee the numbers; one of whom at least must be a qualified accountant with an understanding of GAAP (for the United States) and IFRS (for the rest of the world) principles and financial statements; the ability to use this understanding to evaluate how they have been applied to accounting for estimates, accruals, and reserves. Such an expert should have experience in preparing, auditing, analyzing, and evaluating financial statements of a breadth and depth of complexity comparable to the breadth and depth of the issues the organization will face in reporting its results. To be regarded as a financial expert, the individual must have acquired the relevant attributes as a principal financial officer, chief accountant, controller, or auditor. The committee as a whole must understand internal controls and procedures for financial reporting and the function of the audit committee.[viii]

The role and responsibilities of an effective audit committee have already been covered in Chapter 5, as have the role and responsibilities of the risk committee if there is one. Following in the footsteps of Sarbanes-Oxley, regulators around the world have required companies to implement effective, confidential whistle-blower policies designed to allow concerned individuals submit complaints anonymously to the audit committee regarding questionable accounting, auditing and violations of the company code of conduct:

> It is in every director's interest to ensure that whistle-blower mechanisms are effective and that their efforts visibly contribute to the enforcement of the company's compliance program.[ix]

There are seven areas in financial reporting where directors must dig deep to understand what is really going on.

Unsupported Manual Entry Adjustments

These are entries added "on top" of the automated results by management because they are nonroutine. Nonroutine data and estimates are likely to be more subjective—for example, write-offs of inventory or doubtful debtors, tax liabilities, and other expenses. Much of the fraud at WorldCom was the result of shifting top-side entries of expenses from the income statement to the balance sheet.[x] Directors must challenge top-side adjustments if they are material and, if the answers leave them uncomfortable, they should get independent advice on the treatment of such adjustments. It is important explanations are kept simple. Adjustments that can not be explained in simple language are likely to be aggressive or fraudulent.

Aggressive Revenue Recognition

High quality revenues are those booked *after* the customer has received the product or service, and is required to pay without any further performance required by the company or contingency. *A classic red flag is revenue being booked on purchases that were contingent on future actions.* For example, Qwest incorrectly accounted for $1.1 billion between 1999 and 2001.[xi] The revenues depended on the purchase of fiber capacity and future services; yet they were booked in advance, violating the principle revenues can only be recognized when matching costs are incurred. Tesco in the United Kingdom did the same mismatching of revenues and costs in 2014 which led to a £263 million overstatement of profits.[xii]

Continuous One-Off, Nonrecurring Charges

Companies need to make provisions for future expenses when they are not sure exactly what they will cost. Typical costs needing to be provisioned are merger and acquisition costs, product returns, stock write-offs, nonperforming loans, and lawsuits. Many of these are genuine nonrecurring items, such as damage caused by acts of nature (hurricanes, floods, and earthquakes) or mergers and one-off sales of assets. However, if a company keeps reversing reserves back into operating income, this may be to make the results look better than they really are. In such circumstances, directors should challenge the CFO by asking:
1. Why are the charges nonrecurring and not part of normal operations?
2. How were they determined and how accurately?
3. How likely is it that the charge will not be used?
4. What disclosures regarding these reversals will there be in the financial statements?

Directors should keep challenging the CFO until they are absolutely satisfied they understand the answers and the answers are valid. Opaque or angry answers, hesitant or changing explanations are red flags for fraud.

Regular Changes to Reserve, Depreciation/Amortization or Comprehensive Income Policies

Frequent changes in accounting policies often are designed to hide the truth about the numbers. Numbers may change as the business environment changes, but accounting policies and methods for recording them should not. For example, if sales increase, then the amount set in reserves for bad debts should rise accordingly, but the percentage used for setting aside the reserves should not. If it does, directors need vigorously to question why. For example, WorldCom's fraud was built on many malpractices, but $3.3 billion of fake profits was partially due to reversals of bad debt provisions.[xiii]

Capitalizing expenses and putting them on the balance sheet to be written off over time as opposed to expensing them in the current accounting period is something boards need to look at carefully. For example, it is reasonable to consider capitalizing R&D investments over the lifetime of the project, but judgment is needed to decide what the length of the lifetime might be—the duration of the patent if there is one, or some shorter period to recognize technical obsolescence? Some might even make the conservative case all expenses should be written off in the year in which they occur, because the R&D might not lead to successful projects. This is usually the basis on which A&P investments are written off as expenses rather than being capitalized as part of building the brand asset. Judgment is essential and, as with so much of accounting treatment, it is a matter of expert judgment and interpretation. All the more reason for directors to be skeptical!

Related Party Transactions

Related parties are ones where the policies and management decisions can be affected by another party, resulting in the potential for conflicts of interest between the other party and the company with whom the related party transaction is being done. CFOs should be asked about the ageing of intercompany balances outstanding and the comforting answer they are only in-house debts must be challenged, because the profits recorded may not generate corresponding amounts of cash.[1] This does not mean companies should not do business with related parties. Instead, it means directors must be very clear there are no material conflicts of interest or potential conflicts of interest when approving such transactions:

> Where conflicts arise, they must be well communicated, managed, and subjected to detailed and unimpeachable oversight to ensure that stockholders benefit from doing business with the related party. The board should be able to demonstrate this oversight. What is clear is that employees, officers and directors should be prohibited from (1) taking for themselves personally opportunities that are discovered though the use of corporate property, information or position; (2) using corporate property, information or position for personal gain; and for (3) compet-

---

[1] "Noble had reported much higher net profits over the past five years than it had generated cash. When profits and cash differ significantly for a protracted period, it can be a red flag for analysts because it raises questions about a company's financial performance.

In aggregate, Noble reported net profits of $2.54 billion between 2009 and the first quarter of 2015, yet net cash flows from operating activities amounted to just $118 million over the same period." Hume, N. and Shepard, D. (2015), "Attacks on Noble Group's Accounting Take their Toll," *Financial Times*, July 22, 2015, https://www.cnbc.com/2015/07/22/attacks-on-noble-groups-accounting-take-their-toll.html, accessed on August 24, 2018.

ing with the company. A board needs to show that the company will not tolerate such actions through words and deeds. All executives and directors should be polled regarding their knowledge of related party transactions, personal or otherwise. Oversight of transactions identified should be reviewed, determination made regarding the benefit to the company, and a disclosure in the notes to the financial statements produced.[xiv]

Complex Structured Products

Ever since the treasury function became a profit center, de-emphasizing somewhat its traditional role of protecting the company from the downsides of financial risks, it has been willing to take large positions to help the bottom line by betting on financial upsides offered by structured products—often so complex, treasurers do not understand how they work. This leaves companies open to potentially serious financial surprises. For example, neither P&G nor Gibson Greetings could price the complex derivatives they bought from Banker's Trust, leading to losses of $102 million in the case of P&G[xv] and $20.7 million in the case of Gibson Greetings.[xvi] Even worse, was the bet on future interest rates that bankrupted California's Orange County in 1994, losing it $2.2 billion.[xvii]

As a result, it is essential directors insist on management mapping out the strategies for using complex structured products, explaining clearly the strengths and weaknesses of such products and the downsides, should they go wrong. Directors should be clear the capability exists within the company of "marking to market" such products and *if directors do not understand how they will work or are concerned about the downside, they should not approve their purchase.* Warren Buffett's warning about derivatives in his 2002 annual report to Berkshire Hathaway shareholders should always be heeded. Failure to do so, was a primary cause of the Global Financial Crisis in 2008, as he foresaw in 2002:

> *I view derivatives as time bombs, both for the parties that deal in them and the economic system.* Basically, these instruments call for money to change hands at some future date, with the amount to be determined by one or more reference items, such as interest rates, stock prices, or currency values... Derivatives contracts are of varying duration, running sometimes to 20 or more years, and their value is often tied to several variables.
>
> Unless derivatives contracts are collateralized or guaranteed, their ultimate value also depends on the creditworthiness of the counter-parties to them. But before a contract is settled, the counter-parties record profits and losses—often huge in amount—in their current earnings statements without so much as a penny changing hands. *Reported earnings on derivatives are often wildly overstated. That's because today's earnings are in a significant way based on estimates whose inaccuracy may not be exposed for many years.*
>
> *The errors usually reflect the human tendency to take an optimistic view of one's commitments. But the parties to derivatives also have enormous incentives to cheat in accounting for them. Those who trade derivatives are usually paid, in whole or part, on "earnings" calculated by mark-to-market*

accounting. But often there is no real market, and "mark-to-model" is utilized. This substitution can bring on large-scale mischief. As a general rule, contracts involving multiple reference items and distant settlement dates increase the opportunities for counter-parties to use fanciful assumptions. The two parties to the contract might well use differing models allowing both to show substantial profits for many years. In extreme cases, mark-to-model degenerates into what I would call mark-to-myth...

... Another problem about derivatives is that they can exacerbate trouble that a corporation has run into for completely unrelated reasons. This pile-on effect occurs because many derivatives contracts require that a company suffering a credit downgrade immediately supply collateral to counter-parties. Imagine then that a company is downgraded because of general adversity and that its derivatives instantly kick in with their requirement, imposing an unexpected and enormous demand for cash collateral on the company. The need to meet this demand can then throw the company into a liquidity crisis that may, in some cases, trigger still more downgrades. It all becomes a spiral that can lead to a corporate meltdown.

Derivatives also create a daisy-chain risk that is akin to the risk run by insurers or reinsurers that lay off much of their business with others. In both cases, huge receivables from many counter-parties tend to build up over time. A participant may see himself as prudent, believing his large credit exposures to be diversified and therefore not dangerous. However, under certain circumstances, an exogenous event that causes the receivable from Company A to go bad will also affect those from Companies B through Z.

The derivatives genie is now well out of the bottle, and these instruments will almost certainly multiply in variety and number until some event makes their toxicity clear. Central banks and governments have so far found no effective way to control, or even monitor, the risks posed by these contracts. *In my view, derivatives are financial weapons of mass destruction, carrying dangers that, while now latent, are potentially lethal.* [Emphases mine]

Pension Fund Liabilities

Defined benefit plans are on their way out globally, replaced by defined contribution plans because the pension burden is unsustainable. This is the result of four design flaws.[xviii] Directors need to understand how their company pension plans may be affected by such flaws.

Inflexible Structure to Cope with Ageing Demographics

Pension funds assumed a retirement age of sixty-four on average in the 1960s, when people were expected to live to seventy-eight. Since then life expectancy has risen by around 6.5 years while average retirement ages have only risen to sixty-five. There is a funding need for an added 5.5 years that has not yet been filled. To make matters worse:

> While plan sponsors have been slow to adjust to the longer life expectancy of participants, society in general has not embraced the concept of delaying retirement. Changing workplace requirements during rapid technological change might throw another wrench into the works.

Lower birth rates have exacerbated the problem by significantly altering the ratio of workers to retirees. This puts particular stress on PAYG [pay as you go] systems, as fewer workers will have to contribute for more retirees.[xix]

Unrealistic Discount Rates and Investment Performance Assumptions

The low interest rate regimes adopted by central banks to prevent the Great Recession becoming another Great Depression have driven corporate pension discount rates down to around 4%. Any company using the traditional 7–8% discount rate will face problems when it comes to paying out. Investment performance has been good; achieving around 7.5%, but this has been achieved during one of the longest bull markets. If the "Minsky moment" (discussed in Chapter 10) is correct, it would be unwise to assume such performance can be assumed through to 2050:

> Publicly available data from pension systems globally shows that sponsors frequently use input factors that overestimate the potential asset growth and underestimate the present value of future liabilities.[xx]

Return Targets Drive Asset Allocation Inappropriately

As the proportion of the population shifts toward pensioners away from those working who contribute to pensions on a PAYG basis, so the funds are having to focus more on paying out. Given the yield problems with fixed income created by central banks and QE, trustees have invested in riskier asset classes in order to generate the income needed to pay out without paying due attention to what higher volatility implies:

> Funded global pension plans remain heavily invested in risky assets while the fixed-income component has been steadily declining for years. In short, the traditional shift in asset allocation has not been happening. The drive towards riskier asset allocations has presumably happened out of the necessity to hit return targets and *displays the inability to downplay forward return expectations despite higher expected volatility*.[xxi] [Emphasis mine]

Vested Interests

Companies with defined benefit plans may find themselves in extremis having to choose between paying employees or pensioners and going bankrupt to shed their pension plans, forcing the government take over their liabilities. This is because:

> Unfunded pension liabilities (and deficits in funded pension liabilities) are debts on the company's balance sheet. There are accounting standards that specify exactly how they should be allowed for (IAS19, for example).
>
> While [companies are not] usually required to make interest payments, they are required to make payments. They either pay the pensions as they come due or they pay deficit reduction contri-

butions into the pension scheme. Any requirement to make payments is a liability, regardless of what those payments are...

... If the company has to make large contributions to the pension scheme, it can't pay that money to investors as dividends. It is also possible for a pension liability to drive a company insolvent. Look up what has been happening recently to UK Coal, for example. The coal industry in the UK has been in decline for decades and its pension liabilities became unaffordable (it is liable for the pensions of its large historic workforce even though it is a much smaller company now). *If it hadn't been for the pension liabilities, it may have been able to survive its recent difficulties, but instead the business simply isn't sustainable.*[xxii] [Emphasis mine]

Airlines (United[xxiii] and American[xxiv]) in the United States have chosen bankruptcy to shift their pension liabilities to the Pension Guaranty Corporation, a federal government agency.

In the United Kingdom, Tata Steel has freed itself from a £15 billion pension liability it inherited, when it acquired Corus by paying £550 million to the British Steel Pension Scheme, handing over a third of the company in shares to keep it going. Failure to settle the matter would have led to the closure of Tata Steel in the United Kingdom with a loss of 10,000 jobs.[xxv] The BHS pensions scandal[2] was the result of the company being sold by Sir Philip Green with the express purpose of his family interests avoiding having to shoulder the company's pension liabilities.[xxvi]

It is perhaps fitting the official birth of corporate governance (*The Cadbury Report* in 1992) was a response to one of the biggest pension fund scandals of all time—Robert Maxwell's skimming of more than $900 million from the Mirror Group Newspapers' pension fund:

The wreckage in his wake stretches to both sides of the Atlantic. The sinking New York Daily News, which he owned, is now under Chapter 11 bankruptcy protection in New York. Court-appointed administrators control the media mogul's private holdings in London. His offices have been searched by the British Serious Fraud Squad Office for assets that allegedly have disappeared from his companies... Now it appears that the funds were also used to prop up stock prices of his publicly held companies. The count is still underway, but the current estimate is that Mr. Maxwell [drowned] last month leaving behind an empire also drowning under a $4 billion debt burden.[xxvii]

---

2 "The sale of BHS for £1 in early 2015 to a former bankrupt, Dominic Chappell, and its collapse a year later along with its two pension schemes, led to one of the biggest pension scandals of the past decade.
When the retail chain went bust, with the eventual loss of 11,000 jobs, the pensions of some 19,000 current and past employees of BHS came under severe threat," BBC News, June 28, 2017.

Compliance

Given the seriousness of the consequences of misreporting/malpractices in the seven areas of reporting discussed above, directors should consider adopting six practices for the audit committee to have effective control: regular reporting of key control metrics, executives reporting changes to processes and personnel, executives signing off on the accuracy of their financial statements, identifying and assessing nonroutine processes, supporting a strong IA function, and getting all employees to attest to the code of conduct.

Regular Reporting of Key Control Metrics

Controls can fail when nobody is monitoring what is happening. Indicators are necessary to alert management things are going wrong. They can be simple, such as the number of days lost to accidents; percentage rework; lack of inventory; number of attempted hacks to the system; or more complicated, such as periodic reviews of processes and even stress-testing the system to see where the flaws are. One of the most effective reports is to list all reconciliations, who is responsible for them, when they were last carried out, and the amount of reconciliation taking place. This should cover more than just cash reconciliations and should include system-to-system comparisons, checking physical inventory and comparing it with what the books say:

> Management should have a report that lists the critical controls...a description of the metric for each significant control, the frequency of measurement, the current performance of that metric, and the benchmark or targeted performance. A review of this report will tell the CFO, CEO, or audit committee what is being measured, where, how often, and how well the control is working.[xxviii]

This approach is excellent in theory. However, three factors can create a breakdown in the system: failures of judgment and unconscious biases, deliberate management overrides, and collusion to commit fraud.

Failures of Judgment
There are nine common causes of failures of judgment:
1. *Rush to solve*: This is the unfortunate tendency we all have to want to find an immediate solution without spending enough time on defining the problem; agreeing fundamental objectives or thinking about possible alternatives. We can not rely on the ERM processes to protect us when we are under pressure to find causes for events when none exist;[xxix] given our unwillingness to accept that things really can be random.[xxx]
2. *Judgment triggers*: Every judgment begins with a trigger, which, if not thought about carefully, can lead us to jump to conclusions too early; act too quickly; set

inappropriate objectives; without considering all the available alternatives. This is usually the consequence of "framing effects"—the impact on us of different ways of presenting *identical* information. For example:

> *Choice of statement*: The statement that "the odds of survival one month after surgery are 90%" is more reassuring than the equivalent statement that "mortality within one month of surgery is 10%."[xxxi]

3. *Availability bias*: This limits the alternatives and information we consider to what comes to mind easily. It is also known as "what you see is all there is" (WYSIATI). WYSIATI makes it easier to assume coherence and for us to assume we have the truth. It allows us to make decisions in a fast-moving world, preventing analysis paralysis. However, it excludes the existence of "known unknowns" and "unknown unknowns." Much of the time, it is a good rule of thumb, but it can lead to disastrous mistakes on the basis of statements like "in the time available" or "based on the information available."

4. *Overconfidence bias*: We are all conditioned by evolution to be overconfident about what we know, and our brains suppress doubt and ambiguity:

> Overconfidence: As the WYSIATI rule implies, neither the quantity nor the quality of the evidence counts for much in subjective confidence. *The confidence that individuals have in their beliefs depends mostly on the quality of the story they can tell about what they see, even if they see little*. We often fail to allow for the possibility that evidence that should be critical to our judgment is missing—what we see is all there is. Furthermore, our associative system tends to settle on a coherent pattern of activation and suppresses doubt and ambiguity.[xxxii] [Emphasis mine]

5. *Confirmation bias*: As human beings, we give too much weight to evidence confirming what we already believe and not enough to evidence that challenges our initial prejudices. The election of Donald Trump and the British electorate's decision to vote for Brexit are good examples of this:

> Contrary to the rules of philosophers of science, who advise testing hypotheses by trying to refute them, people (and scientists quite often) seek data that are likely to be compatible with the beliefs they currently hold. *The confirmatory bias of [the unconscious mind] favors uncritical acceptance of suggestions and exaggerates the likelihood of extreme and improbable events*.[xxxiii] [Emphasis mine]

6. *Anchoring bias*: In gathering and evaluating information, the tendency is to anchor on an initial value and stay too close to it when trying to move away from it while making the final assessments. This is particularly critical when doing due diligence in an acquisition; and even more important in a hostile acquisition. For example, when RBS undertook its disastrous bid for ABN AMRO which

bankrupted RBS, the board *were reassured by the anchoring effect of Barclays's competing and overpriced bid.*[xxxiv]
7. *Sunk-cost fallacy*: All economists appreciate the argument fixed costs are sunk costs and past costs should not be the basis for continuing throwing good money after bad. Yet it is one of the most critical reasons for boards failing to write-off obsolete plant, equipment and inventory when the company's own R&D discovers a new process that threatens existing investment. Such a decision ignores the possibility that if the company does not invest in the process, competitors might, at which point the board loses total control of adverse financial impacts of the change.
8. *Endowment effect*: This puts a higher value on losses than on gains, which makes it difficult for us to write off investments, especially if we were emotionally involved in creating them. For, example, the Nokia board's unwillingness to abandon its Symbian mobile phone operating system and go with Google's Android was one of the reasons Nokia went from market dominance to exiting the mobile phone market, crushed eventually by the rise of Apple (with its own operating system) and Samsung (with Android).[xxxv]
9. *Groupthink*: This occurs when people approach the problem with the same assumptions and mental frames of reference. For example, when Toyota had quality problems in the United States with accelerator pedals, the *Economist* featured an article suggesting the initial difficulty Toyota experienced in dealing with PR fallout was because the twenty-nine-member board was all male, all Japanese and all automotive engineers, suffering from groupthink as a result.[xxxvi] (Appendix 12.1 lists the major biases identified by Daniel Kahneman from his book *Thinking Fast and Slow*.)

Deliberate Management Overrides

Any control system is only as good as the people who are responsible for making sure it works as intended. The system can break down *unintentionally* because of misunderstood instructions; errors of judgment, often caused by overworked people; carelessness; inadequate training of new or temporary staff; and changes in processes not properly understood.

Management overrides, however, are *intentional* challenges to the system's integrity. The reasons may be to obtain personal gain or to make the organization look better. Typical overrides are increases in reported revenue hiding a fall in market share, enhancing reported earnings to meet unrealistic budgets, boosting the value of the company prior to an IPO, protecting bonuses linked to unachievable targets, or hiding violations of debt covenants or lack of compliance with regulations.

The creation of off-the-books special purpose vehicles in the case of Enron is an excellent example of management overrides, approved by the board and Enron's auditors. In the case of Lehman Brothers, however, the company did not disclose to the U.S. government, the rating agencies, its investors, or even to its own board it had abused a balance sheet adjustment called "Repo 105" to artificially improve its balance sheet in 2008:

> The use of Repo 105 allowed Lehman to remove $50 billion of assets from its balance sheet temporarily at the end of the first and second quarters of 2008 and declare the cash received as sales rather than financing…Lehman's global financial controller confirmed that "the only purpose or motive for [Repo 105] transaction was reduction in the balance sheet" and that "there was *no substance* to the transactions."[xxxvii]
>
> The justification for doing this was that rather than sell assets at a loss, a Repo 105 increase would help avoid this without negatively impacting our leverage ratios.[xxxviii]

Collusion to Commit Fraud

For management overrides to work, people need to collude actively. However, there is also passive collusion. This occurs when employees know the behavior is noncompliant, but turn a blind eye or condone it. This usually happens when the organizational culture lacks an ethical foundation or because there are inadequate whistleblower mechanisms in place to "protect messengers from being shot." Sometimes it is the result of thoughtlessness, of lack of empathy for the people who are harmed by the bad behavior; they are too far removed; unknown; outsiders. So, the risk they face as a consequence of bad actions are regarded as externalities for which nobody in the organization will be held accountable.[xxxix]

Perhaps the only effective way to prevent passive collusion is to have very clear controls, rigorously enforced, to ensure a strong sense of departmental and organizational discipline as a unifying behavior, regardless of the culture and background. This is no different from the "no broken windows" policy[xl] of crime prevention applied so effectively by the NYPD under Commissioner William Bratton.[xli]

Executives Report Changes to Key Systems, Processes, and People

Change is the biggest threat to a new control system. Segregation of duties is a common element of effective control, dividing tasks into the custody; recording; and approval functions for any process. Should the processes change, the board must be sure segregation is not destroyed as a result. Equally, if effective supervision of a particular process depended on the unique skills of a particular individual, the departure of that individual may jeopardize the entire process.

Consequently, the audit committee must require management to document all changes to key processes, people and systems since they were last certified. Such documentation should include an impact assessment of the changes on the robustness of controls regarding custody, recording, and approvals; whether there is still an independent reconciliation process; and whether staff have been properly trained to implement the changes.[xlii]

Executives Sign Off on their Financial Statements as Being Accurate

Requiring all managers to sign off approving periodic financial reports (monthly, quarterly, and annually) is a good way of making sure what auditors and internal audit check reflects what is going on in the business. However, this assumes the managers are given all the information to do so, which is often not the case. The CEO, on behalf of the audit committee, must make clear managers will be held accountable for what they have signed off.

Identify and Assess Nonroutine Processes

Nonroutine transactions are more likely to be the source of accidental or deliberate errors because controls over these types of transaction are less formal. Therefore, more care must be devoted to nonroutine and estimated transaction operations. The added care taken in these types of operations should include mapping the sources of data; the assumptions underlying any models; challenging the advisers who developed the models and estimates. The finance team should develop and keep an up-to-date list of nonroutine transactions and understand whether the inbuilt assumptions are conservative or aggressive, making sure a qualified person independent from the model's operator reviews it on a regular basis.[xliii]

Support Strong Internal Audit Function

It is essential the board does everything in its power to encourage internal audit to inspect processes and adherence to procedures and service level agreements without fear or favor. However, the audit committee should actively discourage management using internal audit from undertaking nonaudit activities that are not their responsibility and could lead to a conflict of interest, such as helping with accounting analysis or writing SOPs. As discussed in Chapter 5, it is the responsibility of the audit committee to ensure the internal audit function has the authority, resources, and standing in the organization to undertake rigorous inspections to reassure the board all is operating as it should. Internal audit should report to the audit committee with a dotted line to the CEO for "pay and rations." Hiring, firing, promotion, evaluation, and remuneration of the internal audit function is the responsibility of the audit committee; not of the CEO.[xliv] The audit committee must remember most internal auditors do not wish to remain in internal audit for their entire career when trying to create a strong team, which complicates matters.

All Employees Attest their Understanding of the Code of Conduct

All employees need to understand both their obligation to behave in an ethical manner and also that they have an obligation to report any compliance malpractice to the audit committee, and, if necessary, to the appropriate regulatory authorities:

> By having all employees annually attest to a code of conduct, management demonstrates that it takes the code seriously. Protocol for reporting suspected fraudulent behavior or grievances should be spelled out in the code of conduct as well as employee protections.[xlv]

Using text analytics to screen emails can help spot when employee morale is low and pinpoint emerging tensions created by questionable practices in the organization employees feel uncomfortable about or are unsure whether they violate the corporate code of conduct. Obviously, this raises employee privacy concerns, but several U.S. companies are already using text analytics to give them early warning signals of problems.[xlvi]

Introducing COSO[3]

Internal controls overseen by the audit committee must be supported by effective enterprise risk management (ERM) for the system to protect the organization from the consequences of things going wrong at management level. The role of the board in dealing with ERM is as follows:

> The board should discuss with senior management the state of the entity's system of internal control and provide oversight as needed. Senior management is accountable for internal control and to the board of directors, and the board needs to establish its policies and expectations of how members should provide oversight of the entity's internal control. The board should be apprised of the risks to the achievement of the entity's objectives, the assessments of internal control deficiencies, the management actions deployed to mitigate such risks and deficiencies, and how management assesses the effectiveness of the entity's system of internal control. The board should challenge management and ask the tough questions, as necessary, and seek input and support from internal auditors, external auditors, and others. Sub-committees of the board often can assist the board by addressing some of these oversight activities.[xlvii]

Although ERM is mainly the responsibility of management as opposed to the board, directors need to be familiar with the concepts underlying ERM, best articulated by the COSO framework, updated in 2017 to include the following.[xlviii]

---

[3] In 1992, the Committee of Sponsoring Organizations (COSO) of the Treadway Commission in the United States developed a model for evaluating internal controls.

The Need to Consider Risk When Setting Strategy

The revised framework deals with strategy and risk in three ways.

Impact of Risk on Strategy

This explicitly forces management to consider how risks could affect the organization's ability to implement agreed strategy. Previously, the two were kept separate. This allows people to revisit whether the agreed strategy is still suitable (covered in Chapter 8).

Risks Created by the Strategy

This forces the board and management to consider carefully the risks inherent in the chosen strategy and to prepare the organization to deal with them in advance, if, after considering all risk implications, the board still wishes to pursue its chosen route.

Risk of Strategic Misalignment

This forces the board and senior management to check whether the chosen strategy reinforces or undermines the organization's alignment with its agreed mission, vision, and values (preferably using the "Five P" framework to do so).

One of the reasons for this change in approach to risk and strategy was the recognition destruction of shareholder value was primarily the result of choosing the wrong strategy (60%); followed by poor execution (27%); and last and least, failures of compliance (13%),[xlix] the primary focus of earlier ERM frameworks.

Reframing Risk in Terms of Performance

The revised COSO framework reframes risk discussions in terms of setting performance goals and determining acceptable variations in performance. Whereas, previously, risk management was regarded as something different from making business decisions, the revised framework makes it clear risk and risk management are fundamental to business decision making, translating risk-focused language into business-focused language, encouraging more conversations about risk throughout the organization and leading to a more risk-aware culture.

Recognizing the Importance of Culture

The revised framework recognizes the importance of culture in driving desired behaviors in day-to-day decision making. It evaluates the different factors behind where an organization falls on a culture spectrum and the characteristics needed to achieve a risk-aware culture over time and its impact on whether and how well it executes its strategy.

Integrating Internal Control with Risk Management

Focusing on performance brings internal control and ERM together even though they have different objectives. Internal control provides assurance for directors on objectives relating to operations, compliance, and reporting. ERM reassures management when making their strategic planning, resource allocation and risk response decisions. ERM goes beyond periodic risk and process-level control identification to deliver critical insights for high-stakes decisions.

The revised COSO framework applies to any kind of organization at three levels: entity as a whole; operating unit; and function, regardless of industry type. It is a flexible principles-based approach, allowing judgment in how to apply it; considering how principles and components are found in the organization and can be made to work together to identify and analyze risks; and develop appropriate responses to them. It provides an opportunity to extend control beyond just financial controls to other forms of reporting and compliance objectives.[l]

The framework provides for three categories of objectives, which allow organizations to focus on differing aspects of internal control:
1. *Operations Objectives:* These deal with effectiveness and efficiency of the entity's operations, including operational and financial performance goals, and safeguarding assets against loss.
2. *Reporting Objectives:* These deal with internal and external financial and non-financial reporting and may include reliability, timeliness, transparency, or other terms agreed with regulators and recognized standard setters.
3. *Compliance Objectives:* These cover laws and regulations to which the entity is subject.[li]

The new COSO framework has five component parts with twenty principles, shown in Table 12.2.

Table 12.2: COSO: Five components and twenty principles[liii]

1) Governance and culture	2) Strategy and objective setting	3) Performance	4) Review and revision	5) Information, communication and reporting
The board: 1. Exercises risk oversight 2. Establishes operating structures 3. Defines culture 4. Demonstrates commitment to values 5. Attracts, promotes, and retains quality people	The board and management: 1. Analyze business context 2. Define risk appetite 3. Evaluate alternative strategies 4. Formulate business objectives	The board and management: 1. Identify risk 2. Assess severity of risk 3. Prioritize risk Management: 1. Implements risk responses 2. Develops portfolio view	Management: 1. Assesses material changes 2. Reviews risk and performance 3. Pursues improvements in ERM	Management: 1. Leverages information technology 2. Communicates risk information 3. Reports on risk, culture and performance

Using the "Five P" Framework to Cross Check

This chapter has covered the "processes" element of the "Five P" framework. Boards need to cross check whether the "processes" in their organization reflect and reinforce two other elements of the "Five P" framework or undermine them unintentionally.

"Purpose"

The board must review processes developed for internal controls and ERM to ensure they do not unintentionally lead the business away from its agreed "purpose." Should they find there is a contradiction between the processes they are adopting/approving and the agreed "purpose," they will need to consider how to reconcile the apparent contradictions. If they find they can not reconcile "processes" with "purpose," this will be a powerful red flag they either have the wrong "processes" or the "purpose" needs revisiting.

"Principles"

The board must also check the "processes" they approve do not undermine the "principles" (values) they believe are critical to creating the right culture for sustainable success—for example, reward and remuneration systems should not encourage malpractice or excessive risk-taking that could destroy the company's reputation and long-term social "license to operate."

Conclusion

The TLOD approach to internal controls is increasingly being replaced by the FLOA approach because the FLOA approach makes it clear the board and CEO are directly involved in ensuring the integrity of internal controls, as opposed to being stakeholders.

The audit committee needs to ensure it really understands what is happening in the seven areas where things can go wrong in financial reporting: use of unsupported topside adjustments, aggressive revenue recognition, continuous one-off non-recurring charges, frequent changes to accounting policies, regular repeated related party transactions, the use of complex structured products to improve profits, and the impact of pension fund liabilities on the viability of the company.

From a compliance point of view, the audit committee needs to ensure there is regular reporting of key control measures, recognizing there are eight common biases and judgment traps that can lead to poor quality decisions. The audit committee must look out for management overrides, designed to undermine the integrity of the system; and for collusion to commit fraud.

The best ways to do this are to ensure executives report regularly on any changes to systems, processes and people. Managers should be made to sign off on their financial statements; identify and evaluate nonroutine processes and support a strong internal audit function. Finally, all employees must attest they understand and adhere to the agreed company code of conduct.

The board does not need to get too deeply involved in the COSO ERM framework as most of it is the responsibility of management. However, the board is involved in three of the five components: governance and culture (the board's responsibility); strategy and objective setting (shared responsibility with management); and some of the performance review elements. Management is responsible for review and revision and information communication, exchange and reporting.

The "purpose" and "principles" lenses of the "Five P" framework are a useful cross check to ensure nothing material has been forgotten.

Appendix 12.1: Role of the "Unconscious Mind" in Decision Making[liii]

The "unconscious mind" does the following automatically and fast. It:
1. Generates impressions, feeling, and inclinations, which become beliefs, attitudes, and intention when endorsed by the "conscious mind"
2. Is programmed by the "conscious mind" to mobilize attention when a pattern is observed
3. Executes skilled responses and generates skilled intuitions after adequate training
4. Creates a pattern of activated ideas in the associative memory
5. Links a sense of easy mental processing (cognitive ease) to illusions of truth and pleasant feelings, and lowers vigilance
6. Distinguishes the surprising from the normal
7. Infers and invents causes and intentions
8. Neglects ambiguity and suppresses doubt
9. Is biased to believe and confirm
10. Exaggerates emotional consistency through the horns and halo effect
11. Focuses on existing evidence and ignores absent evidence (WYSIATI)
12. Generates a limited set of basic assessments and options
13. Represents sets by norms and prototypes and does not integrate
14. Computes more than intended (mental shotgun)
15. Substitutes on occasion an easier question to answer than the correct, but harder one
16. Is more sensitive to changes in states than to states themselves (prospect theory)
17. Gives too much weight to low probability events
18. Responds more strongly to loss than gain (between 1.5 and 2.5 times more[liv])
19. Frames decision problems narrowly, in isolation from one another

References

[i] Leach, T. J. and Hanlon, L. C. (2016) "Three Lines of Defense versus Five Lines of Assurance," quoted in *The Handbook of Corporate Governance*, edited by Richard Leblanc (Hoboken, NJ: John Wiley & Sons), 335–336.
[ii] Ibid., 351–353.
[iii] Ibid., 337.
[iv] Ibid., 338.
[v] "Defense in Depth: Organizations That Have Adopted the Three Lines Model Experience Collaborative Opportunities to Address Risk," *Internal Auditor* magazine, October 2015 issue, quoted by Leach and Hanlon (2016), op. cit., 339.
[vi] Ibid., 351.
[vii] Ibid., 352.
[viii] Green, S. (2005), *Sarbanes-Oxley and the Board of Directors: Techniques and Best Practices of Corporate Governance* (Hoboken, NJ: John Wiley & Sons), 58.

ix Ibid., 60.
x Ibid., 67.
xi Ibid., 67.
xii Butler, S. (2014), "Criminal Investigation Launched into Tesco's Accounting," *The Guardian*, October 29, 2014, https://www.theguardian.com/business/2014/oct/29/serious-fraud-office-investigate-tesco, accessed on August 24, 2018.
xiii Ibid., 69.
xiv Ibid., 69–70.
xv Reuters (1994), "P&G Reports $102-Million Derivatives Loss: Earnings: The Swaps Charge May be the Largest Ever Reported by a U.S. Industrial Company. Bank that Arranged Contracts Says it Advised Selling," *Los Angeles Times*, April 13, 1994, http://articles.latimes.com/1994-04-13/business/fi-45482_1_bankers-trust, accessed on August 8, 2018.
xvi Hansell, S, (1994), "S.E.C. Faults Gibson Greetings' Accounting in Derivatives Deals," *New York Times*, September 13, 1994, https://www.nytimes.com/1994/09/13/business/gibson-files-lawsuit-over-derivatives.html, accessed on August 8, 2018.
xvii Bagh, C. (2008), "FACTBOX: Largest Derivatives Trading Losses," November 7, 2008, https://www.reuters.com/article/us-derivative-trading-losses/factbox-largest-derivative-trading-losses-idUSTRE4A61ZI20081107, accessed on August 8, 2018.
xviii Boehmer, K. (2018), "The Looming Pension Crisis: Why it Matters and How to Prepare," *Mackenzie Investments*, May 2018, https://www.mackenzieinvestments.com/en/investment-teams/mackenzie-fixed-income-team/looming-pension-crisis, accessed on August 8, 2018.
xix Ibid.
xx Ibid.
xxi Ibid.
xxii Dalton, T. (2014), "Are Large Unfunded Pension Liabilities a Real Liability to Companies?" *Quora*, June 7, 2014, https://www.quora.com/Are-large-unfunded-pension-liabilities-a-real-liability-to-companies, accessed on August 8, 2018.
xxiii Wharton, University of Pennsylvania, (2004), "United Airlines' Pension Problem: Who, Ultimately, Is Going to Pay?" *Knowledge@Wharton*, September 8, 2004, http://knowledge.wharton.upenn.edu/article/united-airlines-pension-problem-who-ultimately-is-going-to-pay/, accessed on August 8, 2018.
xxiv Osorio, I. (2012), "The Pension Guaranty Corporation's Real Crisis," *Forbes*, February 22, 2013, https://www.forbes.com/sites/realspin/2012/02/22/the-pension-benefit-guaranty-corporations-real-crisis/#6de07859416f, accessed on August 8, 2018.
xxv Tovey, A. (2017), "Tata Steel Finally Frees Itself from the £15bn UK Pension Liability," *The Telegraph*, September 11, 2017, https://www.telegraph.co.uk/business/2017/09/11/tata-steel-finally-frees-15bn-uk-pension-liability/, accessed on August 8, 2018.
xxvi "Sir Philip Sold BHS to Dodge Pension Cost, Says Regulator," *BBC News*, June 28, 2017, https://www.bbc.com/news/business-40421414, accessed on August 8, 2018.
xxvii "The Maxwell Scandal," *The Washington Post*, December 9, 1991, https://www.washingtonpost.com/archive/opinions/1991/12/09/the-maxwell-scandal/fa08ac8d-5be3-44f4-b373-bf3d8aa2de93/?noredirect=on&utm_term=.ac2af976ce2a, accessed on August 8, 2018.
xxviii Green (2005), op. cit., 74.
xxix Kahneman, D. (2011), *Thinking Fast and Slow* (London: Allen Lane), 71–88.
xxx Taleb, N. N. (2005), *Fooled by Randomness: The Hidden Role of Chance in Life and in the Markets* (New York: Random House).
xxxi Kahneman (2011), op. cit., 88.
xxxii Ibid., 87–88.
xxxiii Ibid., 81.

xxxiv RBS Group Internal Report cited in FSA Board Report, *The Failure of the Royal Bank of Scotland*, www.fsa.gov.uk/rbs, December 2011, 237, cited in Zinkin, J. (2014), *Rebuilding Trust in Banks: The Role of Leadership and Governance* (Singapore: John Wiley & Sons), 41.

xxxv Doz, Y. (2017), "The Strategic Decisions That Caused Nokia's Failure," *INSEAD Knowledge*, November 23, 2017, https://knowledge.insead.edu/sites/all/themes/knowledge2015/img/share-more-button.png, accessed August 10, 2018.

xxxvi "Accelerating into Trouble," *The Economist*, February 2, 2011, https://www.economist.com/leaders/2010/02/11/accelerating-into-trouble, accessed on October 6, 2018.

xxxvii Examiner's interview of Martin Kelly, October 1, 2009, cited in Lehman Brothers Chapter 11 Proceedings Report, 7, quoted in Zinkin (2014), op. cit., 214.

xxxviii Gentile, J., Lehman (2007), "Proposed Repo 105/108 Target Increase for 2007" (February 10, 2007) atp.1 [LBEX-DOCID 2489498], attached to e-mail from Joseph Gentile, Lehman to Ed. Grieb, Lehman (February 10, 2007) [LBEX-DOCID 2600714], cited in ibid., 214.

xxxix Zuboff, S. (2009),"Wall Street's Economic Crimes Against Humanity," *Bloomberg Business-Week*, March 20, 2009, www.businessweek.com/managing/content/mar2009/ca20090319_591214.htm, accessed January 16, 2013, cited in Zinkin (2014), op. cit., 215.

xl Kelling, G. L. and Wilson, J. Q. (1982), "Broken Windows: The Police and Neighborhood Safety," *The Atlantic Magazine*, March 1982, www.theatlantic.com/magazine/archive/1982/03/broken-windows/304465/, accessed January 16, 2013, cited in Zinkin (2014), op. cit., 215.

xli PricewaterhouseCoopers, "Bill Bratton Transformed Law and Order," Partnership for New York City: Cities of Opportunity (2012).www.pwc.com/us/en/cities-of-opportunity/2012/interviews/pwccitiesopp_brattonweb2012.pdf, accessed January 18, 2013, cited in Zinkin (2014), op. cit., 215.

xlii Green (2005), op. cit., 75.

xliii Ibid., 76.

xliv Ibid., 76.

xlv Ibid., 77.

xlvi Partnoy, F. (2018), "What Your Boss Could Learn by Reading the Whole Company's E-mails," *The Atlantic*, September 2018 Issue, https://www.theatlantic.com/magazine/archive/2018/09/the-secrets-in-your-inbox/565745/, accessed on August 10, 2018.

xlvii COSO (2013), "Internal Control—Integrated Framework: Executive Summary," *Committee of Sponsoring Organizations of the Treadway Commission*, May 2013, 9 https://na.theiia.org/standards-guidance/topics/documents/executive_summary.pdf, accessed on August 11, 2018.

xlviii Chesley, D. and Martens, F., "Gamechangers: Four Reasons Why an Updated COSO ERM Framework Is Good for Your Business," *PwC Global* (https://www.pwc.com/gx/en/services/advisory/consulting/risk/resilience/COSOframework-keychanges.html, accessed on August 11, 2018.

xlix Zinkin, J. (2013), citing Booz, Allen & Hamilton (2004), "Too Much SOX Can Kill You: Resolving the Compliance Paradox," in "Directors as Gatekeepers of Market Participants," Module 1, Session 2, *Security Industry Development Corporation*, 13.

l COSO (2013), op. cit., 1–2.

li Ibid., 3.

lii Based on Kelly, M. (2017), "COSO Debuts Final ERM Framework," *Radical Compliance: Sharp Thinking About Compliance. Audit and Risk*, September 6, 2017, http://www.radicalcompliance.com/2017/09/06/coso-debuts-final-erm-framework/, accessed on August 11, 2018.

liii Zinkin (2014), op. cit., 212.

liv Kahneman (2011), op. cit., 284.

Chapter 13
Engaging Stakeholders

This chapter is presented in five parts: the first covers the board's need to recognize capital market discipline, the second discusses who the stakeholders of the company are, the third explores the best ways of engaging stakeholders in general, the fourth explores how to communicate with stakeholders, and the fifth uses the five lenses of the "Five P" framework to cross check everything material has been covered.

Much of the focus on CG is driven by the need to regulate public listed entities and their reporting requirements to protect investors. As a result, it sometimes underemphasizes the role of capital market discipline on boards, which is achieved through shareholder engagement, but often more immediately through stakeholders altering terms of trade, especially if the company is not listed.

From a regulatory perspective, boards are expected to communicate continuously with stakeholders so they can make properly informed decisions:

> There is continuous communication between the company and stakeholders to facilitate mutual understanding of each other's objectives and expectations.
>
> Stakeholders are able to make informed decisions with respect to the business of the company, its policies on governance, the environment and social responsibility.[i]

Stakeholder engagement can be achieved through investor relations; engagement forums; investor, analyst, and media briefings; website and social media.

Although stakeholder engagement applies to all types of organization, I will discuss the impact of capital market discipline on public listed companies first; and then go on to consider stakeholders in general and the best ways of engaging them.

Capital Market Discipline

Capital market discipline is achieved in three ways: through shareholder-driven market discipline, through stakeholder-driven market discipline, and through regulatory discipline.

Shareholder-Driven Market Discipline

Shareholder engagement is done through general meetings—either at the annual general meeting (AGM) or at an extraordinary general meeting (EGM):

> Shareholders are able to participate, engage the board and senior management effectively and make informed voting decisions at General Meetings.[ii]

Despite the importance assigned to AGMs and EGMs by regulators, boards should remember the stock market is a better source of real-time signals of impending trouble and one that can not be ignored, unlike AGMs where shareholder resolutions critical of management are often non-binding:[iii]

> AGMs and EGMs are few and far between, and can be gamed by errant companies, for example by holding them in remote and difficult to reach locations, to discourage a big showing[1]. A more real-time and transparent forum is the stock market. Disillusioned shareholders can signal their concerns by walking away and pressuring share prices down. Or, an activist investor can buy a stake and follow it up with a critical letter to management.[iv]

Admittedly, this shareholder response is truer of Anglo-Saxon capital markets than in many emerging markets. However, there are signs it is happening elsewhere as well. For example, in Japan, there have been the cases of Sony (2003),[v] Olympus (2011),[vi] and Toshiba (2015);[vii] in Germany the never-ending sagas of Deutsche Bank (2018);[viii] in Switzerland in 2018, the battle between Knight Vinke and UBS[ix] and Dan Loeb and Nestle;[x] in Singapore, Muddy Waters and Olam (2012)[xi] and Goldilocks and Noble (2018).[xii]

Clearly shareholder-driven market discipline works. However, it takes time as the examples above demonstrate; it is expensive to organize; and in the case of "CEO say on pay" resolutions, it is often ignored.[xiii] Sometimes, it reflects underlying problems created by stakeholder-driven market discipline in the first place.

Stakeholder-Driven Market Discipline

In a way, this is the mirror image of the risks discussed in Chapter 10. Boards need to recognize they must engage with all stakeholders who can damage their business model and the assumptions underlying its profitability. Customers can bring a company to its knees by boycotting the business, as they did with Shell in Germany over Brent Star in 1991.[xiv] Counterparties can stop doing business with banks depriving them of essential liquidity and bankrupting them in a weekend, as happened to Bear Stearns in 2008.[xv] Employees can go on strike; key talent can leave damaging the company immediately. Suppliers can change their terms of trade and credit policies,

---

1 The Malaysian Capital Market Development Fund finances the Minority Shareholders' Watchdog Group (MSWG) to attend all AGMs to ask pertinent questions of the board. This approach seems to be quite different from the approach to AGMs discussed in Gillespie, J. and Zweig, D. (2010), *Money for Nothing: How the Failure of Corporate Boards is Ruining American Business and Costing Us Trillions* (New York: Free Press), 195–197, suggesting AGMs were no better than "kabuki theatre" where shareholder questions were dismissed.

causing serious cash flow problems. They may do this because of what they know about the business and act as "canaries in the coal mine" or they may be responding to what other stakeholders are doing, like the rating agencies downgrading the company's creditworthiness or banks putting it through a workout:

> If suppliers begin shortening the terms on which they sell to the company, services such as Dun & Bradstreet or Proudfoot or trade publications pick this up relatively quickly and signal a looming liquidity challenge well before historical financials are published... CDS spreads are also a leading indicator of problems down the road. A good board should track these leading indicators and take preventive action before they become endemic.[xvi]

Regulatory-Driven Stakeholder Engagement

Leading practice is for notice for the AGM to be given at least twenty-eight days before the meeting; all directors must attend the AGM; and the chairs of the audit, risk management, and nomination committees are required to provide meaningful answers to questions raised by participants.[xvii] The presence of all directors allows shareholders to engage with each director. Having the chairs of board subcommittees in attendance facilitates such discussion and allows shareholders to raise questions and concerns directly with the people responsible.

Leading practice requires the board to provide context for, as well as content of, resolutions so shareholders can make informed decisions when voting, including background information and relevant reports or recommendations. The board is also required to take proactive measures to ensure shareholders can participate at general meetings, using technology to facilitate electronic voting because it leads to more accurate and transparent results; quicker turnaround for results, removing the need for ballot papers; reduced administration costs and easier access even for the disabled.[xviii]

Dealing with stock exchanges, boards must follow disclosure guidelines very carefully. When preparing announcements and circulars, boards should present information in a clear and balanced way, providing both positive and negative information. If the circular is long, there should be a summary using plain and simple language that is not emotional or confusing, referring to ranking or position only when supported by the facts.[xix]

Boards must ensure confidentiality is maintained; rumors or unusual market activity are tackled appropriately; equal access to material information is ensured; the impact of fraud or announcements by external parties is dealt with immediately; and profit guidance is given appropriately at the right time to avoid restatements. Boards are expected to provide quality financial information to the market:

Financial statements must be prepared in a timely and accurate manner and must represent a true and fair view of the company's affairs.[xx]

To do this, boards must be financially literate; challenge management proactively on financial and accounting issues; announce results immediately they have been approved by the board; disclose the financial highlights in the annual report and show how the company has done over the previous five years; providing a detailed analysis by segment covering market conditions, level of activities, and factors affecting changes in revenue, margins, costs and cash flows, as well as one-off gains or losses.[xxi] In addition, boards are expected to provide a separate statement in the annual report containing the management discussion and analysis (MD&A) with a holistic discussion of results and financial condition in terms of performance, risks and opportunities focusing on group objectives, strategies and operations, reviewing how these could affect the financials in the financial statement, enterprise liquidity and sustainability and expected future results.[xxii]

Appendix 13.1 lists the questions relating to corporate disclosure that must be answered to ensure disclosure is done properly.

Stakeholders Defined

In general stakeholders can be defined as follows:

> A person, group, or organization [with a] direct or indirect stake in an organization because it can affect or be affected by the organization's actions, objectives and policies.

Key stakeholders in a business organization include creditors, customers, directors, employees, government (and its agencies), owners (shareholders), suppliers, unions, and the community from which the business draws its resources.[xxiii]

Stakeholders can be divided into three groups: primary, secondary, and tertiary stakeholders.

Primary stakeholders have a direct impact on the fortunes of the company. They include all members of the company value chain: employees and union officials, if the employees are unionized. They also include people outside the company: customers and clients (sources of revenue); members of the company supply chain (sources of costs); shareholders, investors; and creditors (sources of funding); as well as pensioners and prospective employees (past and future sources of employees). Regulators must also be considered as primary stakeholders because they literally give the company its license to operate; impose costs of doing business through regulations; and can sanction the company, including withdrawing its license, if the company violates those regulations.

Secondary stakeholders are outsiders involved with the activities or the consequences of the activities of the organization. They can be categorized as service providers: auditors, lawyers, consultants, and advisers. They include three types of endorsers of the company's "license to operate": first, the government, acting through the judiciary to back up enforcement of regulatory constraints; second, civil society: the community within which the company operates; nongovernmental organizations (NGOs); and advocacy groups who may seek to change the way the company operates (e.g., Greenpeace); third, trade/industry associations that can lobby for/against the company's actions depending on whether the company is aligned with its peers. Boards must have a long-range perspective when dealing with these secondary stakeholders, recognizing they provide valuable early warning signals of potential change in the organization's strategic freedom to maneuver.

Tertiary stakeholders are primarily members of the "commentariat" who can influence primary and secondary stakeholders by changing the climate of opinion regarding what is acceptable or not. They include analysts and rating agencies affecting valuations and cost of capital; academics specializing in fields involving the company; individual politicians and legislators who can affect government and regulatory thinking (e.g., Nigel Farage and Brexit in the United Kingdom or Steve Bannon and the rise of Donald Trump in the United States); mainstream and social media which can put pressure on members of parliament or Congress through their impact on how the electorate thinks about a company; and finally, competitors arguing the way they operate is environmentally and socially superior and safer, thereby putting pressure on the board to change the way they do business.[2]

Boards should remember secondary and tertiary stakeholders do matter because they provide input and feedback on the company's strategy, financials, and legal condition. They act as intermediaries in the market of information. Analysts, investment bankers, and media disseminate information to a wider audience; they raise or lower the company's profile (analysts); they convey information to influence the investment community (analysts, fund managers); and they provide supposedly independent reviews of the company.

---

[2] For example, during the Congressional investigations into the BP Deepwater Horizon disaster in the Gulf of Mexico, ExxonMobil and Chevron tried to argue they operated more safely than BP and that such a disaster could not have happened in their companies. In fact, their disaster response systems were equally likely to lead to the same results. The only claim they could perhaps make was they would have stopped operations earlier than BP.
Goldenberg, S. (2010), "We Could Not Have Stopped Gulf Oil Gusher, ExxonMobil Chief Tells Congress," *The Guardian*, June 15, 2010, https://www.theguardian.com/environment/2010/jun/15/exxon-bp-oil-gusher-congress, accessed on August 13, 2018.

Engaging with Stakeholders

Effective stakeholder engagement recognizes all three categories of stakeholder need to be engaged and the ways in which such engagement is undertaken differs by category and by stakeholder. However, just to complicate matters, stakeholders often wear different hats at different times. For example, employees may be customers as may all secondary and tertiary stakeholders. It is important when engaging stakeholders, the organization understands which hat its audience is wearing. This is because, depending on the hat they wear, they have different interests and affect the company in different ways.

Effective engagement seeks to achieve three things:
1. *Build trust and confidence* in the business purpose, mission, vision, and values; the way business is done and with whom; and to highlight mutual interests to create win-win outcomes. This has never been more important, given the low levels of trust generally, shown in Table 13.1.

Table 13.1: Low levels of trust in institutions[xxiv]

	NGOs (%)	Business (%)	Government (%)	Media (%)
Informed public				
2018	67	65	53	53
2017	63	64	53	53
General population				
2018	53	52	41	43
2017	53	52	43	43

What is serious is that although trust in business has risen in half of the markets surveyed by Edelman in 2018 compared with 2017, the public still distrusts business in 16 markets, is neutral in 4 and only positive in 8—all of which, except for the Netherlands, are emerging markets, shown in Table 13.2.

Table 13.2: Trust in business in 28 markets[xxv]

Country	Level of trust (%)	Y-O-Y Change (%)
Global 28	52	0
Trusted markets		
Indonesia	78	+2
India	74	0
China	74	+7
Mexico	70	+3
UAE	68	+4
Colombia	64	0
Netherlands	60	0
Malaysia	60	+4
Neutral markets		
Brazil	57	-4
Singapore	56	-2
Italy	54	-1
South Africa	53	-3
Distrusted markets		
Spain	49	+3
Canada	49	-1
United States	48	-10
Sweden	47	+1
Turkey	46	+3
Australia	45	-3
Germany	44	+1
Argentina	44	-1
United Kingdom	43	-2
Poland	43	+3
Japan	42	+1
France	42	-8
Russia	41	+2
Ireland	40	-1
South Korea	36	+7
Hong Kong	36	+2

Interestingly, the public expect CEOs to lead on policy debates and issues rather than waiting for governments to take the lead in key areas of concern: jobs, the economy, automation, regulations, globalization, corruption, global warming, discrimination, infrastructure, cost of living, education, healthcare, and immigration in descending order of importance.[xxvi]

2. *Solicit support and build alliances:* This is the best way for boards to take the lead in the policy debates the public cares about and can be done by getting stakeholders to understand what the organization is trying to achieve regarding such

policy issues. They can achieve conditional support for its objectives, establishing where the various stakeholders are on a spectrum of "support-versus-oppose," building alliances on that basis.
3. *Create goodwill:* This is important to build business, create a brand premium, increase market capitalization, and have as an "emotional bank deposit" to draw on in times of crisis.

Before discussing how best to communicate, it is critical to consider what should be communicated. There are two elements to communicate so stakeholders understand what makes the organization special.

"Purpose" of the Organization

This will depend on whether the company is a public listed firm, a family firm or a government linked or state-owned enterprise. Each will have different characteristics by which its purpose must be ultimately judged, shown in Table 13.3.

Table 13.3: "Purpose" of three different types of organization[xxvii]

Public listed firm	Family firm	Government linked firm
The ultimate aim is return on shareholder equity better than the return for firms of similar risk characteristics.	The overall aim is shared family wealth and work. The family stays together with appropriate, satisfying, and rewarding work for every adult member who chooses to be in the company.	The overall aim is improved national wealth and work. Society stays united with appropriate, satisfying, and rewarding work for every adult member who chooses to be in the company, which has an obligation to the community as a whole.

In addition, boards should communicate clearly the agreed mission, vision, and values, supported by a clear, honest, and accurate picture of past performance and prospects.

Appropriate Time Horizons and Risk Profiles

Boards must communicate the time horizons they are working to in their strategy to their shareholders, the associated structure of the portfolio over time, the resulting profile of cash flows, and their associated risks. Failure to do this, can lead to a mismatch between investor expectations and the timetables to which management are working. This could lead to the company having the "wrong" kind of shareholders with little or no interest in the long-term approach of the board, leading to trouble between the board and investors.

As Bill Mann of the Motley Fool observed, boards get the shareholders they deserve, because if they are pressured to think only of the short term, it is because they have failed to explain the value of their long-term strategy. If this is done correctly, then the investors will be long-term investors rather than short-term and there will be no mismatch:

> I have a simple, perhaps naïve view of the markets—and it comes, after a fashion, from Warren Buffett. In the long term, companies get the shareholders they deserve.[xxviii]

Boards need to spend much more time thinking through what kind of shareholders they want and whether the shareholders they have, currently, are appropriate; and if not, what they should do about it.

Once the board has agreed what should be communicated and the timing of such communications, directors must consider the best ways of engaging their stakeholders. This begins with stakeholder mapping. Boards must know where key decision makers are on the stakeholder map. The stakeholder map assesses where people and organizations stand on issues of importance to the company and why they feel the way they do about those issues. Typically, both internal and external stakeholders divide into five categories.

Advocates

These are people or organizations who actively promote the proposition to other stakeholders. Even though they are limited in numbers (typically 3–5% of the target population), they make wonderful allies because they have a real desire to make things happen and can make the case for whatever is being proposed. It is important, however, to recognize not all advocates are helpful. This can be because they are ill-informed and make the case based on wrong information and promise things that can not be achieved, discrediting the company. It can also be they bring "baggage" with them and the mere fact they argue for the proposal is a reason for other stakeholders to oppose it. Advocates must therefore be chosen with care, considering who they are; how they behave; and their history with other key stakeholders. They have a significant vested interest in achieving a successful result.

Supporters

These are people or organizations (typically 5–10% of the target audience) who are happy to help when the time is right. However, they need to be energized to act on behalf of the organization and briefed with the right arguments. Then they will help make things happen and will want to see a successful outcome, as they are able to appreciate the benefits of the change.

Spectators
These are people or organizations (the majority of the target audience) who are neutral but prepared to go with the flow, whichever way the flow takes them. Time and effort need to be invested to keep them on board throughout the process, as they have no real interest in a successful outcome but are relatively happy with the status quo.

Saboteurs
These are people or organizations who pretend to agree with what is being proposed but undermine the proposition covertly (typically 5–10% of the target audience). They will practice "malicious obedience," following the letter of the agreement to violate its spirit. For example, if the board decides to sell and lease back its properties over time, but at the right times to optimize the financial impact of such a policy, saboteurs will instead sell the property at the bottom of the market, making the policy look bad; and justify their actions on grounds it was the agreed policy. Directors must appreciate the danger such people present to effective execution of agreed policies. They must know who they are and how to neutralize them by moving them from saboteur to spectator.

Adversaries
These are the rare people or organizations who fight openly to resist what is being proposed (typically 3–5% of the target audience). As it is extremely difficult to convert such stakeholders because they have too much vested interests at stake, the only way to deal with them is to remove them if they are internal stakeholders and isolate them through ally mobilization programs if they are external stakeholders.

It is crucial for directors to remember out of ten possible places stakeholders can be, only two lead to favorable results, two are neutral and six lead to dangerous results, shown in Table 13.4.

Table 13.4: Stakeholder grid[xxix]

Stakeholder category	Understand reason why	Don't understand reason why
Advocates	*Favorable:* Make powerful case why proposed action is good, using correct promises regarding desired outcomes.	*Dangerous:* Undermine case for proposed action, because of faulty arguments; may make promises that can not be kept.
Supporters	*Favorable:* Support advocates effectively because they understand the context and outcomes.	*Dangerous:* Provide support that may undermine the case because they don't understand desired outcomes—see above.
Spectators	*Neutral:* Wait to see which way the wind blows before changing behavior.	*Neutral:* Wait to see which way the wind blows before changing behavior.
Saboteurs	*Dangerous:* Appear to be supportive, but harness vested interests to undermine proposals, using reason and emotion—practice "malicious obedience," understanding enough to do it.	*Dangerous:* Appear to be supportive but use emotional arguments to mobilize vested interests against proposals; not well informed enough to practice "malicious obedience."
Adversaries	*Dangerous:* Mobilize people against what is proposed using powerful rational and emotional arguments.	*Dangerous:* Mobilize people against what is proposed using incorrect and emotional arguments.

What the stakeholder grid makes clear is the importance of moving all stakeholders into the top two left hand boxes where people feel positive about what is being proposed and understand why it is being proposed—with all its implications. The other eight boxes are at best neutral or dangerous. The only way to move people is to keep on communicating why the action is essential, how they will benefit if they make it happen, and how they will be disadvantaged if they do not.

Whichever category stakeholders belong in, they all have the following in common: the need to know "what is in it for them"—professionally in terms of career and personally in terms of extra work and personal risk—if they are to change where they are on the stakeholder grid. This means boards must understand what matters to their stakeholders and who are the people or organizations who can influence them to change their minds. This process of alliance building or lobbying requires the company to map both the stakeholders and their influencers. It is best done by joining trade organizations, funding research to build advocacy platforms, attending government roundtables, networking at industry conferences, lobbying legislators, working with NGOs wherever possible, developing a multimedia PR campaign, writing opinion editorials for key newspapers and magazines, and using social media to reinforce the company positions.

Communicating with Stakeholders

Boards must recognize there are different roles, responsibilities, and channels in developing effective communications with stakeholders. Getting this right, requires the board to agree a communication chain of command; taking responsibility for all major announcements; committing to empathetic, timely, and accurate communications; monitoring stakeholder relations; and using the appropriate channels for each stakeholder audience.

Communication Chain of Command

In dealing with stakeholders, it is absolutely essential there is a clear communication chain of command, articulating explicitly who is responsible for what type of communication to ensure there are not more than one voice speaking for the company at one time and that all messages are internally consistent and coherent. Table 13.5 shows an ideal chain of command.

Table 13.5: Communication chain of command

Role	Authority	Responsibility
Primary spokespersons	Board	Overall responsibility for business, strategic direction and approving accounts and financial statements, stakeholder contact
	CEO	Approves financial reports, announcements, materiality disclosures, media releases, stakeholder contact
	CFO	Treasury, company accounts, financial reporting, and stakeholder contact

Table 13.5 (continued)

Role	Authority	Responsibility
Secondary spokespersons	Head, Corporate Communications	External communications, media relations, press releases, website management, events
	CoSec/Legal	Legal and regulatory compliance, liaison and communication with Stock Exchange
	CEO/MD of BU	Special responsibilities restricted to BU or subsidiary
	IR officer	Investor relations, analyst and financial media relations, presentations, roadshows and investor events

It is also important for boards to appreciate the different roles of investor relations (IR) and public relations to use them effectively given they have different target audiences and different communication objectives. Table 13.6 compares the two functions.

Table 13.6: IR and PR compared

Investor relations	Public relations
Staffed by professionals with finance industry experience: 1. Coordinate *all* communications with *financial community* 2. Prepare financial announcements, financial press releases, presentations, contributions to annual report 3. Anticipate events, stay in touch with key analysts and investors, ensuring selective disclosures are avoided 4. Prepare senior management for meetings with the financial community 5. Initiate structured engagement with analysts, rating agencies, counterparties, and prospective investors 6. Organize roadshows 7. Provide financial market feedback	*Staffed by professionals with communications industry experience:* 1. Handle *all* communications with *press and media* 2. Prepare announcements, press releases, publicity materials, and annual report 3. Anticipate events and prepare FAQs 4. Prepare senior management for press and media interviews 5. Provide senior management with press and media feedback 6. Often in charge of CSR

Taking Responsibility for All Major Announcements

As a result of the James Hardie decision in 2012,[xxx] boards need to be involved in all major media releases to the stock exchange, even if there is a process delegating the release to the IR and PR functions. Regulators now expect boards to get the media release text submitted to them with board papers; ensure the internal process has been followed properly before the release goes public; treat the release to the stock exchange with the same level of care as the underlying substantive decisions; and if the release is material, consider in good faith whether they must approve the final release, even if an approved delegation regime already exists.[xxxi]

Six Principles of Effective Stakeholder Communications

Six elements make for effective communication.

Empathy

Directors must remember to ensure any communication they undertake begins by putting themselves in the shoes of the audience. This means they must integrate three things to be effective. They must appreciate what concerns/interests the *audience*, demonstrate the appropriate *attitude* when seen in the media, and present the correct *angle* to the story.

This is particularly important in the event of a crisis when lawyering up is often the worst thing a board can do,[3] even though it is the natural reaction because the crisis could lead to expensive litigation later. The key spokesperson must show deep concern and care; failure to do so only makes matters worse.[4]

---

[3] When testifying to Congress about the Abacus and Timberwolf deals, the Goldman Sachs witnesses had clearly been prepared by lawyers to minimize the risk of self-incrimination to the point of infuriating Senator Carl Levin. This may have protected the witnesses from prosecution, but led to a change in the law which was much costlier for Goldman Sachs in the long run. This was a failure of both *attitude and angle*.

[4] In the case of the Deepwater Horizon crisis which cost BP an estimated $65 billion (Reuters, January 15, 2018) and the CEO his job, the failure was primarily one of *attitude*. The highly competent Tony Hayward came across as cold in testimony; making matters worse by going back to England to go sailing at the weekend at the Cowes regatta, when the crisis was at its peak. When interviewed on TV, he unfortunately said he "wanted his life back"; outraging the families of the eleven men who had died on the oil rig.

Clarity

Information must be accurate at time of release (omissions/errors corrected as soon as known). Language must be simple; avoiding jargon, legal, and technical phrases if possible.

Transparency

Information must be presented in a fair, balanced way, even if it is unfavorable.

Timeliness

Information must be released as soon as it is known, unless there are legal or very good business reasons not to do so.

Equal Access

Information must be disseminated to the widest possible audience using all appropriate channels, particularly if it affects the share price.

Consistency

Information must be disseminated to the widest possible audience using all appropriate channels; and it must be the same information regardless of who is the spokesperson.[5]

(See Appendix 13.1 for details of what needs to be done for stock exchange disclosures.)

Monitoring Stakeholder Relations

Effective monitoring of stakeholder relations begins with recognizing the topics that matter to stakeholders may change over time as certain issues flare up in the public's consciousness—for example sexual harassment as a result of #MeToo; or climate change as a result of changes in the incidence and impact of severe weather events and wild fires. It then goes on to recognize communications are a two-way process and different parts of the organization interact with different stakeholders shown in Figure 13.1.

---

[5] The MH370 tragedy demonstrated a failure of stakeholder engagement on a number of counts: lack of empathy in the way the Chinese families were handled in Beijing; lack of clarity as different spokespersons from MAS, Air Traffic Control, Malaysian Air Force and Ministry of Defense initially had inconsistent stories; and lack of transparency until the Australian authorities took over. In mitigation, it must be admitted MH370 is a particularly difficult case, as what really happened and why is still unknown.

Orchestrating these interactions can become very complicated in a multidivisional, multilocation organization, especially if there are large time differences between the operations in the event of a crisis, where speaking with one authoritative voice is essential.

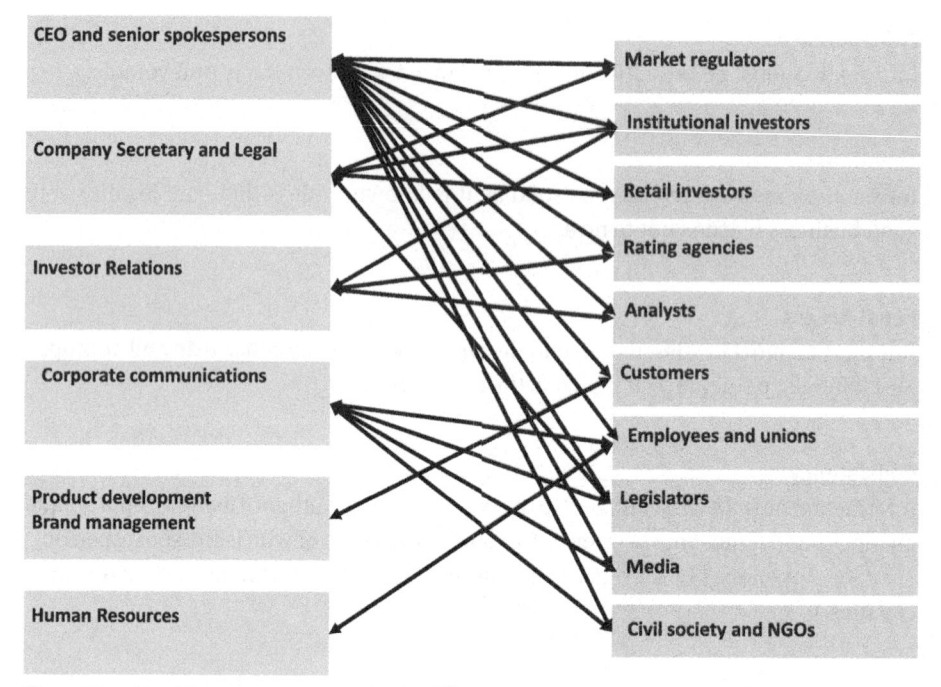

Figure 13.1: Need for two-way communication[xxxii]

Using Appropriate Communication Channels[xxxiii]

Different channels must be used to reach different stakeholders, depending on the message and timing of the message and on whether they are primary, secondary, or tertiary stakeholders.

Customers (Primary)
They are best reached through mainstream and social media and sometimes through face-to-face selling with the communication focusing on products and services, as well as after-sales service. However, there is also a role for employees, their families, and friends to act as brand ambassadors; as sources of recommendation for both the organization's products/services and as a place to work.

Employees (Primary)
The usual channels for communicating with employees are management meetings, performance appraisals; newsletters, intranet; company events and "townhalls"; union negotiations (if unionized) and the annual report. Directors should remember there are these different ways of communicating with employees and must ensure what is communicated is consistent and coherent, as well as remembering the differences in tone needed for a private communication (appraisal) and a public one ("townhall" or intranet) when discussing the communication strategy with corporate communications.

Suppliers (Primary)
They are usually dealt with directly in contract negotiations which stipulate service level agreements, key performance indicators (KPIs) covering volume, value and quality specifications, as well as marketing and training support levels.

Institutional and Retail Investors (Primary)
These are best reached through general meetings (AGM and EGM); quarterly and annual results announcements, press releases, annual reports; the internet using websites, webinars, chatrooms, and blogs. They can also be reached through financial intermediaries, auditors, and analysts.

When dealing with institutional investors only, it is more appropriate to use roadshows; one-on-one meetings (provided it is not to share-price-sensitive information that must be shared with everybody at the same time); conference calls; arranging site visits and company days.

Regulators (Primary)
This should be done through regular face-to-face meetings between top management accompanied by legal staff.

Trade Associations (Secondary)
These are important potential allies so it may be worthwhile being a proactive member, investing time in contributing to industry white papers and research for advocacy platforms. It may mean providing panelists and keynote speakers at industry conferences and association events. It may also require willingness to sponsor trade fairs and industry events.

Civil Society (Secondary)
It is a good idea to institute regular roundtables with NGOs to understand their issues and how they can affect the company's social "license to operate." It may make sense

to go further and provide sponsorship and public support of "win-win" projects such as "Fair Trade," the "Marine Stewardship Council," or the "Roundtable on Sustainable Palm Oil" to show the company is actively engaged in environmental projects.

Important NGOs like Greenpeace or WWF can make a big difference to the acceptability of the organization and its products. However, the board must remember such NGOs have their own objectives and economic drivers which may mean there are times when "win-win" may not be possible. Boards should know when these occasions arise and how to deal with the resulting conflict and adverse publicity. Boards should never treat the disagreement as a purely technical matter; it will become an emotional and political matter, as Shell learned to its cost over the Brent Spar dispute with Greenpeace in 1991:

> A well-orchestrated consumer boycott can hurt companies. The response must be that an ounce of market research is worth a pound of scientific evidence.[xxxiv]
>
> The Royal Dutch/Shell Group of companies owns a petroleum platform, the Brent Spar, in the North Sea. The Brent Spar is an oil storage facility and tanker loading buoy. It came to the end of its useful life and was taken out of commission in September 1991. After a thorough study of the environmental impact of various disposal options, Shell concluded that deep water disposal was the safest strategy. The German arm of Greenpeace mounted an aggressive public campaign against this action, affecting public opinion to the point where Shell changed its disposal plans and opted for on-land dismantling.[xxxv]

Judiciary (Secondary)
It can prove quite helpful to invest time every now and again to educate judges on the unique aspects of the organization's industry; how business is done and trends being faced by the industry so judges have an idea of the issues faced by the board, in the unlikely event of directors being hauled up in front of a judge. This is particularly important in jurisdictions where judges and magistrates do not specialize in company law.

Analysts and Financial Intermediaries (Tertiary)
These people have plenty of time to read reports and do research on the organization. IR and corporate communications should provide them with annual reports; third party research; the external auditor's report; the corporate governance report and the environmental and social report, preferably in one integrated report, following the recommendations of the Global Reporting Initiative (GRI) so they have as much information as they need to form an informed opinion of where the organization is going, what it is doing and how it intends to make good any KPI shortfalls.

Media (Tertiary)

Handling the media is best delegated to corporate communications within the chair's office and they have a range of tools they can use press conferences; media briefings and interviews (off and on the record); arranging media tours of the organization and organizing media lunches with senior management. Building a good long-term relationship with the media is important, offering them newsworthy stories on a regular basis so they respond with good will when the organization needs their help in the event of a crisis or an unfavorable newsworthy event.

For this process to work well, in an integrated, internally consistent way reflecting the interests and priorities of the various stakeholders, it is essential there is a stakeholder communication and engagement plan, allowing the board to track progress, shown in Figure 13.2.

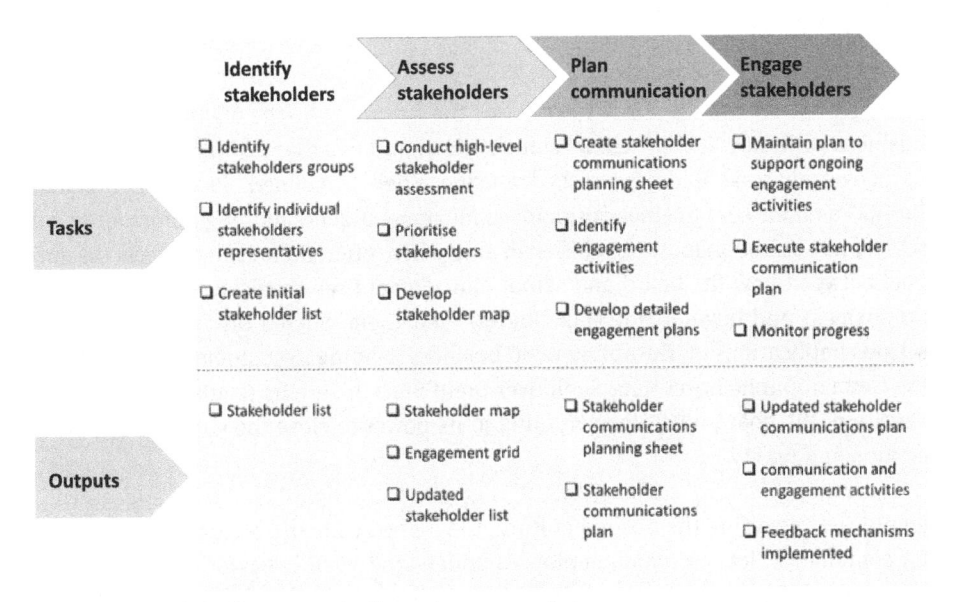

	Identify stakeholders	Assess stakeholders	Plan communication	Engage stakeholders
Tasks	❏ Identify stakeholders groups ❏ Identify individual stakeholders representatives ❏ Create initial stakeholder list	❏ Conduct high-level stakeholder assessment ❏ Prioritise stakeholders ❏ Develop stakeholder map	❏ Create stakeholder communications planning sheet ❏ Identify engagement activities ❏ Develop detailed engagement plans	❏ Maintain plan to support ongoing engagement activities ❏ Execute stakeholder communication plan ❏ Monitor progress
Outputs	❏ Stakeholder list	❏ Stakeholder map ❏ Engagement grid ❏ Updated stakeholder list	❏ Stakeholder communications planning sheet ❏ Stakeholder communications plan	❏ Updated stakeholder communications plan ❏ communication and engagement activities ❏ Feedback mechanisms implemented

Figure 13.2: Stakeholder communication and engagement plan

Using the "Five P" framework to cross check

From an *external stakeholder* communication perspective, "purpose," "principles," "power," "people," and "processes" matter in that order.

Purpose

This is the most crucial element to communicate because it frames why the organization exists; what difference it is trying to make in the lives of its beneficiaries; the value they place on that difference; the costs of so doing and, as a result, the returns to be expected. When engaging with external stakeholders, the board needs to check there is alignment between what they are doing and what stakeholders think they are doing. If there are any discrepancies, the board must find ways to close the gaps.

Regarding *internal stakeholders*, it is vital the board is able to engage effectively with employees to give them a clear "line of sight" between the organizational mission and vison and their jobs.

Principles

These also matter greatly since they define the culture; who the organization will do business with; how it will treat its stakeholders; and whether it will break the law or harm external stakeholder interests. Ever since Shell articulated "People, Planet and Profits" as their core business principles, all stakeholders, and, regulators and civil society pay attention to these. This is an area where often there is the biggest disconnect between how the board and senior management see themselves and how they do business and how outside stakeholders view them. Such a disconnect can have serious implications on the ability to do business, leading to customer boycotts (e.g., the German public boycotting Shell over Brent Star) or serious regulatory sanctions. Here, too, the board must do everything in its power to close the gaps between perception and reality.

Regarding *internal stakeholders*, it is essential the board is able to engage with employees regarding the desired culture; the agreed code of conduct; and the need for compliance. It is essential employees understand what behavior is expected and what behavior is unacceptable—what will be rewarded and what will be punished. It is also essential the board and senior management are *seen to be good role models* of the agreed values.

Power

This is perhaps less important to most external stakeholders since it relates to how the organization is structured and issues of organizational design. However, it matters greatly to investors and analysts and regulators as an early warning signal of potential business difficulties or regulatory malpractice. Here too, any discrepancy between perception and reality must be dealt with by the board. It does also matter to members of the organization's value chain, whether they are suppliers or customers because it can indicate problems of supply and delivery.

Regarding *internal stakeholders*, this may be the most important factor, as it deals with organizational structure and design, their jobs and to whom they report. It also determines whether they live in a culture of fear or one where the "courage to speak truth to power" is valued.

People

By and large, the external stakeholders who care most about this are regulators and the members of the organization's value chain because this is about the board ensuring the right number of people, with the right competencies and the right character are in the right jobs at the right time.

Regarding *internal stakeholders*, this about their jobs, their futures and "what is in it for them." If the board fails to engage effectively on this front through proper succession planning; talent management; reward and recognition of the right people with the right character; and fair and transparent appraisals; the organization will hemorrhage talent and fail.

Processes

Externally, the stakeholders who care the most about this factor are regulators and customers and suppliers who must deal with the organization's procedures before, during, and after the sale. Boards need to be engaged with their external stakeholders only indirectly, as these are primarily operational issues, unless they are matters of policy.

Regarding *internal stakeholders*, the processes are the glue holding everything together to make the organization what it is. So, the board must engage with them regarding SOPs, SLAs, authority limits; the code of conduct and compliance. The board also needs to engage with senior management regarding succession planning; talent management; career planning; appraisals and how they are done; personal development plans; and how these factors reinforce or undermine the agreed "purpose" and "principles."

Conclusion

Boards must pay much more attention to stakeholder engagement than in the past, where the board focus was primarily on shareholders. This reflects the need to recognize the three components of capital market discipline: shareholder-driven, stakeholder-driven, and regulatory-driven discipline. Shareholder-driven discipline takes time and is expensive to organize and often easy to ignore; stakeholder-driven discipline can affect the company almost immediately and can not be ignored; nor can regulatory discipline which can lead to severe penalties and even put the company out of business.

It is also the result of regulators articulating the increased responsibilities of directors to be more open with stakeholders in terms of what they must to disclose in their annual reports, as a result of the Global Reporting Initiative and the demands from analysts and investors to include environmental, social, and governance issues in the annual reports. Boards are now expected to have a detailed MD&A section in the annual report so analysts and investors can get a better "line of sight" regarding future financial projections.

More serious still, is the decline of trust in what were previously respected institutions as a result of the Global Financial Crisis. Boards can no longer just consider what shareholders want; they must consider the impact of their actions on the long-term viability of the social contracts in the leading economies of the world, lest they create a "political tragedy of the commons."

The reasons for engaging with stakeholders are the need to rebuild the lost trust; build support for alliances and engender goodwill. To do this, boards need to communicate the "purpose" of the organization; appropriate time horizons and risk profiles so there can be a good match between what the organization is trying to achieve and the risk-reward appetite of investors.

To do this effectively, boards must recognize there are primary, secondary, and tertiary stakeholders who have different interests; affect the company in different ways; and must be communicated with appropriately using their language and tone of voice rather than the company's. Primary stakeholders have a direct impact on the company; secondary stakeholders are involved with the company as service providers; and tertiary stakeholders are part of the "commentariat" who influence primary and secondary stakeholders.

When communicating with stakeholders, boards should remember they divide into advocates, supporters, spectators, saboteurs, and adversaries. Every effort must be made to try to get them all to become informed advocates or supporters, recognizing maybe the best outcome with saboteurs and adversaries is to get them to become neutral spectators.

Effective communication requires a clear chain of command; with the board responsible for all major announcements and press releases, applying the six principles of effective engagement: empathy; clarity; timeliness; transparency; equal access; and consistency. The board needs to monitor the progress and effectiveness of the engagement plan and proper planning is essential to ensure progress is made using the correct channels to each stakeholder target audience.

Finally, the "Five P" framework's "purpose," "principles," "power," "people," and "processes" are useful to cross check everything needed is included to make stakeholder engagement effective.

Appendix 13.1: Questions Regarding Corporate Disclosure[xxxvi]

1. Immediate disclosure of material information
    a. How did the company determine materiality?
        i. Who was involved?
        ii. What basis did they use?
    b. How did the company determine the impact?
        i. Who was involved?
        ii. What basis did they use?
    c. Who was involved in signing off?
        i. Internally?
        ii. Externally?
2. Contents of announcement or circulars
    a. How did the company put itself in the shoes of the investing public when developing content?
    b. How does the company ensure the language used is easy to understand and not misleading?
    c. How does the company avoid "hiding in plain sight"?
    d. Who is responsible for content?
    e. To whom do they report?
3. Maintaining confidentiality
    a. Who has access to confidential information?
    b. How does the company ensure they understand their responsibility to preserve confidentiality?
    c. What systems and processes are in place to maintain confidentiality?
    d. What sanctions and penalties are in place to deal with breaches of confidentiality?
4. Dealing with rumors or reports and unusual market activity
    a. What is the source of the report or rumour?
    b. How credible is it?
    c. Does it involve any of the company people directly or indirectly?
    d. What action should be taken against the source?
    e. How vulnerable is the company to action being taken against it?
    f. How can the company ensure it does not happen again?
    g. How unusual and large is the market activity?
    h. Who are the beneficiaries?
    i. What relationship do they have to the company?
    j. What is the likelihood of insider trading? If there is any, who is involved?
5. Equal access to material information
    a. How does the company ensure equal access?
    b. If anything goes wrong
        i. What are the contingency plans to mitigate the damage?

ii. How good are the company relations with the regulators?
iii. What will the penalties be?
1. Reputation?
2. Financially?
iv. What lessons can the company learn to prevent it happening again
6. Establishing corporate disclosure policies and procedures (CDPP)
    a. When did the company last review the CDPP?
    b. How adequate and up to date is it?
    c. Who is responsible for
        i. Keeping it current?
        ii. Compliance?
    d. How suitable is the person?
        i. Skills?
        ii. Experience?
        iii. Authority?
7. Profit guidance
    a. Why was it needed?
    b. What happened?
    c. How much warning was there?
    d. How big an impact will it have?
    e. How can the company ensure it does not have to do it again?
8. Fraud/financial irregularity
    a. How serious is it?
    b. Who is involved?
    c. How did it happen?
    d. What red flags were there?
    e. Why were they not spotted?
    f. What can the company do to prevent it happening again?
    g. What lessons can be learned?
9. Announcement by external parties
    a. What impact does the announcement have?
    b. How will the market react?
    c. How does the company mitigate its impact?
    d. How can the company be better prepared next time?
10. Disclosing purpose and utilization of general mandates
    a. Has the company thought about the market reaction?
    b. Has the company explained in simple language what the funds raised will be used for?
11. Quality of financial disclosure
    a. What checks have been undertaken to ensure disclosure is accurate?
    b. Have the external auditors approved the disclosure?
    c. What is done to ensure we met the deadlines and timelines set by Bursa for disclosure are met?

12. Presenting the MD&A
    a. Has the discussion in the annual report been reviewed and signed off?
    b. Is it written in simple language?
    c. How can it be improved?

Appendix 13.2: Questions Regarding Investor Relations[xxxvii]

1. Who are the shareholders?
    a. Summary of shareholder trends?
    b. Changes in registry composition?
    c. Changes in ownership?
2. How is the stock price performing?
    a. Quarterly price performance versus comparable indices?
    b. Quarterly price performance versus peer stock price performance?
3. What are the objectives of the investor relations strategy?
    a. To secure investor interest through timely and clear delivery of appropriate information?
    b. To obtain appropriate coverage of the company, its operations and products?
    c. Create a favorable climate of opinion about the company and its performance?
4. What is the status of the investor relations programs?
    a. What activities have been undertaken and how were they received?
    b. What activities are being proposed?
        i. Who are the target audience?
        ii. Why are we engaging them?
        iii. What are we proposing to communicate?
    c. How comprehensive is the program?
        i. AGM
        ii. Analyst briefings
        iii. Press conferences

Appendix 13.3: Questions Regarding Effectiveness of Stakeholder Engagement[xxxviii]

1. Do stakeholders understand the strategies, as well as the numbers?
2. What feedback are corporate communications and IR providing from
    a. Shareholders?
    b. Regulators?
    c. Employees?

     d. Customers?
     e. Civil society?
     f. Media?
3. What were the concerns of ordinary shareholders at the AGM?
4. When was an independent survey of stakeholder opinion last conducted?
5. What were the results?
     a. Satisfactory?
     b. Early warning of trouble ahead?
     c. Unsatisfactory?
6. What do the markets and analysts say about the company?
7. How easy is it for the company to raise capital?
8. What improvements are there in external opinions and perceptions of the company's
     a. Vision and values?
     b. Strategic intent?
     c. Management?
     d. Ability to
          i. Execute?
          ii. Innovate?
          iii. Recruit and retain top talent?
          iv. Manage risk?
     e. Comparative performance
          i. Within the industry?
          ii. Against benchmarked peers?
9. How much coverage is there of the company?
     a. Which analysts?
     b. How often?
     c. What do they say?
10. How are the shares doing?
     a. Increased liquidity?
     b. Increased frequency of trades?
     c. Increased volatility?
     d. EPS?
     e. Share price?
11. How has share ownership changed over time?
     a. Is the change in the shareholder register in line with company objectives?
     b. What is the level of shareholder loyalty?
     c. Is the company vulnerable to
          i. "Green mail"?
          ii. Activist hedge funds?
          iii. Takeover?

References

i MCCG (2017), 45.
ii Ibid., 47.
iii Gillespie, J. and Zweig, D. (2010), *Money for Nothing: How the Failure of Corporate Boards is Ruining American Business and Costing Us Trillion* (New York: Free Press), 195–197.
iv Nasr, Y. (2018), in an email to the author on August 19, 2018.
v Yonekura, S. (2014), "Poor Corporate Governance Fueled Sony's Meltdown," *Nippon.com*, April 23, 2014, https://www.nippon.com/en/currents/d00113/, accessed on August 20, 2018.
vi Elam, D. et al. (2014), "Olympus Imaging Fraud Scandal: A Case Study," *American Journal of Business Education, Fourth Quarter 2014, Volume 7, No 4*, https://files.eric.ed.gov/fulltext/EJ1053608.pdf, accessed on August 20, 2018.
vii Bloomberg (2018), "Toshiba Board, CEO Blasted by Glass Lewis for Poor Governance," June 20, 2017 https://www.japantimes.co.jp/news/2017/06/20/business/corporate-business/toshiba-board-ceo-blasted-glass-lewis-poor-governance/, accessed on August 20, 2018.
viii Bloomberg (2018), "Deutsche Bank Said to be Cutting Staff in Chicago in US Retreat," *Fortune*, July 28, 2018, http://fortune.com/2018/07/28/deutsche-bank-cutting-staff-chicago/, accessed on August 20, 2018.
ix Turner, G. (2015), "Activist Knight Vinke Fires Latest Salvo Against UBS," *Wall Street Journal*, April 15, 2015, https://blogs.wsj.com/moneybeat/2015/04/15/activist-knight-vinke-fires-latest-salvo-against-ubs/, accessed on August 21, 2018.
x Reuters (2018), "Loeb Pressures Nestle for More Sales, Restructuring," https://www.reuters.com/article/us-nestle-thirdpoint/loeb-pressures-nestle-for-more-sales-restructuring-idUSKBN1JR26K, accessed on August 21, 2018.
xi Grant, J. (2012), "Muddy Waters Issues Critical Olam Report," *Financial Times*, November 27, 2012, https://www.ft.com/content/89709864-3874-11e2-981c-00144feabdc0, accessed on August 21, 2018.
xii Palma, S. (2018), "Noble Wins over Goldilocks for $3.5 Billion Restructuring Plan," *Financial Times*, June 20, 2018. https://www.ft.com/content/b8a27878-7423-11e8-aa31-31da4279a601, accessed on August 21, 2018.
xiii Chiu, N. (2017), "The Drivers that Continue to Dog Say-on-Pay," *Davis Polk, Briefing: Governance*, September 18, 2017, https://www.briefinggovernance.com/2017/09/the-drivers-that-continue-to-dog-say-on-pay/, accessed on August 21, 2018.
xiv Oliver, J. (1995), "Learning the Lessons of Brent Spar Saga," *Politico*, November 1, 1995, https://www.politico.eu/article/learning-the-lessons-of-brent-spar-saga/, accessed on August 21, 2018.
xv Landon, T. (2008), "Run on Big Wall Street Bank Spurs Rescue Backed by US," *New York Times*, March 15, 2008, https://www.nytimes.com/2008/03/15/business/15bear.html, accessed on August 21, 2018.
xvi Nasr, Y. (2018), in an email to the author on August 20, 2018.
xvii MCCG (2017), op. cit., 47-48.
xviii Ibid., 48–49.
xix Bursa Malaysia (2012), *Corporate Disclosure Guide*, 75.
xx Ibid., 83.
xxi Ibid., 84.
xxii Ibid., 85.
xxiii Business dictionary, http://www.businessdictionary.com/definition/stakeholder.html#ixzz25ahfNRnm, accessed on August 13, 2018.
xxiv Based on 2018 Edelman Trust Barometer: The State of Trust in Business, 4, http://cms.edelman.com/sites/default/files/2018-02/2018_Edelman_Trust_Barometer_State_of_Business.pdf, accessed on August 13, 2018.
xxv Based on ibid., 11.

xxvi Ibid., 28.
xxvii Based on Zinkin, J. (2010), *Challenges in Implementing Corporate Governance: Whose Business is it Anyway?"* (Singapore: John Wiley & Sons), 46, 48.
xxviii Mann, B. (2012), "Imaginary Problems: Who Really Benefits from Lower Regulatory Burdens?" *Motley Fool Letter to Shareholders, February 2, 2012.*
xxix Based on Zinkin, J. (2003), *What CEOs Must Do to Succeed* (Petaling Jaya: Prentice Hall), 263.
xxx ASIC v James Hardie, 12-275MR Decision in James Hardie Penalty Proceedings, November 13, 2012, https://asic.gov.au/about-asic/media-centre/find-a-media-release/2012-releases/12-275mr-decision-in-james-hardie-penalty-proceedings/
xxxi Zinkin, J. (2017), *Fundamentals of Corporate Governance: Stakeholder Engagement.*
xxxii Based on Iclif Leadership and Governance Centre (2013), *Fide Good Governance Handbook: Part 7: Engaging Stakeholders*, 30.
xxxiii Ibid., 1–33.
xxxiv Oliver, J. (1995), Learning the Lessons of Brent Spar Saga," *Politico, November 1, 1995,* https://www.politico.eu/article/learning-the-lessons-of-brent-spar-saga/, accessed on August 17, 2018.
xxxv Diermeier, D. (1996), "Shell, Greenpeace, and Brent Spar," *Stanford Graduate School of Business,* Case Study 19, 1996, https://www.gsb.stanford.edu/faculty-research/case-studies/shell-greenpeace-brent-spar, accessed on August 17, 2018.
xxxvi Ibid., 11–14.
xxxvii Ibid., 15.
xxxviii Ibid., 34–35.

Part Three: Creating Value Through Reputation, People, and Processes

The three most important contributors to long-term competitive advantage, the three most important assets any enterprise has are its reputation, people, and processes. Yet they do not feature on the balance sheet and so are often undervalued or forgotten. The following three chapters explore what boards could do differently to create sustainable long-term value provided they gave reputation, people, and processes the attention they deserve. They also explore the issue of a "political tragedy of the commons" caused by individual boards focusing on doing what is best for their own organization at the expense of the environment, community, and economy, if all boards were to follow suit.

Chapter 14
Focusing on Reputation

This chapter is presented in three parts. The first explores why reputation matters; the second discusses the role of reputation in determining strategy, reconciling value creation, and extraction; and the third covers the impact of reputation.

> Reputation, reputation, reputation! Oh, I have lost my reputation! I have lost the immortal part of myself, and what remains is bestial. My reputation, Iago, my reputation.[i]

Henry Ford clearly agreed with William Shakespeare about the importance of reputation:

> The two most important things in any company do not appear in its balance sheet: its reputation and its people.[ii]

Why Reputation Matters

What is reputation and why does it matter? Reputation is defined as:

> The term refers to the observers' collective judgments of a corporation based on assessments of *financial, social and environmental* impacts attributed to the corporation over time.[iii] [Emphases mine]

This definition makes it clear there is more to maximizing the value of a company's reputation than just maximizing shareholder value. Boards must reconcile the impact their companies have on the communities within which they work and, on the environment, as well if they are to maximize their social "license to operate." A good reputation is a valuable business asset because 84% of market value is made up of intangibles.[iv] In 1975, intangibles represented just 17% at US$590 billion. By 2015, the sums involved had risen to US$ 19.8 trillion and 84%. As *The Economist* pointed out in the article quoted below, boards now rate reputation risk as their top risk.[v] This is a new development for which the insurance industry is not yet ready:

> This does not merely reflect the rise of technology giants built on algorithms; manufacturers have evolved too, selling services alongside jet engines and power drills, and crunching data collected by smart sensors.

As the importance of intangibles has grown, so has companies' need to protect themselves against "intangible risks" of two types: damage to intangible assets (e.g., reputational harm caused by a tweet or computer hack); or posed by them (say, physical damage or theft resulting from a cyberattack) …

> ... Companies are not oblivious. *Respondents to a survey last year by Aon, an insurance broker, ranked reputation as their top risk (up from fourth in 2013) and cyber-risk as their fifth (from 18th)* ...

> ...Just as insurance was only part of the answer to fire and maritime risk, it is only part of the answer to modern perils. "Instead of buying insurance against a damaged reputation, firms should be looking at **preventing it in the first place**," says Richard Wergan of Edelman, a communications-marketing firm. Plenty of cyber-breaches could doubtless have been avoided if software had simply been kept up to date. Insurers need to catch up with the intangible age; but so, do their clients.[vi] [Emphases mine]

Boards now recognize they must protect the market value of intangibles[1] and a large part of doing this effectively is to focus on not making the kinds of mistakes that destroy reputation in the first place:

> It takes twenty years to build a reputation and five minutes to ruin it. If you think about that you'll do things differently.[vii]

Moreover, there are five positive reasons for focusing on reputation.

It Increases Growth

The most reputable companies enjoy higher purchase consideration, sales and loyalty (shown in Table 14.1). For every 5-point improvement in the RepTrak score, there is a corresponding 6.3% increase in the propensity to buy and a 5.7% increase in referral rates. When the reputation rating moves from *average* to *excellent*, purchase intent goes up 2.7 times.[viii]

It Makes it Easier to Recruit and Retain the Best People

It shapes public perception of a company as being an "employer of choice":

> Fifty-seven percent of the general public would work for a company with an *excellent* reputation. When a company's reputation shifts from a rating of *average* to *excellent*, there's a 3.0x increase in a willingness to work for that company.[ix]

---

[1] "Something that has value for a business, although it does not exist in a physical way: Intangible capital/property/value. *Examples* of *intangible* property include bonds, shares, copyrights, and patents," *Cambridge English Dictionary.*

It Mitigates Risk

Companies face problems all the time. Even good companies can have problems—poorer results than expected, bad outcomes to good decisions, bad decisions, and unexpected PR problems.

Yet, 63% of the general public give companies with *excellent* reputations the benefit of the doubt in times of crisis. These same companies are also 3.2x more likely to be trusted to manage a crisis than companies with average reputation scores. The result? Reputation acts as an insurance policy against disaster and it pays to have a *strong* or *excellent* corporate reputation.[x]

It Builds Trust Equity

A shift in the RepTrak rating from *average* to *excellent* increases trust by 3.2 times.[xi]

It Enhances the Share Price

As a result of the above, a one-point increase in reputation yields a 2.6% increase in market capitalization, worth an average of US$ I billion; and companies with a good reputation had 2.5 times better performance for the period January 2006–January 2017 than the S&P 500.[xii]

The impact of reputation on a company's performance can be broken down further to show what happens to companies with poor reputations compared with ones with excellent ones, shown in Table 14.1.

Table 14.1: Impact of reputation[xiii]

Given the reputation scores, percentage of people who would:	Poor 0–39	Weak 40–59	Average 60–69	Strong 70–79	Excellent 80+
1. Buy the company's products	9	16	34	55	83
2. Say something positive about the company	8	13	29	50	82
3. Recommend the company's products	8	13	30	50	82
4. Trust the company to do the right thing	8	12	26	44	77
5. Welcome company into the local community	9	14	29	47	78
6. Work for the company	11	17	31	48	73
7. Invest in the company	8	11	23	38	67

From Table 14.1, we can see investing time and effort in getting an excellent reputation is clearly worthwhile. Companies with excellent reputations have nine times more prospects who would buy their products than companies with a poor reputation; just over ten times more positive comments and product recommendations; nearly ten times more people trusting the company to do the right thing and welcoming them in the community; nearly nine times more people willing to invest in the company. This helps explain why the top ten reputed companies in the United States outperformed the S&P 500 by 2.5 times over ten years (January 2006–January 2017).[xiv]

Role of Reputation in Determining Strategy

Given it is so valuable to have an excellent reputation, how do boards ensure the role of reputation is considered thoroughly in setting and implementing strategy so they can avoid making damaging mistakes in the first place?

The board's role in strategy setting and review consists of five tasks: defining a sustainable mission; creating a compelling vision; reconciling creation, extraction, and distribution of value; reviewing implementation; and ensuring compliance with regulations. Reputation is involved in three ways.

Defining a Sustainable Mission

Defining a sustainable mission requires interacting with stakeholders to ensure they agree with or accept the mission. Should key stakeholders reject the mission, they can make it unsustainable. Customers can choose to go elsewhere for their needs; employees can leave (at least in theory); communities can pressure politicians to limit the organization's freedom of maneuver; regulators can close the business; providers of capital (working capital, equity, or long-term debt) can starve the organization of funds. Their decisions to support or impede the company depend on their views of the board's credibility and management's ability to execute—in short, the company's reputation and its impact on each stakeholder group's interest in the company's continued existence shown in Table 14.1. An excellent reputation is essential for a sustainable mission, while a bad reputation is likely to lead to failure. As a result, boards must, among other things, actively choose what kind of reputation they wish to have when defining their mission, if it is to be sustainable.

Creating a Compelling Vision

For a vision to be truly compelling, it must be unique; engage both head and heart; providing a clear "line of sight" from the mission to individual job responsibilities, making individuals feel their roles are more than just a job—that they are not doing it just for the money, but as part of a bigger purpose to make their world a better place. Reputation is an essential ingredient in making the link between the mission and individual responsibilities credible. Boards and management that align the values and purpose of the organization with the values and purpose of individuals in that organization will benefit from greater employee engagement, commitment, and the desire to make a difference. Such employees will be more productive, more loyal, more innovative and excellent brand ambassadors because of their pride in what they do, what they achieve together and for whom they work. Table 14.1 shows the impact of reputation on employees and this can only be the result of a compelling and authentic vision.

Reconciling Value Creation, Extraction, and Distribution

This is far more challenging than defining a sustainable mission and creating a compelling vision because there are real trade-offs to be made between creating value, extracting it, and distributing it. For a company to be successful over time, it must reconcile these three demands. For example, it can develop a reputation for creating value by innovating and satisfying customer needs better than any other company, but if it fails the execute efficiently, it will fail to extract the extra value to be captured through economies of scale and scope. The difference, for example, between Tesla and Apple, both companies with reputations for creating unimagined value through visionary design innovation, lies in the fact Apple has been able not merely to create totally new product markets (like Tesla), it has also been able to capture branding economies of scale and learning efficiencies of scope by outsourcing production to Foxconn, to achieve margins its competitors can not match (not true of Tesla). Unlike Tesla, Apple has cash to distribute to shareholders[xv] as well as increases in share price, while Tesla's shareholders can only ride the roller-coaster of the share price.[xvi]

The reputation of innovative technology companies defines the forward p/e multiples shareholders are willing to pay, based on the future value creation they believe will be achieved. While this is clearly important, boards must remember in their attempts to extract maximum value, they should not damage the company's reputation through offshoring manufacturing or by allowing unacceptable conditions or practices in their supply chain, putting people or the environment at risk.

Equally, companies are beginning to leave themselves open to accusations share buybacks are socially irresponsible behavior, robbing workers of well-deserved pay increases and society of investment in future jobs and new improved products, just to satisfy short-term shareholders and to inflate the remuneration of overpaid CEOs:

> Between 2015 and 2017, U.S. publicly traded companies across all industries spent three-fifths of their profits on buybacks. The low-wage restaurant, retail, and food manufacturing industries spent 137%, 79%, and 58%, respectively. The restaurant industry borrowed money or used cash on its balance sheet to exceed the amount of its bottom line.

> *These actions disproportionately favor senior management and direct funds away from more productive purposes, such as corporate investment, job creation, or increased worker pay.*
>
> *"Lowe's, CVS and Home Depot could have provided each of their workers a raise of $18,000 a year,"* Annie Lowrey writes, covering the report for *The Atlantic*. *"Starbucks could have given each of its employees $7,000 a year, and McDonald's could have given $4,000 to each of its nearly 2 million employees."*[xvii] [Emphases mine]

This accusation does not just damage the reputation of companies practicing buybacks; it undermines the moral case for capitalism and raises questions about the legal basis of companies:

> For much of U.S. history, ...corporations sought to succeed in the marketplace, but they also recognized their obligations to employees, customers and the community. As recently as 1981, the Business Roundtable—which represents large U.S. companies—stated that corporations "have a responsibility, first of all, to make available to the public quality goods and services at fair prices, thereby earning a profit that attracts investment to continue and enhance the enterprise, provide jobs, and build the economy." This approach worked. American companies and workers thrived. Late in the 20th century, the dynamic changed. Building on work by conservative economist Milton Friedman, a new theory emerged that corporate directors had only one obligation: to maximize shareholder returns. By 1997 the Business Roundtable declared that the "principal objective of a business enterprise is to generate economic returns to its owners." That shift has had a tremendous effect on the economy. *In the early 1980s, large American companies sent less than half their earnings to shareholders, spending the rest on their employees and other priorities. But between 2007 and 2016, large American companies dedicated 93% of their earnings to shareholders. Because the wealthiest 10% of U.S. households own 84% of American-held shares, the obsession with maximizing shareholder returns effectively means America's biggest companies have dedicated themselves to making the rich even richer...* ...*Before "shareholder value maximization" ideology took hold, wages and productivity grew at roughly the same rate. But since the early 1980s, real wages have stagnated even as productivity has continued to rise. Workers aren't getting what they've earned.* Companies also are setting themselves up to fail. Retained earnings were once the foundation for long-term investments. *But from 1990 to 2015, nonfinancial U.S. companies invested trillions less than projected, funneling earnings to shareholders instead. This underinvestment handcuffs U.S. enterprise and bestows an advantage on foreign competitors.*[xviii] [Emphases mine]

As a result, Senator Elizabeth Warren has suggested the "Accountable Capitalism Act" which would include a charter for companies with revenue above US$1 billion:

> The new charter requires corporate directors to consider the interests of all major corporate stakeholders—not only shareholders—in company decisions. Shareholders could sue if they believed directors weren't fulfilling those obligations.
>
> This approach follows the "benefit corporation" model, which gives businesses fiduciary responsibilities beyond their shareholders. Thirty-four states already authorize benefit corporations. And successful companies such as Patagonia and Kickstarter have embraced this role.

My bill also would give workers a stronger voice in corporate decision-making at large companies. Employees would elect at least 40% of directors. At least 75% of directors and shareholders would need to approve before a corporation could make any political expenditures. To address self-serving financial incentives in corporate management, directors and officers would not be allowed to sell company shares within five years of receiving them—or within three years of a company stock buyback.[xix]

Were Senator Warren's proposal ever to become law, it would do two things: it would go a long way to reducing the increased inequality undermining the social contract in developed economies and it would improve the reputation of business by refocusing boards on the importance of value creation, as opposed to fixating on value distribution to those who already own a disproportionate percentage of the world's wealth. Support for Senator Warren's approach is to be found in Harald Eia's TED talk "Where in the world is it easiest to get rich?" which explains why Scandinavia has more millionaires and billionaires *per capita* than the United States.[xx]

Minimizing Reputation Risk Across the Value Chain

The new regulatory focus on integrated reporting requires companies to include their environmental, social and governance activities in their annual reports. This is another way of looking at reputation and provides an opportunity for boards to minimize the company's reputation risk across its value and supply chain.

It recognizes there is more to CSR or corporate responsibility than what is done with money once it has been made. That is philanthropy. Spending, time, effort and money on improving the environment, on creating better schools or hospitals, if such activities are not an integral part of the business model, is merely a way of compensating for the externalities society and the environment have to bear, as a result of the company's actions.

If companies were truly persons, such efforts would be a form of "afterlife insurance," allowing the company to be forgiven for what it had done during its daily life. Examples would include the company overcharging for products and services, rent-seeking and creating no added value through its involvement in the supply chain, exhausting nonrenewable resources, polluting the environment, and undermining the social fabric of the community within which it operates by breaking the law and resorting to bribery and corruption to get things done.

Minimizing the reputation risk of everything done across the company's value chain, however, is the first step to a company being responsible. It is the equivalent of a person behaving virtuously in the first place. Figure 14.1 divides reputation risk and its impact into three categories: natural capital, social capital and human capital.

	Raw materials processing	Shipping and Transport	Production	Distribution	Marketing and Sales	Management Policies
1. Natural capital/Environment: • Depletion • Environmental damage ▪ Forestry ▪ Watersheds ▪ Waste ▪ Pollution ▪ GHG emission	• Pollution/spills • GHG emissions • Wasted energy	• Pollution/spills • GHG emissions • Wasted water • Wasted energy • Wasted raw materials • Excessive packaging	• Pollution/spills • GHG emissions • Wasted energy • Excessive packaging	• 'Green' marketing linked to WWF, Marine Stewardship Council, Sustainable Forestry, Roundtable of Sustainable Palm Oil, etc.,	• 3 'R's ▪ Reduce ▪ Reuse ▪ Recycle
2. Social capital/Community: • Corruption • Social inequality • Abuse of indigenous people	• Corruption • Social inequality	• Corruption • Social inequality • Outsourcing • Offshoring	• Corruption • Social inequality • Destroying local capability by providing better products/processes	• Corruption • Truthful selling • Ethical marketing • Tax avoidance	• No corruption • Obey the laws • Pay taxes due • Avoid politics
3. Human capital/Workplace: • Discrimination • Human rights • Union rights • Health & safety • Sexual harassment • Working hours • Child labour	• Discrimination • Human rights • Union rights • Health & safety • Sexual harassment • Working hours	• Discrimination • Human rights • Union rights • Health & safety • Sexual harassment • Working hours • Child labour	• Discrimination • Human rights • Union rights • Health & safety • Sexual harassment • Working hours	• Discrimination • Union rights • Health & safety • Sexual harassment • Working hours	• Diversity & Inclusion • Meritocracy • Pay for performance • Respect union rights • Good working conditions and hours • No sexual harassment

Figure 14.1: Reputation risk areas across the value chain[xxi]

Taking each of the three categories of reputation risk in turn, the following is what boards must consider.

Natural Capital/Environment

First of all, boards must remember *the economy is a subset of the environment and not the other way around*. By calling the environment "natural capital," I am trying to remind directors they must also invest in improving the environment, as opposed to just treating the environment as a disposable source of economic value to be exploited without putting anything back, if it is to continue being a source of wealth. Just as boards must look after the capital assets on the balance sheet to maintain the company's ability to create value, they must do the same for the environment.

Companies in primary industries (mining, energy, plantations, and agriculture) have a unique responsibility to minimize the depletion effects of their activities. If they are in nonrenewables, they need to find a way to compensate for the fact they are damaging the environment and their reputations will suffer, for example, if they cause: landslides (Aberfan),[xxii] destruction of forests (Cargill and Bunge stopping deforestation for soy planting in Brazil, yet allowing it to continue in Bolivia);[xxiii] pollution created by tailings in Indonesia (Freeport McMorran);[xxiv] or rivers being poisoned by the chemical processes needed to extract gold in Romania (Esmeralda Exploration).[xxv]

Companies downstream of primary industries have other environmental concerns, for example: pollution caused by spills during distribution (Exxon Valdez in

Alaska);[xxvi] production processes affecting the water table (Vedanta in India);[xxvii] accidents releasing toxic fumes killing animals in the neighborhood (Seveso in Italy)[xxviii] and killing and disabling people (Bhopal in India);[xxix] radiation (Chernobyl in Ukraine);[xxx] mercury waste being released into the food chain (Minamata in Japan);[xxxi] toxic waste making an area uninhabitable (Love Canal in the United States).[xxxii]

With the recent discovery of the impact of single use plastics on marine life, all companies have to reconsider their use of single use plastics, but most particularly retailers and suppliers of fast foods:

> Most plastics do not biodegrade. Instead, they slowly break down into smaller fragments known as microplastics. Studies suggest that plastic bags and containers made of expanded polystyrene foam (commonly referred to as "Styrofoam") can take up to thousands of years to decompose, contaminating soil and water. The most common single-use plastics found in the environment are, in order of magnitude, cigarette butts, plastic drinking bottles, plastic bottle caps, food wrappers, plastic grocery bags, plastic lids, straws and stirrers, other types of plastic bags, and foam take-away containers... Plastic bags can block waterways and exacerbate natural disasters. By clogging sewers and providing breeding grounds for mosquitoes and pests, plastic bags can increase the transmission of vector-borne diseases like malaria. High concentrations of plastic materials, particularly plastic bags, have been found blocking the airways and stomachs of hundreds of species. Plastic bags are often ingested by turtles and dolphins who mistake them for food. There is evidence that the toxic chemicals added during the manufacture of plastic transfer to animal tissue, eventually entering the human food chain.[xxxiii]

Companies, like Unilever, Nestle, Mars, and Mondelez, sourcing raw materials from biodiverse habitats need to reassure their consumers they are not causing the destruction of those habitats. They can do this by working with NGOs like WWF, Marine Stewardship Council, Sustainable Forestry, RSPO, and others to set sustainability standards on their suppliers. Nowadays, NGOs use data analytics and blockchain to track products in the supply chain to ensure promised standards are upheld.[xxxiv]

As a general principle, boards must insist on management policies adopting the "Three Rs": "reduce, reuse, and recycle" in order to minimize the impact of their operations on the environment, as part of moving toward a "circular economy."[2] In addition, they should also consider how best and how soon their operations can become carbon-neutral, if climate change targets set in Paris on December 12, 2015 are to be met:

> The Paris Agreement's central aim is to strengthen the global response to the threat of climate change by keeping a global temperature rise this century well below 2 degrees Celsius above

---

2 WRAP, "A circular economy is an alternative to a traditional linear economy (make, use, dispose) in which we keep resources for as long as possible, extract the maximum value from them whilst in use, then recover and regenerate products and materials at the end of each service life." http://www.wrap.org.uk/about-us/about/wrap-and-circular-economy, accessed on November 3, 2018.

pre-industrial levels and to pursue efforts to limit the temperature increase even further to 1.5 degrees Celsius. [xxxv]

Social Capital/Community

Pressure to maximize shareholder value can sometimes lead to boards condoning bribery and corruption because without them the company can not do business in certain countries. Even if the company is penalized for engaging in corrupt practices, they might argue the penalties are less than the financial rewards, justifying the malpractice. This was an accepted view until the 1977 U.S. Foreign Corrupt Practices Act (FCPA) was passed in response to the Lockheed scandal in Japan to prevent companies, their representatives, or agents[3] from making corrupt payments to foreign officials to obtain or retain business.[xxxvi]

Similar arguments are often used to justify violating regulations and paying the resulting fine. If the fine is less than the realized profit, the argument goes, it is "the cost of doing business." As governments respond to calls by civil society to minimize the incidence and costs of corruption, this argument becomes untenable. Since the passage of the FCPA, the "OECD Convention on Combating Bribery of Foreign Officials in International Business Transactions" was signed in 2011,[xxxvii] further reducing the "room to maneuver" for companies.

Regulated areas related to finance have also been expanded as a result of actions taken by governments against money laundering and antiterrorism financing, as well as tax evasion. Boards must now pay attention to Anti Money Laundering Act (AMLA) and Foreign Account Tax Compliance Act (FATCA) and the OECD's Common Reporting Standards (CRS) as well, if they want to keep a good reputation.

Following revelations in the leaked Panama Papers,[xxxviii] governments are no longer so willing to allow multinationals to use transfer pricing to report their profits in the lowest tax regimes or for high net worth individuals to use aggressive tax avoidance schemes to minimize their taxes. Companies like Google,[xxxix] Apple,[xl] Starbucks,[xli] and Amazon[xlii] are being criticized for not paying their fair share of taxes in countries where they have substantial revenues.

> The reasons for the change in attitudes toward what had been accepted practice were the discovery of how much money was involved; and the feeling these companies were undermining the social contract in countries where they operate. They benefit from their presence without paying their fair share toward improving the infrastructure of the communities—classic free-riders. It is short-sighted of these companies, as investing in infrastructure raises standards of living, allow-

---

3 "The FCPA can apply to prohibited conduct anywhere in the world and extends to publicly traded companies and their officers, directors, employees, stockholders, and agents. Agents can include third party agents, consultants, distributors, joint-venture partners, and others." US SEC, "Foreign Corrupt Practices Act, 1.

ing their customers to buy more as they get richer. Their boards may well argue it is not their responsibility to do this; it is the job of governments. While true, this argument ignores the fact governments need to raise taxes and citizens resent having to pay more taxes because companies they deal with are avoiding paying their fair share.

Boards also need to be sensitive to charges they have been increasing social inequality and injustice through either paying off rent-seeking elites in emerging markets or by making the richest one percent richer[4] through share buybacks at the expense of their employees. Senator Elizabeth Warren makes a similar point in her interview with Franklin Foer of *The Atlantic*:

> The reason is because the rules are not working now. We were talking about how when GDP goes up, productivity goes up and workers' wages go up. In the '80s, that just flattens out. GDP continues to go up, productivity continues to go up, but workers fall behind and the gap has now become enormous. *Eighty-four percent of the wealth in the stock market goes to 10 percent of the population.*
>
> *Half of all America owns not one share of stock. Not one. Not even in a 401(k) or an employer retirement plan*, and yet a huge portion of the worth of the corporation is being directly diverted to the shareholders. That was not always true. *There was a time in America when that wealth was shared among those who helped produce it. The workers and the investors. That's just not true today.*[xliii] [Emphases mine]
>
> That is, because *the rich and corporate CEOs use their influence to promote their self-interest, inequality is built into the very DNA of capitalism.* And to return to our metaphor, the rich scorpions sting the rest of us[5]—by exacerbating income inequality through pay policies, stock buybacks and other actions—because it's simply their nature.
>
> *But there's plenty of evidence income inequality undermines the economy and, as a result, harms companies and the wealthy too. Eventually, we all sink together.*[xliv] [Emphases mine]

Companies operating in extractive industries and in plantations also need to ensure their policies do not abuse indigenous people, depriving them of their ancient rights to land or forest and river access. What may have been acceptable fifty or a hundred years ago, no longer is.

---

4 "The percentage of total income received by the top 1 percent of earners in the U.S. has risen from under 8 percent in the 1970s to over 18 percent today. The percentage of total wealth held by the richest 0.01 percent (the elite 1 percent of the 1 percent) has soared from under 3 percent to over 11 percent over this interval." Hopp, W. (2016), "How Corporate America Can Curb Income Inequality and Make More Money Too," *The Conversation*, September 21, 2016.

5 Refers to Aesop's fable of the scorpion and the frog: Scorpion met Frog on a river bank and asked him for a ride to the other side. "How do I know you won't sting me?" asked Frog. "Because," replied Scorpion, "if I do, I will drown." Satisfied, Frog set out across the water with Scorpion on his back. Halfway across, Scorpion stung Frog. "Why did you do that?" gasped Frog as he started to sink. "Now we'll both die." "I can't help it," replied Scorpion. "It's my nature."

Boards also need to consider carefully the impact they have on communities when they outsource, if this mean the work leaves the community or goes offshore. They may have little choice, if remaining in the community means the company goes bankrupt as a result of better products at lower prices sourced from abroad, but they still need to consider the impact their decision will have on their reputation. Equally, boards of companies like Walmart need to remember when they open a superstore or logistics center, they tend to depress retail jobs and earnings in their vicinity because they destroy local rivals through their superior processes.[xlv]

Finally, boards need to consider the importance of truthful selling and ethical marketing. Failure to insist on truthful selling was one of the reasons of the subprime crisis and is a recurrent theme in financial services regulation, given the asymmetrical nature of the selling process where most buyers of financial services are not sophisticated enough to understand the pros and cons of what they are being sold. The mis-selling scandals of payment protection insurance in the United Kingdom, for example, destroyed the reputation of the retail banks involved and led to staggering fines totaling an estimated £35 billion on sales of £40 billion[xlvi] in mid-2017, with another eighteen months still to go before the 2019 deadline for claims.[xlvii] It has done the same to the reputations of the banks in Australia in 2018 where the Royal Commission found conflicts of interest in selling, inappropriate incentives, and clients being charged for services they did not receive.[xlviii]

Equally boards must not be tempted to allow cheating when proclaiming standards, they claim they meet. Volkswagen has done immense reputation damage to itself and to German engineering by allowing "dieselgate."[xlix] The same seems to have happened in Japan with Kobe Steel,[l] Mitsubishi Materials,[li] Nissan,[lii] and Subaru[liii] all faking quality standards, lowering the reputation of Japanese engineering as a whole as well as their own.

As a general principle, boards should insist on management policies to ensure their companies: have zero tolerance of corruption, prohibit mis-selling and misrepresentation, obey laws rather than breaking them and later paying fines, pay their fair share of taxes in the communities where they earn revenue, and avoid getting involved in politics.

Human Capital/Workplace

Many of the issues involving reputation risk in the workplace are identical across the value chain. If companies want to have a good reputation as employer of choice, boards must ensure there is no discrimination based on gender, race or religion; people are hired and promoted on merit rather than on crony connections; human rights are respected with the company signing up to the UN principles. It is also important the rights of unions are respected as well, though this will differ by country and jurisdiction, depending on the legal frameworks covering employee rights. It goes without saying the occupational health and safety regulations must be observed and the companies with the best reputation in this area apply the toughest regulatory standards across all their operations wherever they operate to avoid being accused of "racing to the bottom."

Since Harvey Weinstein was fired by Miramax,[liv] allegations of sexual harassment have become an important issue in organizations in the developed world, contributing to the departure of eleven senior managers in Nike,[lv] of Travis Kalanick, founder CEO of Uber,[lvi] of Charlie Rose from CBS, of US Congressman Conyers and Senator Al Franken, actors Bill Cosby and Kevin Spacey, Bill O'Reilly at Fox News and the list goes on.[lvii] The growth of the #MeToo movement, despite all its ups and downs, means boards need to check there are no skeletons in the cupboards of people who matter in their organizations.

Ensuring reasonable working conditions and working hours in supply chain partners is particularly important, as Apple discovered to its cost when the working conditions in the Foxconn Longhua plant came to light as a result of suicides in 2010.[lviii] Even more important, is the need to ensure there is no child labor in the supply chain; something that damaged Nike's reputation when children as young as 10 were found to be making footballs and clothing for the company in Pakistan and Cambodia.[lix]

Boards also must recognize how difficult it is to ensure good working conditions are maintained, as promised by their suppliers in far-off locations. Despite having become a poster child for ensuring good working conditions in their suppliers after their crisis in the late 1990s, Nike found themselves back in the spotlight in 2017 because of poor working conditions in its supplier's Hansae factory in Vietnam.[lx] Nike also now find themselves in the spotlight over sexual discrimination, facing a class action over differentials in women's pay.[lxi]

If the first step is for the board to evaluate the three areas of reputation risk across the company's value chain as they affect natural capital (environment), social capital (the community within which the company operates), and human capital (workplace); the second step is for the board to apply the same analysis to the company's suppliers', distributors', and customers' value chains. The third step is to actively police whatever agreements their suppliers have made to ensure there is no backsliding.

Conclusion

Reputation matters more than ever in a world where intangibles represent over 80% of market capitalization. Boards recognize this, rating reputation risk as their most important risk—a risk for which the insurance industry has yet to create adequate cover.[lxii] This means boards must focus even more on preventing causes of reputation risk.

The positive reasons for focusing on reputation are that an excellent reputation increases growth, makes it easier to recruit and retain the best people, mitigates the downsides of crises, increases trust, and enhances share price (companies with a good reputation outperformed the S&P 500 by 2.5 times over the period January 2006–January 2017). Companies with excellent reputations have nine times more prospects who would buy their products than companies with a poor reputation, just over ten times more positive comments and product recommendations, nearly ten times more people trusting the company to do the right thing and welcoming them in the community, and nearly nine times more people willing to invest in the company.

The board's role in strategy setting and review consists of five tasks: defining a sustainable mission; creating a compelling vision; reconciling creation, extraction, and distribution of value; reviewing implementation; and ensuring compliance with regulations. Reputation is involved in three ways. First, defining a sustainable mission. Second, creating and sustaining a unique and compelling vision to provide a line of sight between the company's mission and the employee's job. Third, reconciling value creation, extraction, and distribution and the needs of the future (investment in R&D and new business models). Focusing on the reputation impact of the trade-offs can help effective reconciliation and enhance the company's reputation as a result. This need for reconciliation between short-term and long-term objectives and the different stakeholder interests has become critically important, as a result of the rise in inequality caused by the doctrine of maximizing shareholder value at the expense of stakeholders who create that value.

Seeking to minimize reputation risk across the company value and supply chain can help find the right balance. To do this effectively, the board should evaluate the reputation risks in the value chain in terms of the environment and the company's impact on natural capital; the community and its impact on social capital; and on the workplace and its impact on human capital.

As far as the environment is concerned, this means adopting policies of "reduce, reuse, and recycle." In the case of the community, this means adopting policies of zero tolerance of corruption, obeying laws, paying taxes, and avoiding politics. In the case of the workplace, this requires policies based on diversity and inclusion, recruitment and promotion based on merit, pay for performance, respect for human and union rights, good working conditions and working hours, no sexual harassment, and no child labor.

References

[i] Shakespeare, W. (1604), "Othello," Cassio, Act 2, Scene 3, lines 255–259, *The Oxford Shakespeare: The Complete Works* (Oxford: Clarendon Press, 1988), 832.
[ii] Ford, H., https://www.azquotes.com/quote/1430055
[iii] Ft.com/lexicon, *Financial Times*, http://lexicon.ft.com/Term?term=corporate-reputation, accessed on August 25, 2018.
[iv] "The Business of Insuring Intangible Risks Is Still in its Infancy," *Economist*, August 23, 2018, https://www.economist.com/ap/printedition/2018-08-25, accessed on August 24, 2018.
[v] Ibid.
[vi] Ibid.

vii Buffett, W., https://www.brainyquote.com/quotes/warren_buffett_108887, accessed on August 25, 2018.
viii LoBue, M. (2018), "The Business Case for Reputation," *Reputation Benchmarks: Insights from Reputation Institute*, August 21, 2018, https://blog.reputationinstitute.com/2018/08/21/the-business-case-for-reputation/, accessed on August 25, 2018.
ix Ibid.
x Ibid.
xi Ibid.
xii Ibid.
xiii Based on Reptrak 2016, *Reputation Institute*.
xiv Ibid.
xv Hansen, D. (2018), "By Tripling its Stock Buybacks, Apple Robs Workers and the Economy," *Forbes*, August 1, 2018; https://www.forbes.com/sites/drewhansen/2018/08/01/triple-stock-buybacks-apple-workers-economy/#74763298808e, accessed on August 29, 2018.
xvi Browne, R. (2018), "Tesla Is a 'Hope Stock' that Is 'Just Not Real,' Fund Manager Says," *CNBC Markets*, August 28, 2018, https://www.cnbc.com/2018/08/28/tesla-is-a-hope-stock-that-is-just-not-real-fund-manager-says.html, accessed on August 29, 2018.
xvii Hansen, D. (2018), op. cit.
xviii Warren, E. (2018), "Companies Shouldn't Be Accountable to Shareholders Only," *Wall Street Journal*, August 14, 2018, https://www.wsj.com/articles/companies-shouldnt-be-accountable-only-to-shareholders-1534287687, accessed on August 29, 2018.
xix Ibid.
xx Eia, H., "Where in the World Is it Easiest to Get Rich?" TEDxOslo, https://youtu.be/A9UmdYOE8hU, accessed on November 27, 2018.
xxi Based on Zinkin, J. (2009), "The Strategic Role of CSR/CR," LBS Bina Group Berhad Workshop, Kuala Lumpur, February 12, 2009.
xxii Edwards, H. (2016), "Aberfan Disaster Still Shadows Lives," *BBC News*, October 19, 2016, https://www.bbc.com/news/av/uk-37698913/aberfan-disaster-still-shadows-lives, accessed on August 29, 2018.
xxiii Hurowitz, G. (2018), "A Most Unlikely Hope: How the Companies that Destroyed the World's Forests Can Save Them," *Eco-Business*, July 2, 2018, http://www.eco-business.com/opinion/a-most-unlikely-hope-how-the-companies-that-destroyed-the-worlds-forests-can-save-them/, accessed on August 29, 2018.
xxiv McBeth, J. (2018), "Indonesian Pollution Charge Piles Pressure on Freeport," *Asia Times*, May 9, 2018, http://www.atimes.com/article/indonesia-pollution-charge-piles-pressure-on-freeport/, accessed on August 29, 2018.
xxv Insurance Journal (2000), "River Danube Poisoned by Cyanide," February 15, 2000, https://www.insurancejournal.com/news/international/2000/02/15/10183.htm, accessed on August 29, 2018.
xxvi Taylor, A. (2014), "The Exxon Valdez Oil Spill: 25 Years Ago Today," *The Atlantic*, March 24, 2014, https://www.theatlantic.com/photo/2014/03/the-exxon-valdez-oil-spill-25-years-ago-today/100703/, accessed on August 29, 2018.
xxvii Varadhan, S. (2018), "Groundwater in Vedanta's Indian Smelter Contains Heavy Metals: Minister," *Reuters*, July 23, 2018, https://www.reuters.com/article/us-vedanta-smelter/ground-water-in-vedantas-indian-smelter-contains-heavy-metals-minister-idUSKBN1KD1LZ, accessed August 29, 2018.
xxviii Cruz, G. (2010), "Top Ten Environmental Disasters: And the Earth Cried," *Time*, May 3, 2010, http://content.time.com/time/specials/packages/article/0,28804,1986457_1986501_1986448,00.html, accessed on August 29, 2018.
xxix Ibid.
xxx Ibid.

xxxi Ibid.
xxxii Ibid.
xxxiii UNEP (2018), "Single Use Plastics: A Roadmap for Sustainability," vi–vii, https://wedocs.unep.org/bitstream/handle/20.500.11822/25496/singleUsePlastic_sustainability.pdf, accessed on August 29, 2018.
xxxiv "New Palm Oil Alliance Initiates Blockchain Solution for Sector." *Digital News Asia*, September 17, 2018, https://www.digitalnewsasia.com/digital-economy/new-palm-oil-alliance-initiates-blockchain-solution-sector, accessed on October 8, 2018.
xxxv UN Climate Change, "The Paris Agreement," https://unfccc.int/process-and-meetings/the-paris-agreement/the-paris-agreement, accessed on August 29, 2018.
xxxvi US SEC, "Foreign Corrupt Practices Act," https://www.sec.gov/spotlight/foreign-corrupt-practices-act.shtml
xxxvii OECD, (2011), "OECD Convention on Combating Bribery of Foreign Public Officials in International Business Transactions," http://www.oecd.org/corruption/oecdantibriberyconvention.htm, accessed on August 30, 2019.
xxxviii ICIJ (2017), "Leaders, Criminals, Celebrities," *International Consortium of Investigative Journalists*, January 31, 2017; Fitzgibbon, W. (2018), "Second Panama Papers Leak: Findings from Around the World," *International Consortium of Investigative Journalists*, August 16, 2018.
xxxix Kahn, J. (2018), "Google's 'Dutch Sandwich' Shielded 16 Billion Euros From Tax," *Bloomberg*, January 2, 2018, https://www.bloomberg.com/news/articles/2018-01-02/google-s-dutch-sandwich-shielded-16-billion-euros-from-tax, accessed on August 30, 2018.
xl Drucker, J. and Bowers, S. (2017), "After a Tax Crackdown, Apple Found a New Shelter for its Profits," *New York Times*, November 6, 2017, https://www.nytimes.com/2017/11/06/world/apple-taxes-jersey.html, accessed on August 30, 2018.
xli Chapman, B. (2017), "Amazon and Starbucks Take Reputation Hit from Tax Avoidance Publicity," *The Independent*, July 26, 2017, https://www.independent.co.uk/news/business/news/amazon-and-starbucks-take-reputation-hit-after-tax-avoidance-backlash-a7861631.html, accessed on August 30, 2018.
xlii Bowman, J. (2018), "Trump is Right. Amazon Is a Master of Tax Avoidance," *Motley Fool*, April 8, 2018, https://www.fool.com/investing/2018/04/08/trump-is-right-amazon-is-a-master-of-tax-avoidance.aspx, accessed on August 30, 2018.
xliii Foer, F. (2018), "Elizabeth Warren's Theory of Capitalism," *The Atlantic*, August 28, 2018, https://www.theatlantic.com/politics/archive/2018/08/elizabeth-warrens-theory-of-capitalism/568573/, accessed on August 30, 2018.
xliv Hopp, W. (2016), "How Corporate America Can Curb Income Inequality and Make More Money Too," *The Conversation*, September 21, 2016, http://theconversation.com/how-corporate-america-can-curb-income-inequality-and-make-more-money-too-62339, accessed on August 30, 2018.
xlv Neumark, D. et al. (2008), "The Effects of Walmart on Local Labor Markets," *Journal of Urban Economics*, 63, 405–430, https://www.socsci.uci.edu/~dneumark/walmart.pdf, accessed on August 30, 2018.
xlvi Treanor, J. (2016), "Bill for PPI Mis-selling Scandal Tops £40bn," *The Guardian*, October 27, 2016, https://www.theguardian.com/money/2016/oct/27/ppi-mis-selling-scandal-bill-tops-40bn-pounds, accessed on August 30, 2018.
xlvii Dunkley, E. and Arnold, M. (2017), "UK Banks Set Aside Further £1.5bn for PPI Rush,, *Financial Times*, July 28, 2017, https://www.ft.com/content/d9f0050a-739c-11e7-aca6-c6bd07df1a3c, accessed on August 30, 2018.
xlviii Chalmers, S. et al. (2018), "Banking Royal Commission Key Findings from Kenneth Hayne's Interim Report," *ABC News*, September 29, 2018, https://www.abc.net.au/news/2018-09-28/bank-royal-commission-kenneth-hayne-key-findings/10317752, accessed on November 27, 2018.

xlix Parloff, R. (2019), "How VW Paid $25 Billion for 'Dieselgate'—and Got Off Easy," *Fortune*, February 6, 2018, http://fortune.com/2018/02/06/volkswagen-vw-emissions-scandal-penalties/, accessed on September 3, 2018.

l BBC (2018), "Japan's Kobe Steel Indicted over Quality Scandal," *BBC News*, July 20, 2018, https://www.bbc.com/news/business-44895564, accessed on September 3, 2018.

li Kyodo (2018), Mitsubishi Materials President to Step Down over Data Tampering Scandal," *Japan Times*, June 11, 2018, https://www.japantimes.co.jp/news/2018/06/11/business/corporate-business/mitsubishi-materials-president-step-data-tampering-scandal/, accessed on September 3, 2018.

lii Ma, J. (2018), "Nissan Says It Found 'Misconduct' In Exhaust, Fuel Economy Test," *Bloomberg*, July 10, 2018, https://www.bloomberg.com/news/articles/2018-07-09/nissan-says-it-found-misconduct-in-exhaust-fuel-economy-tests, accessed on September 3, 2018.

liii Alaniz, A. (2018), "Subaru Boss to Retire Amid Emissions Scandal," *motor 1.com*, June 6, 2018, https://www.motor1.com/news/244206/subaru-ceo-retire-emission-scandal/, accessed on September 3, 2018.

liv Barnes, B. (2017), "Harvey Weinstein Fired on Oct 8, Resigns from the Board," *New York Times*, October 17, 2017, https://www.nytimes.com/2017/10/17/business/media/harvey-weinstein-sexual-harassment.html, accessed on August 31, 2018.

lv Creswell, J. and Draper, K. (2018), "5 More Nike Executives Are Out Amid Inquiry Into Harassment Allegations," *New York Times*, May 8, 2018, https://www.nytimes.com/2018/05/08/business/nike-harassment.html, accessed on August 31, 2018.

lvi Somerville, H. and Menn, J. (2017), "Uber CEO Travis Kalanick Resigns under Investor Pressure," *Reuters*, June 21, 2017, https://www.reuters.com/article/us-uber-ceo-idUSKBN19C0G6, accessed on August 31, 2017.

lvii Warren, K. and Lane, L. (2017), "The Powerful Men in the News Accused of Sexual Misconduct," *NBC San Diego*, October 25, 2017, https://www.nbcsandiego.com/news/national-international/The-Powerful-Men-Accused-of-Sexual-Harassment-452785093.html?_osource=taboola-recirc, accessed on August 31, 2018.

lviii Merchant, B. (2017), "Life and Death in Apple's Forbidden City," *The Guardian*, June 18, 2017, https://www.theguardian.com/technology/2017/jun/18/foxconn-life-death-forbidden-city-longhua-suicide-apple-iphone-brian-merchant-one-device-extract, accessed on August 31, 2018.

lix Boggan, S. (2001), "We Blew It: Nike Admits to Mistakes Over Child Labor," *The Independent*, October 20, 2001, https://www.commondreams.org/headlines01/1020-01.htm, accessed on August 31, 2018.

lx Bain, M. (2017), "Nike Is Facing a New Wave of Anti-sweatshop Protests," *Quartz*, August 1, 2017, https://qz.com/1042298/nike-is-facing-a-new-wave-of-anti-sweatshop-protests/, accessed on August 31, 2018.

lxi Greenfield, R. and Novy-Williams, E. (2018), "Nike Get Tripped Up While Trying To Change its Culture," *Bloomberg Businessweek*, August 1, 2018, https://www.bloomberg.com/news/articles/2018-08-30/nike-gets-tripped-up-while-trying-to-change-its-culture?srnd=businessweek-v2, accessed on September 1, 2018.

lxii "The Business of Insuring Intangible Risks Is Still in its Infancy," *Economist*, August 23, 2018, https://www.economist.com/ap/printedition/2018-08-25, accessed on August 24, 2018.

Chapter 15
Investing in People

This chapter is presented in two parts: The first discusses briefly the underlying assumptions about "people" and their financial impact on the business, and the second considers how best to invest in people.

Every time I ask the question of directors "what is your most important asset?" they answer "people." Incorrectly in my view, because, as I argued in Chapter 14, the most important asset of an organization is its reputation. However, "people" are the second most important asset.

Henry Ford was of the same opinion:

> The two most important things in any company do not appear in its balance sheet: its reputation and its people.[i]

Yet, from my experience, boards spend less than 10% of their time on people issues; at a time where advances in blockchain applications, robotics and AI make people with up to date skills perhaps the most important strategic issue boards must face to stay competitive.

Underlying Assumptions about "People"

Clearly something has gone wrong in the way "people" are discussed at the board. If directors truly believe what they say about the importance of "people" as assets, and I am sure at some level they do, they would put their "people," summarized in the payroll cost, on the balance sheet as well as in the P&L; as an asset to be invested in, upgraded, and protected from obsolescence. They would charge depreciation against the sum allocated, based on the rate at which skills and competencies became outdated. In other words, they would treat payroll in the same way as they treat plant, machinery and goodwill; an aggregated financial sum that is not treated solely as a cost. They might also regard people as a long-term obligation rather than as a variable cost to be disposed of when no longer needed.

People as a Cost

I suspect this difference in accounting treatment has unconscious psychological implications on how boards look at people. They are *expenses only* in the financials and therefore there is subconscious and conscious pressure all the time to minimize

DOI 10.1515/9781547400935-015

these expenses in order to maximize shareholder returns. This pressure can be taken to extremes, as exemplified by Amazon's past treatment of some of its workers in the United States, where despite benefitting from generous tax breaks to set up warehouses in communities, it also relied in part on food stamps provided by the supplemental nutrition assistance program (SNAP) to subsidize its part-time workers who did not get paid enough to buy their groceries:

> The new data showing Amazon employees' extensive reliance on SNAP demonstrates an additional public cost of the corporation's rapid expansion. Even as generous subsidies help its warehouses turn a profit, its workers still must turn to the federal safety net to put food on the table. In Pennsylvania, for instance, an estimated $24.8 million in subsidies support 13 warehouses employing around 10,000 workers[ii]. At the same time, more than 1,000 of those workers don't make enough money to buy groceries, according to public data provided by the state.[iii]

I wondered if Jeff Bezos really believed the people who work for his company were its assets, he would treat them this way. Instead it seemed as though he viewed them as costs to be minimized or externalized in whatever way the law permits. That is a frame of mind encouraged by the way in which financial reporting is done. Perhaps this schizophrenic attitude to people shown by so many boards—regarding them as assets to be treasured but treating them as costs to be minimized or externalized—cannot be changed if financial statements reinforce the assumption people are only costs.

As a result of being targeted by Senator Bernie Sanders who proposed the BEZOS Act to stop him underpaying workers,[iv] Jeff Bezos announced on October 2, 2018 Amazon would raise minimum wages to US$15.00 per hour in the United States from November 1, 2018 and to £10.50 ($13.60) in the United Kingdom for the London area and £9.50 in the rest of the United Kingdom[v] rather than taking several years to do this. This at a time when the U.S. minimum wage was still $7.25, turning Amazon from villain into almost a hero on pay. Maybe Jeff Bezos has had a change of heart. Even if he has not,[1] the reputation gains and improvement in Amazon's image as an employer make the affordable extra cost worthwhile.[vi]

Another category of employers justifies paying their employees less than market rates on the grounds they provide "psychic income" to compensate for the fact they pay less. This applies to all vocational careers—for example, nurses and care givers, teachers and academics, soldiers, police and firemen, and people who work for charities. It also applies to the fashion industry, where except for the owners of the luxury brands and the big-name designers like the late Karl Lagerfeld, there are many people

---

1 The initial favorable reaction to Amazon's announcement was tempered by the realization existing hourly workers would forfeit their monthly bonuses and stock options which would go some way to funding the wage increase. Kim, E. (2018), "Amazon Hourly Workers Lose Monthly Bonuses and Stock Awards as Minimum Wage Increases," CNBC, October 4, 2018, https://www.cnbc.com/2018/10/03/amazon-hourly-workers-lose-monthly-bonuses-stock-awards.html, accessed on October 5, 2018.

lower down in the high fashion value chain who find it difficult to make ends meet because they do not get paid a salary, but in clothes vouchers instead. The justification for this treatment is that fashion is "exceptional," as this quote referring to a book on the fashion industry by Giulia Mensitieri makes clear:

> Mensitieri[vii] ... met "Mia", a successful Italian stylist who had moved to Paris: "She was wearing Chanel shoes and carrying a Prada handbag, being flown across the world in business class. ... Mia couldn't afford to rent a room, so she was couch surfing at a friend's house behind a screen in the kitchen. "Sometimes she had no money for her phone bill. She was eating McDonald's every day. She never knew when she would be paid for a job and how much she would get. For example, for a week's work, a very big luxury brand gave her a voucher for €5,000 (£4,500) to spend in their boutique." True, Mia could have sold it (and, among hard-up fashion workers, there is a lively market in reselling luxury goods) ... This situation is nothing exceptional ...

> ... [As Mensitieri explained:] "The message is, you don't have to be paid because you are lucky to be there at all. Working in fashion is hyper socially validating, even if you're unpaid. ... Fashion presents itself as something exceptional, a world outside the ordinary... There is a kind of confused denial of the norms of labour conditions. *The dream that French fashion, especially, projects is that of a life of effortless luxury—mundane everyday facts of life such as working for a living, or indeed even money, are considered vulgar, taboo, even dirty subjects.*[viii] [Emphasis mine}

The Internet and the gig economy have made matters worse, as they make it much easier for even small companies to look for the cheapest skills in a global market. Platforms like Fiverr[ix] encourage employers of casual labor to race to the bottom:

> While freelance websites may have raised wages and broadened the number of potential employers for some people, *they've forced every new worker who signs up into entering a global marketplace with endless competition, low wages, and little stability.* Decades ago, the only companies that outsourced work overseas were multinational corporations with the resources to set up manufacturing shops elsewhere. *Now, independent businesses and individuals are using the power of the internet to find the cheapest services in the world too, and it's not just manufacturing workers who are seeing the downsides to globalization.* All over the country, people like graphic designers and voice-over artists and writers and marketers have to keep lowering their rates to compete.

> ... Graham and his colleagues have been conducting an extensive study of the digital economy, interviewing hundreds of digital workers and analyzing data about tens of thousands of projects. They found that most buyers are located in high-income countries like the United States, and most sellers are in countries such as India, Nigeria, and the Philippines. While digital-labor markets are intended to allow sellers to auction off their work to whoever will pay the highest price for it, Graham ...found that *they also help buyers find the cheapest sellers.*[x] [Emphases mine]

People Are Disposable

There are many arguments in favor of the "hire and fire" culture typical of Anglosphere free market thinking. Flexible labor laws allow companies to employ people when times are good, making the economy better off because they are not worried about what happens when times are bad. They allow firms to be more innovative because if the risk taken does not pay off, the firm is not burdened with unproductive employees. They allow the young to get a job, even if it is on "zero-hours" contracts[2] (36% of people on zero-hours contracts[3] were between the ages of 16 and 24),[xi] despite zero-hours contracts being bad for physical and mental health.[xii] However, by allowing such flexibility, firms lose continuity—the continuity of engagement with employees that creates loyalty and makes it good economic sense for the company to invest in the skills of its employees long-term.[4] The lack of continuity also allows boards to continue regarding their employees as disposable costs to rise and fall with the market so continuity of engagement does not make sense to them.

There is another way, however, "Rhenish capitalism"; practiced in Austria, Germany, the Netherlands, Scandinavia, and Switzerland:

> The German labour market ... still places more emphasis on employers' freedom to build long-term loyalty between employers and workers. These relationships are embedded in a strikingly different cultural approach to industrial training, closely tied to the German tradition of family-owned Mittelstand businesses buttressed by *long-term savings that take a generational approach to assembling skills and technology...*
>
> *...Employers who do not have a sense of social responsibility for training are unlikely to be durably persuaded to hire apprentices through one-off state payments.* Instead, governments should consider building comprehensive vocational training schemes that could be funded through a reduction in the social costs ensuing from unemployment. Tinkering with apprenticeship programmes on a piecemeal basis, as has been done in the UK, is unlikely to yield long-term results, as such half-hearted reforms result in expensive and wasteful systems that lack both scale and content...

---

2 Q&A: What are zero-hours contracts? "*Zero-hours contracts*, or *casual contracts*, allow employers to hire staff with no guarantee of work. They *mean* employees work only when they are needed by employers, often at short notice. Their pay depends on how many *hours* they work," BBC News, April 1, 2015, https://www.bbc.com/news/business-23573442, accessed on November 3, 2018.
3 "More than half (54.7%) of respondents working on zero-hours contracts were women, supporting previous figures that suggested women, particularly single parents, were more likely to be trapped in more precarious work." Burt, E. (2018), "Women and young people most likely to work on zero hours contracts," People Management, April 24, 2018.
4 Companies choosing to come to countries, like Malaysia, where the primary focus of businesses has been to employ as low-cost labor as possible by importing foreign workers to keep costs low, reinforce the belief it is pointless to invest in skills-building, as they will only move to the next low-cost country when costs get too high. This has happened in the garment, electronics, and sports shoe industries, where Asian OEM and contract manufacturers from, for example, Korea and Taiwan migrated from one country to another as their labor costs rose. If so-called middle income countries are to escape the middle income trap, they must focus on maximizing labor productivity, which requires a judicious blend of upskilling and increased automation, that is, treating employees as assets to be invested in rather than as costs to be minimized.

... One of the main reasons why Germany's economy was able to recover so quickly after the downturn was the system of short-time working support (*Kurzarbeit*), introduced in the 1920s and extended in recent years...

... Imagine a small engineering firm that ran into financial trouble in 2008: rather than letting go of the 17-year-old apprentice who had recently joined the firm, it would have been able to keep employees on board and then benefit from their experience when the economy was back on its feet. *Even if the company had gone bust, the apprentice would by law have been sent to another company.*

Sir Anthony Bamford, chairman of UK excavator maker JCB, points out that his company was forced to shed more than 20% of staff in Britain when production halved in 2009. By contrast, the *Kurzarbeit* system enabled him to keep all his labour force in Germany.[xiii] [Emphases mine]

The key question at the macroeconomic level is which of these two different systems is likely to deliver more sustainable value creation for its people as a whole? Table 15.1 compares the performance of "Rhenish capitalism" with the key economies in the "Anglosphere"—Australia, Canada, the United Kingdom, and the United States with their underlying belief people are disposable, reflected in the relative ease with which they can hire and fire employees:

Table 15.1: Comparison between "Rhenish" and Anglosphere capitalism

Country	2018 percent unemployed[xiv]	Current account % GDP[xv]	2017 GDP per capita PPP US$[xvi]	Estimated GINI coefficient[xvii]	Years of life expectancy[xviii]
Rhenish					
1. Austria	5.2 (February)	+1.9	49,900	30.5 (2015)	81.6
2. Denmark	4.8 (February)	+7.9	49,900	29.0 (2016)	79.5
3. Germany	3.5 (February)	+8.1	50,400	27.0 (2006)	80.8
4. Netherlands	3.9 (March)	+10.3	53,600	30.3 (2015)	81.4
5. Norway	3.9 (June)[xix]	+5.1	71,800	26.8 (2010)	81.9
6. Sweden	5.9 (February)	+3.2	51,500	24.9 (2013)	82.1
7. Switzerland	2.4 (August)	+9.8	61,400	29.5 (2014)	82.6
Anglosphere					
1. Australia	5.3 (July)[xx]	-2.5	50,300	30.3 (2008)	82.3
2. Canada	5.8 (July)[xxi]	-3.0	48,300	32.1 (2005)	81.9
3. United Kingdom	4.1 (January)	-4.1	44,100	32.4 (2012)	80.8
4. United States	3.9 (April)	-2.4	59,500	**45.0 (2007)**	78.7[xxii]

If we compare the two types of economy as job creators, it is interesting to note four "Rhenish" countries (Germany, Netherlands, Norway, and Switzerland) do as well as, or better than the United States or the United Kingdom. The United States, unlike them, relied on a generous tax rebate passed by the Republicans to stoke growth at the top of the economic cycle. This is not sustainable long-term, as it creates a long-term budget deficit that will prove problematic. Except for Sweden, they also all outperform Australia and Canada.

A proxy measure of the relative quality of jobs is the current account as a percent of GDP, since export-oriented jobs in both manufacturing and services pay better than domestic ones:

> The estimates indicate that export-intensive industries pay more on average and that the export earnings premium is larger for blue collar workers in production and support occupations (they earn a 19.0% premium in export-intensive manufacturing industries and a 17.6% premium in export-intensive services industries) than for white collar workers in management and professional occupations (they earn a 9.9% premium in export-intensive manufacturing industries and a 12.0% premium in export-intensive services industries). Overall, the export earnings premium in 2014 is 16.3% on average in the manufacturing industries and 15.5% on average in the services industries.[xxiii]

Interestingly, every "Rhenish capitalist" country in Table 15.1 has a positive current account percentage of GDP, whereas all four Anglosphere countries have a negative current account percentage of GDP. This suggests the Anglosphere model has allowed outsourcing and offshoring to take place in a way that has not occurred in their "Rhenish" counterparts, reflecting the lack of long-term commitment to building skills mentioned earlier. United Kingdom companies that offshored did so on grounds of cost, in particular labor costs (reflecting the view that labor is disposable), whereas the companies that brought business back to the United Kingdom did so to save time to be near big markets with demanding customers.[xxiv] It would appear the drivers of reshoring in general are time to be saved and the need to be near key markets; helped by the rise in the relative cost of labor in China.[xxv]

GDP per capita measured using purchasing power parity (PPP) is another measure of success used by economists, even though it is seriously defective because it only records cash-based exchanges in the formal economy and ignores quality of life measures. Even so, using this measure shows the United States is outperformed by only two "Rhenish" countries (Switzerland and Norway) though all the "Rhenish" countries do better than Australia, Canada, and the United Kingdom.

It is when we compare quality of life, the superiority of the "Rhenish" model becomes most apparent. The GINI coefficient,[5] which measures inequality, shows all the "Rhenish" countries outperforming the Anglosphere countries, except for Austria doing slightly worse than Australia. The United States stands out as an extreme outlier with a score of 45.0, whereas all other countries in the comparison lie between 24.9 (Sweden) and 32.4 (United Kingdom). It is perhaps not so surprising the United

---

5 Low GINI scores indicate less inequality; high scores more.

States and the United Kingdom have had seismic political changes in 2016 based on resentment of the liberal elites by the "Just About Managing" classes (to use UK Prime Minister Theresa May's phrase).

Life expectancy, another measure of the well-being of an economy, also has an interesting story to tell. All the "Rhenish" countries have longer life expectancies than the United States and equal or longer life expectancies than the United Kingdom, except for Denmark. Australia, on the other hand, is only beaten by Switzerland; and Canada is level with Norway and beaten by Switzerland as well as Sweden. Once again, the United States is an outlier, not just because its life expectancy is significantly lower than the others, but because it is falling as a result of the opioid crisis, itself in part a symptom of rising inequality and hopelessness[xxvi] and the difficulty nearly half of Americans have in making ends meet:

> The crisis is fundamentally fueled by economic and social upheaval, its etiology closely linked to the role of opioids as a refuge from physical and psychological trauma, concentrated disadvantage, isolation, and hopelessness.[xxvii]
>
> By virtually any yardstick, the U.S. economy is doing great. Unemployment is near a two-decade low. The stock market is strong. Corporate profits are at record highs.
>
> Yet a report out this week finds that almost half of Americans are having trouble paying for basic needs such as food and housing...
>
> ...In reality, corporations *received 11 times more in tax cuts than they doled out in one-time bonuses or modest wage hikes*, according to the advocacy group Americans for Tax Fairness.
>
> *Moreover, companies are spending 101 times as much on stock buybacks as they are on bonuses and wages, enriching shareholders at the expense of workers...*
>
> ...There's no excuse for millions of working people in the richest country in the history of the world being unable to feed themselves or keep a roof over their heads.
>
> Nor is there a rational explanation for millions being without health coverage, or facing financial ruin in the event of a serious medical problem.
>
> *These are signs of a society that has lost its way, in which the comfort of a relative few has become a higher priority than the well-being of the vast majority.*[xxviii] [Emphases mine]

It is deeply ironic to read nearly half of Americans could not make ends meet in the same week Amazon became a trillion-dollar corporation.[xxix]

If U.S. boards are not careful, even though it may make sense for each individual company to do share buybacks at the expense of their employees; if they think it is OK for Amazon to benefit from taxpayer largesse to locate their warehouses and SNAP programs to lower the cost to them of their workers; they may precipitate a political "tragedy of the commons" creating political pushback they will all come to regret. It has already started in the United Kingdom:

> A radical overhaul of Britain's economy as far-reaching as Labour's post-war reforms and the Thatcherite revolution in the 1980s is needed to address the UK's chronic failure to raise the standard of living of millions of workers since the 2008 financial crash, according to a major report...
>
> ...Although Britain is experiencing record levels of employment, *low wage growth and persistent inequality have been widely cited as reasons for the Brexit vote*.[xxx] [Emphases mine]

How Best to Invest in People?

I believe boards need to invest in people if they are to build successful businesses operating in successful economies rather than treating them as disposable costs. The question is how best to do this?

Apart from instituting effective succession plans and talent management programs (discussed in Chapter 11), I believe boards (the Nomination Committee) must recognize there are several types of leadership, not just one. Management and HR should not waste time, effort and money on trying to "fit square pegs into round holes"; and finally, the top management team must demonstrate training and development really matter.

Recognize There Are Several Types of Leadership

I am surprised how often people think of captains or generals only when they describe leadership and how often the behavior they recommend is that of an extrovert, forgetting there are four types of leaders needed for an organization to succeed: "captains," "navigators," "engineers," and "builders" and many types of behavior.

Just as a ship must have a captain who exercises the ultimate authority over the crew and whose role it is to call them to action, so must a business. The defining role of the ship's captain is to wield power; to articulate the mission and timetable for action; to allocate responsibilities accordingly; to inspire the crew; to lay down the code of conduct and enforce it. It is also to be the focus of energy in a crisis around whom the crew can rally to get things done quickly. It is the captain's responsibility to save the crew in a tempest; that is why the captain is the last to leave a sinking ship. However, if we think only of captains, we miss many other crucial roles contributing to success:

> Part of our difficulty with appreciating the role that effective executive leadership can play in learning is that all of us are used to the "captain of the ship" image of traditional hierarchical

leaders. However, when executives act as teachers, stewards, and designers, they fill roles that are much more subtle, contextual, and long term than the traditional model of the power-wielding hierarchical leader.[xxxi]

Every captain needs a navigator. Once the captain has set the destination and the timetable, it is the responsibility of the navigator to chart the best route, accounting for the wind, weather forecasts, tides, currents and safe channels, reconciling the need for speed with economy and safety:

> To navigate is to chart a course for getting from where you are to where you want to go. Getting there is the process of planning, recording, and controlling the course and our progress to our destination...
>
> ...How you handle your sails, trim your ship...determines the speed and efficiency of how you sail... optimizing the response of your vessel and crew to the changing conditions of wind, water, tides and currents, and the needs of the crew and condition of the vessel itself.[xxxii]

In business, "navigators" are likely to be in staff functions rather than the line. Their responsibility is to develop the key assumptions of the plan, to ask the "what if?" questions, examine scenarios, and develop appropriate contingencies. To do this well, they must look outside the business; understand megatrends and how they could affect the business; establish effective early warning signals; and advise their "captain" when conditions have changed. They do what navigators do on ships when they identify a threatening storm and implement course corrections to avoid the storm yet stay on track to reach the destined port.

Both "captains" and "navigators," however, must rely on "engineers" in the engine room to keep the ship moving—what Peter Senge called "line leaders":

> However, engaging local line leaders may be difficult. As pragmatists, they often find ideas like systems thinking, mental models, and dialogue intangible and "hard to get their hands around...
>
> ...Simon's view is typical of many line leaders at the outset: he was skeptical, but he recognized that he had problems that he could not solve. He also had a trusted colleague who was willing to engage with him. Again, and again, we have found that healthy, open-minded skeptics can become the most effective leaders and, eventually, champions of this work. They keep the horse in front of the cart by focusing first and foremost on business results. *Such people invariably have more staying power than the "fans" who get excited about new ideas but whose excitement wanes once the newness wears off.*[xxxiii] [Emphasis mine]

Senge's points about Simon's skepticism and the excitement of "fans" about new ideas are important caveats. Boards, top management teams, "captains" and "navigators" are persuaded by "big picture" ideas *before* they are applied. Their mental model is "believe, understand, do,"[xxxiv] which is why they listen to consultants and experts and why they move on to the next bright idea or fad so easily. Line managers and "engineers," on the other hand, are more likely to be "little picture" pragmatists *interested in how the idea works in practice*. Their mental model is the reverse: "do, understand, believe," which is why they have staying power once they are convinced. "Captains" and "navigators" need to bear this in mind when communicating new ideas to "engineers" if they are to avoid the weary reaction of "yet another idea from head office; this too will surely pass, like all the other flavor of the month initiatives."

For a ship to do exactly what the navigator has charted, the captain has ordered his crew to do, and the engineer has the engine room running "full steam ahead" to deliver, there needs to be one more type of leader—the "builder." If a ship is not built to spec; if the processes linking all the different parts of the ship to each other are missing, the ship will not respond in the way the captain, navigator, and engineer expect, putting the mission and crew at risk.

So, we must never forget the ship-builder. The reason the *Titanic* was such a disaster was primarily flawed design.[xxxv] In business, "builders" are the planners, enterprise risk managers and auditors whose job it is to ensure there are appropriate processes, procedures, and service level agreements between departments, supported and reinforced by agreed codes of conduct and compliance mechanisms, creating the organizational "infrastructure" for the business model to achieve its agreed mission and vision:

> With little or no infrastructure to support ongoing learning, one might ask, "Why should successful new practices spread in organizations?" Who studies these innovations to document why they worked? Where are the learning processes that will enable others to follow in the footsteps of successful innovators? Who is responsible for creating these learning processes?
>
> There can be little doubt of the long-term business impact of executive leadership in developing learning infrastructure. When the Royal Dutch/Shell Group's central group planning leaders became convinced that "scenario thinking" was a vital survival skill in turbulent, unpredictable world oil markets, they didn't initiate a set of scenario-planning courses for Shell's management. Instead, they redesigned the planning infrastructure so that management teams regularly were asked not just for their budget and their "plan," but for several plans describing how they would manage under multiple possible futures. "Planning as learning" has gradually become a way of life within Shell...[xxxvi]

In addition to realizing there are these different leadership roles to be filled, the nomination committee also must recognize there are different ways of behaving. Table 15.2 compares six possible styles in ascending order of effectiveness.

Table 15.2: Six leadership behavior styles[xxxvii]

Leadership style	Characteristics	Consequences	Areas of improvement
Unpredictable	As an extreme example, Donald Trump's White House according to *Fire and Fury*,[xxxviii] *New York Times* September 5, 2018 op-ed,[xxxix] and *Fear*[xl]	Dysfunctional behavior, lack of focus, inconsistent policies, and flip-flops; Hesitant, fearful, and tentative followers; Back-stabbing, disloyal followers; Churn of key people	1. Focus 2. Work on being consistent 3. Remember words have consequences 4. Ensure actions match words to build trust 5. Recognize loyalty is a two-way street
Passive	Obvious problems persist, because the leader does not know what to do and does nothing about them as a result; Leader appears not to care, so followers cease caring	Disengaged followers; Problems do not get addressed, but are "kicked into the long grass"; Little or no progress	1. Acknowledge the problem 2. Admit to not having the answers 3. Realize leadership is about asking the right questions 4. Engage with subordinates to get answers 5. Develop a plan of action with them and get their "buy-in"
Secretive	"I can't tell you this (You're not important enough to know)." They hoard information because "information is power." Lack of trust is the result: "A team is not a group of people who work together. A team is a group of people who trust each other."[xli] Limited feedback, limiting the success of the leader because of lack of buy-in and care about the leader.	Distrust prevalent; Guarded followers; Silo mentality; Miscommunication; Conspiracy theories; Little buy-in; Weak teams	1. Communicate; share information 2. Be honest, transparent, and vulnerable 3. "Trust, but verify" only when the outcome is more important than the relationship 4. Otherwise simply trust, building trust incrementally with eyes wide open to consequences of failure[xlii]

Table 15.2 (continued)

Leadership style	Characteristics	Consequences	Areas of improvement
Domineering	"It's my way or the highway." They intimidate or threaten people into following them, producing short-term results, but long term, failure. They foster a culture of 'yes' people and weak teams. They get compliance, but not commitment.[xliii]	Management by fear; Compliant, uncommitted followers; No "courage to speak truth to power"; Weak teams; Short-term results and long-term failure	1. Take conscious care not to bully 2. Ask questions rather than providing answers 3. Give credit, take the blame 4. Promote "courage to speak truth to power"; 5. Never "shoot the messenger"
Authentic[xliv]	"People of the highest integrity, committed to building enduring organizations ... who have a deep sense of purpose and are true to their core values who have the courage to build their companies to meet the needs of all their stakeholders, and who recognize the importance of their service to society."[xlv] They: 1. Understand their purpose 2. Practice solid values 3. Lead with the heart 4. Establish connected relationships 5. Demonstrate self-discipline	Clear vision and direction; "Five Ps" aligned with mission and vision; Actions aligned with beliefs; Open, transparent and trusting communication; High levels of engagement between leader and followers leading to active "buy-in"	1. Lead change 2. Ensure organizational alignment remains appropriate when circumstances change 3. Become an empowering leader 4. Develop followers into leaders through empowerment
Empowering	Empowering leaders delegate authority and responsibility; They give subordinates the responsibility and authority to create/ innovate and then get out of their way; However, they remain accountable for everything that happens on their watch	People deep within the organization can say "yes"; Employees experience satisfaction in their work, belief in the mission, a sense of challenge;[xlvi] Front-liners have the freedom to make decisions—to make changes and implement new ideas; "Empowering leaders don't just produce followers—they produce other great leaders"[xlvii]	1. Lead yourself—focus on what you can do to become sharper 2. Lead others—from the heart and soul ensuring alignment between their personal values and purpose and the organization's 3. Train leaders down the organization to create, innovate, and lead

Stop Trying to "Fit Square Pegs into Round Holes"
This tendency manifests itself in two ways: believing the only way to progress in an organization is to become a manager of other people; and force-fitting people into unsuitable roles, ignoring the impact of default personalities on productivity.

The number of people who really do not want to manage other people is surprisingly high.[xlviii] There may be two factors to explain this. The first is the lack of training of managers in managing others:

> A recent study by CareerBuilder.com shows that a whopping 58 percent of managers said they didn't receive any management training. Digest that for a second. *Most managers in the workforce were promoted because they were good at what they did, and not necessarily good at making the people around them better.* This statistic obviously unveils a harsh reality. We have a bunch of leaders who aren't trained on how to lead.[xlix]

The second is that many people do not like managing others because it takes them away from what they love, which is "doing" rather than getting others to do:

> I was merely managing the people who actually did and made things. I no longer operated in my personal sweet spot, where my sense of accomplishment after closing a difficult sale or launching a new product was contingent on my having had a *concrete* deliverable and the sense that my efforts were integral to its success. Being a manager caused me to feel disconnected from what career analyst Daniel Pink has identified as the three primary motivators of behavior: autonomy, mastery and purpose...
>
> ...Why do we reward success on the job with a promotion *out* of the job and into management? ... Companies continue to cling to the notion that one of the *only* mechanisms they have to acknowledge employees' talent is to make them managers and then to continue to promote them into ever-higher levels of management—reflecting the misguided assumption that being good at something also means being able to (and wanting to) manage others doing the same thing. Once in management, its trappings...don't really satisfy many of us who, like me, miss the *doing*... Management titles allow us to mark our growth, and our maturity...
>
> ...I know now ... that as corporate executive I felt like I had to pretend to be something I wasn't—I didn't like being a manager, but I was a manager, so I had to appear to be interested in all the stuff that went along with being a manager. This is something social scientists call "emotion labor"—what you experience when you feel obliged to act differently from your natural inclinations.[l]

One of the most common mistakes of this type is to promote the best salesperson to become an indifferent sales manager, damaging performance twice over: once, by losing the results of the best salesperson; twice, by putting them in a position where they can demotivate their subordinates. This is because of a failure to recognize the skills, involvement and aptitudes needed are quite different.

The best way to avoid making such a mistake is to invest in two career ladders: the traditional managerial ladder which has an ever-increasing number of people to be managed as individuals climb the ladder; and to have a parallel technical ladder where individuals grow and are promoted based on their technical expertise, allowing them to focus on what they do best and like doing.

Professional service firms (e.g., law and accountancy partnerships, management consultants, advertising and PR agencies, and IT companies) have long practiced this approach, where careers are based on becoming the "go-to" technical experts (practice leaders), effective "rainmakers" (client leaders), as well as managerial leaders (office managers). Perhaps this the result of such firms really meaning what they say when, like Narayana Murthy (founder of Infosys) they say:

> Our assets walk out of the door each evening. We have to make sure they come back the next morning.[li]

Too often, management advised by HR departments spend time trying to close performance gaps in staff caused by their default personalities. Instead they should spend more time focusing on harnessing the power of those personalities by putting employees in roles they are temperamentally suited to doing and will enjoy being in. As Aristotle pointed out more than two thousand years ago:

> Pleasure in the job puts perfection in the work.

We know this to be true: a job we do not like is a chore, whereas a job we enjoy doing does not feel like work; it is something we look forward to doing, for which we do not have to be compensated.[6] Peter Drucker has made the same point:

> Altogether, an increasing number of people who are full-time employees have to be managed as if they were *volunteers*. They are paid, to be sure. But...[w]e have known for fifty years that money alone does not motivate to perform... What motivates—and especially what motivates knowledge workers—is what motivates volunteers. Volunteers, we know, have to get *more* satisfaction from their work than paid employees, precisely because they do not get a paycheck. They need, above all, challenge. They need to know the organization's mission and to believe in it.[lii]

This needs to be reinforced by employees feeling temperamentally at home in the roles they are asked to perform, otherwise they expend too much emotional energy reconciling who they are with the emotional demands of the role; energy better spent on becoming more productive. This is even truer of millennials.

---

[6] "Compensate" in English means "give (someone) something, typically money, in recognition of loss, suffering, or injury incurred; recompense." HR should stop using "compensation and benefits" as a mental model as it implies coming to work harms the people who come to work. If people are forced to do work they do not like or that is not suited for their temperament, then maybe it is correct. Personally, I prefer the concept of "reward and recognition" rather than "compensation."

Boards need to recognize there are four primary default personalities, based on a simplification of the Meyers-Briggs profiling tool, called the "DOPE Four Bird Personality Test"[liii] where "D" stands for *dove*, "O" for *owl*, "P" for *peacock*, and "E" for *eagle*.

The *dove* is a *people-oriented introvert* motivated by security, whose focus is maintaining harmony. The *owl* is a *task-oriented introvert* motivated by process, whose focus is accurate data. The *peacock* is a *people-oriented extrovert* motivated by recognition, whose focus is visioning the future. The *eagle* is a *task-oriented extrovert* motivated by challenge, whose focus is achieving results. Nobody is pure dove, owl, peacock, or eagle. We all are mix of each of these four birds. However, the proportion these birds represent in our psychological default makeup will affect our temperamental suitability for given roles.

Just as people are a mix of the four birds, roles require different amounts of the bird characteristics to be done well. For example, the introverted bird default personalities (dove and owl) will feel stressed when placed in roles requiring extrovert behavior such as presenting to a large audience or selling. These are roles the extroverted bird default personalities (peacock and eagle) would feel relatively at ease doing.

The other aspect is where people sit on the task-people orientation spectrum. The people-oriented default personalities (dove and peacock) empathize easily, maybe too easily, and feel the pain of others when they are required to put them under pressure to get things done. The task-oriented default personalities (eagle and owl) will feel no such inhibitions and will be relatively at ease with doing whatever is needed to get people to make things happen.

When investing in personal development of individuals, it makes an enormous difference if the default personalities have been considered. It is far more productive and profitable to match the personality requirements of the role with people with the corresponding default personalities than to try to force fit someone who does not belong and try train them to become someone they are not. However, there may be times in individuals' career development when they need to spend time in roles that will create great personal stress. If they and their superiors appreciate this from the outset and that this will be for a limited time, it can make good sense to place someone in a role that differs markedly from their default personalities.

Demonstrate Training and Development Really Matter

Staff development and training is often neglected under the pressure of day-to-day operations and the belief trained staff leave for better jobs elsewhere, once they have undergone expensive formal training. This is a mirror image of the search for the perfect candidate, who has been trained by some other company.

> The search for the mythical "perfect candidate" has been fueled, in part, by cutbacks in staff training programs, borne out of companies' desire to hire people who essentially don't need any training.

However, what hiring managers are increasingly discovering is that the perfect candidate rarely exists. What is available is good talent that—with some training and coaching—can be shaped into a productive member of a company's workforce.[liv]

Given the "perfect" candidate does not exist, companies should save themselves the frustration of looking for "perfection," recognizing they should hire good candidates who will need to be trained from day one, just as new plant and machinery need to be run in from day one. They should also recognize what could be happening with so-called on the job training:

> While on-the-job training is unquestionably valuable, a problem arises when this becomes an organization's exclusive approach to refining and expanding the skills of its workforce. The dirty little secret about on-the-job training is that *many managers rely on it* because *they don't really have an employee training program.*
>
> That revelation is not lost on employees, who can surely distinguish between such haphazard attempts at skill development, compared to more organized and thoughtful approaches.
>
> There's no substitute for hands-on training. However, it's bound to be more effective when paired with traditional instruction methods, such as those delivered through classroom venues, e-learning tools and formal procedural documentation.[lv] [Emphasis mine]

Companies often conflate new product rollout training with employee development. New product training is important, as people must know how to use or sell new products. However, focusing on product training alone is to ignore the soft skills training and investment in improving competencies needed for employees to become more effective and more loyal:

> A robust employee development program helps staff expand their horizons beyond just the latest product launch. It might help them cultivate much-needed soft skills, such as customer service, communication or negotiation. It might augment knowledge that, while not directly related to their current role, helps position the employee for future opportunities that are aligned with their aspirations (thus improving retention).[lvi]

Finally, they must give employees enough time to engage with their trainers, free of interruptions, when they are being trained and "quiet time" to practice what they have learned, without the pressures of learning it when they are likely to be distracted by the job. "Maintenance on the go" practices come in the form of:

> Directives that employees complete self-training (often delivered online) "as time allows" during their regular workday. It can also be seen in classroom training programs where participants are encouraged to stay in constant touch with the office...
>
> ...It is a disservice to employees when an organization neglects to give them "quiet time" to participate in skill development programs. Indeed, the value of those programs (and the investment a company makes in them) is greatly diminished without the benefit of employees' undivided attention.[lvii]

In my experience, the best way to indicate to employees their training and development is taken seriously is for superiors to attend the entire training of their subordinates. This has two benefits: first, it signals to the subordinates the time they are spending in formal training is not time wasted—it is important enough for their superiors to attend; second, their superiors will know what they have been taught and what they are expected to do differently as a result. Both are effective spurs to paying attention and concentrating on what needs to be learnt, improving training ROI.

Conclusion

The underlying assumption people are costs on the P&L to be minimized or externalized will continue if financial accounts do not find a way of recording them on the balance sheet as assets. As a result, boards often fail to regard people as assets to be invested in from day one to the day they retire. In addition, there is an entire category of employment where the "psychic income" afforded by following a vocation, doing "national service" or working for a nongovernmental organization (NGO) or charity has justified underpaying people.

The Internet and gig economy made matters worse with skilled labor in developed economies competing with workers from emerging markets, reinforcing the assumption workers are a cost to minimized in a global "race to the bottom." This encourages boards to think people are disposable—an attitude most prevalent in the Anglosphere economies. However, "Rhenish" capitalist countries have adopted a different approach, building long-term loyalty through effective apprenticeship programs to develop long-term skills in export-based activities. This has resulted in their creating better paying jobs in export-oriented industries, lower inequality and longer life expectancy than in the United States, where life expectancy is falling. The Anglosphere approach only seems to be superior in delivering short-term GDP growth—a defective measure of the overall well-being of an economy.

The rise in inequality resulting from the view shareholders come first and employees last, demonstrated by companies buying back shares while real wages stagnate or decline for blue collar and lower white-collar workers may lead to a "political tragedy of the commons" where what makes *economic* sense for an individual board does not make *political* sense when all boards follow suit. Brexit, the election of Donald Trump and the rise of populists in Europe are all early warning signals of a political pushback boards may come to regret.

Once we accept, we need to invest in people, the question is how best to do it. It helps if boards recognize there are four types of leader, not just the single "captain of the ship" of our imaginations. "Captains" are essential for giving direction and orders, acting as focus points in times of crisis for the crew to rally round. However, "captains" rely on "navigators" whose role is to chart the best course reconciling safety, speed and economy to reach the destination on time. "Navigators" in turn depend on "engineers" to keep the ship moving and "engineers" depend on "builders" to design and build seaworthy vessels in the first place.

When communicating, directors and senior management must recognize they operate with a "believe, understand, do" model of thinking and communication, whereas line managers, on whom they depend to get things done, operate on a "do, understand, believe" model. Failure to recognize this difference in approach and thought process will lead to miscommunication and cynicism.

It is important to remember there are six types of leadership behavior, in ascending order of effectiveness: unpredictable, passive, secretive, domineering, authentic and empowering. Each has its own characteristics and consequences with its areas of improvement in which companies can invest.

It would help improve morale and productivity if companies stopped trying to "fit square pegs into round holes," by recognizing most people do not want to be managers, either because there is no effective training showing them how to get the best out of people or because they prefer to "do their own thing" rather than facing the problems of managing others. Organizations that recognize this problem have invested in more than one career ladder— people can get to the top of a technical career ladder without having to climb the managerial career ladder they dislike. The other aspect to avoiding trying to "fit square pegs into round holes" is to recognize there are four bird default personalities—dove, owl, peacock, and eagle. Everyone is a mix of these four birds and the combination makes them suited temperamentally to filling roles.

Force-fitting the wrong default personality into the wrong role, justified on the grounds it will be a good developmental experience may be true but comes at the cost of the individual having to invest emotional energy in dealing with the mismatch— energy better spent on enjoying the job and putting perfection into the work, with major increases in productivity as a result. It is important to remember the people best able to judge which person is temperamentally suited to a given role are not HR, but the line managers to whom that person reports. Line managers are responsible for looking after the enterprise's assets and that includes its people.

When investing in training, companies must remember new product training is not the same as training employees in the soft skills and new competencies they need to face the future and companies must stop treating them as the same thing, just as they must also stop searching for the "perfect" employees who need no training— they do not exist. What this attitude reflects is the unwillingness to invest in proper employee development, reflected in the fact companies often neglect to give employees enough "quiet" time to practice what they have learned without the distractions of their daily routine. Finally, senior management must demonstrate their commitment to training and development.

Perhaps there will be no real change in the underlying attitudes of boards to investing in people until accountants find a way of showing people as assets on the balance sheet and capturing the externalities created by treating people as disposable.

References

i Ford, H., https://www.azquotes.com/quote/1430055

ii Douglas, C. (2017), "Tracking Amazon's Rapidly Expanding Footprint," *The Business Journals*, October 11, 2017, https://www.bizjournals.com/bizjournals/maps/the-amazon-effect, accessed on September 3, 2018.

iii Brown, C. (2018).

iv Squawk Box Team (2018), "Sen. Bernie Sanders Targets Low Wages in BEZOS Act," *CNBC Markets*, September 6, 2018, https://www.cnbc.com/video/2018/09/06/sen-bernie-sanders-targets-low-wages-in-bezos-act.html, accessed on October 3, 2018.

v Lauerman, J. and Kahn, J. (2018), "Bezos Blinks and Raises Amazon's Minimum Wage in US, UK," *Bloomberg*, October 2, 2018, https://www.bloomberg.com/news/articles/2018-10-02/amazon-raises-minimum-wage-to-15-for-all-u-s-employees-jmrk3z14, accessed on October 3, 2018.

vi Ovide, S. (2018), "Amazon's Pay Raise Is a Small Price to Pay for its Reputation," *Bloomberg Opinion*, October 2, 2018, https://www.bloomberg.com/view/articles/2018-10-02/amazon-pay-raise-is-a-small-price-to-pay-for-its-reputation?utm_medium=email&utm_source=newsletter&utm_term=181002&utm_campaign=sharetheview, accessed on October 3, 2018.

vii Mensitieri, G. (2018), *Le plus beau métier du monde: Dans les coulisses de l'industrie de la mode* (Paris: Editions de la Découverte), https://fr.calameo.com/read/000215022bc99994c37b5, accessed on September 3, 2018.

viii Marsh, S. (2018), "Chanel Shoes, but No Salary: How One Woman Exposed the Scandal of the French Fashion Industry," *The Guardian*, September 2, 2018, https://www.theguardian.com/fashion/2018/sep/02/academic-exposing-ugly-reality-high-fashion-giulia-mensitieri, accessed on September 3, 2018.

ix "Fiverr—Freelance Services for the Lean Entrepreneur," http//www.fiverr.com/.

x Semuels, A. (2018), "The Online Gig Economy's 'Race to the Bottom': When the Whole World Is Fighting for the Same Jobs, What Happens to the Workers?," *The Atlantic*, August 31, 2018, https://www.theatlantic.com/technology/archive/2018/08/fiverr-online-gig-economy/569083/, accessed on September 3, 2018.

xi Burt, E. (2018), "Women and Young People Most Likely to Work on Zero Hours Contracts," *People Management*, April 24, 2018, https://www.peoplemanagement.co.uk/news/articles/women-young-people-on-zero-hours-contracts, accessed on September 4, 2018.

xii ITV report (2017), "Yong Adults on Zero-Hour Contracts Suffer Worse Physical and Mental Health, Study Finds," *ITV News*, July 5, 2017, http://www.itv.com/news/2017-07-05/young-adults-on-zero-hour-contracts-suffer-worse-physical-and-mental-health-study-finds/, accessed on September 4, 2018.

xiii Marsh, D. and Bischof, R. (2012), "'Hire and Fire' Has Destroyed Britain's Job Economy," *The Guardian*, January 26, 2012, https://www.theguardian.com/commentisfree/2012/jan/26/hire-and-fire-destroyed-uk-jobs, accessed on September 4, 2018.

xiv Eurostat, Bureau of Labor Statistics (2018), https://www.google.com/search?hl=en-MY&ei=T1qOW5TuE4ravgTP1I_IDQ&q=austria+unemployment+rate&oq=austria+unemployment+rate&gs_l=psy-ab.12..35i39k1j0i7i30k1l3j0i7i10i30k1j0i7i30k1l2j0j0i10, https://www.google.com/search?hl=en-MY&ei=HFqOW7KQDovzvgTQuoSoBw&q=denmark+unemployment+rate&oq=den+unemployment+rate&gs_l=psy-ab.1.0.0i7i30k1l10.44947.45805.0.48086.3.3.0.0.0.0.1, https://www.google.com/search?hl=en-MY&ei=3VmOW7zQMsjHvgSh-raoBg&q=germany+unemployment+rate&oq=germany+unemployment+rate&gs_l=psy-ab.1.0.35i39k1j0i7i30k1l3j0l6.55759.57834.0.594. https://www.google.com/search?hl=en-MY&ei=w1mOW8XIFIvvvATI-aSIBg&q=netherlands+unemployment+rate&oq=netherl+unemployment+rate&gs_l=psy-ab.1.0.0i7i30k1l9j0i8i7i30k1.15354.19614.0.23343., https://www.google.com/search?hl=en-MY&ei=IlmOW_uAGorfvATeloCYDQ&q=sweden+unemployment+rate&oq=Sweden+unemployment+rate&gs_

l=psy-ab.1.0.35i39k1j0i7i30k1l2j0i7i10i30k1j0i7i30k1l4j0i30, https://www.google.com/search?hl=en-MY&ei=UlmOW5HrNojUvgSAh7qQDQ&q=switzerland+unemployment+rate&oq=swit+unemployment+rate&gs_l=psy-ab.1.0.0i7i30k1l8j0i8i7i30k1l2.42226.45324.0.4732, https://www.google.com/search?hl=en-MY&ei=FFiOW-6jNIiDvQTSv4aACQ&q=UK+unemployment+rate&oq=UK+unemployment+rate&gs_l=psy-ab.3..35i39k1j0i7i30k1l2j0i67k1j0i7i30k1l6.264790.265569.0.26, https://www.google.com/search?hl=en-MY&ei=flOOW6-9IIrivASBlaD4BA&q=US+unemployment+rate&oq=US+unemployment+rate&gs_l=psy-ab.3..35i39k1j0i7i30k1l6j0i67k1j0i7i30k1l2.1166380.1167211.0.1, accessed on September 4, 2018.

xv World Bank, "Current Account Balance (% of GDP)," https://data.worldbank.org/indicator/bn.cab.xoka.gd.zs, accessed on September 4, 2018.

xvi Central Intelligence Agency, *The World Factbook*, https://www.cia.gov/library/publications/the-world-factbook/rankorder/2004rank.html, accessed on September 4, 2018.

xvii Ibid., https://www.cia.gov/library/publications/the-world-factbook/fields/2172.html, accessed on September 4, 2018.

xviii Ibid., https://www.cia.gov/library/publications/the-world-factbook/rankorder/2102rank.html, accessed on September 4, 2018.

xix Countryeconomy.com, https://countryeconomy.com/unemployment/norway, accessed on September 4, 2018.

xx Trading Economics (2018), "Australia Unemployment Rate 1978–2018," August 16, 2018, https://tradingeconomics.com/australia/unemployment-rate, accessed September 4, 2018.

xxi Trading Economics (2018, "Canada Unemployment Rate 1966–2018," August 10, 2018, https://tradingeconomics.com/canada/unemployment-rate, accessed on September 4, 2018.

xxii Donnelly, G. (2018), "Here's Why Life Expectancy in the US Dropped Again This Year," *Fortune*, February 9, 2018, http://fortune.com/2018/02/09/us-life-expectancy-dropped-again/, accessed on September 4, 2018.

xxiii Riker, D. (2015), "Export-Intensive Industries Pay More on Average: An Update," *Office of Economics Research Note*, US International Trade Commission, April 2015, https://www.usitc.gov/publications/332/ec201504a.pdf, accessed on September 4, 2018.

xxiv Moore, J. (2017), "Realities of Reshoring: A UK Perspective," *University of Warwick in association with Reshoring UK*, https://warwick.ac.uk/fac/sci/wmg/research/scip/networking/26september/wmg_realities_of_reshoring_report.pdf, accessed on September 4, 2018.

xxv Special Report (2013) "Reshoring Manufacturing: Coming Home," *The Economist*, January 19, 2013, https://www.economist.com/special-report/2013/01/19/coming-home, accessed on September 4, 2018.

xxvi Donnelly, G. (2018), "Here's Why Life Expectancy in the US Dropped Again This Year," *Fortune*, February 9, 2018, http://fortune.com/2018/02/09/us-life-expectancy-dropped-again/, accessed on September 9, 2018.

xxvii Dasgupta, N. (2018), Opioid Crisis: No Easy Fix to its Social and Economic Determinants," *US National Library of Medicine, National Institutes of Health*, February 2018, https://www.ncbi.nlm.nih.gov/pmc/articles/PMC5846593/, accessed on September 5, 2018.

xxviii Lazarus, D. (2018), "The Economy May Be Booming, but Nearly Half Americans Can't Make Ends Meet," *Los Angeles Times*, August 31, 2018, http://www.latimes.com/business/lazarus/la-fi-lazarus-economy-stagnant-wages-20180831-story.html, accessed on September 5, 2018.

xxix Stevens, L. and Ramkumar, A. (2018), "Amazon Hits $1 Trillion Valuation," *Wall Street Journal*, September 4, 2018, https://www.wsj.com/articles/amazon-hits-1-trillion-valuation-1536075734, accessed on September 4, 2018.

xxx Inman, P. (2018), "Thinktank Calls for Major Overhaul of Britain's Economy," *The Guardian*, September 5, 2018, https://www.theguardian.com/uk-news/2018/sep/05/thinktank-calls-for-major-overhaul-of-britains-economy, accessed on September 5, 2018.

xxxi Senge, P. (1995), "Rethinking Leadership In The Learning Organization," *The Systems Think-

er, https://thesystemsthinker.com/rethinking-leadership-in-the-learning-organization/, accessed on September 5, 2018.

xxxii Wohl, R. A. and Wohl, L. (2011), *Navigating Organizations Through the 21st Century: A Metaphor for Leadership* (Bloomington, IN: Xlibris), 24–25.

xxxiii Senge (1995), op. cit.

xxxiv Subramaniam, K. (2009), "Seven Deadly Sins in Managing Change," Dynamic Assessment Centre, Securities Commission Malaysia, Kuala Lumpur, May 29.

xxxv Woytowich, R. (2018), "Titanic Sinking Tied To Engineering, Structural Failures (DIAGRAMS)," *Science*, December 6, 2017, https://www.huffingtonpost.com/2012/04/09/titanic-sunk-new-theory_n_1412622.html, accessed on September 5, 2018.

xxxvi Senge (1995), op. cit.

xxxvii Based on Groeschel, C. (2016), *"Leadership Podcast—Episodes 1 &2,"* January 2016; https://open.life.church/training/166-leadership-podcast-the-six-types-of-leaders-part-1, https://open.life.church/training/166-leadership-podcast-the-six-types-of-leaders-part-2

xxxviii Conrad, P. (2018), "Fire and Fury: Inside the Trump White House by Michael Wolff—A Review," *The Guardian*, January 14, 2018, https://www.theguardian.com/books/2018/jan/14/fire-and-fury-michael-wolff-inside-trump-white-house-review, accessed on September 6, 2018.

xxxix Anonymous (2018), "I Am Part of the Resistance Inside the Trump Administration," *New York Times*, September 5, 2018, https://www.nytimes.com/2018/09/05/opinion/trump-white-house-anonymous-resistance.html, accessed on September 6, 2018.

xl Woodward, B. (2018), *Fear: Trump in the White House* (New York: Simon & Schuster).

xli @simonsinek, August 27, 2018, accessed on September 6, 2018.

xlii Russell, N. (2015), "The Problem with a Trust-But-Verify Approach," *Psychology Today*, July 25, 2018, https://www.psychologytoday.com/intl/blog/trust-the-new-workplace-currency/201507/the-problem-trust-verify-approach, accessed on September 6, 2018.

xliii Zinkin, J. (2014), *Rebuilding Trust in Banks: The Role of Leadership and Governance*, Chapter Two: "From Success to Failure" (Singapore: John Wiley & Sons), 25–46.

xliv George, B. (2015), "What Does Authentic Leadership Really Mean?" *Harvard Business Review: Working Knowledge*, November 10, 2015, https://www.linkedin.com/pulse/what-does-authentic-leadership-really-mean-bill-george/, accessed on September 8, 2018.

xlv Ibid.

xlvi Batista, E. (2008), "Peter Drucker on Knowledge Workers, Management and Leadership," http://www.edbatista.com/2008/10/drucker-1.html, accessed on September 9, 2018.

xlvii Groeschel (2016), op. cit.

xlviii Torres, N. (2014), "Most People Don't Want to Be Managers," *Harvard Business Review*, September 18, 2014, https://hbr.org/2014/09/most-people-dont-want-to-be-managers, accessed on September 10, 2019.

xlix Sturt, D. and Nordstrom, T. (2018), "10 Shocking Workplace Stats You Need to Know," *Forbes*, March 8, 2018, https://www.forbes.com/sites/davidsturt/2018/03/08/10-shocking-workplace-stats-you-need-to-know/#67941965f3af, accessed on September 10, 2018.

l Kreamer, A. (2012), "What If You Don't Want to Be a Manager?," *Harvard Business Review*, December 13, 2012, https://hbr.org/2012/12/what-if-you-dont-want-to-be-a, accessed on September 10, 2018.

li "Has Narayana Murthi's Return at Infosys Worked for the IT Major?" *economictimes.indiatimes.com*, quoted in *AZ Quotes*, December 24, 2013, https://www.azquotes.com/quote/771868, accessed on September 11, 2018.

lii Drucker, P. (1992), *Management Challenges of the 21st Century* (Oxford: Butterworth Heinemann), 21.

liii Stephenson, R. (2012), "DOPE 4 Bird Personality Test: Dove, Owl, Peacock, Eagle," April 11, 2012, https://richardstep.com/self-tests-quizzes/dope-bird-personality-test-printable/, accessed on September 9, 2018.

liv Picoult, J. "Your Workforce: The Most Important Asset You're Not Maintaining," *Monster,* https://hiring.monster.com/hr/hr-best-practices/workforce-management/hr-management-skills/employee-engagement-strategy.aspx, accessed on September 11, 2018.
lv Ibid.
lvi Ibid.
lvii Ibid.

Chapter 16
Harnessing Processes to Create Long-Term Value

This chapter is presented in two parts. The first explores how boards can harness processes to create long-term value by improving its creation, extraction and distribution. The second briefly discusses the role of regulators and government in creating a framework or "corporate governance ecosystem" to strengthen long-term value creation.

The processes to create long-term value can be divided into those that are the responsibility of boards of individual organizations and those that are the responsibility of the community, acting through regulators and legislation, endorsing or sanctioning board behavior. Some may argue external sanctions are not necessary—it is solely the responsibility of the board of an individual organization to ensure good corporate governance (CG). However, this is to ignore free-riders who compete with responsible organizations by adopting lower standards of governance. It also disregards externalities imposed on the community at large by boards doing what makes sense for their individual organizations (e.g., firing employees) and not for the economy, if all other companies followed suit. The only way to deal with free-riders and externalities is to create an effective external "CG ecosystem." Both are therefore necessary if a "political tragedy of the commons" is to be avoided.

Board Processes to Deliver Long-Term Value

There are three roles boards must reconcile in delivering long-term value: value creation through the selection of the appropriate strategy, value extraction through efficient execution of the chosen strategy, and compliant distribution of the resulting value to stakeholders. According to a 2004 study by Booz Allen & Hamilton, 60% of shareholder value destruction is the result of boards selecting the wrong strategy; 27% as a result of poor execution; and 13% because of failures of compliance.[i] Boards are therefore right to be concerned they do not spend enough time on strategy:

> A mere 34% of the 772 directors surveyed by McKinsey in 2013[ii] agreed that the boards on which they served fully comprehended their companies' strategies. Only 22% said their boards were completely aware of how their firms created value, and just 16% claimed that their boards had a strong understanding of the dynamics of their firms' industries.[iii]

Put another way, 66% of the directors surveyed did not fully understand the strategies for which they were responsible; 78% were not fully aware of how their firms created value and 84% did not have a strong understanding of the dynamics of the industry to which their firm belonged. These are dismal, but not surprising results, given the problems INEDs have with the asymmetry of information they receive; the limited amount of time they spend on the business; and the increasing complexity of business in today's world.

To improve the situation, the authors of the HBR article suggest a number of process changes. Directors should spend at least 35 days a year on the business,[1] noting private equity directors spend 54 days a year. Directors should go on unstructured strategic offsites so they do not hear and see only what management want them to hear and see; directors should have long-term access to specialist advisers, each of whom brings a deep understanding of the drivers of the business and of issues the industry faces (like Mars, which has five specialists advising the board); and be paid more and be required to hold a significant part of their net worth in the company's stock:

> A few years ago, Johnson & Johnson established minimum ownership guidelines for nonexecutive directors to better align their interests with shareholders'. J&J requires each director to retain the company shares issued upon election to the board and to own shares equal to five times his or her annual cash retainer. Coca-Cola grants nonoption stock awards that become available only after a director has left the board. General Electric follows a similar scheme.
>
> We'd go one step further: To really get directors thinking and behaving like owners, ask them to put a greater portion of their net worth on the table. This could be achieved by giving them a combination of incentive shares, a portion of which vests only some years *after* directors step aside, and requiring incoming directors to purchase equity with their own money.[iv]

I believe director performance in delivering long-term value can be improved further through the following six changes in process: introducing a system of rotating "Devil's Advocacy," using activity-based costing, "reframing" budget and cost control discussions, setting key performance indicators (KPIs) and targets using a ten-step process, adopting an effective innovation process, and recruiting more women directors.

Rotating "Devil's Advocacy"

This deals with the purpose of independent directors. If it is to foster independence of thought and the ability to challenge without fearing the consequences, then being paid in stock could undermine that objective. Fortunately, there is a process solution. It is a variation on Alfred Sloan's method of reviewing important board decisions which he instituted after his first board meeting at General Motors:

---

[1] According to the McKinsey report, U.S. directors on average spend only 22 days a year on company matters, whereas European directors spend 29 days and Asian directors spend 34 days.

If we are all in agreement on the decision—then I propose we postpone further discussion of this matter until our next meeting to *give ourselves time to develop disagreement and perhaps gain some understanding of what the decision is all about.*[v] [Emphasis mine]

The advantage of such a process is clear: the ensuing discussion focuses on all the reasons why the decision might be undesirable, highlighting what could go wrong; and as a result, forcing the board to improve the proposal to overcome identified defects, develop contingency plans in case those defects can not be eliminated and materialize later, or to reconsider adopting the idea.

To do this effectively, directors must spend extra time deliberating diligently. If they are to be a high impact board, they will be forced to understand fully the strategies of their company, how it creates value and the impact of the issues faced by its industry.[2] The benefit of making it an ad hoc rotating process, is no single director gets tarred with the negative halo of always being the naysayer "Devil's Advocate." Making who will be called upon to argue the case against the proposal ad hoc, ensures all directors are well-prepared for the discussion. However, to be able to do their "due diligence" on proposals put before them, they will need to understand the real costs of doing business; the financial assumptions of the budget and how the objectives, KPI and resulting targets and outcomes have been derived.

Adopting Activity-Based Costing (ABC)

Traditional cost accounting assumes the total manufacturing cost is the sum of individual operations and cost of goods sold is that total divided by the number of units sold. However, what matters for a company to be both competitive and profitable is the cost of the total process from end to end, covering the arrival of materials, parts and supplies at the factory loading dock, including what happens after the finished product reaches the end-user. Installation and after-sales service are also costs of the product even though the customer may not have paid for them. It is also important for companies to understand customer and product line profitability so they can shed unprofitable customers and withdraw from unprofitable lines of business. To do this *accurately* requires activity-based costing.

---

[2] "At boards with very high impact, directors spend even more time on their work than their peers at lower-impact boards (40 days per year, compared with only 19 days). Other results suggest that these extra days are not spent on basic compliance but on strategic issues instead. Compared with their peers, the directors at higher-impact boards say they evaluate resource decisions, debate strategic alternatives, and assess management's understanding of value creation much more often. These respondents are also likelier than others to say their boards ensure that organizational resources are in place to deliver on strategy and that they manage strategic performance." Barton, D. and Wiseman, M. (2015), "Where Boards Fall Short," *Harvard Business Review*, January–February Issue, 2015.

The problem with traditional cost accounting is that it only measures what it costs to do something. It does not record the cost of "not" doing something: machine downtime; waiting for delayed shipments of parts or tools needed to complete the job; delays in shipping completed inventory; reworking or scrapping defective parts; the number of calls a salesperson has to make before winning the order or the calls the salesperson made without winning the order:

> The costs of not doing, which traditional accounting cannot and does not record, often equal and sometimes even exceed the costs of doing. Activity-based costing therefore gives not only much better cost control, but increasingly, it gives *result control*...
>
> ...Activity-based costing integrates...value analysis, process analysis, quality management, and costing—into one analysis...
>
> ...Activity-based costing can substantially lower manufacturing costs—in some instances by a full third or more. Its greatest impact, however, is likely to be in services. In most manufacturing companies, cost accounting is inadequate. But service industries...have practically no cost information at all.
>
> ...Service companies cannot start with the cost of individual operations, as manufacturing companies have done with traditional cost accounting. They must start with the assumption that there is only *one* cost: that of the total system...The famous distinction between fixed and variable costs on which traditional cost accounting is based does not make much sense in services... all costs are fixed over a given time period...so that the *total* operation has to be costed.
>
> ...Activity-based costing shows—or at least attempts to show—the impact of changes in the costs and yields of every activity on the results of the whole.[vi]

The importance of measuring yield per customer does not just apply to banks; it applies to hotels and restaurants; to all forms of transport; to Telco's and mobile phone providers; and to all professional service firms. It forms the basis of evaluating the costs of customer acquisition and retention and therefore of customer lifetime value calculations (discussed in Chapter 9, Appendix 9.2). As such, unlike traditional cost accounting, it provides boards and management with a basis for thinking about long-term value creation and extraction.

"Reframing" Budget and Cost Control Discussions

Too often companies do their budgets and discuss appropriate levels of cost based on what happened in the previous year. As a result, they suffer from *anchoring bias*, assuming the previous year's costs were appropriate; without asking whether certain activities or levels of activity are in fact necessary. Often, when boards challenge the validity of the previous year's costs as the basis for the coming year's costs, they will ask for sensitivity analyses requiring only incremental, marginal changes in the way business is done because of *anchoring bias*—by asking what would happen if the resources allocated were the "base case" plus or minus 10–20% around already fixed, anchoring numbers.

Better ways of both creating and extracting value are the result of "reframing" questions to focus on what the appropriate levels of cost and resource are under alternative scenarios with different resulting strategies, ways of doing business and outcomes. Focusing too much on a single approach can lead to boards self-limiting their available strategic opportunities.

Xerox is an excellent example. Its Palo Alto Research Center (PARC) invented a number of new opportunities: Ethernet, personal workstations, PCs, the graphical user interface and laser printing. Xerox chose laser printing for two reasons: it understood how to sell laser printers—a variant on copiers, and it felt it did not have enough resources to develop all the opportunities created for it by PARC:

> Even in the decision to pursue laser printing over workstations, Xerox had a limiting frame. It saw itself as constrained by limited resources. By comparison, the upstart companies that commercialized Xerox PARC inventions had minuscule resources. But they saw themselves as able to raise the resources to pursue these new businesses. Different frames produce different results.[vii]

This is an example of what happens when one firm adopts the incumbent's view of strategy, preventing it from creating new value because of an excessive focus on its legacy and on extracting value by maximizing return on existing resources and costs, while its competitors use a disruptor's approach, seeking resources to create a new business opportunity (discussed in Chapter 8).

If the Xerox board had framed the questions differently, they might have been able to see it was worth seeking additional resources to capture the opportunities created by PARC, but commercialized by Apple, IBM, Adobe, 3Com, and HP instead:

> Many of the inventions that have changed our world, in fact, came from this lab: the personal computer, the mouse, the user-friendly interface, the computer network, and laser printing. Yet Xerox was unable to take advantage of these technical breakthroughs... 'the captains of industry at Xerox headquarters in upstate New York were making too much money the old way—by making copiers—to remake Xerox into a computer company. They took a couple of half-hearted stabs...but did little to promote PARC technology'[viii]. By not investing strategically in their commercialization, Xerox failed to capitalize on the excellent work being done in its lab. Instead Apple, Adobe, 3Com and others saw the potential of these technologies and reaped the benefits.[ix]

One way of avoiding the *anchoring bias* trap implicit in poor "framing," is to encourage management to create at least four viable, nonincremental scenarios, each with a different directive and expected outcome by proposing:

1. *A substantial increase in budget and resources* (say 25–30%) so the company can undertake a different way of doing business to capture new opportunities (to avoid Xerox's self-limiting error)
2. *A dramatic reduction in budget and resources* (say 25–40%), so the company has to change the way it does business; rather than cutting cost by say 10%, leading to no real change in the way business is done, but doing it less well because people belt-tighten and continue doing business as before, but without adequate resources
3. *No change—business as usual*
4. *Exiting the business and cashing in*[x]

The board can then assess the different resulting income streams and decide which to choose. The dramatic difference in the four options forces management to look at them quite differently, requiring them to go back to first principles, answering the cardinal questions of strategy: who are the beneficiaries; what difference do we want to make in their lives; what value will they place on that difference and how much will it cost us to deliver it. This forces management to ask why do we undertake these activities, how much do they cost and what would happen if we stopped doing them.

A variation of the second option is zero-based budgeting which can be done on an ongoing basis to highlight not merely opportunities to reduce cost, but also to allocate resources differently to capture better returns as a result of their redeployment:

> Zero-based budgeting is a repeatable process that organizations use to rigorously review every dollar in the annual budget, manage financial performance on a monthly basis, and build a culture of cost management among all employees. A world-class ZBB process is based on developing deep visibility into cost drivers and using that visibility to set aggressive yet credible budget targets. The annual budgeting process does in fact start from zero and is very detailed, structured, and interactive in order to facilitate meaningful financial debate among managers and executives. Throughout the year, multiple owners are tasked with managing performance and continuing the healthy debate on cost management. Through new system and process controls, and aligned incentive programs, all employees make cost management a part of their daily routine.[xi]

What is more important than the potential savings generated by zero-based budgeting is the way the process forces management to challenge their assumptions about how business should be done and makes them reexamine the extent to which they are prisoners of *anchoring bias*. Zero-based budgeting also provides boards with the data they need to actively reallocate resources, and companies that actively reallocate resources on a regular basis create greater long-term value than companies that do not:

> Dynamic resource reallocation" is a mouthful, but its meaning is simple: shifting money, talent, and management attention to where they will deliver the most value to your company…

83 percent [of senior managers] identify it as the top management lever for spurring growth—more important than operational excellence or M&A. Yet a third of companies surveyed reallocate a measly 1 percent of their capital from year to year; the average is 8 percent.

This is a huge missed opportunity because the value-creation gap between dynamic and drowsy reallocators is staggering. A company that actively reallocates delivers, on average, a 10 percent return to shareholders, versus 6 percent for a sluggish reallocator. *Within 20 years, the dynamic reallocator will be worth twice as much as its less agile counterpart*—a divide likely to increase as accelerating digital disruptions and growing geopolitical uncertainty boost the importance of nimble reallocation.[xii]

The difference in behavior between nimble and passive allocators is caused by executives finding it difficult to calculate where they should reallocate resources, how much they should reallocate, and how to do it successfully. Four factors help them do this: granular evaluation of the costs and revenues for each activity, requiring a mix of activity-based costing and zero-based budgeting; focusing on value creation rather than just looking at cost reduction; overcoming anchoring and overconfidence biases; and being agile.[xiii]

Setting KPIs and Targets Using a Ten-Step Process[xiv]

The first step is for the board to determine who are its beneficiaries and stakeholders, what difference in their lives will our organization make, what value will they place on that difference, how much will it cost to deliver it, and how will we know we have succeeded.

The second step is to translate these beneficiary-stakeholder expectations into strategic objectives, designed to meet each set of beneficiary-stakeholders.[3]

The third step is to develop a "success map":

> A success map is a visual tool that shows how lower level objectives link to higher level strategic objectives. It is a powerful communication tool that explains "what" is to be achieved and "why". It also shows where each part of the organisation contributes to achieving these goals.[xv]

---

[3] This step is critical because, when done properly, it allows the board and management to determine whether a proposed project is within the boundaries set by the agreed strategies—allowing management to devote focused time and attention to doing what they are supposed to be doing rather than chasing after every attractive opportunity and ending up spreading their time and attention too thinly to be effective.

Figure 16.1 illustrates a "success map." Starting from the top, it links the organization's mission and vision to its overriding business objectives via "Purpose." This is where the first two steps of the process for setting KPIs and targets are taken care of.

The overriding business objective is then broken out into its component parts for each element of the value chain, to be translated into subordinate business objectives, which support and reinforce the overriding business objective. The resulting mini-strategies are developed for each element of the value chain using the "5P" framework's "Principles," "Power," "People," and "Processes" to show what needs to be done and why and, as important, by whom and by when:

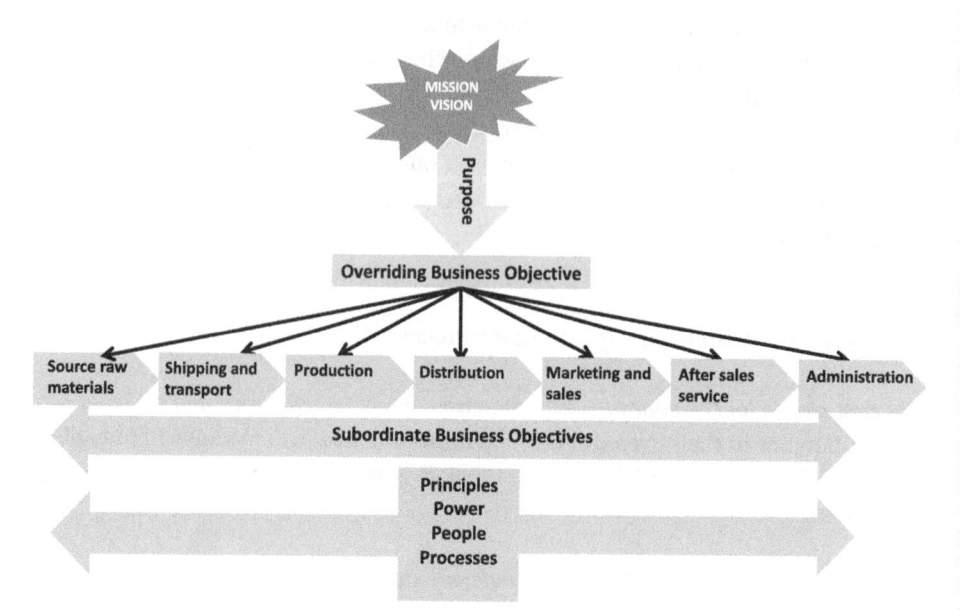

Figure 16.1: Success map[xvi]

Steps 4–10 are taken care of in processes created by using the four lenses of the "Five P" framework to define the priorities; allocate resources; and agree with the people involved suitable milestones, due dates, and accountabilities.

Step 4 is where priorities are agreed, so employees can focus on what is most important. Too few priorities, and work becomes dull and routine; too many, and managers no longer know which matter. The most appropriate number of priorities any one individual can handle effectively is supposed to be seven:[xvii]

> Why seven? If people are given too few challenges, there won't be enough variety in their work to stimulate creativity. If people are given too many challenges, they quickly suffer from overload. Seven falls between these two extremes. And think of all the things in our lives that are config-

ured in sevens: phone numbers, the days of the week, the musical scale. The number seems to contain just the right amount of information for people to remember and process effectively.[xviii]

Step 5 is when the KPIs are set to "operationalize" the processes:

This means designing appropriate performance measures. How you define the measure will drive behaviour. So KPIs must reflect the organisation's goals and encourage the right behaviour from those responsible for delivering the goals.[xix]

Step 6 is the collection of timely and relevant data on which to base targets. This is often overlooked.

Step 7 is data analysis:

You have to draw on your knowledge of the past and of the future to project what is going to happen. You also have to analyse the capability of your processes. Are the processes capable of delivering the forecast? *Most companies forecast, but fewer reassess their capabilities.*[xx] [Emphasis mine]

Step 8 is when targets are set.

Step 9 is developing the action plan with input from those who will have to deliver it, as opposed to handing it down from on high. This may require training/retraining of employees, new IT systems to track progress, and developing new ways of working with customers. In every instance, it is critical to have worked with the people who will make it happen to understand where the barriers are and whether they are obstacles, resolved by allocating resources accordingly or they are objections, which require changing mindsets and persuading vested interests:

Managers who must lead the implementation of observed best practices may resist practices that shift decision-making authority or greater autonomy into the hands of teams or lower level employees... "If we adopt this practice", they may tell themselves, "then I will become less important". Machiavelli may have said it best when he wrote that "The reformer has enemies in all those who profit from the old order", that is, current practices.[xxi]

Step 10 is continuous communication to all who are involved; to remind them of the objectives and why they matter; to advise them of progress toward meeting those objectives and what still needs to be done, by whom and by when.

Adopting an Effective Innovation Process

It is not enough to have a center of innovation in the organization. What matters is the organization's willingness to get behind the new ideas, products, and processes. Innovation requires change in aspirations, expectations and behavior. Consequently, there will always be vested interests rejecting it outright or supporting it half-heartedly. If it is done only half-heartedly, the innovations will remain inventions until somebody else sees their potential and makes them happen.

Eight essential elements must exist for an organization to be able to innovate consistently and successfully.[xxii]

Aspiration

NASA's success in developing entirely new products—the basis of much of the modern world in electronics, communications, and digitization was the result of the bold aspiration set for them by President Kennedy in 1962, to "go to the moon in this decade." Without it and the resulting funding made available to them, NASA would not have been the revolutionary success and incubator for undreamt of commercial innovations. However, the aspirational challenge must connect to departmental financial reality from a business perspective if it is to change behavior:

> But in a corporate setting, as many CEOs have discovered, even the most inspiring words often are insufficient, no matter how many times they are repeated. It helps to combine high-level aspirations with estimates of the value that innovation should generate to meet financial-growth objectives. Quantifying an "innovation target for growth," and making it an explicit part of future strategic plans, helps solidify the importance of and accountability for innovation. The target itself must be large enough to force managers to include innovation investments in their business plans. If they can make their numbers using other, less risky tactics, our experience suggests that they (quite rationally) will.
>
> *Establishing a quantitative innovation aspiration is not enough, however. The target value needs to be apportioned to relevant business "owners" and cascaded down to their organizations in the form of performance targets and timelines. Anything less risks encouraging inaction or the belief that innovation is someone else's job.* [Emphasis mine]

Typically, when linking aspirations to targets, many organizations tend to focus on revenues created by launching new products or entering new markets; requiring them to reach a given percentage of total sales within a given time. It is an obvious choice because new products and their associated revenues are tangible and easy to measure. It engages R&D, marketing and sales who can feel emotionally involved, as it challenges them directly to come up with something new. That is not to deny other people in the organization or outside it often come up with breakthrough ideas of great value. However, it overlooks two other important areas where innovation can have an important and beneficial impact on value creation: the business model processes and the workplace itself, which are more likely to be continuous and incremental in nature.

There are four important advantages in having formal aspirations to improve processes and the working environment. First, it operationalizes the concept of *kaizen*—continuous improvement. Second, innovative improvements in these two areas of everyday working life in the organization affect everybody and make their working lives better, leading to greater employee satisfaction and retention with resulting improvements in profitability. Third, every employee can propose new ways of doing things because they now have three areas where they can contribute, as opposed to just one. More important, their ideas are based on their experience of the efficacy of processes and quality of working conditions. Fourth, as a result, the board is able to create a culture of innovation that makes sense to everybody in the organization, facilitating buy-in and reducing their resistance to change.

Selection

Surprisingly, most organizations have too many creative ideas to choose from rather than too few when it comes to new product ideas:

> Innovation *is* inherently risky, to be sure, and getting the most from a portfolio of innovation initiatives is more about managing risk than eliminating it. Since no one knows exactly where valuable innovations will emerge, and searching everywhere is impractical, *executives must create some boundary conditions for the opportunity spaces they want to explore*...Thoughtfully prioritizing these spaces also allows companies to assess whether they have enough investment behind their most valuable opportunities.[xxiii] [Emphasis mine]

Typically, organizations fail to select well in one or more of three ways. They play safe, filling their product development pipelines with relatively riskless projects, which by their nature will not do more than yield incremental improvements. They spread their resources too thinly, instead of concentrating on those projects with the best returns. They fail to allocate/reallocate enough resources each year, with the resulting stagnation in innovation and its adverse impact on growth compared with companies that actively reallocate resources (discussed earlier in Section 3 on "reframing" budgeting and cost control discussions).

Discovery

Effective discovery of innovative ideas and processes does not depend just on creative genius, however much we would like to believe in "lightbulb" moments. It is the result of a disciplined iterative process, involving the interaction of changes in technology and partnerships with customers to define what they are lacking or what they do not like about either product performance or processes for doing business with the organization. It encourages the active use of prototypes to test and validate improvement hypotheses, be they for products or processes.

Evolution

This concerns adapting the business model to changing circumstances. Established companies have much to fear from upstart disrupters, who threaten their dominance by introducing new products, based in part on having a different business model. They should in theory be prepared to change their business models before the upstarts do it to them, as Jack Welch, one-time CEO of GE put it:

> If the rate of change on the outside exceeds the rate of change on the inside, the end is near.[xxiv]

Yet incumbents find it very difficult to follow this advice. Changing the business model requires changes in behavior; creates political winners and losers in the organization; and may incur expensive write-offs in plant and equipment, resisted vigorously by the finance function. Effective evolution even in companies with a track record of past success in innovation is often blocked by the "Innovator's Dilemma."[xxv] Vested interests will fight such changes when it is not immediately obvious change is required. And when it becomes obvious change is required, it may be too late to do anything about it, as examples like Xerox's, Nokia's, or Sony's fall from grace make clear:

> The problem is they fail to value new innovations properly because incumbents attempt to apply them to their existing customers and product architectures—or value networks. Often new technologies are too new and weak for the more advanced and mature value networks that incumbents operate.
>
> This leads to the ROI needed to advance the innovation to be seen as low. In other words, management acts sensibly in rejecting the continued investment in these new technologies and act in the company's best fiduciary interests. Moving into new markets is rejected as they are seen as too small to make a dent for them and their cost structure prohibitive to enter at sensible margins...
>
> ...Initially these small upstarts don't pose a threat—the new entrants find new markets to apply these technologies largely by trial and error, at low margins. Their nimbleness and [low-cost] structures allow them to operate sustainably where incumbents could not.
>
> However, the error in valuing these technologies comes from what happens next. By finding the right application use and market, the upstarts advance rapidly and hit the steep part of the classic "S" curve, eventually entering the more mature markets of the incumbents and disrupting them.
>
> In essence, the smaller markets are the guinea-pigs and test labs that help the technologies advance enough to play in the big boys' league. In many cases the entry-point markets are left behind as the new technologies move into higher margin upmarket territory disrupting due to their superior performance.[xxvi]

AI and robotics are serious threats to all jobs not requiring creativity and compassion.[xxvii] However, jobs requiring both will not be affected at all; jobs requiring a great deal of compassion or empathy, such as doctors, will change with AI providing the tools to diagnose better, faster and cheaper, turning doctors into the compassionate link between patient and diagnostics. Jobs requiring creativity, such as scientific research, will be enhanced by AI's ability to screen and evaluate data faster, objectively and free from biases, leading to more discoveries. Proponents of blockchain also seem to believe all back-office jobs, regardless of industry, will be threatened by its introduction.[xxviii] Boards will have to understand how these megatrends will affect their business models and the employability of their staff. Sadly, what is right for a single organization may turn out to be wrong for society as a whole.

Acceleration
Ironically the caution created by good governance processes (in marketing, legal, IT, and finance) may stifle the organization's ability to bring a new product to market quickly. Some of the most important innovations have been the result of mavericks refusing to be cowed by the managerial processes of their organizations.[xxix] In these circumstances, it is essential the project has a powerful champion who can withstand the pressures brought to bear to stop the project advancing. For example, the Israeli subsidiary of Intel was able to insist the U.S. operations were wrong to focus on increasing the speed of their computer chips, arguing instead for reducing the size of the chips, saving the company as a result:

> In the early 2000s, Intel's Israeli engineers by most accounts saved the company by stubbornly insisting on a new approach to semiconductor design. The company's philosophy had been that faster clock speed—the rate at which a chip executes instructions—was the only way to measure how well a computer performs. But, looking at the emerging laptop market, the Israelis argued that speed was less important than size. Higher speeds, they contended, generated more heat and required cooling systems that would be too big to squeeze into a thin laptop.
>
> Intel Israel's engineers bulldozed their idea through a wall of opposition in Santa Clara. "We did it the Israeli way; we argued our case to death," Eden recalled in an interview with *Bloomberg News*. "You know what an exchange of opinions is in Israel? You come to the meeting with your opinion, and you leave with mine."[xxx]

Scale
Getting scale right is crucial. Some innovations are suitable for niche markets with small volumes; others are designed to serve mass markets with large volumes. The problem for innovators is how best to move from small start-up volumes to the much larger volumes expected once the market is fully developed. Fast moving consumer goods (FMCG) companies and makers of smartphones typically launch products with mass market scale, with products priced for mature market volume before they achieve corresponding unit costs; burning cash for up to a year before they breakeven. Household electrical goods and computer companies tend to follow a different strat-

egy, pricing high to recover start-up costs with low volumes, dropping their prices as their volumes grow over time and their unit costs fall.

One of the reasons why incumbents find it so difficult to deal with disruptive innovation is their mismatch of scale: their business models are designed to deal with mature markets with corresponding volumes, unit costs and achieved prices, whereas innovative disrupters start with business models designed to serve much smaller volumes.

Extension

It is now a leading practice for companies to work with outside parties to develop proof of concept ideas, prototype them jointly and develop trials to test whether they work as expected. Engineering and life science companies work with universities; FMCG companies work with customers to develop new concepts—for example, Unilever's Sunsilk™ shampoos, codeveloped with leading haircare experts from different countries:

> We work with world-leading experts in every aspect of great hair to bring you Sunsilk. They're the best in the business when it comes to curls, colour, cutting-edge style and everything to do with your hair.
>
> Each one of our Sunsilk Co-Creators specialises in a different element of hair care...
>
> ...With their help, Sunsilk is designed to help you get perfect results, whatever your hair type...
>
> - New Yorker Rita Hazan is one of the most sought-after colourists in the world.
> - Quidad is the first stylist and salon owner in the United States to specialise in curly hair.
> - Teddy Charles creates fabulous looks for premier fashion magazines and catwalks the world over.
> - Thomas Taw is renowned for creating looks for hair shows, fashion shows and educational seminars.
> - Yuko Yamashita created the famous YUKO Hair Straightening System, for super-sleek styles.
> - Dr Francisco Fuscon is an acclaimed scalp and skin care expert, who has been practicing medical and cosmetic dermatology in New York City since 1989.
> - Jamal Hamadi creates sensuous and glamorous hairstyles for celebrities, fashion editorial and international haute couture houses alike.[xxxi]

An increasingly important form of extension occurs when manufacturers agree with their customers what they need are the services provided by the products they offer; rather than selling them as much product as possible:

Meanwhile, some big manufacturers are reorienting from making products to selling services. Martin Stuchtey of SystemIQ, a consultancy, says that nine out of ten boardrooms he visits are debating "how to sell freshness, not fridges; kilometres, not tyres". Rolls-Royce has sold "power by the hour" rather than aircraft engines for years. Rather than flog LED lamps Philips leases them to some customers—including Britain's National Union of Students—with a promise to keep buildings illuminated. By 2020 it wants to double to 15% the share of its profits from such contracts, which can lock in customers for 20 years. Safechem, a chemical company, rents out tanks of fresh solvent rather than selling it to manufacturers for cleaning metal parts. It then collects the tanks, purifies the contents and rents them out again.[xxxii]

Mobilization

This is achieved through providing a clear line of sight between the mission, vision, and values of the organization and the role of innovation in achieving them, including the part everyone is expected to play in creating and sustaining the values of innovation. It is made easier if the concept of innovation includes processes as well as improvements in working conditions so every employee can be incentivized to come up with ideas to be implemented in the three areas of product, process, and place.[4] Larger organizations will set up cross-functional teams to develop new products and processes, often locating them in different buildings or even cities so that vested interests can not obstruct progress, citing legacy and history as reasons why not.

Recruiting More Women Directors

The business case for having more women on boards appears compelling. First, mixed gender balanced teams perform better in terms of sales and profits.[xxxiii] If this is true of teams, it may be true of boards as well. Second, this could be because having women in a group makes the group smarter. Their collective intelligence increased because members were found to be more prone to listen to each other, to be more open-minded, and better able to accept constructive criticism rather than trying to dominate the conversation. This contrasted with groups with high IQs only who did not show the same sense of teamwork.[xxxiv] Third, the more women there are on boards, the better deals they get in mergers and acquisitions, paying less for them:

> Our findings show that the prudence exhibited by women directors in negotiating mergers and acquisitions has had a substantial positive effect on maintaining firm value," says Professor Li. "Female board members play a significant role in mitigating the empire building tendency of

---

4 For example, in the Securities Industry Development Corporation, the training arm of the Malaysian Securities Commission where innovation was one of its core values, every employee was expected to come up with three new ideas a year regarding either product (training programs), processes (business model), or workplace. If they were implemented, the person received Malaysian Ringgit 500 (about US$125) as a reward.

CEOs through the acquisition of other companies. On average, merger and acquisition transactions don't create shareholder value, so women are having a real impact in protecting shareholder investment and overall firm performance.

The researchers say their results suggest women are less interested in pursuing risky transactions and require the promise of a higher return on investment.[xxxv]

A study by Dow Jones of over 20,000 U.S. based venture capital-backed companies within the Dow Jones Venture Source database (between 1997 and 2011), showed the median proportion of female executives was 7.1% in successful companies and 3.1% in unsuccessful companies. The number of women in senior and board positions also increased the likelihood of successful startups:

Companies have a greater chance of either going public, operating profitably or being sold for more money than they've raised when they have females acting as founders, board members, C-level officers, vice presidents and/or directors.[xxxvi]

The European Project on Equal Pay in 2011 was based on data presented by Fortune 500 companies from 1980 to 1998 regarding the number of women in top executive committees and boards. Each industry was evaluated on profit as a percent of revenue, assets, and stockholders' equity. The findings showed when women were promoted, companies did better financially than companies that did not promote women:

Twenty-five subject firms fared better by 34 percent in revenue than companies in the same industry that did not promote women. In terms of assets, companies that promoted women outperformed companies in the same industry by 18 percent. Individually, 62 percent of the subject firms were more profitable in terms of assets than their counterparts. Women friendly firms outmatched their counterparts by 26.5 percent in stockholders' equity. Individually, they outperformed their counterparts by 68 percent."[xxxvii]

Further support for the outperformance of companies with women in senior positions comes from a study by Catalyst of 524 public listed companies with three or more women directors over the period 2004–2008.[xxxviii] It found they achieved 84% better return on sales, 60% better return on capital, and 46% better return on equity. The most recent evidence for the added value women bring comes from the MSCI Asia Pacific Index companies, where companies with at least one female director on the board achieved a five-year annualized return of 8.9% compared with a Bloomberg's 7.3% return for companies with no women on boards.[xxxix]

If the business case for women in senior position appears so compelling, what should boards do to recruit and retain more women in senior positions? McKinsey's *Women Matter* research suggests there are five components boards must introduce if they are to succeed in recruiting more women to boards:

1. *The board, CEO, and senior management must all be committed* to promoting women and developing a talent pipeline for women
2. *The talent pipeline process must be transparent* with effective tracking systems to monitor progress
3. *There must be a formal women's leadership development program*, including training and coaching; sponsorship and mentoring by the top management team and directors; and the establishment of women's networks to parallel those used by men
4. *The establishment of a gender diversity enhancing structure* incorporating flexible working hours, extended leave policies and back-to-work programs to allow women to reenter the workplace without loss of seniority after family-based leaves of absence
5. *Programs to increase awareness of unconscious bias* with formal training and systems designed to debias recruitment, evaluation, and promotion[xl]

In view of the rise of #MeToo, boards must also ensure there is no room for sexual harassment, if they want to protect their organization's reputation as being a good place for women to work and prosper.

"CG Ecosystem" Makes a Difference

In 2016, CLSA, a stockbroker and the Asian Corporate Governance Association (ACGA) published their biennial CG Watch for Asia entitled "Ecosystems Matter: Asia's path to better home-grown governance,"[xli] emphasizing the importance of CG ecosystems:

> Governance matters and the ecosystems that deliver it are key. No single stakeholder can drive the process. It's the collective interaction of all parties that delivers better outcomes...Reforms matter but how companies respond and deliver them is crucial. Investor engagement makes persistent improvement more likely. Asia is getting better and will continue to do so if stakeholders, including agitators, remain engaged. Even the friction adds value... The bottom line is better CG leads to better fundamental outcomes but is distinct from share-price action.[xlii]

The finding that good CG matters, regardless of whether it affects share prices, reinforces the argument the principles of good governance apply to all organizations, regardless of whether they are listed. However, the surveys carried out over the years by CLSA and ACGA highlight the fact the institutions of a CG ecosystem make a big difference:

> If there is a single message from our survey this year, it is that the ecosystem of corporate governance (CG) in any market is not just important, it is *the* differentiating factor between long-term system success and failure. In various ways our previous surveys have always shown this: Hong Kong and Singapore do not consistently top the survey by accident, they do it because they have the best institutions—legal, regulatory and economic—for CG in the region. ..."[xliii]

The report went on to note the importance of the role of capital market regulators who are trying their best to create conditions conducive to good CG, but highlights the constraints imposed on this process by their political masters:

> We would say that the vast majority of regulators we meet around the region are dedicated to their jobs and are doing their best to push reform ahead as far and as fast as they can. Indeed, a trend we have noticed is what one might describe as the "march of the technocrats". This is increasing bifurcation we see in many markets between the open-minded, international and transparent style of capital-market regulators and the closed-minded, parochial and unaccountable behaviour of their political masters.
>
> True the two groups are often serving different ends: financial regulators are trying to cater to a complex array of local and foreign stakeholders, and must be sensitive to international ideas, standards and language. Local politicians on the other hand, have more self-interested populist and domestic preoccupations. It is a hard circle to square.
>
> *...Public governance and government support are critical in the long term for greater accountability in corporate behaviour (private as well as state-owned), and are as important as a free press, an effective justice system and engaged investors[5]. We would argue that the tone set by the public sector matters greatly and can either restrict or foster what regulators are able to achieve in both policy and enforcement.*[xliv] [Emphasis mine]

This lesson applies to good governance everywhere in the world, including developed capital markets in the Organization for Economic Cooperation and Development (OECD), where politicians are tempted to encourage regulatory arbitrage with its inevitable "race to the bottom" in order to attract inward investment.

So, if the CG ecosystem really matters and it is the institutions that make the difference, what institutions are needed for an effective ecosystem? Figure 16.2 illustrates the process components of an effective CG ecosystem and how they work on each other to deliver good CG.

---

[5] This comment was in part the result of the 1MDB scandal and the then Malaysian government's response to it; it affected the rating and ranking given to Malaysia.

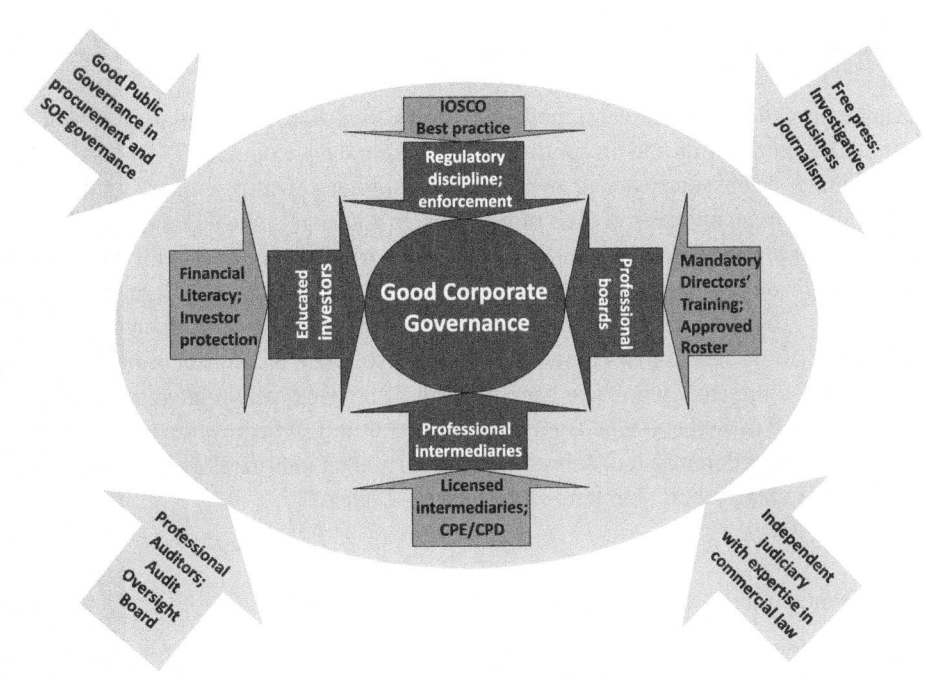

Figure 16.2: Process components of an effective "CG ecosystem"

Starting at the center of Figure 16.2, we see good CG depends on four components:

Effective Regulatory Discipline

In the case of public listed companies, regulatory discipline is determined by IOSCO international best practices, administered by national securities commissions and stock exchanges. In general, listed companies are regulated by stock exchanges and securities commissions; financial intermediaries are also regulated by central banks or their equivalents. Although most companies by far are not listed, they all come under their respective national companies acts. Charitable organizations and not-for-profit societies are registered in one way or another and laws apply to how they conduct themselves. Regulatory discipline, however, does not just apply to capital market rules; it applies to the enforcement of all legislation and regulation affecting organizations, including occupational health and safety; environmental; consumer protection; workplace legislation; and antimoney laundering and bribery laws.

Professional Boards

Leading practice is to professionalize directors, insisting on mandatory training before they join boards and on continuing professional development (CPD) once they have joined, in the same way as members of any profession must embark on CPD to maintain their membership of their professions. In addition, some jurisdictions maintain a *roster of professionally qualified directors* from which candidates for INEDs are drawn for listed companies (e.g., New Zealand, Australia, and Malaysia). In Malaysia, in addition, the financial sector is regarded as being of greatest systemic importance, as a result of the 1998 Asian Financial Crisis; and so, there is a subset of professionally qualified directors who have been through CPD specifically related to banking, insurance and capital markets. Their mandatory training and education are overseen by the Securities Commission Malaysia for capital market intermediary boards and by Bank Negara Malaysia for banking and insurance boards.

Professional Intermediaries

Capital markets are currently short of trust, when trust is the most important attribute looked for by buyers. In order to rebuild the trust lost by the malpractices selling subprime mortgages during the Global Financial Crisis, PPI mis-selling in the United Kingdom, and the current banking malpractices in Australia, all driven by wrongly structured incentives,[xlv] regulators look to professional behavior from licensed intermediaries. They must be trained in the products they sell so they can explain them properly and honestly to their clients; *to whom they now owe a fiduciary duty as opposed to the more traditional duty of care*. They must follow "Know Your Customer" (KYC) processes, lest they lose their licenses. Regulators aim to eliminate the malpractices of people like Jordan Belfort, the "Wolf of Wall Street." They also are trying to eliminate front-running and insider trading. The reputation of the capital market depends on minimizing the impact of scams and other forms of malpractice. Gone are the days when the whole point of being an intermediary was access to information outsiders did not have.

Educated Investors

Perhaps as important, is the investment in educating investors regarding the inherent risks of capital markets to ensure they have realistic expectations regarding investing and their own exposures to risk and their ability to live with the consequences of investment downsides. Regulators spend a great deal of time effort and money on educating the general public about investing and the more governments have financial inclusion as an ambition, the more money will need to be spent on educating and protecting investors.

Figure 16.2 also shows there are four forces for good or bad with a major impact on the "CG ecosystem." The first force is the behavior of the government and its entities in setting the tone of public governance. If governments are corrupt; if governments violate the most basic principles of CG in their companies; if governments turn a blind eye to malpractice because it is undertaken by cronies; their bad example corrodes and undermines the entire "CG ecosystem." To quote an ancient Chinese proverb:

> The fish goes rotten from the head down.

The only forces preventing this from happening are the second and third forces: a robust free press and an independent judiciary. To be effective, a free press must have good investigative journalists who understand business and how it works and who are not afraid of "following the money" regardless of where or how high it leads—exemplified by *The Sarawak Report* in the 1MDB case.[xlvi] An independent judiciary must have judges who are specialists in commercial law and white-collar crime who can therefore come to proper judgments and who are then not afraid of punishing malefactors, regardless of who they are. Whenever governments intimidate the press and the judiciary, there is bound to be an erosion of CG—with 1MDB as a tragic object lesson.

The fourth force are professional external auditors. Their processes must be robust and reflect professional independence to ensure accurate and timely financial reporting. To achieve this requires adhering to high standards, reinforced by an independent audit oversight board to ensure external auditors fulfill their roles competently, without fear or favor.

Conclusion

Directors admit they do not spend enough time on strategy with dismal results: 66% in the HBR study did not understand the strategies of their companies, 78% did not understand how their companies created value, and 84% did not understand the dynamics of their company's industry.

There are two solutions to this problem. First directors should spend more time on the business. The HBR study recommended they should spend at least thirty-five days a year per board on which they sit. Second, there are six areas where boards can increase long-term value by harnessing changes in processes: introducing rotating "Devil's Advocacy" in board deliberations; using activity-based costing to understand the financials; "reframing" budget and cost control discussions to remove *anchoring biases*; setting KPIs using a ten-step process; adopting an effective innovation process; and recruiting more women directors.

These six operational areas of improvement need, however, to be reinforced by processes, outside the organizations, designed to create a "CG ecosystem." For it to deliver good CG, an effective "CG ecosystem" must have effective regulatory discipline, based on international best practice and effective enforcement of all relevant legislation for all regardless. It requires the existence of *professional* boards, with directors who are properly trained and committed to a lifetime of CPD, as with all other professions. It must invest in educating, training, and certifying intermediaries and it must enforce correct behavior. It must also invest in investor education and protection so investors can engage appropriately with boards.

This can only be done effectively, if there is a good "CG ecosystem" with the government setting a good example; with boards and government held to account by a robust free press with fearless investigative journalists who understand business; and an independent judiciary with judges who understand commercial law and who are truly independent; supported by a body of professional auditors to ensure accuracy and timeliness of financial reporting.

References

[i] Booz Allen & Co. (2004), "Too Much SOX Can Kill You: Resolving the Compliance Paradox," November 18, 2004.

[ii] "Improving Board Governance: McKinsey Global Survey Results," cited by Barton, D. and Wiseman, M. (2015), "Where Boards Fall Short," *Harvard Business Review*, January–February Issue, 2015.

[iii] Barton and Wiseman (2015), op. cit.

[iv] Ibid.

[v] www.brainyquote.com/quotes/quotes/a/alfredpsl194029.html#fzMXMKty3pvGPiRW.99

[vi] Drucker, P. (1998), "The Information Executives Truly Need," *Harvard Business Review on Measuring Corporate Performance* (Boston, MA: Harvard Business Review Paperback), 5–8.

[vii] Matheson, D. and Matheson, J. (1998), *The Smart Organization: Creating Value through Strategic R&D*, (Boston, MA: Harvard Business School Press), 40.

[viii] Cringley, R. X., (1992), *Accidental Empires*, (Reading MA: Addison Wesley Publishing Company), 91, quoted in Matheson and Matheson (1998), op. cit., 5.

[ix] Matheson and Matheson (1998), op. cit., 5.

[x] Ibid., 41.

[xi] Callaghan, S., Hawke, K., and Mignerey, C. (2014), "Five Myths (and Realities) about Zero-Based Budgeting," *McKinsey & Co., Strategy & Corporate Finance, McKinsey Quarterly*, October 2014, https://www.mckinsey.com/business-functions/strategy-and-corporate-finance/our-insights/five-myths-and-realities-about-zero-based-budgeting, accessed on September 27, 2018.

[xii] Atsmon, Y. (2016), "How Nimble Resource Allocation Can Double Your Company's Value," *McKinsey & Co, Strategy & Corporate Finance, McKinsey Quarterly*, August 2016, https://www.mckinsey.com/business-functions/strategy-and-corporate-finance/our-insights/how-nimble-resource-allocation-can-double-your-companys-value, accessed on September 27, 2018.

[xiii] Ibid.

[xiv] Based on Cranfield School of Management (2012), "How to Set the Right Performance Targets: A Ten Step Target Setting Tool," published by Association of International Certified Professional Accountants, joint venture of American Institute of CPAs, New York and Chartered Institute of Management Accountants, London https://www.cgma.org/content/dam/cgma/resources/tools/downloadabledocuments/target-setting-tool.pdf, accessed on September 23, 2018.

xv Ibid., 2.

xvi Based on Zinkin, J. (2015), "Performance Driven Leadership," Star Newspaper Senior Management Program, Kuala Lumpur, September 1, 2015.

xvii Miller, G. A. (1956), "The Magic Number Seven, Plus or Minus Two: Some Limits on Our Capacity for Processing Information," *The Psychological Review,* Vol. 63, No. 2, 1956, 81–97, cited in Simons, R. and Davila, A. (1998), "How High is Your Return on Management?" *Harvard Business Review,* "Measuring Corporate Performance," 86.

xviii Simons and Davila (1998), op. cit., 86.

xix Cranfield School of Management (2012), op. cit., 2.

xx Ibid., 3.

xxi Matheson and Matheson (1998), op. cit., 83.

xxii De Jong, M., Marston, N., and Roth, E. (2015), "The Eight Essentials of Innovation," *McKinsey & Co, Strategy & Corporate Finance, McKinsey Quarterly,* April 2015, https://www.mckinsey.com/business-functions/strategy-and-corporate-finance/our-insights/the-eight-essentials-of-innovation, accessed on September 27, 2018.

xxiii Ibid.

xxiv Welch, J., https://www.goodreads.com/quotes/185636-if-the-rate-of-change-on-the-outside-exceeds-the, accessed on September 27, 2018.

xxv Christensen, C. (1997), *The Innovator's Dilemma* (Boston, MA: Harvard Business Review Press).

xxvi Thrasyvoulou, X. (2014), "Understanding the Innovator's Dilemma," *Wired,* https://www.wired.com/insights/2014/12/understanding-the-innovators-dilemma/, accessed on September 27, 2018.

xxvii Lee, K-F. (2018), *AI Superpowers: China, Silicon Valley and the New World Order* (Boston, MA: Houghton Mifflin Harcourt).

xxviii Tapscott, D. and Tapscott, A. (2016), *Blockchain Revolution: How the Technology Behind Bitcoin Is Changing Money, Business, And the World* (New York, NY: Portfolio/Penguin).

xxix De Jong, Marston, and Roth (2015), op. cit.

xxx "Intel in Israel: A Fab Relationship Faces Criticism," *Knowledge@Wharton,* September 29, 2014, http://knowledge.wharton.upenn.edu/article/intel-israel-old-relationship-faces-new-criticism/, accessed September 28, 2018.

xxxi https://www.unilever.com.my/brands/our-brands/sunsilk.html, accessed on September 28, 2018.

xxxii "Businesses Are Trying to Reduce, Reuse and Recycle," *The Economist Special Report,* September 29, 2018, https://www.economist.com/special-report/2018/09/29/businesses-are-trying-to-reduce-reuse-and-recycle, accessed on September 29, 2018.

xxxiii Hoogendorn, S. et al. (2014), "The Impact of Gender Diversity on the Performance of Business Teams: Evidence from a Field Experiment," *Management Science,* Articles in advance, published online, March 4, 2013, 13, https://papers.tinbergen.nl/11074.pdf, accessed on September 29, 2018.

xxxiv Wooley, A. and Malone, T. W. (2011), "Defend Your Research: What Makes a Team Smarter? More Women," *Harvard Business Review,* June 2011 Issue, https://hbr.org/2011/06/defend-your-research-what-makes-a-team-smarter-more-women, accessed on September 28, 2018.

xxxv Li, K. (2013), "Women Directors Get Better Deals in Mergers and Acquisitions," *University of British Columbia, Sauder School of Business,* December 2, 2013, https://www.sauder.ubc.ca/News/2013/Women_directors_get_better_deals_in_mergers_and_acquisitions, accessed on September 28, 2018.

xxxvi Dow Jones (2012), "Women at the Wheel: Do Female Executives Drive Startup Success?," *Dow Jones Venture Source,* 2012, https://www.pedrad.org/Portals/5/Subspecialties/Diversity%20and%20Inclusion/Women%20Executives%20Dow%20Jones%20Report.pdf?ver=2018-02-14-115459-767&ver=2018-02-14-115459-767, accessed on September 28, 2018.

xxxvii Adler, R. D. (2011), "European Research Project on Equal Pay," cited by, French, A. (2012), "Research Summary: Women in the Executive Suite Correlate to High Profits," *InPower Coaching,* January 25, 2012, https://inpowercoaching.com/study-women-in-the-executive-suite-correlate-to-high-profits/, accessed on September 28, 2018.

xxxviii Carter, N. M. (2011), "The Bottom Line: Corporate Performance and Women's Representation on Boards, 2004–2008," Catalyst, March 11, 2011.

xxxix "Fund Manager Wants to Prove Gender Equality Is Good for Profits," *Star Online*, January 1, 2019, accessed on January 1, 2019.

xl McKinsey & Company (2017), "Women Matter: Time to Accelerate: Ten Years of Insights into Gender Diversity," 51, https://www.mckinsey.com/~/media/mckinsey/featured%20insights/women%20matter/women%20matter%20ten%20years%20of%20insights%20on%20the%20importance%20of%20gender%20diversity/women-matter, accessed on September 28, 2018.

xli Cochrane, S. and Allen, J. (2016), *CG Watch: Ecosystems Matter: Asia's Path to Better Home-Grown Governance*, CLSA and ACGA September 2016, 3.

xlii Cochrane, S. (2016), *CG Watch: Ecosystems Matter: Asia's Path to Better Home-Grown Governance*, CLSA and ACGA September 2016.

xliii Allen, J. (2016), *CG Watch: Ecosystems Matter: Asia's Path to Better Home-Grown Governance*, CLSA and ACG September 2016, 12.

xliv Ibid., 15–16.

xlv Ralston, D. (2018), "The Problem with Australia's Banks Is One of Too Much Law and Not Enough Enforcement," *The Conversation*, September 29, 2018, https://theconversation.com/the-problem-with-australias-banks-is-one-of-too-much-law-and-too-little-enforcement-103996, accessed on September 30, 2018.

xlvi Wright, T. and Hope, B. (2018), *Billion Dollar Whale: The Man Who Fooled Wall Street, Hollywood and the World* (New York: Hachette).

Chapter 17
Conclusion: Achieving Better Governance Across the Board

Definitions of corporate governance (CG) have evolved over twenty-five years to include a wider range of stakeholders and their interests, moving away from just considering shareholders. Increasingly regulators, investors, and directors are being forced to recognize the importance of CG, if only because the costs of failure can be so dramatic. These costs are rising because of the increased interconnectedness resulting from the financialization and globalization of business.

CG Matters Regardless of the Type of Ownership

From the perspective of developing the right strategy; implementing it effectively; managing risk; planning succession and managing talent; ensuring proper internal controls; and engaging stakeholders, CG matters regardless of the ownership structure or the cultural differences between "Anglosphere" capital markets and others.

Integrating Ethics and Branding

Ensuring their enterprise satisfies the needs of customers in ethical ways is the responsibility of the board, as are its culture and its codes of conduct that define how customers are treated. It is essential clients' needs are satisfied ethically and the role of regulations is to help companies do this. Given there are two approaches to regulations each with its own issues, directors need to find the best way to reconcile them. Universalists and particularists view the role and relevance of regulations differently and directors need to reconcile these different worldviews, if they employ people from the two different backgrounds.

Directors are the custodians of their corporate brand. The corporate brand promise captures what makes the organization unique in terms of what it does, whom it does business with and how it does that business. It defines how the enterprise interacts with its stakeholders and provides the reasons why its stakeholders should believe the claims it makes. Failure to deliver the brand promise affects the value of the company and can destroy its social "license to operate."

Redefining Boundaries of Responsibility

As far as the boundaries of responsibility between the board and management are concerned, the board has the strategic responsibility for defining and overseeing critical elements in the "Five P" performance framework, whilst management is responsible operationally for making sure they are implemented. There is a difference of opinion and practice regarding where the boundaries lie. Traditional thinking is that the board "governs and directs," whereas more modern thinking in the Commonwealth states directors "manage and direct" the affairs of the business for which they are responsible. Boards in such jurisdictions must demarcate clearly where the boundaries lie and document them in the board charter.

Chairing an Effective Board

The chair must decide on the best way for the board to work with management, reflecting the drivers of the business; life-stage of the business; or most suitable engagement style. The chair's personal contribution to the effectiveness of the board is immense: defining the board's purpose and values; applying his or her understanding of the drivers of the business; seeing the "big picture"; being open to ideas whatever their source; engaging regularly with senior management; defining the standards for creating value; setting the board agenda, managing the business of the board and ensuring accurate and timely information; and last and *most important*, creating positive board dynamics within the board and between the board and management, *by maximizing constructive cognitive disagreement over ideas and minimizing disruptive affective disagreement about personalities.*

The board sits at the top of the organization and is accountable for everything that happens on its watch. The board does not just advise or supervise; it has six core responsibilities: setting strategy, reviewing its implementation, managing risk, planning succession, ensuring sound internal controls, and engaging stakeholders. Collectively, it is the sole source of authority and can not blame the chair, CEO, or its committees for failures of CG. *The buck stops with the board.*

Being an Effective Board Member

The twenty-first century standards to which boards are being held are much more demanding. There is greater focus on directors being effective board members. The spotlight is firmly on the two key members of the board: The chair and the CEO. The chair is responsible for ensuring the board is properly governed, fulfilling ten fiduciary duties, acting as the link between the board and the CEO, energizing internal stakeholders with the help of the CEO, and engaging external stakeholders. The CEO *is answerable to the board* for achieving the organization's agreed "purpose," while working within executive limitations set by the board. The CEO *works with the board* in setting the company direction, articulating its values, and allocating resources to create long-term value. The CEO *has board-delegated authority to work alone* on setting performance standards; protecting the company's reputation; representing the organizational brand to employees and setting the appropriate "tone at the top"; creating an integrated communication architecture, so the company speaks with one voice to its many audiences.

Effective directors understand they act as business advisers and coaches to the CEO, while at the same time being overseers and watchdogs. These roles can sometimes be in conflict. Directors must fulfil their duties as fiduciaries, most important of which, are the duties of care, loyalty, skill, and diligence. Effective INEDS are characterized by four attributes: the ability to reconcile independence of mind with a deep understanding of the business, commitment to and passion about what the company does, experience and appropriate competence, and above all good EQ.

Reconciling Leadership and Governance

Quick and decisive action in business has been the justification for combining the roles of chair and CEO in U.S. companies. Companies need good CG, however, to protect them from the follies of corrupt, incompetent or excessively risky but powerful CEOs. Leadership and CG must be reconciled, if companies are to avoid failures of CG on the one hand; and good CG with mediocre performance on the other.

"Five P" Framework

The framework captures the need for the board to define "purpose," "principles," "power," "people," and "processes." It provides five lenses through which the board can review performance; establishing whether things are going according to plan; and where more investment and corrective actions are needed, if they are not. It also helps directors assess new proposals brought to the board by management, allowing directors to check whether all aspects of the organization are aligned with the board-agreed mission and vision. If any of the five elements are not aligned, directors have an early warning of potential failure.

Setting Strategy

When setting strategy, directors must question the assumptions regarding the PESTLE and Five Forces environments in which the company operates and use this to analyze the company's internal environment to establish whether its business model and capabilities are adequate. Directors must decide how to compete—as low-cost leaders or by investing in differentiation. There are four further options: to remain in the existing market with existing products, to take existing products into new markets, to launch new products in existing markets, or to diversify.

The board still needs to consider whether it will act as an incumbent seeking to "improve the game" or as a disruptor seeking to "change the rules of the game." The board can then choose low-cost leadership, differentiation or focus as their route. When considering which of these three routes to take, they must remember to avoid getting "stuck"; with assets and a business model that does not allow them a way out, should circumstances change.

Reviewing Strategy Implementation

As far as the financials are concerned, the board has tools to assess the value of investments: payback, IRR, and NPV using the appropriate risk-adjusted WACC as the discount or hurdle rate. Each of these tools has advantages and drawbacks: payback is simple but ignores the time value of money; IRR does not consider the materiality of the project when used for comparison purposes; NPV can be fudged by assuming optimistic revenues; conservative costs and too high a terminal value.

From an operational perspective the board must look at both the income statement and the balance sheet, remembering the critical importance of the working capital cash-cash cycle. The appropriate financial focus depends on three business unit lifestages: growth, maturity, and decline. Directors also need to remember traditional financials ignore the "voice of the customer" and the elements affecting the "voice of the customer" need to be tracked as well as the financials to evaluate the effectiveness of strategy execution. Finally, there are the soft metrics and key performance indicators (KPIs) to be considered as they affect innovation, process quality, and employee satisfaction.

Managing Risk

Boards must take risks; grouped into four families: "cultural," "systemic," "traditional," and "earnings driver" risks. The first three are primarily issues of policy, while "earnings driver" risks are operational in nature and the responsibility of management. Given Warren Buffett's explanation for his success that "culture + leadership + trust = wealth," "cultural" components of risk are the most important. Most boards recognize this, but in practice pay lip service to the idea they are responsible for it. "Cultural" risks are created by ethical conflicts often caused by "imperial CEOs" with simple, overambitious goals and a top-down fear-based style of management;

misaligned incentives and strategy and inappropriate KPIs; inappropriate rewards and remuneration; and differences in social culture.

"Systemic" risks are an area where boards have tended to pay insufficient attention. The reasons why directors allow their companies to ignore "systemic" risks, apart from ignorance, are herding behavior; failures of systemic integrity; moral hazard and the belief the company is "too big to fail" leading to excessive risk-taking.

Boards deal with the "traditional" risks reasonably well from a policy perspective. "Traditional" risks cover financial and credit risk; market risk; natural hazards, physical security; legal/regulatory risk; compliance and fraud risks; and IT and cybersecurity risks, to which boards will need to pay *much, much more attention in future*.

Working with management, boards need to be briefed on operational issues occurring in "earnings driver" risks. These are failure to innovate; brand impairment; pricing pressure; changes in supplier relationships; changes in distribution channels; the impact of alternative technologies on either revenues or methods of distribution; and customer churn.

Planning Succession and Managing Talent

Boards are responsible for both succession planning and talent management. When choosing directors, it is important to recognize experience is not enough. Directors must be able to think strategically; work with their colleagues; be willing to "speak truth to power" and bring an independent, objective perspective to deliberations. In annual board assessments, there are eleven attributes to be evaluated.

CEO succession is the most important responsibility of the board. It is critical to recognize effective CEOs are no longer "commanders in chief," running a top-down command and control type of organization. Instead they are "enablers," relying on distributed leadership across and down the organization to create collaborative "teaming," bringing together relevant skills from across the organization to solve problems.

This raises the question of how they should be rewarded. Clearly the focus on TSR alone and shareholder value maximization does not work well, as it allows CEOs to indulge in financial engineering to maximize the value of their stock options in the name of shareholder value. Instead, they should be remunerated through a system providing a clear "line of sight" linking current value to future value creation, encouraging them to build sustainable value by investing in the future.

The NRC process for managing talent involves four steps: developing the strategy and defining who the talent is; agreeing current and future pivotal positions with their associated competencies with the CEO; identifying and developing the talent pipeline; and monitoring and evaluating its effectiveness. Finally, the NRC must check whether the agreed business strategy is still feasible by reviewing regularly the suitability of organizational design and individual talent.

Ensuring Effective Internal Controls

The "three lines of defense" approach to internal controls is increasingly being replaced by the "five levels of assurance" approach. The audit committee needs to really understand what is happening in the seven areas where things can go wrong in financial reporting: use of unsupported manual journal entries, aggressive revenue recognition, continuous one-off nonrecurring charges, frequent changes to accounting policies, regular repeated related party transactions, the use of complex structured products to improve profits, and the impact of pension fund liabilities on the viability of the company. From a compliance point of view, the audit committee needs to ensure there is regular reporting of key control measures, recognizing, however, there are eight common biases and judgment traps that can lead to poor quality decisions. The audit committee must also be on the lookout for management overrides, designed to undermine the integrity of the system; and for collusion to commit fraud.

Although the enterprise risk management framework is the responsibility of management, the board is involved in three of the five components: governance and culture (the board's responsibility), strategy and objective setting (shared responsibility with management), and some of the performance review elements. Management is responsible for review and revision and information communication, exchange, and reporting.

Engaging Stakeholders

Boards must pay much more attention to stakeholder engagement than in the past, where the board focus was primarily on shareholders. Shareholder-driven discipline takes time and is expensive to organize and often easy to ignore; stakeholder-driven discipline can affect the company almost immediately and can not be ignored; nor can regulatory discipline which can lead to severe penalties and even put the company out of business.

It is also the result of regulators articulating the increased responsibilities of directors to be more open with stakeholders in terms of what they must to disclose in their annual reports, as a result of the Global Reporting Initiative and the demands from analysts and investors to include environmental, social and governance issues in the annual reports. Boards are now expected to have a detailed MD&A section in the annual report so analysts and investors can get a better "line of sight" regarding future financial projections.

The reasons for engaging with stakeholders are the need to rebuild lost trust; build support for alliances and engender goodwill. To do this, boards need to communicate the "purpose" of the organization; appropriate time horizons and risk profiles so there can be a good match between what the organization is trying to achieve and the risk-reward appetite of investors.

To do this effectively, boards must recognize there are primary, secondary, and tertiary stakeholders who have different interests; affect the company in different ways; and must be communicated with appropriately using their language and tone of voice rather than the company's.

Effective communication requires a clear chain of command; with the board responsible for all major announcements and press releases, applying the six principles of effective engagement: empathy, clarity, timeliness, transparency, equal access, and consistency. The board needs to monitor the progress and effectiveness of the engagement plan and proper planning is essential to ensure progress is made using the correct channels to each stakeholder target audience.

Focusing on Reputation

Reputation matters more than ever in a world where intangibles represent over 80% of market capitalization. The positive reasons for focusing on reputation are that an excellent reputation increases growth, makes it easier to recruit and retain the best people, mitigates the downsides of crises, increases trust, and enhances share price. Companies with excellent reputations have nine times more prospects who would buy their products than companies with a poor reputation, just over ten times more positive comments and product recommendations, nearly ten times more people trusting the company to do the right thing and welcoming them in the community, and nearly nine times more people willing to invest in the company.

Reputation is involved in three ways. First, defining a sustainable mission. This requires stakeholder engagement, which in turn depends on their views of the board's credibility and management's ability to execute. Second, creating and sustaining a unique and compelling vision to provide a line of sight between the company's mission and the employee's job. Third, reconciling value creation, extraction and distribution. This is the hardest to achieve as it requires trade-offs between achieving a reputation for creative innovation while at the same time demonstrating efficiency in delivering new products and services on the one hand, and on the other the appropriate allocation of resources to create current value while building future value. Focusing on the reputation impact of the trade-offs can help effective reconciliation and enhance the company's reputation as a result.

Seeking to minimize reputation risk across the company value and supply chain can help find the right balance. To do this effectively, the board should evaluate the reputation risks in the value chain in terms of the environment and the company's impact on natural capital; the community and its impact on social capital; and on the workplace and its impact on human capital.

Considering the environment, community and workplace as areas of natural, social and human capital will help boards remember they need to invest in them as a capital stock, if they are to run a sustainable operation. As far as the environment is concerned, this means adopting policies of "reduce, reuse, and recycle." In the case of the community, this means adopting policies of zero tolerance of corruption, obeying laws, paying taxes, and avoiding politics. In the case of the workplace, this requires policies based on diversity and inclusion, recruitment and promotion based on merit, pay for performance, respect for human and union rights, good working conditions and working hours, no sexual harassment, and no child labor.

Investing in People

The underlying assumption people are costs on the P&L to be minimized or externalized will continue as long as financial accounts do not find a way of recording them on the balance sheet as assets. As a result, boards often fail to regard people as assets to be invested in from day one to the day they retire. In addition, there is an entire category of employment where the "psychic income" afforded by following a vocation, doing "national service," or working for an NGO or charity has justified underpaying people. The internet and gig economy made matters worse, reinforcing the assumption workers are a cost to be minimized in a global "race to the bottom." This encourages boards to think people are disposable—an attitude most prevalent in the Anglosphere economies. However, "Rhenish" capitalist countries have adopted a different approach, which has resulted in their creating better paying jobs in export-oriented industries, lower inequality, and longer life expectancy than in the United States, where inequality is rising and life expectancy is falling.

The rise in inequality resulting from the view shareholders come first and employees last, demonstrated by companies buying back shares while real wages stagnate or decline for blue collar and lower white-collar workers may lead to a "political tragedy of the commons" where what makes *economic* sense for an individual board does not make *political* sense when all boards follow suit.

Once we accept that we need to invest in people, the question is how best to do it. It helps if boards recognize there are four types of leader, not just the single "captain of the ship" of our imaginations. "Captains" rely on "navigators" whose role is to chart the best course reconciling safety, speed and economy to reach the destination on time. "Navigators" in turn depend on "engineers" to keep the ship moving and "engineers" depend on "builders" to design and build seaworthy vessels.

It would help improve morale and productivity if companies stopped trying to "fit square pegs into round holes," by recognizing most people do not want to be managers. Organizations that recognize this problem have invested in more than one career ladder—people can get to the top of a technical career ladder without having to climb the managerial career ladder they dislike.

Force-fitting the wrong default personality into the wrong role, justified on the grounds it will be a good developmental experience may be true but comes at the cost of the individual having to invest emotional energy in dealing with the mismatch—

energy better spent on enjoying the job and putting perfection into the work, with major increases in productivity as a result.

When investing in training, companies must remember new product training is not the same as training employees in the soft skills and new competencies they need to face the future.

Harnessing Processes to Create Long-Term Value

Directors admit they do not spend enough time on strategy with dismal results: 66% in the HBR study did not understand the strategies of their companies, 78% did not understand how their companies created value, and 84% did not understand the dynamics of their company's industry.

There are two solutions to this problem: First directors should spend more time on the business. The HBR study recommended they should spend at least thirty-five days a year per board on which they sit. Second, there are six areas where boards can increase long-term value by harnessing changes in processes: introducing rotating "Devil's Advocacy" in board deliberations, using activity-based costing to understand the financials, "reframing" budget and cost control discussions to remove anchoring biases, setting KPIs using a ten-step process, adopting an effective innovation process, and recruiting more women directors.

These six operational areas of improvement need, however, to be reinforced by processes, outside the organizations, designed to create a "CG ecosystem." For it to deliver good CG, an effective "CG ecosystem" must have effective regulatory discipline, based on international best practice and effective enforcement of all relevant legislation for all. It requires the existence of professional boards, with properly trained directors, committed to a lifetime of continuous professional development as with all other professions. It must invest in educating, training, and certifying capital market intermediaries and enforce correct behavior. It must also invest in investor education and protection so investors can engage appropriately with boards.

This can only be done effectively, if there is good public governance with the government setting a good example; with boards and government held to account by a robust free press with fearless investigative journalists who understand business; and an independent judiciary with judges who understand commercial law and who are truly independent; supported by professional auditors to ensure accurate and timely reporting of the financials.

Index

A

AC (audit committee) 56–57, 61–62, 76–79, 87, 100, 171–72, 190, 192, 210–11, 247, 249, 256, 259–61, 265, 368
Accountability 3, 29, 32, 53, 55, 64, 70, 221, 243, 248, 346, 348, 356
Accounting policies 250, 265, 368
ACGA (Asian Corporate Governance Association) 355, 362
Achieving better governance 363–64, 366, 368, 370
Acquisitions 6, 73, 117–18, 175, 183, 198, 223, 257, 353–54, 361
Activities, key 156, 166
Activity-based costing (ABC) 179, 183, 340–42, 345, 359, 371
Advocates 108, 277, 279, 290
Agents 9, 308
AGMs (annual general meetings) 63, 88, 97, 117, 269–71, 285, 293–94
AICD (Australian Institute of Company Directors) 221, 241, 243, 245
Alignment, organizational 138, 328
Amazon 41, 208, 232, 314, 318, 323, 335
American companies, large 304
American companies and workers 304
AMLA (Anti Money Laundering Act) 96, 308
Analysts 5, 9, 91, 172, 192, 201, 212, 269, 273, 281, 285–86, 288, 290, 293–94, 368
Analyzing organizational capabilities 152–53, 155
Anglosphere 14, 321
Anglosphere capital markets 11, 16, 363
Annual board of directors study 79
Annual report 77, 79, 97, 220–21, 252, 272, 281, 285, 290, 293, 368
Anti Money Laundering Act (AMLA) 96, 308
Apple 21, 41, 43, 109, 128, 151, 160, 181, 218, 232, 258, 303, 311, 314, 343
Asian Corporate Governance Association (ACGA) 355, 362
Asia's path 355, 362
Assessments, annual board 239, 367
Asset classes 204
Assets 89–90, 133, 174–75, 177, 179, 204, 212, 214, 254–55, 259, 317–18, 320, 333–34, 354, 370
– average business 175, 178
– fixed business 176, 178
– important 38, 219, 239, 297, 317
– total 176
– total business 178–79
Assumptions 13, 15, 128, 141–42, 162, 173, 204, 258, 260, 317, 319, 321, 323, 342, 344
– management's 101, 153
Assurance 57, 210, 247–48, 263, 266
AT&T 41, 202
Audit 76–78, 100, 170, 175, 268, 271
Australia 13, 58–59, 96, 104, 192, 275, 310, 321–23, 358
Austria 320–22, 335
Authority 8, 15, 37, 47–48, 59, 63, 77–78, 88–90, 98, 109, 112, 120, 131, 205, 211–12
– board-delegated 102, 365

B

Bad leaders 106, 108–9
– great 107–9, 112, 120
Bad leadership 109, 119–20
Balance sheet 145, 149, 173–79, 185–86, 249, 251, 259, 297, 299, 303, 306, 317, 333–34, 366, 370
Balances 5–6, 15, 56, 63, 68, 79, 105, 112, 116, 120, 144, 242
Banks 17, 20, 29, 31, 43, 118–19, 121, 177, 199–201, 203, 206, 267–68, 271, 337, 342
BBC News 83–84, 167, 218, 255, 267, 313, 315, 320
Beneficiaries 48, 51, 56, 95, 106, 126, 129, 288, 291, 344–45
Better home-grown governance 355, 362
Blankfein, Lloyd 30–31, 44
Board agenda 74, 82, 86, 364
Board charter 47, 63, 67, 70–72, 76, 81, 83, 96, 364
Board committees 76–77, 79, 87, 220
Board composition 16, 72, 103
Board deliberations 359, 371
Board directors 79
Board dynamics 67–68, 70
– creating positive 82, 364
– good 67–68
Board effectiveness 67, 72–73, 75, 103
Board evaluations 72, 86, 222

Board focus 289, 368
Board governance 17, 100
Board governance processes appendix, regarding 83
Board in risk management oversight 216
Board involvement 68
Board meetings 59, 69, 71–72, 75, 80, 82, 89, 96, 110, 170–71, 237, 242, 340
Board meetings directors 96
Board members 14, 27, 53, 71, 74, 80, 82, 85, 95, 97, 171, 194, 220, 354
Board processes 339, 341, 343, 345, 347, 349, 351, 353
Board responsibility 47, 49, 51, 53, 55–57, 59
Board risk management 83
Board risk management committee TOR Appendix 83
Board risks cross-subsidizing 174
Boardroom 55, 65, 75, 96, 220–21, 242, 244–45, 353
Boards 47–50, 52–65, 67–77, 85–90, 93–103, 127–38, 141–47, 197–211, 219–25, 236–45, 258–62, 286–90, 305–12, 339–45, 362–71
- accountable 6
- challenger 69, 71
- engaged 68–70, 115
- good 7, 271
- individual 297, 333, 370
- intervening 69, 71
- large 79
- manages risk 61
- new 203, 225
- organization's 248
- parent 224
- professional 358, 360, 371
- remembering 191, 229
- scout 68–71
- sets strategy 61
- subsidiary 79, 224–25
- traditional risks 191
- watchdog 69, 71
Board's approval 60, 114
Boards function 70, 221
Boards oversee management 54
Board's strategy review process 169
Boards that lead 65, 70, 83
Boss 47, 88, 135, 268
Boston 109, 120, 151, 190, 218, 360–61

Boundaries of board responsibility 47–48, 50, 52, 54–56, 58, 60–62, 64, 125, 135, 137–38, 364
Brand 19, 37–39, 41–43, 89, 91, 129, 133, 158, 164, 177, 181–82, 186–87, 207, 215, 233
- corporate 39–40, 207, 363
- distributor's 129
- organizational 19, 91, 102, 365
- owner of 187
- valuable 36, 39
Brand name reassurance 180–81
Brand promise 36–38, 40, 363
Branding 19–20, 22, 24, 26, 28, 30, 32, 34, 36–38, 40, 42, 44, 92, 129, 363
Brands' volume market shares 186–87
Budget 57, 61, 100, 119, 169–70, 178, 180, 187, 222, 227, 326, 341–42, 344
Buffett, Warren 83, 168, 313
Builders 324, 326, 334, 370
Business 20–25, 29–31, 35–40, 43–44, 80–83, 127–28, 130–33, 143–44, 175–77, 197–202, 208–12, 214–16, 268–76, 343–44, 363–65
- big 159, 190
- company's 96, 99, 154
- new 21, 343
- practice 131
- successful 194, 324
Business advisers 93, 103, 365
Business conduct and ethics 44
Business decisions 44, 262
Business education 139, 295
Business enterprise 31, 36, 304
Business judgment rule 14, 44, 63–64, 94–95
Business leadership 128, 224
Business model 96, 147, 158, 162, 165, 181, 186, 207–8, 234, 270, 305, 326, 350–53, 366
- company's 91, 156, 166
- existing 152, 162
- new 146, 312
Business model processes 348
Business objectives 264, 346
Business opportunities 145
Business plans 61, 348
Business portfolios 202, 234
Business purpose 21, 23, 31, 36, 43, 109, 197, 210, 213, 220, 238, 274
Business roundtable 57, 65, 304
Business schools 23, 130
Business strategy 94, 131–32, 211, 230, 236, 238

– agreed 236–37, 239, 367
– current 133
Business units, strategic 197
Buyers 30–31, 145, 148, 151, 154, 181, 187, 310, 319, 358
Buy-in 159, 327–28, 349

C
Calculating customer lifetime value 189
Canada 13, 85, 103, 275, 321–23
Candidates 79, 220, 229–30, 244, 358
– high potential 236–37
– perfect 331–32
Capital 3, 7, 12, 115, 118–19, 174, 212, 233, 294, 302, 345, 354
– human 223, 305, 311–12, 369
– natural 305–6, 311–12, 369
Capital market discipline 269, 271, 289
Capital markets 13, 89, 356, 358
Career ladders, managerial 334, 370
Carver 55, 64–65
Cash 90, 121, 175–78, 186, 212, 251, 259, 303
Caveats regarding implementation 11, 13
CDOs (collateralized debt obligations) 114–15
CEMs 177
CEO 47–48, 62–63, 68–74, 79–82, 85, 87–91, 93–94, 99–100, 102–3, 105–6, 118–20, 225–36, 238–39, 244–48, 364–65
CEO and senior management 61, 69, 93, 233
CEO succession 219, 225, 227, 239, 245–46, 367
CFO 48, 62–63, 96, 100, 115, 130, 248, 250–51, 256, 280
CG. See Corporate governance
– definitions of 3–4, 15
– failures of 10, 48, 63, 119, 364–65
– principles of 4, 16
CG ecosystem 339, 355–57, 359–60, 371
CG failure 10
CG Watch 362
Chair 14, 47–48, 63, 67–69, 71–76, 79–82, 85–89, 101–3, 113–14, 116, 119, 222, 244, 271, 364–65
– job of 72–73
Chair and NRC 221, 224, 226, 229, 238
Chairing 67–68, 70, 72, 74, 76, 78, 80, 82, 84, 364
Chairman 85, 103, 105, 113, 116, 119, 321
Challengers 68, 76

Challenges 16, 21, 43, 47, 83, 104, 209, 257, 296, 346, 348
Channels 156, 166, 177, 183, 215, 234, 280, 284–85
– appropriate 280, 283
Characteristics of effective leadership 108–9, 111
Charitable organizations and not for-profit societies 357
Citi 29, 42, 201, 203
Clients 30, 33, 40, 43, 56, 79, 99, 113, 147, 154, 175, 180–81, 198, 358, 363
Climate change 101, 150–51, 283, 307, 314
CLSA 355, 362
CLV (customer lifetime value) 183, 186, 189
Collaboration 131, 226, 228
Combined Chairman and CEO 103
Committee of Sponsoring Organizations. See COSO
Committees 16, 48, 57, 63, 65, 76–77, 79–80, 82, 171, 190, 192, 210, 249, 364
Commonwealth 13–14, 58
Communication architecture, integrated 90–91, 102, 365
Communications 100, 248, 264, 277, 280–84, 332, 334, 348
– corporate 101, 281, 285–87, 293
– stakeholder 287
Communities 22, 25–26, 28, 127, 132, 272–73, 276, 297, 299, 302, 304–5, 308, 310–12, 339, 369–70
Companies 3–8, 35–40, 56–61, 67–73, 87–100, 126–33, 152–58, 175–84, 194–208, 250–55, 269–74, 290–94, 299–313, 328–34, 365–71
– chemical 167, 353
– dictatorship 6–7
– gas 49
– good 21, 301
– government-linked investment 67
– individual 4, 151, 323
– leading 79, 101, 177, 198, 220
– manufacturing 342
– profitable 21, 175
– reputable 300
– successful 22, 304, 354
– traded 303, 308
Companies Act 23, 35, 58–59, 65, 222
Companies Ordinance 58, 65
Company brand promise 39
Company brands 20, 36, 38–39

376 — Index

Company business model 155, 224
Company reputation 90–91
Company secretary 63, 71, 74–75, 81–82, 96–97, 171
Competencies 64, 83, 104, 134, 157–58, 209, 220, 236, 245, 317
Competition 24, 32, 44, 97, 129, 148, 150, 153, 160, 163–64, 179, 184, 191, 202, 206
Compliance 19, 34–36, 56, 62, 89, 94, 205, 210, 214, 247–48, 256–59, 262–63, 268, 288–89, 292
Compliance objectives 263
Compliance officers 35, 200
Computer companies 343, 351
Conduct, code of 19–20, 25, 29, 36–37, 39, 53, 62, 64, 89, 91, 110, 131, 138, 256, 261
Confidentiality 82, 98, 241–42, 271, 291
Conflicts 25, 28, 30, 50, 55, 64, 79, 82, 85, 96, 98, 102–3, 242, 251, 260
– potential 242, 251
– principal-agent 9, 11, 15, 25
Conglomerate 41–42, 157, 199
Congress 29–30, 44, 56, 273, 282
Conservation 150–51
Constraints, board-defined 86, 88
Continuing professional development (CPD) 358, 360
Continuity 141, 188, 320
Contracts 23–24, 28, 93, 97, 150, 172, 252–53, 353
– zero-hours 320
Control 9, 11–12, 16, 47, 100, 102, 105–6, 129, 179, 181, 248, 253, 256, 259–60, 263
Core director attributes 241, 243
Core responsibilities Board's role 61–63
Corporate boards 64, 88, 97, 121, 270, 295
Corporate directors onboarding program 104, 126
Corporate governance 3–4, 6, 8, 10–12, 14, 16–19, 64–65, 83–86, 94, 96, 104–5, 123, 216, 245–46, 266
Corporate governance (CG) 1, 3–12, 14–20, 47–48, 53–55, 64–65, 82–86, 94, 96–98, 103–6, 245–46, 295–96, 339, 355, 363
Corporate governance, good 4, 67, 82, 339
Corporate governance matters 5, 7, 9
Corporate performance and women's representation on boards 362
Corporate/product apparel 41–43
Corporate/product automotive 41–42

Corporate/product beer 42
Corporate/product financial services 41–42
Corporate/product FMCG 41–43
Corporate/product luxury 41–42
Corporate/product retail 42
Corporate/product technology 42–43
Corporations 4, 44, 93, 95, 253, 299, 304–5, 309, 318, 323
– for-profit 23
Corrective actions 55, 61–62, 74, 78, 110, 125, 135–36, 138, 176, 222, 365
Corruption 26, 32, 38, 275, 305, 308, 310, 312, 370
COSO (Committee of Sponsoring Organizations) 191, 261, 263–64, 268
COSO enterprise risk management framework 247
Cost management 344
Costs 10, 129, 144, 164–66, 173–75, 177, 183–84, 196–97, 250, 272, 317–18, 320, 333–34, 341–45, 370
– acquisition 175, 183, 189, 250
– agency 6, 95
– appropriate levels of 342–43
– correct 174
– year's 342
Costs of failure 10, 15, 363
Counter-parties 29, 252–53
Countries 4, 12, 24, 35–36, 49–50, 57–58, 76, 145, 192, 196–97, 222, 275, 308, 310, 319–22
Courts 60, 94–95, 150
CPD (continuing professional development) 358, 360
Create long-term value 339–40, 342, 344, 346, 348, 350, 352, 354, 356, 358, 360, 362, 371
Create value 55, 64–65
Creating long-term value 232, 235
Credibility, board's 302, 369
Creditors 15, 98, 176–78, 272
Credo 22, 24–25, 43
Crisis 10, 69, 113, 115, 227–28, 282, 284, 287, 301, 311, 323–24
Crisis CEO 227, 229
Crisis management 70, 228
Cultural differences 16, 36, 363
Cultural risks 191, 194–95, 197, 199–200, 209–10, 213, 366

Culture 19–20, 36–37, 39, 43–44, 112, 157–59, 163–64, 194–95, 198–200, 236, 263–65, 288–89, 363, 366, 368
– organizational 200, 259
– risk-aware 262–63
Culture eats strategy for breakfast 194, 216
Customer churn 208, 210, 215, 367
Customer lifetime value (CLV) 183, 186, 189
Customer relationships 156, 165–66, 208
Customer segments 165
Customer value proposition 166
Customers 24–25, 31, 36–39, 90–92, 126–27, 142–43, 148, 154–55, 160–61, 165–66, 179–85, 188–90, 302–4, 341–42, 352–53
– dissatisfied 183
– individual acquired 189
– new 157, 179, 183, 234
– voice of the 173, 180, 182, 186, 366
CV (Current value) 231, 234, 367, 369
Cycle, product life 37, 129

D
Data General 159–60
Data General and DEC 159–60
Data processing, distributed 159–60
Debt 130, 144–45, 163, 174, 179, 191, 204, 254
Debtors 176–78, 212, 249
DEC 159–60
Decisions 22–23, 25–28, 68, 70–76, 82, 94–96, 108, 110–13, 132–33, 199, 227, 235, 240–41, 257–58, 341
– informed 269, 271
– right-good 27–28, 40
Defense 7, 29, 205, 247–48, 266, 283
– second line of 247–48
Deliberate management overrides 256, 258
Deliberations, board's strategy 143
Deliver long-term value 339, 341, 343, 345, 347, 349, 351, 353
Demographics 157, 163, 213
Departments 20, 45, 90, 139, 141, 160, 197, 199, 211, 213, 326, 330
Derivatives 118, 252–53, 267
Derivatives contracts 252–53
Designing performance 246
Determining strategy 302–3
Differentiation 37–38, 128, 156, 160–62, 164, 366
Diligence 92, 96, 103, 242, 365

Direction 12, 34, 56, 58–59, 74, 132, 225, 228, 328, 333
– board-agreed 61, 93
Director defendants 116
Director independence 83, 104, 245
Directors 9, 27–28, 34–36, 39–40, 57–60, 71–76, 91–104, 129–32, 169–72, 215, 219–25, 238–46, 248–52, 339–41, 363–68
Directors & Boards Magazine 83
Directors
– corporate 55, 95, 103, 304
– executive 20, 80, 91
– fellow 100–101, 243
– five possible approaches 25
– individual 79, 224
– marketing 36, 38–39
– nominee 98, 100
– qualified 358
Directors Statement of Internal Control (DSIC) 171, 247
Directors work 224
Disagreements 76–77, 86, 102, 110, 195, 286, 341
Discipline 289–90, 368
Disclosure 63, 250, 252, 272, 291–92
Discounts 176–78, 185, 366
Discovery 307–8, 349, 351
Disney 38, 41, 94
Disruptors 156, 158–59, 162, 366
Dissent 28, 112, 114–15
Dollars 6, 111, 173, 193, 344
Dove 39, 331, 334, 337
Downsides 10, 252, 319
Drivers 14, 57, 67–68, 72–73, 81, 91, 96, 110, 144, 191, 232, 295, 322, 340, 364
DSIC (Directors Statement of Internal Control) 171, 247
Duties 12, 23, 30, 58, 82, 92–95, 97–98, 103–4, 211, 241, 243, 259, 365
Duties and Liabilities of directors 23, 104
Dynamics 32, 157, 339, 359, 371
– best board-management 75

E
Earnings 144, 209, 232, 252, 267, 304, 310
Earnings driver risks 194, 206–10, 213, 215, 222, 366–67
Economic profit (EP) 231–32

Economies 10, 15, 129–30, 144, 146, 150, 160, 179, 303–7, 309, 313, 320–21, 323, 325, 333
Ecosystems matter 355, 362
EDP (Electronic Data Processing) 159
EDP departments 159–60
Effective board 57, 67–68, 70, 72, 74, 76, 78–80, 82, 84, 222, 364
Effective board member 85–86, 88, 90, 92, 94, 96, 98–102, 104, 364
Effective CEOs 90, 226–28, 239, 367
Effective chairs 72–75, 88
Effective director 91, 93, 95, 97, 103–4, 173, 365
Effective leadership 107–9, 111, 241
Effectiveness 78–79, 81, 85, 89, 169, 173, 185–86, 237, 239, 261, 263, 326, 364, 366–67, 369
Effects
– legacy 110–11, 141, 143, 158–59, 163
– network 160–61
EGMs (extraordinary general meeting) 63, 269–70, 285
Electronic Data Processing (EDP) 159
Emphases 3–5, 20–22, 30–31, 33–34, 57, 92, 98–99, 131–32, 194–97, 229–31, 253–55, 257, 319, 323–25, 347–49
Employee satisfaction 183–84, 186, 349, 366
Employees 22–25, 30, 37–38, 52–53, 88–91, 130–31, 196, 200, 272, 284–85, 288, 302–5, 320–21, 329–30, 332–34
Employers 98, 146, 318–20
Energy 53, 105, 109, 112, 155, 306, 324, 330, 334, 371
Engagement 68, 70, 242, 274, 320, 328
Engaging stakeholders 269–70, 272, 274, 276, 278, 280, 282, 284, 286, 288, 290, 292, 294, 296
Engineers 21, 188, 196–97, 324–26, 333–34, 370
Enron 5, 10, 21, 57, 70, 97, 171–72, 190, 258
Ensuring internal controls 247–48, 250, 252, 254, 256, 258, 260, 262, 264, 266, 268
Enterprise risk management. See *ERM*
Enterprise risk management framework 78, 368
Enterprise value (EV) 231
Entities 12, 125, 197–98, 261, 263, 359
Entrants, new 155, 163, 350
Environment 5, 20, 22, 25, 39, 63, 73, 167, 169, 297, 299, 303, 305–7, 311–12, 369

– external 142–43, 145, 147, 149, 151, 162
EP (economic profit) 231–32
EP approach 232
Equity 80–81, 95, 130, 174–75, 179, 198, 214, 242, 302, 354
ERM (enterprise risk management) 192, 261, 263–64
Errors 7, 10, 60, 199, 252, 258, 350
Ethical basis 20–21, 23, 25, 27, 29, 31, 33, 35, 92
Ethical foundation 19, 21, 25, 38–39, 259
Ethical framework 25, 40
Ethics 4, 19–21, 25–27, 36, 44, 70, 72, 196–97, 200
Ethics conflicts 195, 213
Europe 107, 157, 195–96, 333
EV (enterprise value) 231
Existing markets 157, 162, 366
Existing products 157, 162, 366
Expected behavior 52, 241–43
Expenses 8, 12, 23, 25, 146, 202, 232, 249–51, 297, 309, 312, 317–18, 323
Experience 56–57, 71, 73, 86–88, 92–93, 96, 100–101, 103, 114–16, 220–21, 223–24, 228, 230, 239, 348–49
External auditors 57, 62, 77, 82, 247, 261, 292, 359
Extraction 299, 302–3, 312, 339, 342, 369

F
Facebook 7–8, 17, 41, 105, 151, 205, 232
Failure 25, 28–29, 90, 97–98, 105–6, 108–10, 112–13, 121–22, 162, 171–72, 196–97, 210, 223, 255–56, 282–83
Fair share 22, 308–10
Families 7, 11–12, 15, 48–49, 51, 64, 194, 210, 276, 282, 284, 366
Family firms 7, 11–12, 47, 49
Family-owned companies 12
FATCA (Foreign Account Tax Compliance Act) 96, 308
FCPA (Foreign Corrupt Practices Act) 308, 314
Feasibility feedback for business strategy xlvii 237
Fiduciaries 94–95, 103, 365
Fiduciary duties 15, 35, 94–95, 97, 101–2, 171, 222, 241, 358, 364
Financial economics 16–17
Financial services 41–43, 131, 310

Index — 379

Financial Services Authority (FSA) 118–19
Financials 16, 65, 70, 170, 175, 185–86, 272–73, 317, 359, 366, 371
Firm performance 16, 354
First directors 359, 371
Five forces framework 24, 178
Five p 123, 125–38, 169, 185–86, 191, 208–10, 219, 238–39, 247, 262, 264–65, 269, 287, 290, 364–65
Flexibility 4, 128, 162, 177, 228, 320
FLOA approach 248, 265
FMCG (fast moving consumer good) 41–42, 158, 351
Forces management 262, 344
Ford, Henry 51, 299, 317
Foreign Account Tax Compliance Act (FATCA) 96, 308
Founders 7, 21–22, 48–49, 51, 68, 110, 130, 142, 244, 330, 354
Framework to cross check 208–9, 238, 247, 264, 269, 287
Fraud 77, 175, 195, 205, 215, 249–50, 256, 265, 271, 368
Friedman, Milton 21–22, 31
FSA (Financial Services Authority) 118–19
FSA Board Report 122, 268
Fuld, Dick 113, 115, 120
Fund manager 273, 313, 362
Funds 60, 176, 222, 254–55, 292, 302
FV 231, 233
FV creation 234, 239

G

GAAP (generally accepted accounting principles) 56, 249
Gaps 237–38, 288, 309
– board performance 221–24
GDP 309, 322, 336
General duties and powers 82
General meetings 63, 97, 269, 271, 285
Generally accepted accounting principles (GAAP) 56, 249
Germany 5, 16, 45, 196, 270, 275, 320–21, 335
Goldman Sachs 30, 43, 113, 115, 282
Goldman Sachs code of business conduct and ethics 44
Good CEOs 226–30
Good CG 4–8, 35, 86, 105, 112, 119, 197, 356–57, 360, 365, 371
Good governance 5, 8, 64, 123, 355–56

Good leaders, great 108–9, 112
Goodwin, Fred 113, 117, 120–21
Governance 3–5, 7, 17, 43, 55, 65, 91–92, 105–6, 108, 120–22, 211, 225–26, 264–65, 268–69, 365
Governance and culture 264–65, 368
Governance framework, corporate 4
Governance policies 243
Governments 11–13, 29, 32, 48–49, 64, 100, 142, 144–46, 167, 225, 253–54, 258, 272–76, 308–9, 358–60
GPAC (gross profit after commission) 176, 178
Greenpeace 273, 286, 296
Gross profit after commission (GPAC) 176, 178
Groupthink 110, 258
Growth 7, 12, 69, 73, 81, 146, 163, 179, 186, 203, 231, 233, 311, 366, 369
Guardian 146, 190, 216–18, 267, 273, 314–15, 335–37

H

Handbook of Corporate Governance 23, 65, 70, 83, 94, 104, 216, 245–46, 266
Harnessing processes 339–40, 342, 344, 346, 348, 350, 352, 354, 356, 358, 360, 362
Harvard Business Review 120, 337, 341, 360–61
Harvard Business Review on measuring corporate performance 360
HBR 359, 371
Health Maintenance Organizations (HMOs) 145
HMOs (Health Maintenance Organizations) 145
Hoboken 23, 65, 70, 83, 94, 104, 168, 216, 245, 266
Hong Kong powers and duties of directors 58
HP 42, 148, 225, 238, 244, 343

I

IBM 41, 111, 128, 148, 159–60, 343
Income statement 174–76, 178–79, 185–86, 206, 249, 366
Incumbents 119, 147–48, 158–60, 162, 225, 343, 350, 352, 366
Independence 14–15, 57, 77, 79, 82, 98–99, 240, 340
Independent directors 57, 68, 103, 113, 340
India 21, 196, 275, 307, 319
Industry 41–43, 45, 49, 143–44, 150, 153, 155, 201, 203, 222, 224, 285–86, 339, 341, 354
– export-intensive services 322
Industry economics 163

380 — Index

INEDs (independent non-executive director) 14–15, 70, 72, 75, 77, 79–80, 85, 91, 93–94, 96, 98–101, 240, 358
Inequality 309, 312, 322–23, 333, 370
Innovation 7, 36, 52, 159, 165, 183, 186, 206, 215, 223, 231–34, 348–51, 353, 361, 366
Insurance companies 9, 145, 201
Intangibles 299–300, 311, 369
Integrating Ethics and Branding 19–20, 22, 24, 26, 28, 30, 32, 34, 36, 38, 40, 42, 44, 363
Integrity 57, 70, 72, 87, 91, 106, 131, 137, 202, 221, 241–42, 247, 265, 368
Interest rates 144, 214, 252
Interests 3, 5–6, 12, 15, 23, 25, 30, 33, 49, 79, 85–86, 95–98, 189, 242, 251
– best 15, 44, 75, 94–95, 98, 197
Interface, board-management 86
Internal audit 35, 131, 134, 192, 199, 212, 214–15, 247–48, 260
Internal auditors 77, 119, 247–48, 260–61, 266
Internal controls 3, 16, 38, 62–63, 87, 94, 171, 185, 249, 261, 263–65, 268, 363–64, 368
International business transactions 308, 314
International corporate governance 16, 54, 65
International organization 16, 84
Inventory 30, 176–77, 212, 249, 256, 258
Investment banking 118, 202
Investments 14–15, 116, 118, 125, 128, 130, 133, 160–61, 173, 175, 179, 303–4, 332, 349–50, 365–66
– prior 158–59
Investor relations 63, 87, 101, 269, 281
Investors 3–8, 197–98, 201, 255, 258, 269, 272, 277, 281, 288, 290, 360, 363, 368, 371
IRR 174, 185, 366

J

James Hardie Industries Ltd. (JHIL) 60
JHIL (James Hardie Industries Ltd.) 60
Jobs 35, 57, 131, 133–34, 137, 146, 214–15, 227–28, 238, 288–89, 302–4, 319–20, 329–30, 334–35, 350–51
– employee's 312, 369
Johnson 22, 130, 167–68
Judgment 34, 58, 92, 95, 214, 251, 256–58, 263, 359
Judiciary, independent 359–60, 371
Justified underpaying people 333, 370

K

Key decisions 63, 69–71, 116, 118
Knowledge and performance areas 221–24
Knowledge workers 226, 330, 337
KPIs (key performance indicators) 86, 88, 90, 135, 170, 173, 183, 186, 192, 197, 213, 285, 340–41, 347, 366
Kraft Heinz 146–47

L

Labor costs 320, 322
Language 141, 283, 290–91, 356, 369
Large companies 29, 97, 178, 220, 240, 305
Laws 17, 19–20, 29, 32, 34–36, 56, 58–59, 88–89, 91–93, 95–96, 149, 241–42, 305, 318, 321
– black letter 14, 34
Leaders 62, 91, 106–12, 116, 120, 226, 314, 324–29, 333, 370
Leadership 8, 17, 43, 105–9, 111, 119–21, 221, 227, 236, 241, 245–46, 324, 327, 336–37, 365–66
– resonant 107–9
Learning processes 326
Lehman board 116
Lehman Brothers 6, 10, 94, 113, 115, 117, 121, 258
Lessons 292, 295–96, 356
Leverage 113, 115, 129–30, 159, 164
Liabilities 23, 35, 60, 102, 104, 174–77, 186, 191, 212, 254–55, 267
Licensed brand 129
Life expectancy 145, 253, 323, 333, 336, 370
Life stages, business unit 186, 366
Line management 48, 60, 64
Line managers 325, 334
Listed companies 9, 11–12, 14, 18, 50, 56–57, 64, 98, 235, 357–58
– public 5–6, 9, 15, 77, 88, 96, 269, 354, 357
London Business School 23, 117, 203
London-based directors and board members 194
Long-term value 3, 39, 48, 64, 102, 232, 246, 339–40, 344, 359, 365, 371
Losses 10–11, 34, 118, 130, 146, 154, 177, 191, 252, 255, 258–59, 263, 266, 330, 355

M

Malaysia 12–13, 35, 44, 49–50, 58, 104, 144, 199, 225, 275, 320, 356, 358

Malaysian code of corporate governance 104
Malaysian companies act 60, 83, 98, 104, 240
Malicious obedience 278–79
Management 47–48, 55–61, 63–65, 67, 69–71, 73–78, 99–103, 125–27, 135–39, 206–7, 209–10, 220–21, 258–65, 328–30, 364–68
– company's 4, 106, 240
– executive 89, 119, 236
– operational 248
Management challenges 65, 245, 337
Management compensation 57, 211
Management controls 247
Management manages 14, 55, 57, 60
Management performance 55, 87
Management policies 307, 310
Management power 6
Management responsibilities 54
Management teams 8, 55, 326
Management's ability 302, 369
Management's role 61–63
Managers 6, 8–9, 11, 25, 55, 128, 131, 260, 265, 329, 332, 334, 337, 344, 346–47
Managers in big companies 159
Managing 24, 57–60, 64, 80, 82, 86, 89, 242, 329, 334, 364
Managing risk 191–92, 194, 196, 198, 200, 202, 204, 206, 208, 210, 212, 214, 216, 218, 363–64
Managing talent 16, 219–20, 222, 224, 226, 230, 232, 234, 236, 238–40, 242, 244, 246, 363, 367
Manufacturer's brand 129
Margins 90, 147, 154–55, 160, 175, 189, 206, 215, 233–34, 272, 303
Market activity 271, 291
Market discipline 269–70
Market failure 33
Market margin 24, 153–55, 157–58, 202
Market model 13
Market share 145, 154, 179–82, 186–87, 258
Market value 16, 38, 40, 174, 299–300
Marketing 36, 45, 52, 100, 145, 164, 285, 348, 351
Marketing and innovation 36
Markets 12–14, 16, 32–33, 47, 114–15, 128, 155, 157, 160–61, 197–98, 230, 234–35, 273–74, 277–78, 350–51
– emerging 12, 32, 270, 274, 309, 333
– new 157, 162–63, 233, 348, 350, 366
Matheson 360–61

Maximizing shareholder value 10, 23, 39, 232, 299, 312
MBS 114–15
MCCG 220, 240, 295
MCI 190, 202
McKinsey & Co 360–61
McKinsey Quarterly 17, 360–61
Measures, key 183–85
Measures Matter 171, 173, 175, 177, 179, 181, 183
Measuring corporate performance 360–61
Media 41–42, 91, 207, 274, 280–82, 287, 294
Meeting 52–53, 60, 69, 77, 82, 86, 96, 101, 110, 135–36, 240, 243, 341, 347, 351
Megatrends 145–46, 325, 351
Members 47–48, 55, 71, 77–79, 82, 95, 98, 101, 225–26, 238, 242–43, 272–73, 288–89, 353, 358
– adult 49, 276
Mental models 23, 106, 325–26, 330
Mergers 114, 117, 198, 223, 250, 353–54, 361
Merrill Lynch 6, 113–14, 121

Metrics 141, 172–73, 234, 256
Minding the numbers 247, 249, 251, 253, 255
Minimizing reputation risk across 305, 307, 309
Minority shareholders 15, 242
Minority Shareholders' Watchdog Group (MSWG) 270
Minutes 28, 59–60, 74, 77, 102, 119, 150, 171
Mission 38, 48, 50, 52, 55–56, 109, 138, 164, 169, 222, 242, 302, 324, 326, 328
– board-agreed 138, 36organization's 330, 346
– sustainable 50, 302–3, 312, 369
Mission and vision 50–52, 91, 125–26, 135–38, 184–85, 328
Mistakes 22, 94, 108–11, 128, 217, 228, 300, 302, 307, 315, 329
Models 14–15, 68, 148, 152–53, 155, 194, 226, 248, 253, 260–61, 334
Money 21, 23, 29, 113, 120–21, 147–48, 154, 173, 180–81, 235, 305, 308–9, 318–19, 330, 358–59
MSWG (Minority Shareholders' Watchdog Group) 270

N
Net revenue 176, 178–79, 212
Netherlands 192, 274–75, 320–21

New products 22, 157, 162–63, 179, 183–84, 215, 233–34, 329, 332, 348, 350–51, 353, 366, 369
New York 16, 43–44, 51, 64, 88, 97, 113, 120–21, 138–39, 151, 245, 255, 267, 270, 361–62
New York Times 43–44, 121, 217, 267, 295, 314–15, 337
Nike 41, 207, 311, 315
Nomination committee 71, 87, 271, 324, 326
Nonexecutive directors 80, 340
Norton 120, 190
Norway 321–23
NPV (net present value) 174, 183, 185, 233, 366
NRC 62, 76, 100, 133, 220–21, 224, 226, 229–30, 235, 238–39, 367
Number 51–52, 79, 172, 175–76, 178, 182, 184–85, 188–89, 236, 238, 249–50, 256, 340–43, 347–48, 354
– greatest 25, 27–28
– large 51, 146, 205

O

Objectives 4, 9, 49, 52, 86, 90–91, 170, 230, 242, 248, 263, 269, 272, 276, 347
Obligations 22, 35, 98, 107, 243, 261, 276, 304
OECD (Organization of Economic Cooperation and Development) 4, 11, 16, 64, 356
OEMs 177
Officers 96–97, 244, 251, 281, 305, 308
Offices, chair's 101, 287
Oil spills 151, 167–68
O'Neal, Stan 113–15
Operating boards 70–71
Organization 19–20, 47–53, 88–92, 125–26, 141–43, 183–86, 201–3, 225–27, 241–43, 258–64, 272–79, 286–90, 328–29, 348–50, 367–68
– individual 201, 339
– nongovernmental 55, 126, 196, 273, 333
– single 199, 351
Organization design 89, 133, 137, 185, 237
Organization employees 261
Organizational brand values 90
Organizational culture and leadership 111
Organizational design 125, 129, 132–33, 170, 238–39, 288, 367
– agreed 185, 209
Organizational hierarchy 110, 226
Organizational objectives, board-agreed 88

Oversight 169, 251–52, 261
Owners 5, 9, 11–12, 15, 25, 47–48, 50, 88, 128, 142, 187, 191, 197–98, 340, 348

P

Palo Alto Research Center (PARC) 343
Particularists 35–36, 40, 134, 363
Partners 25, 69–70, 77, 166, 213
Passive boards 70
Pensions 85, 143, 254–55
People management 320, 335
People trusting 302, 312, 369
People value 24
Performance 6, 52–53, 55–56, 73–74, 79–80, 82, 85, 87, 90, 92–94, 170–71, 173, 230–31, 243–44, 262–64
Performance areas 221–24
Performance framework 125–26, 128, 130, 132, 134, 136, 138, 364
Performance measurement 219, 229, 231, 233, 235
Petronas 49–50
Planning succession 219–20, 222, 224, 226, 228, 230, 232, 234, 236, 238, 240, 242, 244, 246, 363–64
Policies 27–28, 53, 55–56, 61–62, 64, 76, 78, 83, 189, 192, 220, 222, 278, 309, 355–56
– adopting 312, 370
– agreed 89, 278
– board-approved 134, 138
Policy issues 213, 276
Pollution 33, 127, 132, 150–51, 306
Power 17, 20, 58–59, 82, 102, 109–10, 112–13, 125, 127, 132, 136–39, 185, 287–88, 290, 325–26
Power structure 125, 133
Power wielders 106, 109
PPP (purchasing power parity) 322
Pressure 5, 9, 12, 23, 25, 144–45, 147, 196, 202, 215, 235, 273, 308, 318, 331–32
Prices 22, 24, 37, 51–52, 155, 160, 165, 181, 197, 199, 252, 352
Principles 3, 25–26, 28, 35–36, 125, 130–32, 134, 136, 138, 185, 209, 238–39, 263, 265, 287–90
Principles-based approaches 13, 35
Principles-based regulations 34–35
Process Board's role, CEO's role 236–37
Process components 356–57

Processes 72, 125–26, 137–38, 164, 184–85, 238, 258–60, 264–65, 289–91, 297, 339–41, 346–49, 353, 358–60, 371
Product brands 36, 39, 129
Product line profitability 179, 341
Product market 24, 154–55, 157, 179, 222
Product mix 144–45
Productivity 52, 172, 183–85, 304, 309, 329, 334, 370–71
Products and services 22, 50, 127, 143–45, 154, 165–66, 234, 284, 305
Professed business principles 29–30
Profitability 24, 91, 96, 132–33, 145, 176, 183–84, 206, 211, 270, 349
Profits 6–7, 21–23, 43–44, 154, 157, 175, 177, 200, 207, 210, 212, 251, 253, 303–4, 353–54
– gross 176, 178
Proposal 15, 102, 110, 277, 341
Purchase 182, 250, 252
– frequency of 182–83, 187
Purchasing power parity (PPP) 322
Purpose, board's 81, 364
Purpose checklist 213, 215, 217

Q

Quality 37, 49, 67, 100, 118, 164, 179–81, 183, 188, 225, 230, 232, 248, 257, 322
Quality risk management 247
Quarterly price performance 293
Questions, directors 133, 156, 213
Questions regarding business model appropriateness 156, 165, 167

R

RBS (Royal Bank of Scotland) 6, 113, 117–18, 121–22, 206, 257, 268
Rebuilding Trust 17, 43, 121, 246, 268, 337
Recommendations 76–78, 103, 188, 220, 271, 284, 286
Reconciling leadership and governance 92, 105–6, 108, 110, 112, 114, 116, 118, 120, 122, 365
Red flags 28, 205, 211–12, 250–51, 264, 292
Regulations 4–5, 11, 14, 19, 29, 31–35, 40, 56–57, 63, 144, 146, 149, 241–42, 272, 363
Regulators 4–5, 19–20, 38–39, 197, 206, 236, 238, 247–49, 270, 272, 288–90, 292–93, 339, 356, 358
Relationships, supplier 207, 210, 215, 367

Remuneration 70, 76–77, 82, 85, 97, 100, 130, 135, 170, 172, 199–200, 229–31, 233, 235, 238
Remuneration committees 87, 220
Rents 32, 178, 319, 353
Reputation 38, 150, 155, 195–96, 199, 207, 210, 242, 292, 297, 299–306, 308, 310–14, 317, 369
– excellent 300–302, 311–12, 369
– good 130, 299, 301, 308, 310, 312
– impact of 299, 301, 303, 312, 369
– poor 301, 312, 369
Reputation Institute 313
Reputation risk 129, 192, 208, 224, 305–6, 310–12, 369
Reserves 22, 118, 249–50
Resigning 99, 102
Resources 8–9, 62, 64, 77, 79, 125, 137, 141, 158–60, 162, 222, 227, 343–44, 346, 349
– key 156, 166
– necessary 78, 214–15
– reallocate 344–45, 349
Responsibilities 19–20, 36, 47–48, 52–64, 69–71, 76–80, 86–88, 92–93, 95–96, 134–35, 242–43, 260–61, 324–25, 339, 363–64
– board's 24, 47, 50, 95, 205, 219, 265, 368
– businesses fiduciary 304
– chair's 71, 86
– chair's board governance 86
– core 47, 60, 63, 219, 223, 225, 364
– operational 135–38
– strategic 135–38, 364
– taking 202, 280, 282
Restaurants 41, 43, 342
Retail 41–42, 133, 303
Retention 183–85, 342, 349
Return 9, 33, 37, 49, 95, 106–8, 130, 136, 159, 174–75, 178–79, 276, 345, 354, 361
– better 49, 354
– fair 22–23, 25, 198
Revenue streams 156, 165–66
Revenues 12, 143, 173–75, 179, 183, 185, 215, 233–34, 244, 250, 272, 308, 310, 345, 354
– gross 176, 178
Review 53, 57, 61–62, 74, 77–78, 131, 135, 137, 142, 146, 169–70, 191–92, 237, 241, 264–65
Review performance 136, 138, 142, 365
Review processes 169, 264

Reviewing Strategy 169–70, 172, 174, 176, 178, 180, 182, 184, 186, 188, 190
Rhenish capitalism 321–22
Rhenish countries 321–23
Right character 134, 137, 289
Right people 145, 170, 219, 289
Risk management 3, 70, 72, 76, 78, 87, 94, 100, 106, 114, 164, 176, 185, 262–63, 271
Risk management committee. See RMC
Risk management framework 242
– organization's 248
Risks 28–29, 34, 78, 89–90, 114–16, 118–19, 157, 173–74, 177, 191–95, 199–206, 210, 213–15, 248, 261–64
– legal/regulatory 210, 367
– macroprudential 201
– market 204, 210, 214, 367
– microprudential 78, 201
– residual 203, 247–48
– systemic 201, 209–10, 213, 367
– top 299–300
– traditional 194, 203, 205, 210, 213–14, 367
RMC (risk management committee) 61, 76–79, 82, 87, 100, 192, 210
ROABA 178–79
ROE 130, 179, 198, 200
ROIC 232, 234
Roles 54–55, 64–65, 71–72, 76–80, 85–86, 88, 102–3, 105–6, 190–91, 235–37, 249, 280–81, 323–25, 330–31, 333–34
– board's 81, 153, 192, 302, 312
– chair's 222
– distinct 85, 87, 89, 93, 101
– important 55, 248
Roles, boards 339
Roles of chair and CEO 73, 119, 365
Rolls-Royce 203, 217, 353
Ruining American business 64, 88, 97, 121, 270, 295
Rules 3–4, 12, 25–26, 32, 34–36, 69, 94, 99, 134, 195, 226, 257, 309
Rules-based approaches 13–14, 35
Rules-based regulations 34

S

Saboteurs 278–79, 290
Sample board charter 82–83
Sample board charter table 72
SBUs (strategic business units) 197–98, 213

Scale 50, 119, 129–30, 147, 151, 160, 166, 179, 303, 320, 351–52
Scandals 5, 8, 12–13, 85, 190, 197, 245, 335, 356
Sellers 31, 319
Senior management 49, 57, 61–62, 69, 73, 81, 87, 93, 189, 195, 248, 261–62, 281, 287–89, 334
Senior management team 20, 204, 225
Senior managers 25, 79, 118, 159, 171, 220, 311, 345
Senior positions, women in 354
Separate Chairman-CEO Post in Companies 103
Setting strategy 141–44, 146, 148, 150, 152–54, 156, 158, 160, 162, 164, 166, 168, 302, 312, 364–65
Shareholder engagement 269
Shareholder return, total 231
Shareholder value 9, 63, 70, 224, 239, 262, 354, 367
– long-term 3, 89
Shareholder value maximization 239, 367
Shareholders 3–4, 6–9, 15, 22–23, 25, 29–31, 55, 63, 75, 89, 97–100, 130, 270–72, 276–77, 304–5
– dispersed 11–12, 48–49, 64
– large 240
Shell 270, 286, 288, 296, 326
Ship 147, 157, 324–26, 334, 370
Sight, line of 90, 233, 288, 290, 302, 368
Singapore 13, 16–18, 43, 54, 59, 64–65, 83, 104, 121, 192, 246, 268, 270, 275, 296
Skills 71, 73, 79, 82, 92, 94, 96, 158, 161, 224–25, 239, 241, 317, 365, 367
SOEs (state-owned enterprises) 50, 67, 69, 230
Staggered boards and long-term firm value 17
Stakeholder contact 280
Stakeholder contexts 142
Stakeholder engagement 70, 72, 185, 269, 283, 289–90, 295–96, 368–69
Stakeholder grid 279
Stakeholder interests 4, 39, 63, 211, 312
Stakeholder map 277
Stakeholders 3–4, 15–16, 38, 40, 63, 90, 127–28, 159, 241–43, 269–72, 274–81, 283–85, 287–90, 363–64, 368
– external 86, 90, 102, 277–78, 288–89, 364
– internal 88, 102, 278, 288–89, 364
– primary 31, 272, 290
– secondary 272–73, 290
– tertiary 272–74, 284, 290, 369

Stakeholders defined 272–73
Stock exchanges 212, 220, 271, 281–82, 357
Stock market 270, 309, 323
Stockholders 11, 22, 95, 308, 354
Strategic business units (SBUs) 197–98, 213
Strategic decisions 70, 268
Strategic objectives 169, 191, 345

Strategy & Corporate Finance 360–61
Strategy 55–57, 70–72, 100, 158–62, 169–70, 194, 199–200, 210–11, 220, 222, 236, 262–65, 339, 343–44, 367–68
– business unit 179
– business unit life stage 179
– differentiation 161
– financing 89
– role of reputation in determining 299, 302–3
– talent management 137
Strengths 73, 107, 143, 148, 152–54, 164, 177, 182, 252
Structured products 116, 118, 252
– complex 252, 265, 368
Subordinates 53, 105, 110–11, 115, 137, 196, 227, 327–29, 333
Subsidiaries 211, 224, 281
Success map 345–46
Succession planning 38, 50, 70, 72, 106, 164, 170, 185, 219–21, 223, 225, 236, 238–39, 289, 367
Superiors 132, 196, 331, 333
Supervision 59, 82
Supine board 116, 121
Suppliers 3, 5, 22, 24, 90–91, 127, 130, 132, 154, 177–78, 181, 270–72, 289, 307, 311
Supply chain 24–25, 132, 163, 177, 202, 223, 303, 305, 307, 311–12, 369
Supply chains, global 147–48
Supporters 99, 108, 277, 279, 290
Sustainable value 10, 19, 92, 94, 105, 235, 239, 367
Sweden 275, 321–23, 335
Switzerland 270, 320–23, 336
SWOT 152, 192

T
Talent management 50, 70, 80, 94, 131, 135, 170, 185, 219, 223, 225, 236–39, 289, 367
Target audience 277–78, 281, 293
Taxes 22, 100, 130, 144, 200, 308–10, 314, 323
Teaming 228, 239, 367

Teams
– board-management 55
– weak 327–28
Technologies 41–42, 90, 147, 163–64, 206, 208, 210, 215, 226, 234, 271, 343, 349–50, 361, 367
Temptation 8, 48, 102, 105, 112, 174–75, 181
Threats 33, 91, 93, 143, 145–46, 151–52, 158–59, 191, 201, 203, 208, 215, 255, 259, 350
Tipping point for combined chairman and CEO 103
TLOD approach 247–48, 265
Too big to fail 203, 210, 214, 367
Top management 236, 285
Top management team 225, 324–25, 355
TOR 76–78
Toyota 41, 195–96, 258
Traditional cost accounting 341–42
Training 79, 82, 135, 225, 241, 266, 320, 324, 329, 331–34, 355, 360, 371
Transactions 30, 119, 171, 174–75, 251–52, 259–60, 354
– party 211–12, 251–52, 265, 368
Treatment 35, 96, 100, 248–49, 318–19
Trust 24, 30, 69, 72, 74, 131, 194, 274–75, 290, 295, 301, 327, 358, 366, 369
Trust in business 275, 295
Trustees 55, 95, 254
TSR (total shareholder return) 231–32, 235, 239, 367

U
UK Companies Act 58, 92, 96, 104
Understanding board's role in strategy and risk management 222
Unemployment 320, 323, 335–36
Unilever 8, 146–47, 157, 198, 202, 307
Unit costs 352
United Kingdom 5, 13–14, 56–57, 81, 85, 107, 113, 145–46, 199, 250, 255, 273, 275, 318, 321–24
United States 5, 8, 10, 13–14, 29, 57, 85, 113, 115, 150–51, 172, 196–97, 199, 318–19, 321–23
Universalists 35, 40, 134, 363
Unsuitable people 116

V

Value chain 144, 157, 202, 213, 305, 307, 309–12, 346, 369
– organization's 289
Value creation 73, 83, 89, 230–31, 233, 235, 303, 305, 339, 341, 345, 348, 367
– long-term 8, 87, 147, 231, 233–34, 339, 342
Value investor 7
Value propositions 156, 164–66
Values 48–50, 52, 90–91, 109–12, 125, 130–31, 164–66, 175–77, 180–85, 189, 232–33, 235–36, 302–3, 305–6, 363–67
– agreed 64, 200, 238, 288
– creating 73, 80, 100, 165, 297, 303, 360, 364
– current 231, 367, 369
– extracting 343
– functional 37
– organization's 90
– organization-wide 227
– personal 91, 109, 328
Vested interests 15, 33, 158–60, 170, 198, 229, 254, 277–79, 347–48, 350, 353
VIP boards 69–70
Vision 48, 50–52, 55–56, 90–91, 109, 125–26, 133, 135–38, 164, 184–85, 236, 274, 276, 326, 328
– compelling 302–3, 312, 369
Volkswagen 38, 195, 197, 310
Voting 77, 95, 97, 102, 271
VW 195–97, 315

W

WACC 174, 232
Wall Street 25, 44, 113, 116, 121, 362
Wallace, P. 17–18, 64, 106
Where Boards Fall Short 341, 360
Women 22, 36, 145, 311, 320, 353–55, 361
Women and young people most likely to work 320, 335
Women directors 220, 340, 353–54, 359, 361, 371
Work 22, 24, 77–78, 100–102, 166–67, 187, 198, 230, 299–301, 303–4, 318–20, 327–28, 330, 352, 364–65
– life science companies 352
– rewarding 49, 276
Workers 172, 207, 254, 304–5, 309, 318, 320, 323–24, 333, 335
Working capital 90, 175, 178, 302
– positive 177, 185–86
Working conditions 22, 132, 172, 208, 311, 349, 353
– good 311–12, 370
Workplace 53, 172, 196, 310–12, 349, 353, 355, 369–70
World Bank 23, 32, 336
World's Most Valuable Brands 41, 43, 45

X, Y

Xerox 149, 172, 343–44, 350

Z

Zero-based budgeting 169, 344–45, 360
Zinkin 16–18, 43–45, 64, 83, 104, 121, 126, 138–39, 167–68, 190, 246, 268, 296, 313, 361

Made in the USA
Monee, IL
04 April 2023